Race News

THE HISTORY OF COMMUNICATION

Robert W. McChesney and John C. Nerone, editors

A list of books in the series appears at the end of this book.

Race News

Black Journalists and the Fight for Racial Justice in the Twentieth Century

FRED CARROLL

UNIVERSITY OF ILLINOIS PRESS
Urbana, Chicago, and Springfield

Library of Congress Cataloging-in-Publication Data
Names: Carroll, Fred, 1971– author.
Title: Race news: black journalists and the fight for racial justice
    in the twentieth century / Fred Carroll.
Description: Urbana : University of Illinois Press, 2017. | Series:
    The history of communication | Includes bibliographical
    references and index.
Identifiers: LCCN 2017020955 (print) | LCCN 2017034231 (ebook)
    | ISBN 9780252050091 (ebook) | ISBN 9780252041495 (cloth :
    alk. paper) | ISBN 9780252083037 (pbk. : alk. paper)
Subjects: LCSH: African American press—History—20th century.
    | Civil rights movements—Press coverage—United States—
    History—20th century. | Racism in the press—United States.
    | African American journalists—History—20th century. | Press
    and politics—United States.
Classification: LCC PN4882.5 (ebook) | LCC PN4882.5 .C38 2017
    (print) | DDC 071.308996073—dc23
LC record available at https://lccn.loc.gov/2017020955

Contents

Acknowledgments

I first thank those who sacrificed so I could write—my wife Lisa, daughters Emma and Melissa, and parents Fred and Brenda.

I also thank those who improved what I wrote. During my journalism career, my writing and reporting benefited from working alongside numerous editors, reporters, and photographers. I particularly owe gratitude to Kevin Ellis, Earl McDaniel, Mark Di Vincenzo, and Dave Hendrickson. When I transitioned to higher education, conversations with professors and students at the College of William and Mary deepened my understanding of the process of historical inquiry. Kimberley Phillips and Scott Reynolds Nelson helped me develop this book's core historical arguments, while James La Fleur and Earnest L. Perry Jr., of the University of Missouri, also offered valuable suggestions. The American Journalism Historians Association reinforced my commitment to this project in 2012 when it recognized the significance of my research. The manuscript improved as I weighed the questions and comments made by panelists and attendees at conferences organized by the American Journalism Historians Association, African American Intellectual History Society, Association for the Study of African American Life and History, and School of Journalism and Mass Communications at the University of South Carolina. Cindy Hahamovitch, a mentor in the fullest sense, and Jane Rhodes offered crucial insights as I pitched my proposal to publishers. The University of Illinois Press saw promise in the manuscript and improved it during the production process. The press's readers, including Patrick Washburn and a reviewer who remained anonymous, provided sound criticisms and suggestions.

And I thank those who assisted my research. The John Hope Franklin Research Center for African and African American History and Culture at Duke University awarded a generous travel grant that allowed me to access its relevant archives. The archivists with the Moorland-Spingarn Research Center at Howard University and Vivian G. Harsh Research Collection at the Chicago Public Library graciously supported my research over several visits. I also received assistance from librarians with Swem Library at the College of William and Mary; Harvey Library at Hampton University; Tamiment Library at New York University; Schomburg Center for Research in Black Culture at New York Public Library; Rare Book and Manuscript Library at Columbia University; University Archives and Records Center at the University of Louisville; Oberlin College Archives; and Library of Congress in Washington, D.C.

Race News

Introduction
Political Pressures and Black Newswriting

Marvel Cooke, a newspaper editor whose friends included leading civil rights activists and Harlem Renaissance writers, protested in the streets and in print during the Great Depression for better pay and employment conditions for herself and other black workers. Locked out of the *New York Amsterdam News* in October 1935 for attempting to unionize the newsroom, Cooke and other journalists picketed eleven weeks for better pay and better hours. As Cooke marched, an article she cowrote with activist Ella Baker appeared in the *Crisis*, the influential journal on race relations published by the National Association for the Advancement of Colored People (NAACP). The writers accused well-to-do white women in New York of underpaying and cheating day-laboring black domestics who were "pressed to the wall by poverty, starvation and discrimination." They characterized this modern-day labor arrangement as a return of the antebellum slave market. As Cooke marched, a lifetime of progressive influences—a father who voted for a socialist presidential candidate; a mother who hosed down cranky segregationists; a past supervisor, W. E. B. Du Bois, who elaborated upon his political convictions in private conversations; and her own union activism—culminated in the central political decision of her life: Cooke joined the Communist Party at age 32.[1]

Although Cooke avoided propagandizing in her journalism, her politics informed her newswriting. "The reason I was possibly successful," she recalled decades later, "is because they said I wrote well, you know, and you should never project your opinions in a news story, and I never did that. But I might have emphasized some part of a story that somebody else might not have emphasized, the work conditions or something like that." Cooke's politics shaped her career ambitions. She eventually left the *Amsterdam News* to work for "social-minded" leftist newspapers, including the *People's Voice*, a Harlem-based weekly that filled key positions with Communist Party supporters, and the *Daily Compass*, a white-owned newspaper that also employed I. F. Stone, a prominent critic of the Cold War. Both papers folded as hostilities with the Soviet Union escalated and a rising anticommunism movement reshaped American politics. Cooke was called to testify in 1953 before a Senate committee about her political beliefs. She invoked her constitutional right against self-incrimination and refused to answer questions. She never worked in journalism again. Cooke's newswriting defined the reportage of a generation of black journalists that came of age in the 1920s and 1930s as Black America relocated to northern industrial cities, modernist sensibilities reordered racial protest, and economic destitution inspired a fervent search for alternatives to American capitalism and racism. This type of newswriting coincided with the modernization of black journalism as an industry and helped transform the commercial black press into one of the integral black-led institutions agitating for racial justice.[2]

As Cooke exited the newspaper business, Ethel Payne covered the emerging Civil Rights Movement as the Washington bureau chief for the *Chicago Defender*. Progressive influences had also shaped Payne's newswriting. She protested discrimination in the early 1940s by supporting A. Philip Randolph's March on Washington Movement, and, while writing for the *Defender*, she worked for the Democratic National Committee and a political education committee for the American Federation of Labor and Congress of Industrial Organizations (AFL-CIO). "Maybe I'm wrong," she recalled, "but I just believe that Black journalists have a responsibility to be advocates. Because we're Black first of all before we're journalists, and there's so much out there that isn't reported adequately, or so much that is distorted." Unlike Cooke, though, Payne began her reporting career after World War II—after black activists had gained acceptance for continued racial protest by supporting the war effort and characterizing their demands as patriotic. The repressive nature of the Cold War discouraged journalists like Payne—regardless of race—from expressing support for communism.[3]

Although sharply skeptical and frequently disappointed, Payne believed America's governing institutions could surmount the nation's racist past. Pacing the corridors of the U.S. Capitol and attending press briefings at the White House, she scrutinized national leaders' commitment to integration and civil rights. She irked President Dwight D. Eisenhower in July 1954 by asking whether his administration would support a ban on segregation in interstate travel. Eisenhower seldom called on her again. Payne's reporting took her across the nation and abroad, from Chicago to Birmingham, from Bandung, Indonesia, to Saigon, South Vietnam. She witnessed the signing of milestone civil rights legislation and helped integrate broadcast journalism when CBS hired her as a radio and television commentator. Her commitment to political reform compelled her to criticize Black Power activist Stokely Carmichael in 1972 after he urged Howard University students to not vote in the upcoming presidential election. Payne called such advice "shopworn" and "suicidal." "You all run—don't walk—to the nearest polling place," she told her listeners. Payne's newswriting style represented the sensibilities of black journalists who reached adulthood in the 1940s and 1950s. These journalists avoided Marxist-style politics to better demand full inclusion within American society. They won grudging recognition from the federal government and eventually opened new employment opportunities in segregated white newsrooms but disappointed black radicals who doubted integration would lead to equality.[4]

Race News: Black Journalists and the Fight for Racial Justice in the Twentieth Century analyzes the commercial black press's problematic working relationship with the alternative black press and its thorny interactions with a repressive federal government and hostile white media to explain how shifting toleration of progressive politics reconfigured how black journalists wrote and covered the news. The commercial and alternative black presses were observably distinctive in their emphasis on profitability, sophistication of production and distribution systems, and guiding orientation toward the American political economy. However, black journalism as an industry was an integral component of an expansive and permeable black print culture that expected writers to publish in various genres and across multiple print forums. Thus, the boundaries of the commercial and alternative presses were never rigid, and the definition of journalist was broad. Segregation constrained black writers' careers and earnings and often compelled authors, poets, scholars, and activists to publish alongside working reporters, infusing black journalism with an unexpected cultural vibrancy and cosmopolitan character. W. E. B. Du Bois, a scholar, editor, and activist, was in his mid-60s when he resigned in 1934 as the editor of the *Crisis*, but he maintained national relevance by continuing to publish columns and essays in newspapers and magazines for another quarter-century. While celebrated for his poetry, Langston Hughes reached his largest readership through his weekly column in the *Chicago Defender*. Ida B. Wells was known as a memoirist, pamphleteer, educator, and international orator, but her activism was rooted in her journalism career and her association with other journalists. Other writers and editors who worked at the fulcrum of literature and journalism included James Weldon Johnson, Pauline E. Hopkins, George Schuyler, Claude McKay, Wallace Thurman, Frank Marshall Davis, Ellen Tarry, Horace Cayton, Alice Childress, Lorraine Hansberry, Julian Mayfield, and many more. Black writers' willingness to shift genres and platforms imbued the alternative black press with journalistic legitimacy and fostered friendships between alternative and commercial journalists, who frequently wrote and edited for both presses. This familiarity and camaraderie eased the transition of radical political ideas—the politics of anticolonialism, anticapitalism, and Black Nationalism—into the commercial black press in the first half of the twentieth century and promoted the formation of a progressive reporting style not tolerated in white-owned daily newspapers.[5]

Commercial publishers proudly traced their lineage back to black journalism's beginnings in the United States, to its very first newspaper, *Freedom's Journal*, which was founded in 1827. By the mid–twentieth century, though, leading publications were markedly different from their nineteenth-century predecessors. The commercial press included hundreds of weekly newspapers, as well as two significant daily papers and some prominent magazines and journals. National newspaper publishers—including Carl Murphy of the *Baltimore Afro-American*, Robert Abbott and John Sengstacke of the *Chicago Defender*, C. B. Powell of the *New York Amsterdam News*, P. B. Young of the *Norfolk Journal and Guide*, and Robert Vann of the *Pittsburgh Courier*—printed multiple editions and sold hundreds of thousands of copies each week. Their success stemmed from the commercial black press's central attributes—its capitalistic outlook and racial autonomy. The black news industry was owned, produced, and consumed primarily independent of white oversight. Commercial publishers and their editorial departments packaged their mission of ending racial discrimination and securing citizenship rights within a profit-oriented, objective presentation of current events designed to cater to the many interests of the largest possible black readership. According to Roy Wilkins, a onetime Kansas City editor who became the executive secretary of the NAACP, the commercial black press was a "business proposition first, and an uplift agency, second." Profits and protest went together. Rising newsstand sales ensured the continued distribution of dissent by bankrolling the next issue. Circulation gains spurred the modernization of mechanical operations and the professionalization of newsroom employees, who increasingly aspired to lifelong careers in the news industry. Together, publishers, editors, and reporters broadened their papers' appeal by covering sports and women's issues, theater and books, and community news and social events—as well as news stories concerning politics, crime, money, and racial abuse.[6]

As the sole disseminators of news for and about African Americans whose coverage was not shaped primarily by racial prejudice and stereotypes, commercial black journalists established the parameters of political debate for millions of readers. Leading newspapers often tempered commonplace platitudes of racial uplift, which touted hard work and self-improvement as the remedies for discrimination, by more assertively demanding inclusion within American society and reveling in sensation and scandal, splashing murders, celebrities, and divorces across their pages. The astonishing surge in newspaper circulation during the interwar years financed a transnational communications network that informed, inspired, and mobilized black activism. "Only through the agency of the Negro Press," boasted the *Pittsburgh Courier* in 1930, "can public opinion in our group be swiftly organized." Maintaining this outsized influence in black political life created a practical incentive for commercial publishers to provide expansive coverage of radical political views that were frequently at odds with their personal commitment to the nation's political system and its capitalist economy.[7]

A partisan and idiosyncratic alternative black press existed to advocate for racial and political perspectives that its editors believed the commercial black press—as well as other establishmentarian black institutions—either mischaracterized, unfairly denounced, or simply ignored. Its writers aimed to broaden black political discourse by informing readers—including commercial journalists—about political views that challenged the legitimacy of the American status quo. Alternative editors questioned African Americans' faith in integration and explored cultural and political connections with people of color elsewhere in the world. They described socialism and communism as empowering alternatives to capitalism's inherent impulse to create wealth by exploiting the oppressed and disadvantaged. Unlike commercial journalists, alternative writers often intended to directly intervene in political affairs. They structured the radical political movements of their times, including the New Negro Movement of the 1910s and 1920s and the Black Power Movement of the 1960s and 1970s. "We know from our own experience," the Black Panther Party asserted, "that no one can depict a struggle better than those who are actively engaged in that struggle." Like commercial publishers, alternative editors pursued profitability, but most struggled to maintain their publishing operations. Advertisers avoided associating their products with controversial political views, and alternative writers secured their credibility by positioning themselves as outsiders who refused to compromise editorial integrity for fiscal solvency. Despite his desperate need for cash, Hubert Harrison, a leading voice of the New Negro Movement, promised his readers that his paper "remained manly and independent" and "would not cringe before the Exalted Ones." Impaired by unreliable financing, alternative publications lacked the longevity of commercial newspapers. These frequently fleeting publications usually ceased operating when their politics either became too passé to sustain sufficient reader interest or were popular enough to percolate in mainstream black political discourse.[8]

Alternative editors' influence among commercial journalists expanded or contracted as toleration for progressive politics shifted within the United States. Early alternative editors—including socialists like A. Philip Randolph, communists like Cyril Briggs, and Black Nationalists like Marcus Garvey—emerged after World War I to advocate a radicalized brand of racial militancy that enlarged African Americans' denunciation of Western racism. Although criticized by conventional black political leaders and scrutinized by federal authorities, these editors' seemingly marginal viewpoints gained wider acceptance in the interwar years as ordinary men and women grappled with extreme economic hardship and unrepentant racism. Commercial black journalists—like Marvel Cooke—crafted a progressive newswriting template that infused their reporting with the militancy of the New Negro Movement, modernist sensibilities of the Harlem Renaissance, and Marxist critiques of the American political economy. By 1940, the alternative black press had effectively folded into an increasingly progressive commercial black press.

Two national institutions—the federal government and the white press—worked to silence, or at least moderate, black journalists' outspokenness. Government officials and white journalists closely monitored this dissident press, shifting the boundaries of what was considered acceptable public discourse in a democratic nation according to their whims, needs, and concerns. State surveillance and press criticism intensified during wars and other moments of perceived national peril. Government pressure—frequently applied by the military or Federal Bureau of Investigation (FBI) but also other federal agencies—forced commercial black publishers during World War I and World War II to modify their newspapers' political positions. Publishers who pushed too aggressively for reform risked losing their mailing privileges, quarreling over gratuitous censorship, or defending themselves against criminal charges of sedition. Publishers, though, rarely capitulated outright to ominous threats leveled by state authorities. They could not abandon the fight for racial justice without being forsaken by their readers. Instead, they promoted patriotic appeals for service and sacrifice in war years while continuing campaigns to end segregation and other forms of racial discrimination. Such tactful negotiations concerning news coverage helped refashion the working relationship between state power brokers and commercial publishers. The open antagonism displayed during World War I evolved into a mutually rewarding but contentious co-option of one another during the Civil Rights Movement. However, commercial publishers maintained their status as legitimate political actors only by narrowing the terms of acceptable political debate and removing their papers' most radical voices.[9]

After World War II, rising anticommunism sentiment shattered the journalistic convergence that had united the alternative and commercial black presses. National commercial publishers distanced their newspapers from progressive writers who had written favorably about communism or had ties with leftist organizations. These publishers intended to protect their businesses and curry favor with federal officials amid Cold War repression. A parade of prominent journalists exited commercial black journalism—including poet Frank Marshall Davis, former communist George Padmore, foreign-affairs columnist John Robert Badger, onetime war correspondent Ollie Harrington, and publisher Charlotta Bass. Unlike those journalists, reporters like Ethel Payne avoided praising communists in the 1950s and 1960s for rejecting racial discrimination. Instead, they accused white segregationists of aiding the Soviet Union by championing segregation and alienating potential allies worldwide. This new framing of news stories robbed the commercial press of its most urgent, most radical possibilities for reform. Progressive writers countered by reviving the alternative black press in the 1950s, but they struggled to finance publications, most notably Paul Robeson's *Freedom*, that reiterated familiar Marxist broadsides against Western capitalism and imperialism. By the late 1960s, though, the escalating militancy of the Civil Rights Movement and commercial publishers' cautious response pushed countless young activists to their typewriters. These new alternative editors and writers included confrontational student protesters, advocates of armed self-defense, Depression-era leftists, and Black Nationalist groups, such as the Nation of Islam and Black Panther Party. They denounced commercial black publishers for too readily abandoning the fight for global equality for insufficient domestic political gains. The reemergence of the alternative black press ensured the fullest possible airing of black political thought, but it also symbolized the marginalization of black progressives. Exclusion from the commercial black press cast black radical thought as aberrant.

Amid these political maneuverings, black journalists encountered unyielding criticism from white reporters and editors who reinforced journalism's color line by withholding from commercial black newspapers the imprimatur of professionalism. White journalists often characterized black reporters as uncredentialed amateurs who worked for marginal publications prone to spelling errors and sloppy design. They dismissed black innovation as mere emulation. Most devastatingly, white press critics accused black journalists of violating the news industry's faith in objectivity by exaggerating racial wrongs and needlessly inflaming racial relations—an unpardonable lapse of professional integrity that most white journalists believed black reporters could never overcome. "Extremist Negro leaders and Negro newspapers in this country are demanding an overnight revolution in race relations," warned Virginius Dabney, the respected editor of the *Richmond Times-Dispatch*, during World War II. Such criticisms, though, ignored how African Americans' experience with racism and exclusion led them to create a distinctive "Afro-modernity," which scholar Michael Hanchard defines as "the selective incorporation of technologies, discourses, and institutions of the modern West within the cultural and political practices of African-derived peoples to create a form of relatively autonomous modernity distinct from its counterparts of Western Europe and North America." Black journalists embraced and tweaked prevailing journalism practices to suit the needs of undercapitalized publications serving a distinctive readership. In particular, they exposed the fundamental fallacy of journalistic objectivity, a professional doctrine that claimed racial neutrality but reinforced white supremacists' efforts to erase African Americans' participation in the modern world. As a sympathetic white journalist observed, "When a white man first reads a Negro newspaper, it is like getting a bucket of cold water in the face."[10]

The white press's commitment to a narrow definition of objectivity blinded its journalists and their readers to the full extent that racism configured American society. Blithely unaware of the news industry's institutionalized racism, few white editors seriously considered integrating their newsrooms until African Americans' protests escalated in the late 1960s into violence and property destruction. Embarrassed by their inadequate coverage of the era's urban uprisings, white news executives began to hire a few black reporters. They expected them to better explain the causes of black anger without fundamentally altering how their newspapers reported race news. Black journalists in white newsrooms, though, demanded equality in the workplace and pushed to eliminate biased reporting and expand coverage of African American communities.

The historical sweep of *Race News* illuminates how commercial black journalists responded to the countervailing forces that pressured them to revise how they wrote the news—the progressive political perspectives advocated by the alternative black press versus the repressive status quo upheld by the federal government and white press. The story of modern black journalism opens in the late 1800s with the commercial black press poised to take advantage of ongoing demographic changes by adopting the editorial practices that would

Ethel Payne, of the *Chicago Defender*, on her trip to China in 1973. Courtesy of the Library of Congress, Prints & Photographs Division, Washington, D.C.

create publications of national influence. It concludes in the late 1970s when black reporters' bruising battles to integrate white newsrooms marked the end of the black press's near exclusive access to the skills and talents of African American journalists. This timespan covers the working lives of four generations of journalists—focusing primarily on those who, like Cooke, shaped black journalism in the decades between the world wars, and those who, like Payne, wrote at the beginning of the Cold War, during the Civil Rights Movement, and beyond. It also covers the careers and politics of late-nineteenth-century editor-proprietors and late-twentieth-century integrationists working in white newsrooms. These reporters, editors, and publishers struggled to reconcile the assimilationist aims of a black middle class seeking to integrate into American society and the global agendas of black radicals who endorsed the politics of anticapitalism, anticolonialism, and black separatism. Black journalists engaged in these debates knowing that the federal government and white press stood ready to obstruct racial reform through surveillance, censorship, and ridicule. However, more than personal values, outside pressure, and changing political currents tempered black newswriting. Business concerns also shaped editorial decisions. The black news industry modernized in the twentieth century, expanding its circulation, advertising, and distribution capabilities while also professionalizing journalism as a career field. New competitors surfaced, seeking to diminish weekly black newspapers' near monopolistic grip on race news. Black journalists' responses to these political and economic changes reveal that journalistic agitation was never an inert constant of a dissident press. Black newswriting was ever-changing.

Chapter 1, "'Negro Subversion': Solidifying a Militant Press," examines how commercial publishers expanded their influence in the early 1900s as black families left the poverty and violence of the rural South for the promise of better jobs and better lives in industrial cities in the North and elsewhere. New publishers competed against established black weeklies for a share of this emerging market of news consumers by adopting crusading editorial policies and modern journalism practices. The era's premier examples of this new journalism were Robert Abbott's *Chicago Defender* and the *Crisis*, which under the editorship of W. E. B. Du Bois was the rare black-oriented publication with significant interracial financing and readership. During World War I, military investigators and postal censors hoped to bully journalists into delaying their demands for racial reform until after the war ended. They soon learned, though, that the stunning proliferation of newspapers with militant editorial policies taxed even the federal government's powers and resources.

Chapter 2, "Enter the 'New Crowd' Journalists," explores how the print culture of the New Negro Movement, in both its political and cultural arenas, imbued the commercial black press with modernist sensibilities, a keener sense of "Negro consciousness," and a more critical, more progressive political outlook. Doubting the United States' commitment to truly fulfill the democratic beliefs its soldiers had fought abroad for, radical editors established the alternative black press to promote progressive options to unrelenting racism. Alternative writers helped spread their ideas into the commercial black press in the 1920s and 1930s by waging public debates with its editors and joining its newsroom staffs. Chapter 3, "Popular Fronts and Modern Presses," describes how the commercial black press as an institutional entity appropriated the politics of the alternative black press in the 1930s by advancing Marxist-inspired critiques of capitalism, colonialism, and racial exploitation—even as individual publishers and writers rejected progressive criticisms of the American political economy. The commercial press's participation in this "leftward turn," which reshaped black activism nationwide during the Great Depression, occurred as millions of readers propelled black newspapers to their peak popularity. As profits surged, leading publishers enlarged their editorial departments, modernized their print-ing equipment, and expanded their distribution networks, establishing news-papers of regional, national, and international significance.[11]

However, the outbreak of World War II forced black journalists to recalibrate their reportage to avoid familiar charges of disloyalty and sedition lobbed by military officers, federal administrators, and white columnists. Chapter 4, "The 'New Crowd' Goes Global," studies how publishers and journalists attempted to reconcile white officialdom's distrust of black journalism during World War II with readers' refusal to moderate their demands for equality. Black publish-ers won grudging acceptance from the nation's governing elites by endorsing the war effort. They secured readers' loyalty by allowing reporters to denounce segregation at home while also condemning Western imperialism abroad. In particular, war correspondents eluded state censure because they praised the bravery of African American troops as they crafted a global critique of white supremacy that united Black America with subjugated people of color around the world.

Commercial publishers, though, failed to maintain this delicate balance during the Cold War. Chapter 5, "'Questionable Leanings': The 'New Crowd' Driven Out," describes how the politics of the Cold War unraveled the tem-plate for progressive black newswriting in the late 1940s and early 1950s. As the anticommunism movement strengthened, publishers rid their newsrooms of left-leaning journalists and suppressed coverage of radical political perspec-tives. This pragmatic capitulation to Cold War politics transformed commercial publishers into "establishmentarian dissidents" who protested nonviolently to integrate into American society. This changeover constrained how black journalists reported on the Civil Rights Movement—just as the white media seized control of the black protest story. As black militancy escalated in the 1960s, commercial publishers shifted from attempting to moderate student protests to condemning the Black Power Movement. Chapter 6, "Black Power Assaults the Black Newspaper," details the politics and popularity of a reborn and recast alternative black press that challenged the values and outlook of the statesmanlike commercial black press. Frustrated by commercial publishers' comparative conservatism, marginalized activists founded inflammatory, and frequently profane, alternative publications to challenge the politics of inte-gration and endorse the Black Power Movement. The most popular alterna-tive publications—the Black Panther Party's *The Black Panther* and the Nation of Islam's *Muhammad Speaks*—claimed sales that rivaled the circulations of the largest commercial papers. Despite declining readership, commercial black newspapers sustained sizable circulations by remaining the most reliable and widely available source of news treating African Americans as concerned citizens, not just subjects of controversy.[12]

In the early 1970s, though, the commercial black press lost its monopoly over the labor of black journalists, guaranteeing it would never see the return of its World War II–era heyday. The white press began to acknowledge how deeply its reporters, editors, and columnists misunderstood the nature of racism in the United States. White editors moved cautiously to repair their flawed coverage of racial matters by tepidly integrating their newsrooms. White hesitation provoked conflict. Chapter 7, "Into the White Newsroom," details how black journalists fought for fairer news coverage and equal employment opportunities at white newspapers, as well as radio and television stations. Black journalists challenged story assignments, filed employment discrimination lawsuits, and formed professional organizations. While the problems of institutional and individual discrimination persisted, newsroom integration marked the culmination of a century's worth of protest by black journalists. They had gained unprecedented recognition of their professional standing and expanded opportunities to improve mainstream news coverage of African Americans and other minority groups.

Race News provides the first sustained scholarly analysis of the political and professional evolution of black journalism in the twentieth century. It accomplishes this by synthesizing a rich historiography on the black press, accessing fourteen manuscript collections at nine research centers, reviewing seven published archival collections, and examining extensive runs of national and regional black newspapers. Prior monographs on the black press generally divide into three categories: personal and institutional biographies of publishers, writers, and newspapers; studies that examine publishers' interactions with federal officials who attempted to censor newspapers during World War I and World War II; and textbooks and reference works. *Race News* contributes to its field by consistently challenging a tendency to depict publishers as top-down arbiters of newsgathering decisions (a reflection of the very nature of biography as a genre) and attributing greater significance to the influence of the alternative black press on national commercial newspapers. By qualifying publishers' authority within their own newsrooms, *Race News* recognizes the expanded editorial independence enjoyed by journalists as their industry professionalized and emphasized writers' intellectual creation over owners' control of mechanical production. This shift in perspective enlarges the collective responsibility for editorial decision making, which in turn explains how perspectives advocated by alternative writers helped shift news reporting conventions over time.[13]

This book also engages recent historical scholarship on black radicalism and black internationalism. Its intellectual structuring owes debts to Nikhal Pal Singh, who explains how the Great Depression inspired African American scholars, activists, labor leaders, and journalists to embrace the tactics of leftist political organizing, and Bill V. Mullen, whose suggestive interpretation of the *Chicago Defender* as a front for communist ideals spurred my search for more authoritative evidence of communism's influences on black journalism. Regarding black internationalism, Brenda Gayle Plummer and Penny M. Von Eschen identified journalists as integral promoters of Pan-Africanist perspectives. They requested a substantive examination of the black press and its reconfiguration by the Cold War to fill a void in the historiography. This book answers their call.[14]

Race News explores the rich history of black journalism in the twentieth century by describing how contested political outlooks shaped the conventions of black newswriting as the modernization and professionalization of the news industry inflated the significance of writers' words. It reveals how journalists' coverage of milestone events in African American history shaped ordinary readers' understanding of the world around them and explains how critics and competitors attempted to invalidate these reporters' influence. The columns, stories, and editorials in black newspapers inspired debate and activism and provoked surveillance and retribution. Black journalists fought for racial justice, and, in doing so, they changed readers' awareness of the world and their place in it.

CHAPTER 1

"Negro Subversion"

Solidifying a Militant Press

Week after week, postal censors and military intelligence officers read black newspapers from around the United States, riffling through pages for seditious statements as American soldiers fought and bled and died in boggy European trenches. They believed the editors and reporters who criticized the nation's practices of racial oppression during World War I threatened to undermine the morale of African Americans called to support the war effort despite racism's injustices. In private meetings and personal letters, censors attempted to intimidate editors, warning them of the fines and jail sentences they faced if their editorials and articles were deemed sufficiently unpatriotic. A San Antonio editor was convicted for attempting to cause mutiny among military forces after publishing a column that encouraged black soldiers to retaliate against civilian harassers. The military's concerns mounted as the war continued.[1]

National officials called about thirty editors to Washington, D.C., in June 1918, hoping to improve what they characterized as "the bitter tone of the colored press." Deadly race riots had already erupted in East St. Louis and elsewhere. A military court had already hanged black soldiers accused of murdering police officers during the so-called "Houston mutiny," which had erupted amid extensive racial harassment and allegations of police brutality. Wherever African Americans organized for workers' rights and adequate housing, their efforts were checked by indifference or violence. Military officers routinely mistreated and abused black enlistees. Regardless, federal officials—including Secretary of

War Newton Baker, Committee on Public Information Chairman George Creel, and Assistant Secretary of the Navy Franklin D. Roosevelt—appealed to the publishers' sense of loyalty and duty. They encouraged the editors to use their publications—the *Chicago Defender, Crisis, New York Age, Pittsburgh Courier, Baltimore Afro-American, Richmond Planet, Washington Bee,* and *St. Louis Argus,* among others—to fully mobilize black resources and increase America's odds of winning the Great War. The publishers defended themselves and their race. They explained how lynching, segregation, and discrimination dampened enthusiasm for the war among their readers.[2]

While "heated argument was not infrequent," both sides considered the conference a success and afterward frankly acknowledged their shared interests and unresolved differences. Col. Marlborough Churchill, the head of military intelligence, told the Army's chief of staff that "the leaders of the race are intensely loyal, but feel keenly their inability to carry the great mass of their race with them in active support of the war unless certain grievances receive immediate attention." The editors reaffirmed their loyalty and promised to aid the war effort. Carefully noting that their combined weekly circulations topped one million copies, they aimed to preempt their critics but also reassure their readers. "German propaganda among us is powerless," their joint statement read, "but the apparent indifference of our own Government may be dangerous."[3]

The nation-state's intense wartime scrutiny of black publishers revealed the remarkable transformation that had occurred within black journalism since the beginning of the twentieth century. A skeletal national communications network of news by, about, and for African Americans solidified in the early 1900s as black men and women left sharecroppers' shacks for industrial jobs in southern and then northern cities. As African Americans' journeys acquainted them with modern urban living and greater daily freedoms, illiteracy plummeted and a mass consumer marketplace emerged for race news. Upstart editors competed for readers' pennies and nickels by adopting modern journalism practices and emboldening their demands for racial justice. These editors condemned lynching, denounced segregation, and defended citizenship rights with an audacious militancy. They demanded integration, asserted African Americans' humanity, and safeguarded an expansive conception of freedom claimed since Reconstruction. Circulations surged as new competitors intensified the pursuit for news. During World War I, military investigators and federal censors fixated upon the sensational headlines, critical editorials, and soaring popularity of a robust dissident press. The nation-state's agents attempted to quiet editors by drawing connections between criticisms of American racism and potential acts of sedition, perhaps even treason. While editors often moderated their news coverage when confronted by state authorities, they refused to abandon their mission of protest. Abject editorial capitulation guaranteed bankruptcy.

Crusading Journalism in the Late Nineteenth Century

Aspiring editor-proprietors struggled to establish black journalism as a viable community institution between the Civil War's smoldering aftermath and the dispiriting collapse of Reconstruction. Emancipation fulfilled abolitionists' aims and eliminated most white financial support for publications devoted to African Americans' concerns. Antislavery editors silenced their presses or joined other reform causes. Freedmen and women valued the written word after being forbidden by owners from learning to read and write. They viewed literacy as a means to personal empowerment. But illiteracy and poverty prevented them from subscribing to local black newspapers, which typically folded within two years of publishing their first issue. Ratified in 1868, the Fourteenth Amendment enabled black men to vote and inadvertently expanded African Americans' access to the First Amendment's freedom of the press. Partisan black newspapers often appeared several months before elections to tout the particular politician that bankrolled them. Such papers, though, typically ceased publishing soon after Election Day. Although the number of black newspapers nearly quadrupled in the 1870s, none published before 1880 existed three decades later.[4]

White supremacists intensified efforts to strip black men and women of their circumscribed political and economic independence after Reconstruction ended and federal troops decamped from the South. Unrepentant Confederates moved to consolidate their control over southern society through violence, social ostracism, and denial of civic rights. Vigilantes lynched thousands of African Americans. State prisons overflowed with black men convicted of petty property crimes. The U.S. Supreme Court upheld laws that mandated racial segregation in public places under the pretense that equal facilities would be provided for both races. State legislators drafted new constitutions across the South and disenfranchised most African Americans by tying voting rights to property and literacy requirements. White voters then swiftly replaced officeholders endorsed by black editors.[5]

White editors nationwide reinforced the South's racial agenda by distorting, demeaning, and ignoring African Americans. They depicted black men and women in the abusive stereotypes assigned to them by white southerners. Using the same tropes as literary authors, reporters depicted black men as either rapacious brutes or lazy fools. Black women were loving mammies or flirty

Jezebels. Black families were contented in slavery but wretched in freedom. Newswriting style guidelines subtly marked black men and women as outside American citizenry. Editors refused to follow the standard practice of using courtesy titles when writing about African Americans. Instead of referring to a black woman as "Mrs. Smith" or "Miss Jones," a reporter might identify her as "the Smith woman" or "the Jones woman." Reporters typically reserved such language for outing prostitutes. White newspapers seldom capitalized the word "Negro," despite a relentless campaign of protest by black editors. But mostly, white journalists ignored African Americans, obfuscating the daily, interracial commitment required to build and grow communities. Daily newspapers did not announce black births or marriages or deaths. They did not post notices of black fraternal lodge meetings or women's club fund-raisers or church dinners. They did not recognize black students' academic achievements.[6]

White editors traded in stories that highlighted the supposedly inherent nature of black criminality, which implicitly justified extralegal racial violence. They featured race prominently in crime news, often flashing a black assailant's color in the headline and then mentioning the suspect's race again in a story's first or second paragraph. While they seldom identified white assailants by race, they always identified by color the white victims who were allegedly attacked by black suspects. Editors frequently cast petty crimes involving black perpetuators as humorous reaffirmations of stereotypes. They wrote, for example, about thefts of watermelons or chickens with an exaggerated, knowing tone of condescension. Writers could demean entire neighborhoods to explain away unsolved crimes. A *New York Times* correspondent described in 1880 how white residents in Washington, D.C., blamed "horrible assaults upon young women" on "a large class of colored people here who live by burglary and begging, and who cannot be induced to go into the country and work, even for good wages." Such news coverage validated and intensified white readers' racial prejudices.[7]

White editors aimed to titillate and enrage their readers when they described allegations of interracial rape and murder. They slanted their stories with fanciful language that contrasted the white victim's supposed good character with the black suspect's alleged cruelty. In a story with the subheading, "Another Negro Fiend Finds Death at the End of a Rope," the *Macon* (Georgia) *Telegraph and Messenger* reported that "a burly negro" stopped two children on the way to school and "laid violent hands upon the little girl and dragged her to the woods." Outraged editors often encouraged extralegal retribution. The *Wheeling* (West Virginia) *Register* did not wait for a jury to decide the fate of a 20-year-old black man arrested for rape. Describing the suspect as someone with "a mean sneaking look" who "would commit any devilish crime," the newspaper headlined its story, "Work for Judge Lynch." While black perfidy was unforgivable, vigilante lawlessness was explained away by the victim's pain. The *St. Louis Post-Dispatch* commended a lynch mob for remaining "orderly" as it hanged "a Negro brute."[8]

Location and financial solvency often determined how aggressively black editors refuted white journalists' lies, distortions, and innuendos. Most black newspapers operated in the South where 90 percent of African Americans lived. Southern editors either tempered their words or jeopardized their lives. A mob destroyed the *Memphis Free Speech* in 1892 after its 30-year-old editor, Ida B. Wells, suggested white women solicited interracial sexual relationships. Traveling on the East Coast when the attack occurred, Wells never returned to Memphis. Instead, she moved north and intensified her campaign against lynching. "Having lost my paper, had a price put on my life, and been made an exile from home for hinting at the truth," she recalled, "I felt I owed it to myself and to my race to tell the whole truth now that I was where I could do so freely." Similarly, Alexander L. Manly of the *Wilmington* (North Carolina) *Record* sparked a riot in 1898 after writing during a racially inflamed election season that, "Our experience among poor white people in the country teaches us that the women of that race are not any more particular in the matter of clandestine meetings with colored men than are the white men with colored women." Rampaging white citizens burned Manly's offices, destroyed other black businesses, murdered an uncertain number of African Americans, and forced elected officeholders to resign. In the riot's aftermath, a group of prominent black ministers, politicians, and educators blamed Manly for instigating the riot and apologized for his editorial. Rather than capitulate, hundreds of other black residents abandoned the city.[9]

Northern editors wrote more freely but still struggled to sell newspapers. By the mid-1880s, editor-proprietors published dozens of papers in northern and border-state cities with sizable black populations. They established publications that would enjoy several decades of success, including T. Thomas Fortune's *New York Age*, W. Calvin Chase's *Washington Bee*, Harry C. Smith's *Cleveland Gazette*, John Mitchell Jr.'s *Richmond Planet*, Christopher Perry's *Philadelphia Tribune*, and Edward E. Cooper's *Indianapolis Freeman*. Northern editors wrote with greater militancy and urgency, but small circulations and limited advertising imperiled their papers' existence. To appease patrons and advertisers, even the most pugnacious editors moderated their opinions when necessary. Even so, northern editors enjoyed larger circulations than editors in southern states because of their editorial forthrightness and readers' higher rates of literacy. Successful newspapers sold just several thousand copies each week but circulated in all regions of the country and overseas. Editors extended the reach of their columns by exchanging copies with one another, reprinting excerpts from other newspapers, and engaging in long-distance political debates.[10]

Crusading black editors denounced white supremacists' efforts to reassert a master's control over black lives and advocated a fulsome definition of freedom. While some publishers retained childhood memories of slavery, most reached maturity amid heady expectations of full citizenship and political participation. They expected their talent, ambition, and connections to advance multifaceted careers. They often worked full-time as lawyers, printers, teachers, ministers, or political appointees. They created their newspapers to promote racial justice, supplement their incomes, and build their leadership credentials. They styled themselves as "race men" and "race women"—middle-class entrepreneurs who believed acceptance of the Victorian values of thrift and sobriety would lead to their race's material and intellectual betterment and, ultimately, assimilation into American society. They saw their publications as community trusts, platforms for uplift and self-improvement, not mere commercial ventures. They seldom engaged in original reporting but printed local social news and announcements unavailable elsewhere. They condemned white oppression in scathing editorials that defined the era's journalism and praised black achievement in flowery platitudes.[11]

Living in a supposed "age of accommodation," these editors often trumpeted a bracing militancy and bombastic indignation. At the *New York Age*, Fortune emerged as his generation's most influential journalist. Delicate-looking but hot-tempered, Fortune argued that the best way to avenge racial atrocities was to emulate the oppressors. He urged African Americans to "look at the white papers of the South and learn from them the necessary lesson, that the only way we can hope ever to win our fight is to arm ourselves as our opponents do, support those newspapers alone that support us, and support those men alone who support us." Mitchell, an honor student born to enslaved house servants, took over the *Richmond Planet* in 1884. He advocated armed self-defense from the Confederacy's onetime capital, and his early exploits earned him fame as the "Fighting Negro Editor." Mitchell once holstered his Smith & Wesson revolvers and investigated a lynching, despite receiving an anonymous death threat warning him to stay away. He then wrote about the lynching and publicly ridiculed the threat. Readers applauded the stunt. Mitchell was just 22. Such editorial brazenness established a tradition of journalistic outspokenness that would expand in the twentieth century as the successors to these crusading editor-proprietors benefited from financial stability, greater personal safety, and improved production standards.[12]

"Calm, Deliberate, and Critical Thought"
Modern Race Journalism in the *Crisis* and *Chicago Defender*

The Great Migration evolved more modestly than its historical moniker implies but also fomented a cultural transformation far greater than that label allows. This mass movement of African Americans began in the 1880s and 1890s when a single workingman or a young family or a small group of relatives decided to quit the rural South's entrenched poverty and racist caste system for factory wages and greater freedom in industrialized cities, particularly those in the North. While the vast majority of African Americans still lived in the South, muckraking journalist Ray Stannard Baker observed in 1908 that black population increases in northern cities were "not short of extraordinary." Then World War I came, and the movement accelerated. Friends and family in Chicago, New York, Pittsburgh, Cleveland, Norfolk, Baltimore, St. Louis, Kansas City, Los Angeles, Oklahoma City, and elsewhere opened their homes to newcomers recruited to fill vacancies at plants manufacturing munitions and armaments. Black men and women still encountered discrimination and violence, but they also had more money in their pockets, more choice in their daily lives, and greater access to schooling. Black illiteracy rates sank from 70 percent in the 1880s to 45 percent in 1900 to about 30 percent in 1910. Northward migration, industrial employment, and increased educational attainment combined to establish sizable local markets of urban news consumers. "It is a difficult matter to find a Negro who can read, who does not read one or more of these race papers," said L. M. Hershaw, an editor and educator. "He may not always be a subscriber, but failing this he has an unfailing faculty for borrowing his neighbors' papers."[13]

By the early twentieth century, American journalism little resembled what it had looked like just three decades earlier. The development of industrial capitalism and the creation of a national market economy remade cultural perceptions, a process that historian Alan Trachtenberg calls the "the incorporation of America." Industrialization promoted the rapid growth of cities, propelled a surging rise in immigration, and created a class of professional, middle-class managers. Industrialists moved to solve a crisis of overproduction by searching for new markets and creating new categories of consumer goods. They developed and refined marketing and advertising techniques to entice new groups of people to buy their products. These changes culminated with the development of a modern mass culture built upon consumption. Consumer culture altered people's perceptions and values, and the nation gradually transitioned from emphasizing agrarian independence and Victorian notions of character to concentrating on personality and appearance.[14]

A revolution in communications helped fashion this mass consumer culture. Modern American journalism traced its origins to the penny press of the 1830s, but it was reshaped when publishers and advertisers responded to industrial capitalism's transformations by overhauling daily metropolitan newspapers and creating mass-circulation magazines. These changes occurred as a dramatic drop in the cost of newsprint spurred rapid expansion within the publishing industry. The number of daily newspapers in the nation quadrupled between 1870 and 1900. Average circulation leapt from 2,600 to more than 15,000. No modern national magazines existed in 1880, but about 20 circulated by 1900. Monthly magazine circulation tripled in fifteen years, leaping from 18 million to 64 million by 1905.[15]

In appearance and content, newspapers and magazines appealed to readers in new ways. Publishers attracted consumers' gaze with sophisticated layouts and designs and more illustrations and advertising. The nature of newswriting also changed. Reporting was becoming an esteemed occupation, a profession. Sociologist Michael Schudson argues that journalists "saw themselves, in part, as scientists uncovering the economic and political facts of industrial life more boldly, more clearly, and more 'realistically' than anyone had done before." Reporters' conception of their work borrowed from literary realism, which contended that facts could be seen and documented. It also drew upon progressivism's reformatory tendencies, which sought to hold power brokers accountable for their actions—but seldom questioned the ongoing structural change within American society. The over-the-top ostentatiousness of "yellow journalism," as seen in William Randolph Hearst's *New York Journal* and Joseph Pulitzer's *New York World*, reinvigorated debates about the role of press sensationalism. Hearst characterized such reporting as "journalism of action." Publisher Adolph Ochs purposely contrasted his *New York Times* against its competitors by emphasizing news as information, not entertainment, and refraining from sensationalism's ceaseless self-promotion.[16]

Editorial decisions shaped mass-market readerships by catering to the interests and worldviews of certain groups of readers while ignoring others. The exclusion of African Americans from the emerging mass media reflected a larger effort to mitigate the social changes rocking the United States by containing and silencing perceived outsiders. Scholar Richard Ohmann describes how national magazine editors defined an emerging, modern "professional-managerial class" by providing "their readers with a range of information and interests that linked them conversationally to other readers in the same circle of acquaintance, and culturally to like-minded readers across the nation." Among these white, urban middle-class readers, African Americans were seen as "increasingly irrelevant to the social project of industrial capitalism." Fittingly, then, editors avoided stories about racial repression, which would have undermined their magazines' aspirational tone by challenging white readers' claims to privilege. Instead, advertisers reinforced conceptions of African Americans—as well as other ethnic and racial groups—as premodern through the stereotyped images of the happy servant and irascible pickaninny. Such depictions protected the interests of white entitlement—just like southern newspaper editors' lurid lynching stories, which transformed white lawlessness into a sacred duty to protect white womanhood. Denied a voice in mainstream journalism, racial, ethnic, and political minorities strengthened their own dissident presses.[17]

Black editors participated in the sweeping changes that recast American journalism, even though racial barriers deprived them of the capital needed to fully modernize their publications. Novelist and editorialist James Weldon Johnson characterized the black press as "a feeble and struggling medium." The typical newspaper still employed only a handful of people—the proprietor, perhaps an assistant editor, a secretary who handled bookkeeping and read copy, and two or three part-time agents who claimed a percentage of the papers they sold. Many editors still had full-time careers in other professions. Publishers typically contracted out their mechanical work to white printers who could afford to buy printing presses.[18]

Even so, black journalism expanded at an unprecedented rate in the early 1900s. Publishers saw newspapering as a way to participate in the nation's political discourse, even though disenfranchisement and segregation curtailed their direct involvement in electoral politics. Aspiring journalists launched at least 1,320 newspapers between 1890 and 1910. That figure exceeded the total number of papers started in every other decade—combined—from 1860 to 1940. The cheapness of ink and paper made newspapers, at least financially, a low-risk, high-reward entrepreneurial venture. Most newspapers appeared in the South and folded quickly. The typical newspaper in Mississippi, for example, survived just one or two years. Northern editors, though, experienced more lasting success. They established the black press's first long-running secular periodical and several newspapers that would circulate nationally by World War II.[19]

The most successful editors aspired to fulfill the spirit and aims of the Niagara Movement, whose organizers demanded full political rights and integration into American life. Founded in 1905, the movement countered Booker T. Washington's rhetoric of accommodation. Washington, the politically connected and well-financed president of Tuskegee Institute, achieved national acclaim in 1895 by telling appreciative southern white businessmen that African Americans should pursue educational and economic success before they insisted on social and political equality. Washington urged black editors to moderate their views to protect interracial goodwill, and he waged a relentless public relations campaign to silence those who criticized his advocacy of delayed equality. The Niagara Movement's founders, led by W. E. B. Du Bois, an editor, activist, and academic, denounced Washington's manipulative press dealings by adopting a constitution that called for "freedom of speech and criticism" and "an unfettered and unsubsidized press." Among Du Bois's journalistic allies who attended the movement's founding conference were William Monroe Trotter of the *Boston Guardian*, J. Max Barber of the *Voice of the Negro*, Chase of the *Washington Bee*, Smith of the *Cleveland Gazette*, columnist John E. Bruce (known as Bruce Grit), and Wendell P. Dabney of the *Cincinnati Union*. Although the all-black Niagara Movement folded in 1909, its supporters inaugurated an era of enhanced militancy and pointed black journalism in a new direction.[20]

Fleeting but sophisticated monthly magazines, in particular, illustrated the coalescence of a racial outlook shaped by militancy, modernity, and the marketplace. Magazine editors aimed their eclectic mix of opinion, news, fiction, and poetry at a readership of elite blacks and sympathetic whites who could afford to pay upfront for a yearly subscription. They consciously depicted their periodicals as an erudite and cosmopolitan expansion of black print culture—the product of what a writer in *Alexander's Magazine* described as "the outcome of calm, deliberate, and critical thought." Leading magazines reinforced a broader intellectual commitment to an international conception of modern racial activism. Publishing from Atlanta, J. Max Barber and J. W. E. Bowen evaded southern parochialism in the *Voice of the Negro* (1904–1907) by commenting upon "Current History, Educational Improvements, Art, Science, Race Issues, Sociological Movements, and Religion." They commissioned articles on the Dominican Republic, Haiti, and the Philippines, and boasted that their magazine was read on every continent except Antarctica. Under the editorship of Pauline E. Hopkins, Boston's *Colored American Magazine* (1900–1909) developed into a first-rate literary journal that critiqued American racism and its consequences through fiction and poetry. Hopkins wrote a series of biographical sketches that countered white editors' stereotypes by depicting black men—and especially black women—as heroic defenders of a universal humanity that defined the modern age. "The dawn of the Twentieth century finds the Black race fighting for existence in every quarter of the globe," Hopkins wrote in 1903. "But the Negro still lives, and while life remains, Hope lifts a smiling face."[21]

Debuting in November 1910, *The Crisis: A Record of the Darker Races* emerged as the nation's foremost black publication thanks to editor W. E. B. Du Bois's

straightforward and unrelenting attacks on racism and inequality. As the official journal of the interracial NAACP, the Crisis was the rare black-oriented
publication with reliable funding from white supporters and a readership that
included many white subscribers. A prickly intellectual and tireless activist,
Du Bois earned a doctorate degree from Harvard University and taught sociology at Atlanta University before becoming the NAACP's director of publicity
and research. Like other editors, Du Bois had struggled for years to establish
a national platform from which he could denounce racism and urge African
Americans to greater achievements. Several months after founding the Niagara
Movement, Du Bois and two associates launched Moon's Illustrated Weekly. It
folded after thirty-four issues. One cofounder complained that the publication
might have survived if Du Bois had toned down his editorials. Du Bois then
wrote regularly for The Horizon, the magazine of the Niagara Movement. Despite
funding concerns, Du Bois persuaded the NAACP's board of directors to finance
a journal of "opinion and literature" that would "record important happenings
and movements in the world which bear on the great problem of interracial
relations and especially those which affect the Negro-American." The magazine
sold for ten cents a copy or one dollar for a yearly subscription. The first issue of
one thousand copies sold out. More success followed. By early 1914, the Crisis
claimed 33,000 monthly subscribers, and Du Bois operated nearly independent
of the NAACP's governing board. Circulation topped 45,000 in April 1916.[22]

Written from a black perspective for an interracial audience, the Crisis contradicted stereotyped images of African Americans by showcasing black men
and women as participants in modern life and as citizens active in shaping
the destiny of the United States. Du Bois argued that whites misjudged blacks
because they ignored "the educated and intelligent of the Negro people that have
led and elevated the mass." In its early years, the Crisis ran only a few photographs
of poor sharecroppers—a purposeful avoidance of images that a white reader
could quickly reduce to well-honed caricatures of wretchedness, ignorance, and
servility. Instead, Du Bois featured the educated black elite, whom he labeled
the "Talented Tenth." The journal's covers frequently displayed a photograph
or engraving of a carefully composed clubwoman—her expression, whether
smiling or sober, reflected her Victorian bearing, and her hairstyle and clothing spoke to her prosperity. A "Men of the Month" feature celebrated the civic,
educational, and business accomplishments of black professionals, regardless
of gender, through short biographical sketches. Accompanying photographs
reiterated the subjects' claims to respectability.[23]

Special editions associated elite African Americans with the white middle-
class's emphasis on learning and domesticity. Du Bois devoted the July 1913

W. E. B. Du Bois in the offices of the *Crisis*. Courtesy of the Photographs and Prints Division, Schomburg Center for Research in Black Culture, The New York Public Library, Astor, Lenox, and Tilden Foundations.

issue to the topic of education and published on its cover a formal portrait of thirteen students attending Indiana University. He used six inside pages to list the achievements of outstanding high school and college students and also ran fifty photographs of students and teachers. Similarly, Du Bois printed eighty-nine photographs of infants and children in the October 1914 issue. He argued that the images disproved racist assumptions linking skin color to hereditary deficiencies. "As social problems these children are of greatest interest," he wrote. "They are beautiful, bright and wholesome. There is no reason in the world why in any civilized human society they should not easily, gracefully, and effectively take their place and do their work, receiving the respect due to decent human beings." These children, Du Bois claimed, would be well educated, well fed, and well-groomed but also "compelled to prove before a prejudiced jury that they have a right to be treated as normal American citizens." The simple abundance of such images countered the perspective of white editors who treated black achievement and respectability as exceptional. Through such pictorials,

Du Bois attempted to expose sympathetic white liberals to their racial prejudices by asserting the ordinariness of black achievement.[24]

The *Crisis* also revealed how white editors transmitted stereotypes by dissecting articles and headlines to expose the manipulation of news coverage. Du Bois routinely excerpted columns, editorials, and articles from white newspapers and critiqued their racial biases. He argued that white journalists believed racial inferiority was an inherent, verifiable truth, and this assumption compelled them "to make the facts prove this thesis . . . and when stubborn facts appear that simply will not support this thesis there is almost complete silence." Du Bois unmasked journalistic bias in an occasional *Crisis* feature, "The Manufacture of Prejudice." The May 1911 issue illustrated how white reporters exaggerated and sensationalized racial conflict by comparing stories about three different incidents with testimony from other sources—a letter written by the NAACP chairman, firsthand reports from eyewitnesses, and a contradictory news story. In February 1913, Du Bois paired sensational headlines from white newspapers—including "WOMAN CLUBBED AND LEFT TO DIE; POSSE SEEKS NEGRO," and "RACE WAR IN A HIGH SCHOOL"—with less incendiary follow-up accounts printed in black newspapers. Regarding the clubbing, only a black newspaper reported that a white farm laborer confessed to the crime. The *Chicago Tribune* later admitted the school riot (initially reported as instigated by a black student) never occurred and printed a correction. A black editor, though, observed that the retraction appeared "in an obscure corner of the paper."[25]

Writing bluntly about racism for an interracial readership caused Du Bois to clash often with white readers and benefactors who accused him of excessive negativity and racial chauvinism. A regular feature, "The Burden," recounted incidents of white abuse and showed how racism manifested itself through violence, economic sanction, political fraud, courtroom manipulation, and accepted custom. Such articles were common fare in black newspapers, but they stunned uninformed white readers. Du Bois also wrote editorials with unsparing frankness. One satirical piece bemoaned the loss of white privilege and the right of white men to rape black women. Du Bois concluded this editorial by sardonically conceding he had been wrong to oppose lynching: "Hereafter we humbly pray that every man, black or white, who is anxious to defend women, will be willing to be lynched for his faith. Let black men especially kill lecherous white invaders of their homes and then take their lynching gladly like men."[26]

Readers' response to such editorials revealed the limits of racial understanding among white liberals. One white reader said she was "truly shocked" at Du Bois's outlook and warned that his journal "only creates discontent among your people." White NAACP board members constantly pressured Du Bois to moderate his editorials. Board chairman Oswald Garrison Villard wanted Du Bois to balance his recounting of white atrocities by printing news about black crimes. The suggestion infuriated Du Bois, who already fumed at Villard's paternalistic demeanor. Board member Mary W. Ovington pinpointed the cause of tensions: *"The magazine is the organ of two races, but its psychology is the psychology of the colored race."* She, too, urged Du Bois to placate his critics. He refused. Du Bois defended himself against charges of racial bitterness by restating his belief that stereotypes hid the depths of racial injustice from white readers. "This is a newspaper," Du Bois wrote. "It tries to tell the Truth. It will not consciously exaggerate in any way, but its whole reason for being is the revelation of the facts of racial antagonism now in the world, and these facts are not humorous."[27]

In the same year that Du Bois launched the *Crisis*, little-known publisher Robert S. Abbott moved to distinguish the *Chicago Defender* from its rivals by applying the modern journalism techniques of metropolitan dailies to a weekly black newspaper. In doing so, he established the template followed by the most successful black newspapers for much of the twentieth century. The son of former slaves, Abbott was born in 1868 in coastal Georgia. He studied printing at Hampton Institute and moved to Chicago in 1897 to attend law school.

Robert Abbott, founder of the *Chicago Defender.* Courtesy of the Yale Collection of American Literature, Beinecke Rare Book and Manuscript Library, Yale University.

His legal career stalled when he was unable to attract clients because of his dark complexion. He founded the *Defender* in 1905. It began as a four-page sheet published out of a boardinghouse by Abbott and friends who occasionally volunteered their time. A poor speller prone to awkward phrasing, Abbott seemed unlikely to triumph over a crowded field of competitors that included the venerable *Conservator*, best-selling *Appeal*, and intemperate *Broad Ax*. Little distinguished Abbott from his established rivals. That began to change in 1910 when he hired J. Hockley Smiley, a caterer-turned-journalist and the *Defender*'s first full-time employee, to overhaul his newspaper.[28]

Abbott and Smiley led the way in transforming black newspapers into commercial ventures of mass appeal by emulating the appearance and news conventions of the nation's most popular daily papers. Other editors also experimented with new layouts, provocative headlines, and more images, but none did so as quickly or as successfully as Abbott. (The *Defender* so resembled the Hearst newspapers that unfounded but persistent rumors alleged Hearst was Abbott's secret partner.) Abbott and Smiley deployed elements of sensationalism to imbue the weekly *Defender* with a sense of urgent immediacy rarely conveyed by their competitors. Banner headlines, often printed in red ink, ran the full length of the front page, morphing standard stories of racial abuse and achievement into breathless, breaking news. Out of inclination and calculation, Abbott refrained from overt partisanship as he condemned racial abuses. Tellingly, he was one of the few editors to avoid siding with either Washington or Du Bois in their long-running feud. In September 1914, the *Defender* became the first black newspaper in Chicago to expand to eight columns across eight pages. Abbott swelled with pride: "New and original matter coming from all parts of the world has necessitated this action. To make room for the growing business it hopes to do this fall and winter. The outlook is bright and the time is ripe." Seven months later, Abbott divided the newspaper into sections, promising consistent coverage of sports, churches, clubs, society, books, art, music, drama, fashion, health, legal aid, and housekeeping. A cartoon appeared on the editorial page. Reporters were hired. The *Defender* soon provided news coverage comparable in breadth to a small daily newspaper. Circulation grew to about 30,000.[29]

To a degree unmatched by its rivals, the *Defender* was a racialized consumer product purposely designed to appeal to the largest possible readership. Abbott cultivated working-class readers. He ran columns devoted to the doings of janitors, hotel workers, and railroad porters. He listed activities sponsored by minor churches and clubs, not just those attended by the city's prominent citizens. He printed regular dispatches from other states, keeping newcomers in touch with their hometowns. He ran promotions that offered prizes and brief celebrity to ordinary readers. Such material seemed to personalize the news even as the paper's content grew more impersonal—a result of Black Chicago's population growth and the staff's increased attention to a national circulation. Abbott touted the *Defender* as the reader's personal guide to understanding the impersonal city. A 1916 promotion, for example, boasted about the *Defender's* role in telling a Chicago woman about the death of an aunt in Nashville and informing another woman about the whereabouts of her estranged stepson. Learning of a relative's death or location through the newspaper, though, revealed the disruptions, not the connections, of modern black life.[30]

Billed as the "WORLD'S GREATEST WEEKLY," the *Defender* functioned as a promoter of modernity and urban life. Abbott's pathbreaking success stemmed from his vision of marrying the militancy of racial protest to the spectacle of modern life. Articles about lynchings, riots, and other racial wrongs appeared alongside news about celebrities, high-society scandals, and commercialized leisure. The juxtaposition served to exclude the racist South from modern life and optimistically cast the accoutrements of city living—such as musical performances, theatrical acts, and professional sports—as symbols of racial advancement.

The *Defender* was perfectly positioned to exploit the quickening of black migration out of the South after 1916. Abbott ran classified advertising that listed industrial job openings across the Midwest. Reporters and editors wrote news articles about groups' planned departures and southern white officials' concerns about the loss of black labor. Southern authorities enhanced Abbott's standing whenever they accused him of aggravating racial tensions and wherever they confiscated his newspapers. The *Defender's* editorial militancy imbued Abbott with the credibility of a race leader. "I love and honor the *Defender*," one reader wrote, "because it is the one concern that lives exactly up to its name, and further because it defends the virtue, honor, rights and dignity of a worthy people." Abbott's stature as a protector of black rights persuaded many southern readers who had never visited Chicago to trust editorials, columns, and articles that urged them to leave behind southern violence and discrimination for the promise of better work and more opportunities in the North. Among African Americans who remained in the South, the *Defender* fueled dreams of greater freedom and modern living incompatible with southern segregation.[31]

Abbott built the *Defender's* circulation with a far-flung distribution network that ceaselessly wooed potential customers. Newsboys hawked papers on the streets. Railroad porters sold them on trains and delivered bundles to sales agents across the nation. Musicians and actors carried them from town to town. Abbott hired Roscoe Conkling Simmons, a popular Republican orator better known than the *Defender*, to write a column and promote the paper on his speaking tours. Circulation leapt to 50,000 in late 1916, then to 90,000 in 1917, and to 125,000 in 1918. Roughly two-thirds of the *Defender*'s readers lived outside of Chicago. Ironically, circulation growth deepened readers' sense of personal connection to the *Defender* as African Americans nationwide consumed the same news stories.[32]

The stunning success experienced by the *Crisis* and the *Defender* emboldened other publishers to win circulation from established rivals in metropolitan markets by embracing greater editorial militancy and adopting modern journalism techniques. These editors crusaded against local discrimination, broadened news and feature coverage, and expanded business operations. They condemned the same racist practices criticized by their nineteenth-century predecessors. However, they wrote their editorials in the straightforward language of modern journalism rather than the flowery formalism of Victorianism. They also paired editorial opinion with original reporting on local discrimination in education, housing, employment, and government. Such reporting forced northern municipal officials to acknowledge a racial double standard and respond to complaints. Ray Stannard Baker warned in 1916 that black editors "have shown an increasing impatience and boldness of tone." Publishers' growing influence alarmed white authorities who accused them of arousing racial resentment.[33]

Cash-strapped but enduring newspapers now dotted the country. In Pittsburgh, lawyer Robert L. Vann, a pragmatic entrepreneur and Republican operative, partnered with five others in 1910 to found the *Courier*. He soon became the paper's editor and used its pages to promote his legal cases and build his clientele. Located above a funeral parlor, the *Courier* grew slowly because Vann rejected sensationalism. Even so, circulation climbed to 12,000 by 1919 thanks to his crusades for better housing and schooling, more job opportunities, improved medical care, and reduced crime. When the *Baltimore Afro-American* went bankrupt in 1897, the paper's printing foreman, Civil War veteran John H. Murphy Sr., bought it. Murphy later merged with a competitor, reincorporated to raise capital, and gained readers by campaigning to defeat state disenfranchisement amendments. In 1919, two years after adopting a sensationalistic format, the *Afro-American*'s circulation topped 19,000.[34]

James H. Anderson, a onetime bill poster, bellhop, baker, sailor, and sexton, founded the *New York Amsterdam News* in 1909 in a cellar on Amsterdam

Avenue. The paper teetered on bankruptcy and struggled to compete against the *New York Age*, which remained one of the nation's most respected black papers, even though Fortune had sold his stake two years earlier. The *Amsterdam News*'s circulation rose after Anderson moved his offices to Harlem, added society news, and printed a popular minister's sermons. Financial solvency, though, was not achieved until Edward A. Warren, an awning-maker, subsidized the paper's production. Warren reputedly pawned a large diamond ring three times to keep the presses rolling. Elsewhere on the East Coast, P. B. Young moved to Norfolk in 1907 to work as plant foreman for the *Journal and Guide*, a fraternal paper published by the Supreme Lodge Knights of Gideons. Young's father, a North Carolina slave-turned-editor, was a member. Young bought the paper in 1910 when state insurance regulations restricted the lodge's business activities. Located in the former Confederacy and serving a conservative business community, Young championed Tuskegee-style accommodationism but also organized the local NAACP branch. By 1919, the *Journal and Guide*'s circulation had grown from 500 to 4,000.[35]

In the Midwest, Joseph E. Mitchell launched the *St. Louis Argus* in 1912 with the backing of a small insurance company he had organized. An Alabama native who served in the Spanish-American War, Mitchell began his journalism career after a Republican sheriff refused to appoint more black deputies, saying the loyalty of black voters was not enough reason to reward them with patronage jobs. On the opposite side of Missouri, Chester A. Franklin moved to Kansas City in 1913 after helping his parents edit and print Denver's *Colorado Star* (formerly the *Statesman*). He hoped Kansas City's sizable black population could support a profitable publishing venture and operated a print shop for six years before establishing the *Call* in 1919. In Oklahoma, vegetable farmer Roscoe Dunjee founded Oklahoma City's *Black Dispatch* in 1915, even though his formal education ended in the fourth grade. Dunjee had worked in a print shop, and he learned about newspapering from his father, a Baptist minister who had published a newspaper three decades earlier in West Virginia. The *Black Dispatch* served as the official news organ of the local lodge of the Knights of Pythias. Like Young, Dunjee supported Booker T. Washington but became a driving force in the state's NAACP activities.[36]

And on the West Coast, Charlotta Bass bought California's oldest black newspaper, where she worked as an editor, in 1912 after its founder died. She renamed it the *California Eagle* and hired her future husband as a reporter. Bass gained national attention when she protested the filming of *Birth of a Nation*, a movie based on D. W. Griffith's novel *The Clansman* that depicted African

Americans in offensive stereotypes. In every major region of the nation, black journalists stood ready to condemn racial abuse and demand fairness and equality.[37]

"Rights Are Seldom Granted Except in a Crisis"
The Black Press in World War I

Civilian and military officials clashed with these surprisingly influential and contentious publishers during World War I when they attempted to censor press criticisms concerning racial discrimination in foreign and domestic affairs. The United States declared war on Germany in April 1917, despite widespread reluctance among its citizens to become involved in what many characterized as a European conflict. President Woodrow Wilson attempted to persuade skeptical Americans to commit themselves fully to the war effort by depicting the attacks of German U-boats on American merchant ships as the actions of a "selfish and autocratic power" and "natural foe to liberty." Germany's actions, Wilson claimed, jeopardized freedom everywhere. "The world," the president told Congress, "must be made safe for democracy." Mobilization included the construction of a vast state propaganda bureaucracy that manipulated Americans' sense of obligation to their nation to obtain their voluntary cooperation. Dissenters endured societal reproach, violent vigilantism, and state surveillance and prosecution, whether they were labor organizers, conscientious objectors, communists, draft dodgers, socialists, or African Americans staking a personal claim to Wilson's rhetoric of freedom. Propagandists and censors expected the nation's critics to delay their supposedly selfish concerns until after the war. Most black editors, though, refused to postpone their demands for full citizenship rights. They agreed with Harry Smith of the *Cleveland Gazette*, who observed, "Rights are seldom granted except in a crisis."[38]

World War I provoked racial unrest across the United States as the draft and industrial production relocated hundreds of thousands of African Americans at a time of heightened anxiety about German espionage. Unfamiliarity, job competition, overcrowding, and harassment led to assaults, riots, and murders. Authorities speculated that German agents instigated racial discord among black men and women to disrupt the American war effort. Southern politicians struggled to reconcile their demands for black loyalty in wartime with fears that black military service would pose a postwar challenge to segregation. The Selective Service system drafted nearly 400,000 black men into an army of almost 4 million soldiers and sailors. Black draftees joined a segregated military that deemed them inferior and refused to appropriately train and arm them. They were mostly confined to service details and excluded from combat. White soldiers refused to obey orders from black officers, who were never promoted higher than the rank of captain. Despite Wilson's call for national unity, racial discrimination and repression intensified during the war years.[39]

A vicious riot erupted in East St. Louis, Illinois, in July 1917, spurring protests across the nation by African Americans, including journalists. Racial tensions had simmered for months after the Aluminum Ore Company, which held military contracts for manufacturing airplane parts, replaced striking white workers with nonunion black workers. Physical attacks occurred. Rumors spread. When a carload of white men fired guns in a black neighborhood, residents shot back at the next car with white males, killing two police officers. Thousands of white men, as well as women, then stormed through black communities, burning homes and businesses, and attacking any African American they saw. When it was over, nearly forty blacks and eight whites were dead. Hundreds of black families lost their homes. Later in the month, the NAACP organized a silent march in New York City to protest lynching and racial violence. Ten thousand African Americans participated. "What shall we do to be saved?" asked Benjamin J. Davis Sr.'s *Atlanta Independent*. "If we don't work South we are jailed; if we do work North we are mobbed."[40]

Black editors denounced the rampage, criticized white press coverage, and accused the federal government of dispiriting indifference. As she had done twenty-five years earlier after a lynching in Memphis, Ida B. Wells packed her bags and set out to find the truth. She interviewed black refugees, learning that community leaders had asked the Illinois governor for protection a month before the attack. She accused the city police and state militia of participating in the riot. She urged the state to conduct a vigorous prosecution of white rioters. Wells published her investigation as a pamphlet. The military censored it. Back in Chicago, Wells's husband, lawyer and editor Ferdinand Barnett, urged the city's black residents to arm themselves in self-defense. At the *Defender*, Abbott criticized white editors who blamed the riot on black men and women. Southern editors often characterized the riot as proof that Northerners treated African Americans too leniently and integrated too easily. For Abbott, too many northern editors agreed. A few even speculated about the involvement of German instigators who aggravated black dissatisfaction. The *Defender* dismissed those editors for failing to understand the desires of African Americans: "The main thing we ask and have been asking for is to be let alone that we may work out our own salvation. We want nothing more, nothing less than every other American citizen is entitled to."[41]

The weekly edition of Joseph Mitchell's *St. Louis Argus* did not appear until four days after the violence and destruction started. "So much has been said in the daily press about the affair," the *Argus* reported, "that it would be a waste of time to review the facts in the horrible massacre were it not for the false reports made and the probable result on the minds of the people." The paper's banner headline labeled the riot "a national disgrace," and the lead story reassured readers in large print that "NEGROES DID NOT START TROUBLE." A reporter who visited East St. Louis dismissed rumors printed in daily newspapers that accused African Americans of orchestrating an ambush. Mitchell observed that police officers confiscated weapons from black men but seized none from the white mob. His paper reported that white attackers avoided "the thickly popu-lated district" and vented their "fury on isolated spots and helpless victims." Mitchell subtly highlighted that the city's white residents had failed to live up to the nation's ideals, noting that the riot occurred just before Independence Day and happened in the state most associated with President Abraham Lincoln, who authorized the Emancipation Proclamation. Mitchell argued that "city officials gave license to the rioters by their partiality in favor of the whites," but he also urged black residents to return to East St. Louis to prevent riot-ers from claiming a white supremacist victory. As the weeks passed, Mitchell resumed his editorial campaign to end military segregation and secure black soldiers' right to fight in combat. "It is enough for the Negro to be compelled to fight continuously against local prejudices," he wrote, "but when it is carried so boldly into the United States government service, it is just a little more than we can stomach without protest."[42]

Mitchell and other black editors urged President Wilson to condemn the riot in East St. Louis and reaffirm the federal government's commitment to prevent-ing racial violence and upholding the law equally. When Wilson failed to act, they accused him of hypocrisy and challenged his rationale for fighting overseas. In the *Crisis*, Du Bois described Wilson as "that silent man in the White House who wants Home Rule for Ireland, Freedom for Poles, and Justice for Arme-nians, but has no single word for the 3,000 American citizens lynched North and South." If Wilson failed to act, P. B. Young of the *Journal and Guide* argued that "the United States government should renounce its purposes for entering the world war and stand convicted among the nations of the earth as the great-est hypocrite of all times." The U.S. Post Office refused to deliver the *Richmond Planet* when Uzziah Miner, a former editor of the *Howard University Journal*, linked Wilson's silence with an act of civil disobedience—evading the draft. "I fail to see how I can conscientiously volunteer to fight for a 'World Democracy,'" Miner wrote, "while I am denied the fruits and blessings of a Democracy at home." The issue went out only after publisher John Mitchell hired a lawyer and traveled to Washington, D.C., to defend his publication.[43]

The month after the East St. Louis riot, publishers crafted a more circumspect editorial stance after black soldiers at Camp Logan in Houston attacked a police station in retaliation for rampant and prolonged racial abuse. The incident began when a black soldier attempted to stop two white policemen from beating a black woman. The officers clubbed and arrested the soldier for interfering with an arrest. He was later released. Rumors, though, spread that the police had killed him. Desiring revenge and fearing a white attack, more than 150 armed black soldiers marched through Houston. About twenty people died in the ensuing clashes, including five police officers and four soldiers. The Army court-martialed 118 soldiers. Military tribunals found 110 soldiers guilty of mutiny and riot. Nineteen were hanged and sixty-three received life sentences. Without condoning the soldiers' actions, editors decried the merciless sentences. They judged the soldiers' violence within the context of American racism. John Murphy's *Afro-American* published an editorial that compared the rioting soldiers to southern lynch mobs. Both were guilty, he concluded, but only black men were punished for their crimes. "It will never be forgotten that these bold regulars who broke the law and merited the punishment," the paper observed, "were the victims of southern crackers and copperheads, who baited them on and taunted them beyond human endurance." Abbott's *Defender* published a more conciliatory editorial and generally avoided directly commenting on the incident. The *Defender* also characterized the soldiers' actions as an inappropriate response to legitimate grievances. While deploring the "ignorant, cracker element," Abbott encouraged African Americans to pursue reform by voting, not violence. Despite racial abuse, he asked them to wholeheartedly support the war effort. "If after the smoke of battle has cleared away we are not accorded the same rights and privileges other peoples enjoy, it will be time then to gather our forces, white and black, and crush every form of segregation in this broad land."[44]

Amid deadly riots, mutinous soldiers, and extensive press criticism, civilian and military authorities quit viewing black editors' attacks on the racial status quo as special pleading and instead regarded their written statements as potential calls for domestic insurrection. Wartime legislation aided state surveillance. Congress had already passed the Espionage Act of 1917. The act punished statements that could cause "insubordination, disloyalty, mutiny, or refusal of duty" among troops with a fine of up to $10,000 and twenty years in prison. The amending Sedition Act of 1918 went further, essentially making it illegal to criticize the United States if that criticism could be construed as harming the war effort. The acts authorized the Postmaster General to censor and impound offending publications and suspend second-class mailing permits. Black journalists and their publications, regardless of size or prominence, were monitored for disloyalty by the Post Office, State Department, Bureau of Investigation, and military intelligence divisions. Agents filed classified reports, combining personal interviews and press clippings with rumor, innuendo, and misunderstanding to link black journalists to "Negro subversion." Censors read black newspapers with exaggerated suspicion, particularly accounts of racial violence, criticisms of military segregation, and comparisons of southern racism to German atrocities. "The fomenting of race hatred among the negroes [sic] at this time," a postal lawyer wrote, "is extremely unfortunate and flavors strongly of German propaganda."[45]

Surveillance was extensive, but prosecution was rare. Investigators routinely met with publishers to express the government's concerns and outline possible consequences. They intended to intimidate, relying on threats of legal action and the loss of mailing privileges to achieve editorial moderation. The financial toll of either action threatened to bankrupt a small newspaper. As the nation's most influential black publisher, Abbott met repeatedly with government authorities. White southerners knew the *Defender*'s editorial mission jeopardized the future of segregation, which they considered a threat to national security. They pressured federal authorities to investigate. A Bureau of Investigation agent in Chicago asked Abbott about his paper's finances and checked his credit record. Postal officials forwarded copies of the *Defender* to Washington, D.C., for legal review. Major Walter H. Loving, a black Army investigator, visited the *Defender*'s offices in May 1918 and warned Abbott that "the eye of the government is centered upon his paper, and caution should be his guide."[46]

Editors, though, evaded punishment mostly because they seldom condemned the war itself, despite significant black opposition to it. Although an outlet of protest, black newspapers also served as a forum for state propaganda. Editors drew a clear line between advocating for racial justice and denouncing the United States. They rarely challenged President Wilson's contention that the war was fought to make the world safe for democracy. Instead, they asked why African Americans were excluded from democratic discourse. While they questioned why black men should join a discriminatory military, they avoided encouraging draft evasion or registering as consciousness objectors. They cautiously—and repeatedly—reaffirmed their patriotism. Abbott responded to

Loving's warning by touting proofs of his loyalty and distinguishing the difference between the *Defender*'s attacks on "the evils of the South" and its loyal support for "the great cause of Democracy." He reminded Loving that he "gave unlimited space" to promote the sale of Liberty Bonds. The same month Loving visited Abbott, he also warned the *Argus*'s Mitchell to moderate his editorials or lose his mailing privileges. Mitchell stood accused of "professing loyalty" but publishing news that "proved both harmful and injurious to the morale of the negroes [*sic*] of St. Louis." The accusation came after Mitchell paired an editorial that supported an antilynching bill with an editorial asking readers to buy Liberty Bonds. Mitchell dared Loving to identify any treasonous statements, asking "whether it is considered disloyal for us to tell of the wrongs that are being daily directed against us." Surveillance and intimidation led editors to temper their words but seldom silenced their criticisms.[47]

G. W. Bouldin, editor of the *San Antonio Inquirer*, became the exception when a jury found him guilty of attempting to cause mutiny among military forces. A local Bureau of Investigation agent obtained a criminal complaint against Bouldin for publishing a guest column in November 1917 that defended the soldiers court-martialed in Houston. In an open letter to those soldiers, Clara L. Threadgill-Dennis claimed, "It is far better that you be shot for having tried to protect a Negro woman, than to have you die a natural death in the trenches of Europe, fighting to make the world safe for a democracy that you can't enjoy." The author told the soldiers that she had needed them in Austin that week to stop a streetcar conductor from insulting her. Proximity and timing seemingly mattered in Bouldin's prosecution. Threadgill-Dennis's sentiment was widely shared among African Americans, and other black newspapers had printed similar statements, although not so bluntly. Bouldin, though, published in the state where the riot had occurred, and the column praised soldiers then being court-martialed. Federal officials in Texas likely saw themselves as deterring a second riot—an imminent danger—when they arrested Bouldin. Court testimony indicated Bouldin never saw the column before it was published. It did not matter. A jury found him guilty. A judge sentenced him to two years in a federal penitentiary. He was paroled after about one year.[48]

Editors who appeared to capitulate to state pressure endured fierce criticism. Du Bois jeopardized his reputation as a leading civil rights activist in July 1918 when he wrote in the *Crisis*, "Let us, while this war lasts, forget our special grievances and close our ranks shoulder to shoulder with our own white fellow citizens and the allied nations that are fighting for democracy." Other black editors had routinely vowed to not allow racial wrongs to hamper black participation in the war. However, those editors lacked Du Bois's national stature, and they avoided the appearance of compromised integrity. Critics accused Du Bois of abandoning his principles for personal gain—a captaincy in the Army's military intelligence branch. NAACP Board Chairman Joel Spingarn, also an Army major, had informally offered the commission to Du Bois, pitching it as a way to help win the war and secure civil rights. After Du Bois agreed to accept the position, Spingarn assured the commander of military intelligence that Du Bois had promised to "change the tone" of the *Crisis*. By then, Du Bois likely had little choice but to temper his words: White NAACP board members were scandalized by being associated with a potentially seditious publication. Federal investigators had already visited NAACP offices and written letters warning of possible prosecution. The Post Office bolstered the government's case when it twice declared the *Crisis* unsuitable for mailing. (The declarations came after the controversial issues were delivered.) Du Bois defended his call to suspend civil rights agitation until after the war and vowed that black military service would be rewarded in the future. "If this is OUR country," he wrote in August, "then this is OUR war." Amid the ensuing controversy, the military commission was never formally offered. After the war, Du Bois redoubled his demands for equality, depicting racial reform as the price to be paid for the black soldiers who died to protect democracy.[49]

Press relations were not one-sided. Federal authorities also listened. Black editors' conversations and correspondence with government officials led to modest consideration of African Americans' concerns. Federal officials expected their June 1918 meeting in Washington, D.C., with thirty-one editors and ten other black representatives to have "an excellent effect on the colored press," resulting in more favorable coverage. However, conference organizers knew they had to make concessions toward racial reform to prove their sincerity and win over skeptical publishers. The editors identified fourteen demands they believed would bolster African Americans' support for the war. Most of their demands aimed to alleviate discrimination within the military, such as equalizing the racial distribution of service and support details, enlisting black doctors, training and promoting more black officers, and employing black nurses in the Red Cross. They also requested clemency for the soldiers sentenced to death or prison for their involvement in the attacks in Houston. Two other demands concerned news coverage of African Americans involved in the war effort. Editors wanted military officials to obtain and distribute news about black troops, and they wanted them to correct distortions and omissions printed in white newspapers about black soldiers' service. The editors' top concern, though, was presidential support for antilynching legislation. Several editors described lynching as "producing a dangerous feeling among the colored people of the country."[50]

Wilson's administration delivered enough concessions to give the appearance of support without promoting significant social change. Most notably, Wilson condemned lynching for the first time in July 1918. Although he neither mentioned race nor singled out the South, Wilson observed that every lynching was "a blow at the heart of order, law, and humane justice." He accused the vigilante of emulating the German soldier, his actions proving he was "no true son of this great democracy, but its betrayer." Wilson reiterated the theme of national hypocrisy trumpeted by black editors. "How shall we commend democracy to the acceptance of other peoples," he asked, "if we disgrace our own by proving that it is, after all, no protection to the weak?" Other government actions also occurred. Col. Charles Young, the Army's highest-ranking black officer until he was discharged in June 1917 for medical reasons, was reinstated. The War Department ordered the Red Cross to employ black nurses. The president commuted the death sentence of ten soldiers who participated in the Houston riot. The Committee on Public Information accredited Ralph W. Tyler, a conference participant and editor of the *Cleveland Advocate*, to report from France. Tyler was the only officially credentialed black war correspondent. Although Wilson never endorsed antilynching legislation, his compromises allowed black editors to claim their efforts had gained a measure of recognition for black concerns unseen at the federal level since Reconstruction ended.[51]

• • •

The state's intense surveillance and Wilson's conciliatory gestures showed how an escalating racial militancy in the early twentieth century had expanded commercial black newspapers' influence. The hallmarks of nineteenth-century journalism remained but were altered amid proliferating publications, soaring readerships, modern living, and unrequited demands for wartime sacrifices. Condemnations of racial violence were still journalists' stock-in-trade. Political partisanship continued to shape news coverage but less frequently defined it. More editors challenged Tuskegee-style accommodationism, especially outside of the South. Editors still urged readers to embrace Victorian values and racial uplift, but their bromides were increasingly undercut by urban lifestyles, leisure activities, and consumer products promoted and advertised in metropolitan newspapers. When the twentieth century began, white authorities viewed black editors mostly as an annoyance and occasionally as a localized threat. During World War I, civilian and military officials realized they could not silence publishers' criticisms even amid the precariousness of combat. As individuals, editors and reporters were susceptible to white wrath and discipline. As a group, they claimed to rival ministers as Black America's preeminent leaders. Commercial journalists strengthened that assertion over the next two decades with newswriting emboldened by alternative editors who aggressively enlarged the meaning of racial justice and extended the fight against white supremacy beyond the United States' borders.

CHAPTER 2

Enter the "New Crowd" Journalists

Wallace Thurman, a novelist, editor, and failed publisher, launched in November 1928 what he described as "an independent magazine of literature and thought." He called it *Harlem: A Forum of Negro Life*. In his first (and next-to-last) editorial, Thurman criticized an older generation's spent reportage as "nothing else but preaching and moaning." For Thurman, modern black journalism was inextricably linked to the sensibilities of the "New Negro"—that idealized figure symbolizing the forward-looking African American forged from the dissonance of twentieth-century industrialism, urbanism, and mobility. Thurman urged journalists to emulate the convention-shattering authors and poets of the Harlem Renaissance by embracing "new points of views and new approaches to old problems."[1]

That same month, literary benefactor Eugene Gordon outlined similar parallels between the professionalization of black journalism and the trope of the New Negro. He praised reporters for developing a new sense of professional standing and converting to political radicalism. Gordon, a leftist press critic and the only black editor at the white-owned *Boston Post*, credited young college graduates with redesigning sloppily edited and poorly composed weeklies. He contended that young journalists, inspired by Harlem's radical orator-editors, "dared to state baldly on the printed page what had hitherto been only whispered in secret and dark places: a desire for complete social equality; an admiration for the Bolshevisitic experiment in Russia; and contempt for all Negroes who were less radical than the writers themselves were." Realistic depictions of black life in fiction freed journalists to more forcefully scrutinize and chastise real-life race leaders. Like their more celebrated literary colleagues, reporters used text and image to interrogate stereotypes as well as conventions concerning class, culture, and citizenship. "They all breathed that same fierce fire of independence and radicalism," Gordon claimed, "independence of thought on sacrosanct questions of the day; radicalism with relation to the social and economic condition of the workers."[2]

Thurman and Gordon trumpeted the perspective of a young cohort of journalists whose political radicalization and unsparing criticism of a racist nation-state during the interwar years eventually established a new template for black newswriting. The outlines of this reporting style first appeared in the pages of a fledgling alternative press that formed during World War I. Radical editors, frustrated by an exclusionary war effort and escalating postwar violence, equated compromise and conciliation with the continuance of American racism. They instead searched for alternatives to the status quo, advancing race-first concepts like "Negro consciousness" and "back to Africa," as well as socialist and communist critiques of the nation's discriminatory political economy. Commercial journalists extended the alternative press's influence by providing news coverage of radical editors' political views and cultivating a network of personal friendships and professional relationships that encouraged writers—whether they considered themselves political activists, professional journalists, or literary authors—to write for different mediums within an expansive black print culture. The young writers of the Harlem Renaissance further refined black newswriting in the 1920s by developing a modernist literary aesthetic that explored the meaning of black life and identity in its fullest terms, regardless of possibly inviting white condescension. These authors and poets challenged established writing conventions by highlighting the hypocrisy of conservative Victorian values and exposing the sins and scandals of their race. The controversies stoked by radical polemicists and literary superstars reinforced decisions by many commercial newspaper publishers to shift to tabloid sensationalism, the era's defining journalistic mode, amid bruising competition for circulation.

The "New Negroes" of Newsprint

World War I ended in November 1918 with an Allies victory but few significant gains for the oppressed and colonized people who had aided the winners. The victorious European nations swiftly reaffirmed their commitment to maintaining imperial empires and ignored President Woodrow Wilson's support in peace negotiations for a "free, open-minded, and absolutely impartial adjust-ment of all colonial claims." Despite their contributions and sacrifices, African Americans received no meaningful recognition from either the military or the federal government. W. E. B. Du Bois's plea to "close ranks" with white citizens produced no amelioration of black grievances. Instead, a wave of racial violence gripped the nation in the summer of 1919 amid high unemployment, climbing inflation, and exaggerated fears of anarchist terrorism. More than twenty riots occurred, with black victims suffering at the hands of white attackers in cities as diverse as Knoxville, Tennessee, Omaha, Nebraska, and Washington, D.C. Federal officials routinely characterized black expressions of dissent as "race hatred." White authorities who had blamed wartime racial unrest on the provo-cations of German spies now feared African Americans were being duped by communist infiltrators inspired by the Russian Revolution.[3]

The most violent attacks happened in Chicago, and federal investigators and municipal officials accused journalists—white and black—of inflaming racial tensions there with inaccurate, exaggerated, and prejudiced news cover-age. The rioting started with a drowning. A black swimmer died after he was pelted with rocks thrown by young white men angered when he drifted into waters reserved for whites. Days of mounting violence erupted. Several dozen African Americans died, and hundreds were wounded. City leaders formed a commission to examine the riot's causes. Commission members recommended changes in how newspapers covered racial issues. They urged white journalists to present African Americans in a more objective and positive manner. They similarly encouraged black publishers to abandon sensationalism and report with greater accuracy on interracial incidents. The commission, though, also revealed how white citizens perceived black journalism as a threat to the pre-vailing social order. Its members paternalistically asked black publishers to muffle their militancy by devoting "more attention to educating Negro readers as to the available means and opportunities of adjusting themselves and their fellows into more harmonious relations with their white neighbors and fellow-citizens." By asking African Americans to conform to white expectations, the statement amounted to an endorsement of Booker T. Washington's rhetoric of racial uplift and accommodation. *Chicago Defender* publisher Robert S. Abbott, a commission member, signed off on the recommendation.[4]

The onslaught of racial violence swelled the popularity of radical editors who predicted the nation's entrenched racism would remain unwavering once the war ended. At first, speaking atop small stepladders, street orators like Hubert Harrison, A. Philip Randolph, and Marcus Garvey, among others, greeted tens of thousands of migrants—whether from the South, the Caribbean, or elsewhere—as they arrived in Harlem for new jobs and new lives. From 1910 to 1920, New York witnessed a staggering surge in its black population, jumping from 90,000 black residents to more than 150,000—a 66 percent increase. Like native-born New Yorkers, the migrants lived lives constricted by low wages, overcrowded and dilapidated housing, poor access to medical care, and limited opportunities for improvement. They encountered hostility from white workers who believed the newcomers threatened their jobs, families, and neighborhoods. Amid the postwar unrest, radical editors exerted a cultural influence that far exceeded their mostly modest circulations and erratic publication runs. Their editorials came to define the "New Negro," who chose confrontational opposition to continued oppression.[5]

As their crowds swelled, the orators turned to print, establishing the alternative black press to extend their influence to readers they would never meet in the street. Despite sharp political differences and frequent feuding, these orator-editors shared broadly similar racial and political outlooks. They jointly promoted racial pride, condemned racism, demanded full equality, and advocated armed self-defense. "The New Negro is Negro first, Negro last, and Negro always," Harrison wrote. "He needs not the white man's sympathy; all he is asking for is equal justice before the law and equal opportunity in the battle of life." Radical editors attributed the origins of World War I to capitalism's ceaseless drive for new markets and Western imperialism's worldwide exploitation of people of color. They recognized that shared oppression and common cultural traits united African-descended peoples, regardless of their nationality, in a Pan-African freedom movement. They repudiated black leaders who asked African Americans to moderate their demands and pursue interracial cooperation. They believed black soldiers returned from fighting for democracy abroad ready to more aggressively demand their personal freedoms. "The New Negro has arrived," declared Randolph's *Messenger*, "with stiffened backbone, dauntless manhood, defiant eye, steady hand and a will of iron."[6]

Alternative editors rejected half-measures and ridiculed activists whom they believed too readily abandoned their principles. Hubert Harrison, a West Indian orphan dubbed "the father of Harlem radicalism," was among the most influential of New York's black militants. Harrison migrated from St. Croix to the United States in 1900 at age 17, lost a comfortable career as a postal clerk after publicly criticizing Booker T. Washington, and became a formidable socialist organizer and thinker. Frustrated with white socialists' refusal to acknowledge the importance of race and racism in the workers' struggle, the dark-skinned Harrison founded the Liberty League of Negro Americans in 1917. The league was a radical, all-black alternative to the NAACP. Harrison promoted his political views in *The Voice*, a four-page newspaper that sold for a penny. Harrison described his paper "as the medium of expression for the new demands and aspirations of the new Negro," a figure who represented "a breaking away of the Negro masses from the grip of old-time leaders." In *The Voice*'s first issue, Harrison characterized the riot in East St. Louis as a "pogrom." "How can America hold up its hands in hypocritical horror at foreign barbarism," he asked, "while the red blood of the Negro is clinging to those hands?" Harrison claimed white editors concealed reports of black men repulsing white attackers because they feared other African Americans might emulate the defenders. "If white men are to kill unoffending Negroes," he wrote, "Negroes must kill white men in defense of their lives and property." Within a month, *The Voice*'s circulation topped eleven thousand.[7]

President Wilson's call to defend democracy worldwide unleashed a more determined effort among African Americans to denounce colonialism and capitalism as exploitative systems rooted in white supremacy. This unexpected twist on the president's words troubled civilian and military authorities even more than the unrelenting demands to protect the civil rights of black men and women. The fight for civil rights was an argument for inclusion within American society. The politics of anticolonialism and anticapitalism jeopardized the foundation of Western civilization and aimed to create a liberation movement that united African-descended peoples from around the world. State censors and investigators monitored the radical editors who espoused these beliefs, intending to minimize their influence and moderate their politics. Federal officials, for example, did not invite radical editors to the June 1918 editors' conference in Washington, D.C., that inaugurated a new relationship between federal agencies and the black press. This deliberate exclusion reinforced perceptions that alternative editors were dogmatic political activists of marginal influence—illegitimate racial representatives. In contrast, the meeting positioned integrationist-minded commercial publishers as race leaders and businessmen who understood the value of compromise and deal-making in a democratic-capitalist political economy.

Harrison distinguished his brand of radical politics from other strains of socialism and communism through his conception of "Negro consciousness." Propaganda billing World War I as a campaign for democracy, he claimed, exposed the degree to which Western capitalism exploited people of color worldwide. "Whether in the United States or in Africa or China," he wrote, "the economic subjection is without exception keener and more brutal when the exploited are black, brown and yellow, than when they are white." This realization led the New Negro to intensify demands for full democracy and racial equality. Harrison contended that black radicals who embraced socialism or communism did so not so much because those ideologies promised to level the wealth disparity between owners and workers, but because "the dogma of Race-Consciousness" positioned those ideologies as a means to defeat a capitalistic system that upheld white supremacy. Harrison believed radicals who were explicitly racial—those who nurtured "racialism, race-consciousness, racial solidarity"—would attract more black followers than either socialism or communism because only they understood that "the roots of Race-consciousness must of necessity survive any and all changes in the economic order." Harrison's disillusionment with socialism stemmed from his belief that racism would persist even if workers eliminated capitalism's economic inequalities. "Any man today who aspires to lead the Negro race," Harrison wrote, "must set squarely before his face the idea of 'Africa first.'"[8]

Harrison's adamancy on keeping "Africa first" sparked feuds with other editors and attracted government surveillance. Harrison joined William Monroe Trotter, the uncompromising publisher of the *Boston Guardian*, in June 1918 to sponsor the National Liberty Congress, a six-day conference held to denounce lynching and argue for expanded civil liberties for African Americans. Attendees cast the Liberty Congress as a militant alternative to the government-organized meeting where editors like Abbott and Du Bois were "wined and dined at the government's expense for the sole purpose of muzzling them." The Bureau of Investigation monitored the conference, and a military intelligence informant described Harrison, a naturalized citizen, as a person of "questionable" loyalty. The conference concluded with a petition asking the U.S. Congress to outlaw segregation and discrimination anywhere under federal authority, pass anti-lynching legislation, and uphold constitutional amendments concerning black civil liberties. The signers claimed congressmen needed to fulfill these demands so "our country may not be weakened in moral position, prestige, and power by violations here of the noble pronouncements of its President." While attendees reaffirmed their loyalty, they refused to turn their conference into a rally for the war effort. Soon afterward, Harrison denounced Du Bois for his "Close Ranks" editorial, which asked African Americans to set aside their "special grievances." Encouraged by Major Walter H. Loving, the black military investigator, Harrison publicly linked Du Bois's softening editorial stance to his promised military commission. "This ruins him," Harrison declared, "as an influential person among Negroes at this time."[9]

Harrison's ideas and actions inspired other radicals, including a pair of southern transplants touting "scientific radicalism." A. Philip Randolph and Chandler Owen were socialists in their late twenties, searching for steady work, when they launched the monthly *Messenger* in November 1917. Backed by the Socialist Party of America, they pitched their publication as "The Only Radical Negro Magazine in America." They defined scientific radicalism as an unapologetic attack on American racism founded upon an interracial class consciousness that would "build a new society—a society of equals, without class, race, caste or religious distinctions." Randolph and Owen saw signs of their ultimate success in the rise of the Soviet Union, fall of the German empire, and unrest in the British colonies. They advocated mass protest, endorsed the Russian Revolution, demanded integrated unions, and supported women's suffrage. Both men opposed World War I. They also rejected Du Bois's plea to halt racial protest until after victory was achieved. "Since when has the subject race," Owen asked, "come out of a war with its rights and privileges accorded for such participation?" Randolph and Owen were arrested in Cleveland in August 1918 for violating the Espionage Act after urging black men to avoid the draft and fight for their rights at home. A judge, though, dismissed the charges. According to Randolph, the judge saw the young editors as unsophisticated dupes misled by savvy white socialists. Regardless, the Post Office suspended the *Messenger*'s second-class mailing privileges.[10]

As doctrinaire socialists, Randolph and Owen criticized militants like Harrison who emphasized the intransigence of racial difference and the fragility of class solidarity. They contrasted the class-oriented militancy of the "New Crowd Negro" against the "Old Crowd Negro," a dismissive label for established leaders who failed to recognize African Americans as "the most exploited of the American workers." Randolph derided the Old Crowd as "false leaders" whose advocacy of racial chauvinism threatened to stall a socialist uprising by discouraging black workers from recognizing that white workers shared their economic anxieties. Denouncing Harrison's "Race First" outlook as "an indefensible doctrine," Randolph and Owen argued, for example, that the true cause of race riots was not racial hatred, but capitalism and "the exploitation of human labor-power and the natural resources of the country, for private profits." Racial prejudice was just one of many weapons used by capitalists to divide workers. Race riots worked to undermine support for interracial unions, which in turn weakened the labor movement's ability to achieve its goals of higher wages and shorter hours. Racism protected owners' profits, and racial violence would persist for as long as capitalism existed. "The capitalist system must go," the *Messenger*'s editors wrote, "and its going must be hastened by the workers themselves."[11]

Another radical editor, West Indian activist Cyril Briggs, evolved into a communist committed to forging a revolutionary liberation movement among

African-descended peoples. Briggs immigrated to the United States in 1905 when he was 18. Unlike other radicals, he avoided public speaking because he stuttered. Briggs joined the fledgling *New York Amsterdam News* in 1912 and eventually took on editing duties. His editorials caught the attention of postal censors and military intelligence agents in May 1918 after he questioned why black soldiers should fight in the war and warned that a true black man would "no longer be satisfied to bite his tongue and hide his resentment in connection with the grievous wrongs suffered by his Race at the hands of American fiends who seem bent on out-Prussianising the Prussians!" Confronted by state authorities, Brigg's supervising editors claimed he had published his editorials without their knowledge. They promised to avoid writing future editorials that might violate the Espionage Act. Briggs later resigned. He began publishing the monthly *Crusader* in September 1918 to promote "Africa for the Africans." Briggs advocated "government of the Negro by the Negro and for the Negro" through the creation of an independent African nation, which he believed could be carved into existence through support of Wilson's call for self-determination among colonized peoples. Briggs briefly aligned his publication with the Hamitic League of the World, a Black Nationalist organization cofounded by three employees of an Omaha newspaper. To better advance his political views, Briggs organized the secretive African Blood Brotherhood for "the liberation of Africa and the redemption of the Negro race." An open admirer of the Russian Revolution, Briggs increasingly viewed an alliance with the international communist movement as the surest way to fulfill his editorial mission. He most likely joined the Communist Party in mid-1921, hoping to tap its resources and global network of activists to strengthen a black working-class movement that acknowledged but transcended disputes arising from diverse national origins.[12]

Marcus Garvey emerged as the era's most influential black radical and the founder of a mass back-to-Africa movement. Born in Jamaica in 1887, Garvey worked as a printer in Kingston, a timekeeper on a banana plantation in Costa Rica, and a messenger for the London-based *African Times and Orient Review*, an early advocate of Pan-Africanism. Inspired by his study with anticolonialists in England, Garvey returned to Jamaica in 1914 and organized the Universal Negro Improvement Association (UNIA) "with the program of uniting all the Negro peoples of the world into one great body to establish a country and Government absolutely their own." Garvey sailed to New York City in 1916 to raise money for a Jamaican trade school, but he decided to stay in the United States after recruiting about one thousand new members in Harlem. "Industrially, financially, educationally and socially," Garvey said, "the Negroes of both hemispheres have to defer to the American brother, the fellow who has revolutionized history in race development." State authorities monitored Garvey closely for sedition during and after World War I, infiltrating his meetings, reading his newspaper, and interviewing supporters and critics. White officials regarded Garvey with a mix of arrogance and anxiety. They scoffed at his rhetoric concerning the creation of an independent, black-led nation in colonized Africa but also feared the violence and upheaval that could result from armed men attempting to fulfill those ambitions. Garvey's surging popularity further worried them. Within a few years, the UNIA boasted more than seven hundred chapters worldwide.[13]

Garvey created the world's largest organization of black, working-class men and women—a group that historian Steven Hahn says "left its mark on every major black social and political movement of the twentieth century." With its uniforms and conventions and declarations, the UNIA stoked racial pride by assuring its members that they deserved better treatment. Unlike Du Bois and his emphasis on the educated well-to-do who belonged to the "Talented Tenth," Garvey placed janitors, bellhops, waitresses, and clerks in prominent leadership positions. Unlike the white-led NAACP, the UNIA was an all-black organization that never compromised its ideals to satisfy the concerns of wealthy white patrons. While Garvey appreciated aspects of socialism and communism, he preferred to nurture and expand black-owned businesses, their profitability enriching African Americans and refuting racist stereotypes. Garvey's persistence and popularity won over some critics. John Edward Bruce, a respected columnist known as "Bruce Grit," initially dismissed Garvey as a "*glib* phrase maker and a dreamer," telling a military investigator the UNIA's plans for redeeming Africa were "impracticable, utopian, and jackassical." Ten months later, though, Bruce reconsidered his opposition as Garvey spoke atop a stepladder at the corner of Lenox Avenue and 135th Street in Harlem. Garvey again outlined his mission, which Bruce summarized as an effort "to draw all Negroes throughout the World together, to make one big brotherhood of the Black Race for its common good, for mutual protection, for commercial and industrial development, and for fostering of business enterprises." Ill-served by the Republican Party and unconvinced by socialism, Bruce realized he had no reason to oppose Garvey, particularly since no one else had offered a better plan for fighting racism. Bruce believed critics mischaracterized the true intent of Garvey's "back to Africa" movement. He told Garvey, "I think I see with tolerably clear vision that your purpose is to lay the foundation broad and deep, so that the Negroes of the coming day will know better than we . . . how to possess and hold and develop the heritage which the Almighty has given to the black race."[14]

Garvey communicated with his followers around the Atlantic basin—and fostered a sense of transnational communal connection—through the weekly

Negro World. Its editors reprinted Garvey's speeches, devoted the front page to his extended essays, covered national conventions, and reported on local chapters. While unswervingly focused on reaffirming Garvey's leadership, the *Negro World* also reinforced readers' militancy and infused them with a sense of their own significance. A Garvey biographer observes that "pledges, promises and proclamations were laid before the reader much as they'd previously been laid before the King." Editors solicited reader-written poems that expressed spiritual connections to Africa, skewered the Ku Klux Klan, and celebrated the UNIA. Letters to the editor linked isolated readers—perhaps in a Cuban village, South African city, or Alabamian whistle-stop—to a worldwide movement. "Kindly allow me a small spot in your big world," began a letter from a reader in Bermuda. Bold banner headlines—"AFRICA THE LAND OF HOPE AND PROMISE FOR NEGRO PEOPLES OF THE WORLD" and "THE NEGRO DESIRES COMMERCIAL AND INDUSTRIAL PROSPERITY, EDUCATIONAL AND SOCIAL PROGRESS AND POLITICAL LIBERTY"—nurtured pride in ancestral heritage and future prospects. Garvey claimed a peak unaudited circulation of more than two hundred thousand. British and French colonial authorities banned the newspaper. They feared the *Negro World* would provoke unrest with its demands for self-governance and support for a return to Africa where black-majority rule could prevail.[15]

"You Must Be a Wide-Awake Racial Man"
Extending the Radicals' Reach

Alternative editors and their publications—whether *The Voice*, *Messenger*, *Crusader*, *Negro World*, or others—transformed the supposedly fringe perspectives of the New Negro Movement into a widely understood, if hotly debated, political movement. Briggs encouraged members of the African Blood Brotherhood to convert others to their political views by organizing literary clubs that discussed black history and news about racial problems. He instructed members to "build up a strong public opinion against the serviles of the race, against ignorance, against immorality and race debasement." Briggs also attempted to shape news coverage more directly by establishing a mimeographed weekly news service. He distributed the Crusader News Service to more than two hundred black newspapers in the United States, West Indies, and Africa. Small publishers with limited budgets were especially eager to fill blank space by printing Briggs's free editorials and dispatches. Newspapers such as the *Savannah* (Georgia) *Tribune* and *St. Paul* (Minnesota) *Appeal*, for example, published brief articles about the Communist International's proposal to fight racial discrimination, radical poet

Claude McKay's trip to Europe, and Garvey's founding of a daily newspaper. By the early 1930s, Briggs's news service had offices in New York, Paris, and Cape Town and served as a key distribution center for the *Negro Worker*, a communist-backed trade union publication edited by George Padmore, a prominent communist organizer and staunch anticolonialist.[16]

Other radical editors goaded better-known commercial publishers into acknowledging them and their viewpoints every time they contrasted the militancy of the "New Crowd" to the alleged docility of the "Old Crowd." Randolph and Owen subversively inverted black journalism's practice of lauding race leaders with a regular "Who's Who" feature that abandoned nuance to ridicule prominent race men as conservative accommodationists, regardless of their actual politics. In the *Messenger*, the Old Crowd included journalists like Du Bois; veteran editor T. Thomas Fortune; *New York Age* editorialist James Weldon Johnson; NAACP organizer, orator, and columnist William Pickens; and Howard University educator and columnist Kelly Miller. The editors skewered Roscoe Conkling Simmons, the well-known Republican speaker and *Chicago Defender* columnist, as representative of others who were "bankrupt in information, poverty stricken in ideas, intellectual Lilliputians, and mental midgets." Randolph labeled Fortune "a peddler of editorial slush." Floyd J. Calvin, the *Messenger*'s assistant editor, claimed that the influence of Fred R. Moore, editor of the *New York Age* since he bought it in 1907 with money borrowed from Booker T. Washington, was "rapidly waning, in proportion as the New Crowd demonstrates to the Negro public the difference between *brain*-work and *guess*-work."[17]

Commercial publishers popularized alternative editors' viewpoints—even as they rejected them—by excerpting radicals' editorials, writing rebuttals, covering conventions and lectures, and reporting on personalities and scandals. Garvey's fame as the nation's leading black militant threatened the standing and credibility of "Old Crowd" leaders, who were genuinely baffled by his mass popularity. His journalistic critics often depicted Garvey either as a fraud who fleeced unsuspecting black men and women of their hard-earned wages or as a vainglorious troublemaker who jeopardized legitimate racial reform in the United States. James Weldon Johnson argued that "the whole history of African colonization schemes" was "a colossal failure." "Mr. Garvey and those with him," Johnson wrote in the *Age*, "are either deceiving themselves or deceiving others."[18]

Garvey's scandals invited skeptical coverage from a sensationalist press. An assassin attempted to kill him in 1919. The State Department refused to issue a visa in 1921, preventing him from returning to the United States for several months after traveling abroad. His shipping line went bankrupt in 1922 amid allegations of mismanagement and corruption and the filing of mail fraud charges. Garvey even met with leaders of the Ku Klux Klan that same year and validated its members' acceptance of segregation—a mistake that severely diminished his popularity. In 1923, two Garveyites were convicted of murdering James Eason, an expelled UNIA leader who founded a rival organization. Each incident received extensive coverage in commercial newspapers.[19]

Amid these controversies, Du Bois's *Crisis* and Abbott's *Defender* seemed to rival the *Negro World* in their coverage of Garvey and the UNIA. "Marcus Garvey is, without doubt," Du Bois wrote in May 1924, "the most dangerous enemy of the Negro race in America and in the world. He is either a lunatic or a traitor." The *Defender* gleefully reported on Garvey's legal woes and exchanged insults with him. Abbott saw himself as protecting African Americans' ability to fight racial discrimination in the United States. To emphasize Abbott's point, the *Defender* published a supposedly private exchange between a UNIA official and one of its reporters. The official asked, "Why do you fellows insist upon exposing us?" The reporter replied, "We are simply attacking your system of operation. We know that your plans are not feasible and that you are only taking money from people who can ill afford to lose it." The *Defender* routinely demeaned Garvey personally and often reminded readers that he was a foreigner who could not truly know their concerns. Abbott even hired a detective agency to turn up evidence that the Black Star Line was a swindle. Garvey responded by frequently suing newspapers and accusing his press critics of jealousy. Garvey poked at Abbott by claiming that the *Defender*'s opposition had increased his stock sales by "2000 per cent." "Why not be fair and constructive in your criticism of good and new movements?" he asked. "Why not support a thing for the good that is in it, rather than condemn it because you are not at the head of it?"[20]

Garvey received more favorable news coverage from rival editors looking to win the business of other newspapers' readers. In Chicago, Abbott's unyielding opposition to Garvey's movement provided editors at the *Broad Ax* and *Whip* with an opportunity to lure local readers away from the nation's largest black newspaper. Both newspapers regarded Garvey favorably until his meeting with Klan leaders. The *Broad Ax* tempered the *Defender*'s criticism of Garvey's alleged stock swindles by drawing comparisons to questionable business ventures pursued by a hustling Abbott early in his career. In New York, the *Crusader* and *Amsterdam News* countered the *New York Age*'s forthright opposition to Garvey with pragmatic support. Despite Garvey's personal shortcomings, the *Crusader* contended that even "his avowed enemies" must recognize his "genius for organizing." The *Amsterdam News* established a measured editorial position in the mid-1920s by distinguishing the UNIA's accomplishments from Garvey's mistakes. Editors urged UNIA members to separate themselves from Garvey, warning they would "succeed or fail in proportion to their ability to see Marcus Garvey as he really is — a gigantic blunderer, whose tactics are compelled to fail, and whose wisdom is exceeded by his foolhardiness."[21]

Radical editors also influenced the commercial press through their friendships and professional relationships with journalists. Alternative publications like the *Negro World* achieved a measure of mainstream respectability when esteemed journalists joined their staffs. Garvey's newspaper began publishing John Edward Bruce's column in May 1920, not long after the popular columnist endorsed the publisher's racial agenda. Bruce brought respectability and an international network of contacts to the *Negro World*. Born in 1856 to enslaved Marylanders, Bruce started his writing career in 1875 as a special Washington, D.C., correspondent for a New York newspaper. Over the ensuing decades, he wrote for numerous papers, participated in Republican politicking, and celebrated a black history rooted in the African Diaspora. An early promoter of Pan-Africanism, Bruce had cultivated personal and professional correspondences with African-descended men and women in Africa, the Caribbean, Central and South America, and Europe. The *Negro World* also hired T. Thomas Fortune as an editor in 1923. The hire was made mostly to associate the newspaper with Fortune's reputation for journalistic excellence. By then, though, Fortune was a shell of his former self, crippled by alcoholism and apparent bouts of mental instability.[22]

Journalists often moved between the alternative and commercial presses, continually recalibrating the balance between political advocacy and professional ambition as they switched jobs. Brothers Robert and Ulysses Poston established the *Hopkinsville* (Kentucky) *Contender* in 1919 with their father. Another brother, the teenager Ted, worked as a copy boy. The older brothers had already established a reputation for outspoken militancy. The Army had demoted them during World War I when they protested discrimination by a white southern sergeant. After they were discharged, the brothers angered Hopkinsville's white leaders by writing an editorial that criticized the city for relegating black soldiers to the end of a parade celebrating the return of local troops. The ensuing uproar forced the brothers to relocate to Nashville. They moved to Detroit in September 1920 in hopes of finally earning a profit. After covering several speeches by Garvey, the brothers again folded their newspaper, moved to Harlem, and joined the UNIA. Both worked for the *Negro World* and became high-ranking UNIA officials. In May 1922, Ulysses Poston was named managing editor of a short-lived UNIA publication, the *Daily Negro Times*. Back in Hopkinsville, Ted read the newspapers his older brothers mailed home. Family history and UNIA agitation encouraged him to pursue journalism as a career. He attended Tennessee Agricultural and Industrial College in Nashville, working as a railroad porter to pay his tuition. He applauded editorials in the *Messenger* that endorsed the porters' efforts to unionize. On work layovers, Ted stayed at Ulysses's Harlem apartment. After a falling out with Garvey, Ulysses rejoined the commercial press, contributing to the *Pittsburgh Courier* and *Inter-State Tattler* and publishing the *New York Contender*. (Robert Poston died of pneumonia in 1924.) After graduating, Ted moved to Harlem in 1928 and helped put out the *Contender* from a bedroom office. Three years later, Ted joined the *Amsterdam News*, where his pro-union stance eventually clashed with the publisher's anti-labor views.[23]

Journalists with radical sympathies gradually expanded the parameters of acceptable public discourse within commercial newspapers and magazines. Perhaps the most conspicuous example was Joel Augustus "J. A." Rogers, a self-taught Jamaican born sometime in the early 1880s. After serving in the British Army, Rogers migrated in 1906 to the United States. While working as a railroad porter, Rogers suffered the insults of American racism for the first time. Those humiliations motivated him to pursue a career as an independent researcher studying the history of race and racism. In 1917, Rogers published his first book, *From Superman to Man*, which refuted the supposed scientific origins of white supremacy. It sold more than ten thousand copies and appeared serially in many newspapers. Rogers called Harrison a friend, served as Garvey's confidante, and contributed to Randolph's *Messenger*. He also published widely throughout the 1920s in commercial newspapers—writing for the *Pittsburgh Courier*, *New York Amsterdam News*, and *Baltimore Afro-American*, among others. His syndicated articles financed his research at leading libraries and museums across North America, Europe, and Africa. He eventually became a weekly columnist for the *Courier*.[24]

Rogers played a central role in popularizing the concept of the African Diaspora. In 1934, the *Courier* began running his popular "Your History" feature, which paired facts about black history with sketches drawn by an illustrator. The cartoon feature fostered an assertive racial pride and a Pan-Africanist perspective by tracing the lineage of African Americans to ancient empires in Egypt and Ethiopia. "Your history dates back beyond the cotton fields of the South," read the feature's introduction, "back thousands of years before Christ." Rogers explicitly refuted stereotypes by championing example after example of black manliness, bravery, dedication, intellectualism, and physical prowess. (Rogers was also known to counter white erasure of black historical involvement by exaggerating the significance of black milestones or unearthing dubious evidence of a historical figure's blackness.) One early feature paired sketches of muscular black men building the Great Pyramid with the exploits of a champion boxer and record-breaking cyclist. Another touted the intellectual achievements of agricultural chemist George Washington Carver and the popularity of a Mexican poet born to Congolese parents. That feature also listed the nine black boxers who had held championship belts, their names accompanied by a drawing of a triumphant black pugilist standing above a concussed white opponent. A third feature noted that two black soldiers were the first Americans awarded a French military decoration for heroism in combat. Their achievement was acknowledged with an illustration of a black soldier bayoneting a German infantryman.[25]

Readers praised "Your History." A New Orleans fan encouraged others to clip the feature and paste it in scrapbooks for children and pin it to bulletin boards at lodges, libraries, schools, and civic clubs. Another reader thanked Rogers's editor for running his work. "As an editor," she wrote, "you must be a wide-awake racial man to pick up such a value, for believe it or not, the only way of saving the Afro-American, who is fast sinking, is by awakening his racial pride through facts of his past achievements." The *Courier* inculcated generations of readers with an appreciation for Pan-Africanism by running "Your History" regularly into the mid-1970s, nearly a decade after Rogers's death.[26]

"Thrusts and Lunges"
Modernist Sensibilities and Tabloid Sensationalism

As the 1920s progressed, the New Negro moniker was gradually appropriated—much to the chagrin of political radicals—for a coalescing literary aesthetic eventually labeled the Harlem Renaissance. English professor and literary promoter Alain Locke claimed authors and artists symbolized the potent cultural and psychological changes that had occurred "in the internal world of the Negro mind and spirit." Although informed and impelled by political radicalism, writers and artists—including Wallace Thurman, Langston Hughes, Claude McKay, Eric Walrond, Walter White, Zora Neale Hurston, Aaron Douglas, George Schuyler, and others—strove for a more personal understanding of the New Negro. They drew inspiration from a vibrant working-class culture and staked a claim to national citizenship by asserting the centrality of black culture to the American experience. These young artists represented African Americans in an array of media—novels, poems, essays, reviews, music, drama, and journalism. Scholar Anne Elizabeth Carroll describes their works as "an on-going, ever-changing exploration" of how texts could most effectively undermine racism.

"Race for them," Locke optimistically wrote, "is but an idiom of experience, a sort of added enriching adventure and discipline, giving subtler overtones to life, making it more beautiful and interesting, even if more poignantly so. So experienced, it affords a deepening rather than a narrowing of social vision."[27]

White publishers helped develop and publicize the Harlem Renaissance, but segregation, discrimination, and indifference restricted the opportunities they offered. Poet Arna Bontemps described the excitement as "almost unbearable" when frontline book publishers began recruiting black writers and nurturing long-lasting relationships with them. "The walls of Jericho were toppling," he recalled. Workplace segregation, though, prevented qualified black applicants from landing full-time editing and writing positions. Poet and author Langston Hughes defined the New Negro literary movement with his blues poems and his defense of black artists' right to depict black culture—flaws and all—without embarrassment. Despite his obvious qualifications, Hughes struggled to find employment, while less talented friends were hired to write books, radio scripts, and Hollywood screenplays. "But they were white," Hughes wrote, "I was colored." Book publishers' profit motives also worked against black writers. Disappointing book sales convinced publishers that white readers would never buy enough black-themed books to make them profitable. Like other black authors and poets, Hughes subsidized his literary work with paychecks earned in journalism.[28]

Black periodical editors, particularly Du Bois and sociologist Charles S. Johnson, proved more crucial in buoying the literary movement. Both men edited monthly journals backed by white philanthropists who funded literary prizes and confided with top-line publishers. In the NAACP's *Crisis*, Du Bois and literary editor Jessie Fauset commended art and literature that depicted black middle-class values as normative and downplayed racial differences to avoid inflaming negative stereotypes. Du Bois touted art for its value in dismantling racial injustice and advancing integration. "I stand in utter shamelessness," he wrote in 1926, "and say that whatever art I have for writing has been used always for propaganda for gaining the right of black folk to love and enjoy. I do not care a damn for any art that is not used for propaganda." Johnson evaluated art and literature differently in *Opportunity: A Journal of Negro Life*. *Opportunity* was a monthly magazine founded in 1923 by the National Urban League, an interracial organization dedicated to improving race relations and removing barriers to black employment. Trained at the University of Chicago, Johnson approached art with the dispassion of a sociologist. He argued that attempting to use art as propaganda distorted the "authenticity" of self-expression. Instead, Johnson described the New Negro literature "as an integral part of a single tradition and as a unique collective experience. Only as these different expressions of the racial life are viewed as parts of a whole is it possible to arrive at any true estimate of the Negro's cultural achievement or his traits."[29]

The Harlem Renaissance further eroded the pervasive influence of racial uplift ideology, with black newspapers and magazines serving as a primary arena for the contestation between conservative Victorian values and modernist sensibilities. While *Crisis* and *Opportunity* generally reflected the outlook of their editors, commercial newspapers fostered a wider-ranging debate about the movement's merits, as illustrated by coverage of Claude McKay's *Home to Harlem* (1928). McKay was a celebrated poet, onetime Garveyite, and a former associate editor of the *Liberator*, a socialist monthly founded in 1919. He was best known for his militant sonnet, "If We Must Die," which was widely reprinted in radical publications. He later converted to communism and toured the Soviet Union. His controversial first novel aired the tawdriness of Harlem street life. Critics in several leading newspapers panned *Home to Harlem* for denigrating the community's citizens. The reviewers undoubtedly knew the book had already received favorable coverage in New York's leading dailies. They had been similarly scandalized just two years earlier by Carl Van Vechten's *Nigger Heaven*, a white author's foray into Harlem's underbelly. Saying "Harlem is not as bad as painted," the *Courier*'s critic accused McKay of being "solely after the shekels, shekels and still more shekels." In the *Defender*, Dewey R. Jones contended the novel violated common decency and possessed "few redeeming features." "Pimps, whores, chippies, parade themselves along in a fashion never before encountered in fiction," Jones wrote. "There is even the undercurrent of contempt, expressed and implied, for everything that savors of respectability." The *Baltimore Afro-American* ran a nonjudgmental summary review, but columnist Ralph Matthews dismissed the novel four months later as "merely obscenely dirty." Matthews accused McKay of actualizing stereotypes that could slow racial progress.[30]

Such criticisms were common enough that provocative authors expected commercial black newspapers to publish negative reviews. McKay said black writers understood their work would be perceived by an average reader in general terms and by a black reader in racial terms. A writer could pretend to ignore racial opinion, McKay wrote, but "very likely he has his social contacts with the class of Negroes who create and express this opinion in their conversation and through the hundreds of weekly Negro newspapers and the monthly magazines." McKay considered reviewers' emphasis on race as "a kind of censorship" and claimed his critics seemed "afraid of the revelation of bitterness in Negro life."[31]

Fellow author Wallace Thurman agreed. For Thurman, black middle-class disgust for realistic literature was comparable to "those American whites who protest against the literary upheavals of a Dreiser, an Anderson, or a Sandburg." Thurman challenged this perspective by founding two short-lived but critically acclaimed journals—*Fire!!* and *Harlem*—that refuted Du Bois's proscription that artistic creation should function as racial propaganda. (Thurman also worked as the managing editor of the *Messenger* in the mid-1920s after its editors had abandoned socialist politics and the magazine resembled what Hughes described as "a kind of Negro society magazine and a plugger for Negro business, with photographs of prominent colored ladies and their nice homes.") After a lifetime combating stereotypes, most African Americans, Thurman argued, could not distinguish between "sincere art and insincere art." "The mass of American Negroes," he wrote, "can no more be expected to emancipate themselves from petty prejudices and myopic fears than can the mass of American whites. They all revere Service, Prosperity and Progress." Tellingly, McKay's and Thurman's commentary appeared in white publications—the *New York Herald-Tribune Books* and *New Republic*, respectively.[32]

And yet, newspaper coverage as a whole amplified and normalized the literary writers' modernist outlook. Not all reviewers, for example, condemned *Home to Harlem*. The *Amsterdam News*'s Aubrey Bowser, a writer and educator married to T. Thomas Fortune's daughter, referred to McKay's novel as "dirt for art's sake" and called it "the best novel of Harlem ever written." In the *Defender*, poet Donald Jeffrey Hayes praised the work of writers like McKay. Then McKay won the Harmon Gold Award for Literature, one of eight awards established in 1926 to recognize black achievement. The honor prompted newspapers to run a spate of complimentary notices. As Thurman observed, "Negro newspapers reprinted every item published anywhere concerning a Negro whose work had found favor with the critics, editors, or publishers." Controversy and public recognition led editors to demand more copy. A personal remembrance by James W. Ivy appeared in the *Courier* and *Afro-American*. J. A. Rogers interviewed McKay while traveling in Paris. Commercial reporters ultimately helped transform a radical poet into a mainstream celebrity, ensuring that his work and political reviews received wide coverage in the future.[33]

More broadly, scenes in *Home to Harlem* were no more shocking, exploitative, or commercially oriented than the crime-and-scandal stories splashed across the front pages of black newspapers nationwide. Editors filled inside pages with short articles about corrupt ministers, gruesome murders, and adulterous divorces. These editors saw themselves at the forefront of modern journalism. Sensational tabloid newspapers reshaped American journalism in the

1920s as editors energized disposable print publications to compete more effectively against radio and movies for the leisure dollars of modern urban readers.
Tabloid-style news coverage scandalized middle-class America, irrespective of
race. An industry observer noted that such reporting was nicknamed "jazz journalism" because both forms were "denounced as vulgar, depraved and vicious."
Kelly Miller, a widely syndicated columnist and Howard University dean, knew
daily newspapers in the South had a well-deserved reputation for maligning
African Americans, but claimed to "find in them no such display of Negro crime
and misdeeds as one sees in any ordinary Negro paper." Thomas W. Young,
son of the *Norfolk Journal and Guide*'s publisher, feared an excessive emphasis
on tabloid journalism among New York's black weeklies undermined the fight
for racial justice. "Pure dirt and atrocious scandal pervaded the columns of the
real voice of the Negro," Young wrote, "pictures displaced the written word,
and sensationalism displaced a rising tide of progress among our people." The
Pittsburgh Courier's editors, though, offered no apology to sensationalism's critics. Only black newspapers accurately covered African Americans, and those
papers would fail if they did not sell. "Where an editor knows that his public
is interested in crime and scandal," the *Courier* said, "he would be a very poor
businessman not to capitalize upon that interest." While some groaned, many
readers applauded in 1929 when the *Afro-American* shifted to a tabloid format.
"Get out of the old beaten path, pioneer, do things in a new and more modern
way," a hairdresser told the editors. A decade's worth of sensational journalism likely inoculated many readers to McKay's alleged carnality. As the *Afro-
American*'s Matthews observed, "Mr. McKay is guilty of the same crime that
most Negro writers commit, newspaper men being the greatest violators, that
of giving the whites a look into our garbage cans and toilets, but never allowing
them to see us when we are cleaned up and sitting on the front porch." From
this perspective, newspapers and literature complemented one another.[34]

The early career of George Schuyler exemplified how sensationalism, political radicalism, and literary modernism informed the temperament of black
newswriting in the 1920s. Schuyler quit high school in 1912 at age 17 and enlisted
in the Army to escape limited work opportunities in Syracuse, New York. He
reenlisted in 1915 but deserted three years later after encountering discrimination. He surrendered himself after three months and served nine months in a
military prison. After his release, Schuyler returned to New York, worked odd
jobs, and joined the Socialist Party of America. For Schuyler, socialist politics
"was exhilarating and just the type of stimulation I had been hungering for." He
soon met fellow socialist A. Philip Randolph, who asked him to help around the
Messenger's offices. Schuyler swept floors, answered mail, delivered magazines,

corrected copy, and wrote a caustic column. He eventually became managing editor and hobnobbed with the nation's leading black journalists, radicals, and literary writers. He began writing regularly for the *Pittsburgh Courier* in 1924. His work won the admiration of another satirist and iconoclast, H. L. Mencken, the legendary Baltimore newsman who edited *American Mercury*. Schuyler published frequently in Mencken's magazine, which earned him freelance assignments in other white-owned outlets. Schuyler cemented his literary reputation with *Black No More* (1931), a satirical novel that critiqued America's fixation on race.[35]

Although Schuyler later became a zealous anticommunist who denied his youthful radicalism, the militancy of his early reporting and stinging sarcasm of his early columns reflected the journalistic temperament, but not necessarily the politics, of the New Negro. His *Courier* column, the appropriately named "Thrusts and Lunges," intensified the *Messenger*'s spirited combativeness. (The column was soon renamed, becoming the more modest "Views and Reviews," but Schuyler maintained his acerbic tone.) Schuyler claimed to hold an objective

George Schuyler, reporter and columnist for the *Pittsburgh Courier*, in the 1930s. Courtesy of the Photographs and Prints Division, Schomburg Center for Research in Black Culture, The New York Public Library, Astor, Lenox, and Tilden Foundations.

sense of detachment that allowed him to transcend color prejudice and see the good and bad in both blacks and whites. He neither loved nor hated either race. While humans could be "patient, self-sacrificing, dutiful and loyal," Schuyler believed, "The bulk of people, white or black, are boresome, ordinary, paltry, superficial, ignorant, commonplace and often repugnant." He stood ready to mock everyone and everything. He cultivated a purposely contrarian political perspective that defied easy categorization. He challenged race leaders like Du Bois who ceaselessly touted the merits of the black middle class and urged working-class African Americans to live faultless lives to convince whites of their worth. "We shouldn't be trying to make people believe that we are angels of light and sweetness wholly," Schuyler wrote, "what we should try to empha- size is that we are just human beings striving as best we can to cope with the extraordinary difficulties confronting us in our environment." Schuyler also sparred with ministers, claiming African Americans were "too much concerned with God." Instead of wasting time in church, he encouraged his readers to devote more energy to organizing labor unions. Fellow radicals did not escape Schuyler's scorn. He invited disgruntled UNIA members to join "The Associa- tion of ex-Garvey officials," guaranteeing their acceptance by promising to not administer an intelligence test. He dismissed Pan-Africanism as an offshoot of white supremacy, arguing that racial concerns could never unite people divided over national interests. "When we get our own house in order," he wrote, "it will be time enough to consider the other fellow, whether black or white, in other parts of the globe."[36]

. . .

As the Jazz Age closed, the New Negro Movement's racial militancy and Har- lem Renaissance's modernism had undermined the popularity and profitability of more conservative commercial newspapers. The declining relevance of the reputable *Washington Bee* allowed the *Baltimore Afro-American* to open a bureau and build its readership in Washington, D.C. The *Richmond Planet* maintained its circulation, but publisher John Mitchell Jr.'s reputation as the "fighting editor" was a distant memory. He had shifted his attention from politics to business, prompting the *Messenger* to dismiss him as a "*hat-in-hand* Negro." "John Mitchell's day is done," Randolph and Owen wrote. "Negroes need shed no tears over it. When one loses his courage and devotes most of his time urging the victims of oppression to be polite to the prosecutors, it is time for him to go." In New York, the *Amsterdam News* claimed a circulation nearly one-third larger than Moore's venerable *New York Age*, which critics lampooned as a "Negro weakly." In Los Angeles, the *California Eagle* emerged as the most influential black newspaper on the West Coast. Its publisher, Charlotta Bass, belonged to the NAACP and organized the local chapter of Garvey's UNIA.[37]

Competition among Chicago's newspapers illustrated the ascendance of militancy and modernism among black urban readers—but also the persistence of racial uplift and respectability. By the mid-1920s, the *Defender*'s strongest local rival was the *Chicago Whip*, a newspaper launched in 1919 by two college-educated southerners, Joseph D. Bibb and William C. Linton. Besides supporting Garvey, the editors enjoyed deflating the pretensions of black leaders. Frank Marshall Davis, a journalist and aspiring poet who briefly worked at the *Whip*, described the paper as "the South Side's most militant journal." Chicago readers, though, also supported the *Chicago Bee*, which finished a distant third in Chicago-area circulation. Cosmetics tycoon Anthony Overton established the paper in 1925 to boost his merchandise sales. The *Bee* purposely aimed for a middle-class readership alienated by its competitors' stridency and sensationalism. Its editors promised to pursue "good, wholesome and authentic news" and "cordial relations between races." "This *Bee* had no stinger," Davis recalled. "Overton wanted nothing controversial in its columns. There were enough sacred cows to stock a Texas ranch." The business prospects of comparatively conservative publishers like Overton, though, would worsen in the 1930s when economic collapse led some working-class African Americans to explore aspects of communism, which moved the political radicalism of the alternative black press more directly into the mainstream of commercial black journalism. This leftward shift occurred as mechanical modernization enabled journalists to reach an unprecedented national—and even transnational—readership that numbered in the millions.[38]

CHAPTER 3

Popular Fronts and Modern Presses

Throughout the spring and summer of 1935, Italy's fascist dictator Benito Mussolini amassed an army on Ethiopia's borders in anticipation of invading one of the last independent nations on the African continent and forging a runt-sized Roman Empire. A hemisphere away, up-and-coming heavyweight boxer Joe Louis, an Alabama sharecropper's son who grew up in blue-collar Detroit, polished his undefeated record and maneuvered for a title shot. Week after week, stories about Ethiopia's plight and Louis's fight dominated the front pages of black newspapers across the United States. On the night of June 25, before a record crowd for a nontitle fight at Yankee Stadium in New York, the two stories collided as the soon-to-be champion pounded the proxy for the never-to-be Caesar. Louis defeated the hulking Italian Primo Carnera, a former titleholder and onetime carnival attraction, in the sixth round of a fight he controlled from the opening bell. Black America celebrated. Its journalists worked.[1]

The nation's two largest black weeklies rushed special editions into print, bragging as much on themselves as on Louis. A crowd of ten thousand stopped traffic outside the offices of the *Chicago Defender* as a blow-by-blow description of the fight, wired direct from ringside, was read over a loudspeaker. Office workers then telephoned the account to crowds gathered at a Bronzeville theater and a hall in suburban Evanston. A special, eight-page extra edition hit the streets twenty minutes after the fight ended, supposedly beating the city's daily newspapers by ten to fifteen minutes. None of the employees working in

Chicago was paid that night. All volunteered. "It was a mighty triumph for Race journalism," the *Defender* crowed on its front page. The first copy was rushed to publisher Robert Abbott, who was home sick. A specially installed wire let him track from his bedside what happened at the office. "I knew Joe would win," Abbott said. "Ethiopia is truly stretching forth her arms."[2]

Meanwhile, somewhere 10,000 feet over Pennsylvania, William G. "Bill" Nunn, city editor of the *Pittsburgh Courier*, typed his story to the drone of a chartered plane's engines, winging back to Pittsburgh with what was billed as the "first" pictures of the fight. The *Courier*'s presses started rolling one hour after Nunn landed. Six hours after the fight, newsboys hawked a special edition with three pages of fight photos and stories by seven correspondents reporting from New York. The words Nunn wrote for the fight also resonated for his profession: "Tonight, I am proud that I'm a Negro."[3]

By year's end, the *Courier* had more than doubled its circulation and surpassed the *Defender* as the largest black newspaper in the nation. It printed more than 150,000 copies each week and put out seven zoned editions. A one-week snapshot of sales showed that just slightly more than twelve thousand copies were sold in Pennsylvania, with the rest distributed in every state except Idaho and North Dakota. The *Courier* was truly a national newspaper. Percival L. Prattis, the ambitious new city editor, pondered the reasons for the newspaper's growth, seeking to sort the sizzle from what he saw as self-satisfaction. Prattis believed overnight success was decades in the making. Publisher Robert Vann and his staff had built goodwill among subscribers over many years. More immediately, though, Prattis attributed circulation gains to quality content. The *Courier* locked up exclusives with Louis's camp after nimble-fingered sports columnist Chester Washington, who excelled at shorthand, began working as Louis's secretary while churning out a weekly series recounting the boxer's life story. And since no other black newspaper (and only a few dailies) had sent its own reporter to Ethiopia, the *Courier* promoted J. A. Rogers's coverage by touting the authenticity of firsthand experience that establishes a war correspondent's credibility. At the end of Prattis's first year with the *Courier*, the newspaper paid shareholders their first common stock dividend since 1929. Prattis's friend and former boss, Claude Barnett, who ran the Associated Negro Press (ANP), the main national news service for black newspapers, was impressed. "Whew but the *Courier* is jumping." It was just the beginning.[4]

Excluded from U.S. citizenry and staggered by global depression, black activists in the 1930s fortified the institutions and communication networks that united a newly national minority population—just as severe economic deprivation inspired intellectuals, labor leaders, and journalists to embrace the tactics of leftist political organizing. By 1940, more than two million African Americans had quit the rural South since the early twentieth century, mostly moving northward and concentrating in the nation's largest industrial cities. This dramatic demographic shift promoted the expansion of newspapers, colleges, unions, civil rights organizations, and other venues for racial protest. When confronted by economic crisis, these institutions participated in what historian Nikhal Pal Singh calls "a sharp leftward turn" to more effectively communicate and coordinate reform efforts with working-class men and women. Journalists, in essence, yoked the sensibilities of Marxist racial politics to the business orientation of the commercial newspaper, an incongruous and tempestuous pairing of radicalism and capitalism that occurred because newspapers operated autonomously of white oversight. The nation's most read papers increasingly framed world affairs as a contest pitting the forces of white supremacy and class exploitation against the united resistance of people of color. Journalists at leading newspapers so effectively incorporated radicals' debates and criticisms concerning Western capitalism, imperialism, and racial exploitation into their regular news coverage that the alternative black press essentially folded into the commercial black press.[5]

Progressive news coverage helped double and possibly triple total circulation within fifteen years, transforming leading black newspapers into publications of regional, national, and transnational significance by the outbreak of World War II. To capitalize on this stunning growth, major publishers modernized their printing and distribution capabilities and expanded their advertising and administrative operations. In turn, editors and reporters assumed greater control of newsroom responsibilities. Journalists' newfound workplace independence inspired escalating demands for recognition of their professional status—and reinforced their commitment to politics that advocated for black liberation and workers' rights within and beyond America's borders.

"The Only Party Going Our Way"
Black Newspapers and Communism

Racism exacerbated the hardships of the Great Depression for African Americans and reordered their political alliances. Blacks had earned and accumulated significantly less than whites in the prosperous years before the 1929 stock market crash. Meager savings and restricted employment opportunities accelerated families' descent into poverty and businesses' collapse into bankruptcy. As the depression worsened, black men and women lost their jobs earlier and more frequently than white workers. In the North, about half of black laborers could not find employment in major cities. In the South, poor sharecroppers fell deeper into debt, and most urban families survived on public aid. African Americans initially continued to vote for Republican presidential candidates, despite President Herbert Hoover's indifference to civil rights reforms and his reluctance to involve the federal government in economic relief efforts. *Courier* publisher Robert Vann, a Republican stalwart turned Democrat, famously predicted in 1932 that the descendants of slaves would no longer vote for the party of the "Great Emancipator," Abraham Lincoln. "I see millions of Negroes," Vann said, "turning the picture of Lincoln to the wall." Vann's speech was largely ignored by daily newspapers but widely reprinted in black weeklies. Four years later, three-quarters of black voters cast ballots to reelect Democratic President Franklin D. Roosevelt. The president responded to the economic catastrophe by more than doubling federal spending by World War II. He created an array of programs to reduce joblessness and establish a minimum standard of subsistence. He promised racial equity in divvying up aid and met regularly with black advisors. Under Roosevelt, the federal government acknowledged the legitimacy of black concerns for the first time since the reconstruction of the post–Civil War South.[6]

Regardless, Roosevelt's gestures toward racial reform failed to produce significant change for African Americans desiring full inclusion as citizens. While New Deal policies and politics affirmed the notion of black citizenship, they proved inadequate in alleviating actual black needs. Roosevelt viewed African Americans as just one of many interest groups vital to his party's electoral ambitions. His administration repeatedly abandoned or moderated civil rights legislation to secure the allegiance of a more influential group—the white southern legislators who chaired key congressional committees. The price of those legislators' votes was the maintenance of segregation and discrimination. Southern politicians repeatedly blocked efforts by the NAACP and other organizations to pass federal antilynching legislation. They moved to exclude African Americans from New Deal programs and deprive them of their fair share of assistance. The Agricultural Adjustment Act paid southern farmers to not plant cotton, but payments went to landowners, who were mostly white. The National Recovery Act aimed to revive manufacturing through price and wage controls that ensured fair competition, but African Americans lampooned it as the "Negro Removal Act" because white employers often ousted black workers when wages increased. The Social Security Act did not cover domestics and farm workers, preventing nearly two-thirds of the black workforce from receiving old-age benefits. The Federal Housing Administration refused to guarantee home mortgages in black neighborhoods, meaning homeownership remained unaffordable for most black families. Despite unprecedented recognition from the federal government, African Americans remained marginal participants in the nation's political discourse.[7]

White newspaper and magazine editors displayed exclusionary tendencies similar to those held by New Deal administrators. Although few publications deployed the crudest stereotypes that had been commonplace decades earlier, *Time* could still josh in 1940 that, "Everybody knows that pickaninnies can be smart as paint," when it reported academically gifted black children might not be an anomaly. However, like federal officials, white editors also realized that African Americans' changing demographics and mounting protests merited serious examination. Northern editors once regarded articles about race as regional news from Dixie. Now they assigned their own reporters to explain how local black residents intensified housing shortages, demanded government services, and filled factory jobs. Increased press attention was not a gesture of interracial goodwill but a tacit acknowledgment that black men and women had become a hard-to-ignore segment of society. News coverage tended to depict African Americans as a problem that threatened the well-being of the United States, which was implicitly construed as a white nation. This framing exemplified the liberal view of race in the era of "managed race relations," a euphuism for what passed as interracial dialogue in the segregated mid–twentieth century. The goal of race relations was to grant just enough concessions to black activists to prevent flash eruptions of violence while blocking any systematic change to white dominion of the status quo.[8]

Reporting framed by the concept of race relations usually portrayed African Americans as objects of fascination or consternation. Such reporting could treat black men and women with sympathy, curiosity, humor, and fear—but seldom with fairness and empathy. This perspective permeated Stanley High's factual, yet menacing and paternalistic, two-part series "Black Omens." High told the *Saturday Evening Post*'s readers in the spring of 1938 that African Americans were overcoming their economic and social divisions to agitate in unison for racial justice. Such assertiveness belied white expectations of black complacency. Black defiance moved High to warn that the "the Negro himself—in both his temper and his objectives—is a very different person from the docile servant of the pre-migration, pre-depression period." High concluded that black unity posed an ominous but vague threat to (white) America. "The Negro is out for a new place in the sun," High wrote. "He does not expect to get it, like Emancipation, on a silver platter. He plans to make or take it for himself."[9]

Black journalists had few opportunities to counter such news coverage in white publications. White editors seldom hired them. Novelists, poets, and academics occasionally contributed to small but influential literary journals and liberal political magazines, such as *The Nation*, *New Republic*, and *American Mercury*. Reporters sometimes placed freelance articles in magazines or ghosted articles for major dailies, allowing a white journalist's byline to appear over their words. A few prominent exceptions landed full-time jobs. Lester Walton, a former *New York Age* editor who helped convince the Associated Press in 1913 to capitalize the word Negro, covered general assignment news for the *New York World* in the 1920s. Eugene Gordon worked at the *Boston Post* from 1919 to 1935, leaving to write for the English-language *Moscow Daily News.* However, when the liberal *New York Post* hired Ted Poston in 1937, he was the only black reporter working full-time for a major metropolitan newspaper. Poston went weeks without getting a story from City Hall or police headquarters after he was hired because white reporters excluded him when they compared notes on breaking news or shared tips on potential stories. Poston eventually forced them to treat him as a colleague by scooping them on news. "That broke the ice," he recalled, "and they began asking me what was going on." Knowing he held his job with a tenuous grip, Poston never severed his ties with the black press.[10]

Denied full participation in politics and the press, some influential African Americans listened sympathetically to political radicals, especially communists. The Communist Party of the United States of America (CPUSA) broadened its appeal among African Americans in 1928 when the Sixth World Congress of the Communist International, also known as the Comintern, brushed aside decades of racial indifference and recognized blacks in the American South as an oppressed people entitled to the right of self-determination. The recognition funneled party finances and expertise into racial protest. Communists won African American converts and sympathizers when their racial progressiveness was touted by a small but disproportionately influential cadre of black writers and intellectuals. This black leftist vanguard helped shape the Harlem Renaissance and was well acquainted with the black press's leading editors. Its members—including Langston Hughes, Claude McKay, Jean Toomer, Eric Walrond, Walter White, and others—edited and wrote for various leftist publications and joined radical writing groups. Their political beliefs encompassed a hodgepodge of progressive ideologies critical of American democracy and capitalism. Frequently at odds with the official dictates of the Communist Party, these writers taught newspaper and magazine readers to appropriate for their own purposes the racial righteousness of communism specifically and political radicalism generally.[11]

Communism's popularity grew in the early 1930s as its followers' new racial activism and the catastrophic failure of capitalism established its political legitimacy. Unlike the New Dealers, communists promised to remedy economic inequality and correct racial injustice. Communists' sense of a worldwide battle against capitalism and the exploitation of workers tapped into black radicals' sentiments concerning Pan-Africanism and the global nature of racism. "It was not the economics of Communism, nor the great power of trade unions, nor the excitement of underground politics that claimed me," recalled novelist Richard Wright, who joined the Communist Party before becoming a literary sensation, "my attention was caught by the similarity of the experiences of workers in other lands, by the possibility of uniting scattered but kindred people into a whole." The CPUSA gained more black supporters after communist-affiliated lawyers defended African Americans' legal rights in two politicized court cases. Lawyers challenged the prejudiced trials of nine black men accused of raping two white women in Scottsboro, Alabama. They also represented party member Angelo Herndon after he was convicted in Atlanta of fostering insurrection for attempting to organize industrial workers. Communists' brash racial advocacy contrasted sharply with the cautious activism of the interracial NAACP, which blunted its criticisms to avoid angering wealthy white philanthropists. Eugene Gordon of the *Boston Post* participated in street demonstrations demanding justice for the accused men. "I was beginning to embarrass the editors of the *Post*," he recalled, "and that embarrassed me." Gordon heeded his convictions and moved to the Soviet Union, joining the newsroom at the *Moscow Daily News*. Soon, Alabama sharecroppers, Harlem maids, and West Coast lawyers agitated for civil rights through grassroots organizations with ties to the Communist Party. "The Communists appear to be the only party going our way," said Carl Murphy, a studious Harvard University graduate who succeeded his father as publisher of the *Baltimore Afro-American*. "They are as radical as the NAACP were [*sic*] twenty years ago."[12]

Communist tactics inspired new modes of journalistic agitation in black newspapers. Scholar Bill V. Mullen contends that the *Chicago Defender* functioned as a cultural front during the Great Depression and World War II. Mullen argues that the *Defender* "undertook a revolution in personnel, editorial strategy, and marketing" that blurred distinctions between journalism and advertising, fiction and poetry to recast each genre with a political purpose that "assaulted commercial and journalistic convention in order to undermine representations of white hegemony." The *Defender*, though, was hardly alone. The formation of cultural fronts allowed people blocked from full participation in the political system to fight for social and political change by applying outside pressure in public arenas where they had access, talent, and influence. Workers picketed. Consumers boycotted. Artists painted. Writers wrote. The commercial black press as an industry—regardless of individual publishers' halfhearted denials or outright opposition to communism—fit within the coalition of progressive institutions that operated as cultural fronts. The press's mission of racial justice coincided and overlapped with the general aims of socialists, antifascists, labor unionists, and communists—all of whom advocated economic, political, and social reform to better the lives of minority groups and the working class. While most publishers likely restrained their papers' radicalism to protect advertising revenue from white businesses, William O. Walker, editor of the *Cleveland Call and Post*, concluded, "At heart, I would claim two-thirds of our editors as radicals of varying degrees." Communism's progressive influence was everywhere, even if communists themselves were not.[13]

Black newspapers operated as passive and active agents of progressive reform. Editors acted as passive change agents when they responded to a story's news value and likely reader interest by covering activities and controversies involving progressive groups, including the Congress of Industrial Organizations, Federal Writers' Project, National Negro Congress, Council on African Affairs, Socialist Party, and Communist Party, among others. They functioned as active brokers through actions that directly shaped editorial content—hiring reporters and columnists, assigning and laying out news stories, and writing supportive editorials. The *Afro-American* offered readers friendly coverage of the Communist Party in the 1930s. The *Defender*'s columnists consistently endorsed progressive views in the 1940s. The Associated Negro Press balanced owner Claude Barnett's conservative tendencies with editor Frank Marshall Davis's leftist sympathies. The *New York Amsterdam News* employed a radicalized editorial staff in the mid-1930s that covered the labor movement favorably and fought for better wages and work conditions in its newsroom. Aspiring publisher Leon Washington launched the *Los Angeles Sentinel* in 1933 with assistance from his cousin Loren Miller, a lawyer who supported communist policies and attended the local John Reed Club, a leftist writing group.

Commercial publishers aimed to mobilize readers in other public arenas when they appropriated front techniques of agitation by sponsoring parades and rallies for racial equality—which also happened to attract publicity and boost sales. Most famously, several newspapers endorsed and helped coordinate "Don't Spend Your Money Where You Can't Work" campaigns in the 1930s, simultaneously advocating racial equality and condemning class exploitation. The movement seized national attention in 1929 when *Chicago Whip* editors A. C. MacNeal and Joseph Bibb, who recalled being labeled "Red, radical, revolutionary," asked readers to boycott and picket white-owned businesses that refused to hire black employees. Pickets paced in front of Woolworth's Five and

Ten stores, wearing wooden placards that called the company "UNFAIR TO COLORED LABOR" for refusing to hire black clerks. Woolworth's relented after seventeen weeks. The *Whip*'s success encouraged other newspapers, including the *Cleveland Call and Post, Los Angeles Sentinel, Minneapolis Spokesman*, and *New York Age* to endorse similar campaigns in their cities.[14]

The Communist Party recruited African American writers to join its leading publications and report on racial discrimination, celebrate black workers and their culture, and link racism to capitalistic exploitation. These writers, though, remained part of the larger black print culture that included the commercial black press, even as they wrote for the *Daily Worker* and *New Masses*. Richard Wright worked for six months in 1937 as the full-time Harlem editor of the *Daily Worker*. He reveled in the opportunity to discuss literature and current affairs with people who seemed to consider his views seriously, although he often wondered whether white communists were merely humoring him. While there, he befriended Ralph Ellison, an earnest, soft-spoken Oklahoman who moved to New York after dropping out of Tuskegee Institute when he could no longer afford tuition. Ellison often slept in the *Daily Worker*'s offices. Wright and communism were formative influences on Ellison, who contributed many articles and reviews, as well as short stories, to *New Masses* between 1938 and 1942. Independent-minded writers like Wright and Ellison, though, soon ran afoul of party commands governing the opinions they could express. Wright bitterly renounced his party membership, while Ellison simply moved on. Despite its appeal for interracial unity, the Communist Party never shook itself of segregation and racism. "For all the Communist Party's racial concern in those years," recalled Ben Burns, who worked at three communist daily newspapers before becoming an editor at the *Chicago Defender* and *Ebony*, "I—like most white party members—remained ignorant of black institutions and society, of black businesses and churches, of black universities and fraternal groups."[15]

Other communist-influenced writers enjoyed prestigious positions within the commercial black press, although their ties to the Communist Party itself were often either undisclosed or identified as a past affiliation. Born Malcolm Nurse around 1903 to middle-class parents in Trinidad, George Padmore wrote regularly for black newspapers and magazines in the 1930s and 1940s. He moved to the United States in 1924 after condemning British exploitation of the island's peasants. Padmore later enrolled in law school at Howard University, where the *Defender*'s future leftist editorial writer, Metz T. P. Lochard, was one of his professors. Soon afterward, he joined the Communist Party, and took his radical pseudonym. A prolific writer, stirring speaker, and tireless organizer, Padmore was called to Moscow and charged with coordinating the party's involvement in racial issues. He recruited and organized black members across Europe and Africa. He helped found the International Trade Union Committee of Negro Workers (ITUCNW), which aimed to coordinate anticolonialism activities in Africa and the Caribbean. Padmore publicized black workers' shared struggles and touted their revolutionary zeal in the organization's monthly publication, *The Negro Worker*, which he edited in Hamburg, Germany. He ceaselessly emphasized the international dimensions of the black liberation struggle. Even so, Padmore clashed frequently with party leaders. He expected them to make self-determination among minority populations a party priority—as they had promised. When his advice was ignored, Padmore planted critical stories in black newspapers. In 1933, the Nazis raided *The Negro Worker*'s offices, and Padmore was deported to England. He resigned from the Communist International when party leaders softened their opposition to colonialism to gain favor with the West. Soviet officials responded by labeling him a Black Nationalist, a dismissive epithet reserved for someone unable to rise above racial difference to achieve worker solidarity.[16]

Freed from the constraints of Communist Party doctrine, Padmore never wavered in his criticism of capitalism but amplified his belief that black freedom worldwide depended upon unity among African-descended people. Excluded from communist publishing circles, Padmore became a regular contributor to the *Crisis* in 1935 and joined the *Chicago Defender* as its European correspondent in 1938. He also wrote a syndicated column for the ANP news service. Barred from entering the United States, he wrote from London. The transition into black journalism forced the practiced communist pamphleteer to tailor his writing style to the nonpartisan standards of crusading journalism. Padmore adjusted to writing for black newspapers, but a friend said he "used to laugh much about their lamentable outlook." A change in tone did not alter his political outlook. Padmore urged African Americans to rally to Ethiopia's aid as it prepared in 1935 to battle Italy, depicting the independent African nation as an unwilling sacrifice offered to maintain political stability in Western Europe. "In this hour of danger," he wrote in the *Crisis*, "it is the duty of every black man and woman to render the maximum moral and material support to the Ethiopian people in their single-handed struggle against Italian fascism, and a not too friendly world." Four years later, Padmore saw himself as vindicated when World War II erupted after Great Britain and France rushed to protect Poland from German invasion as quickly as they had abandoned Ethiopia to Italy. He scoffed at claims that Western powers sought to defend democracy. "What they *are* concerned about is the preservation of their colonial empires and the monopoly which they enjoy in the exploitation of cheap colored labor." No peace would last, Padmore warned, until imperialism was abolished.[17]

Another prominent communist journalist worked in the communist press and black commercial press simultaneously, reluctantly using a pseudonym to avoid provoking controversy at the *Chicago Defender*. John Pittman left his hometown Atlanta after graduating from Morehouse College to earn a master's degree in economics from the University of California, Berkeley. His thesis examined the relationship between railroads and black workers. In 1931, the 28-year-old Pittman founded the *San Francisco Spokesman*, an eight-column broadsheet whose editorial staff denounced segregation and discrimination and endorsed union activism among longshoremen and railroad workers, even though leading unions refused to integrate. Pittman's politics radicalized as the years passed and the depression persisted. By 1934, rumors circulated that the Soviet Union subsidized his newspaper. A local post of the Veterans of Foreign Wars asked whether "the *Spokesman* actually advocates subversive propaganda in connection with our Constitution and Government." Pittman defended himself and the Communist Party in an open letter printed on the front page. He characterized the *Spokesman* as an independent paper that reserved the right "to tell either Mr. Roosevelt or Mr. Stalin to go to the devil." He described the nation's rhetoric of democracy as "the mask behind which lurks as tyrannical and ruthless an oligarch as ever made profits from war or sold men into slavery." He pointed to the need for a labor party that was independent of business-minded Republicans and Democrats. "The *Spokesman* regards Communism in the United States as a healthy symptom of peoples' awakening," Pittman wrote. "Social change usually requires extreme measures. There is much exaggeration in Communist propaganda; but exaggeration is necessary to win attention for doctrines little known, generally unpopular, and denounced by the nation's rulers." The "real danger" to the United States, Pittman contended, was not the political beliefs of communists but the often violent and illegal efforts to silence those perspectives. Pittman witnessed political repression firsthand in 1934 during a general strike initiated by unionized longshoremen. San Francisco ground to a halt in early July as police and strikers battled in the streets and the governor mobilized the National Guard. Pro-ownership vigilantes destroyed the printing press used by the *Spokesman* and *Western Worker*, a communist newspaper. Pittman later wrote for the *Western Worker*, which became *People's World*, the West Coast's daily communist newspaper. Pittman was named editor in 1941.[18]

While editing *People's World*, Pittman wrote a weekly foreign-affairs column from 1942 to 1946 for the *Chicago Defender*, using the pseudonym John Robert Badger. *Defender* editor Ben Burns asked Pittman to take a pen name because "you are known as a Communist on the West Coast." Pittman resented hiding his identity, arguing that "the political importance of doing the column attaches primarily to the fact that the *Defender* sees fit to publish a view by a person like myself." Pittman was especially galled that former communist George Padmore, whose politics he disputed, was not required to take a fictitious name. Burns, though, told Pittman he had to be "cautious and careful" since some *Defender* executives opposed allowing communist influences in the newsroom and on the printed page. Pittman accepted the terms. After all, the *Defender* sold about 175,000 copies each week, while *People's World* distributed only 15,000 copies. As Badger, Pittman consistently depicted the Allied nations' desperate desire to expand an international coalition against fascism as a decisive step toward ending colonialism. He viewed wartime alliances with the Soviet Union and China as safeguards to postwar self-determination. He criticized the United States and Great Britain for fostering racial hatred in the Pacific theater and possibly jeopardizing victory to maintain imperial footholds in Asia. He depicted the end of military segregation and discrimination as a necessary precondition for "winning allies and utilizing the assistance offered by peoples of diverse national and racial origins." Pittman believed everyday people could influence foreign affairs, and he repeatedly urged his readers "to mobilize and increase pressure for a correct policy toward the colonial people."[19]

The encroaching influence of communist politics encouraged one opportunistic publisher to launch a Harlem tabloid that he called the "Lenox Avenue edition of the *Daily Worker*." Founded in 1942, the *People's Voice* was published by the Reverend Adam Clayton Powell Jr., a New York City councilman who desired to expand his political constituency, with Charles Buchanan, the general manager of the Savoy Ballroom. Communist Party members and supporters filled key positions: Doxey Wilkerson, a former Howard University professor of education, was general manager; Max Yergan, a leader in the National Negro Congress and cofounder of the Council on African Affairs, was treasurer; and Marvel Cooke, a former *Amsterdam News* reporter, was assistant managing editor. Cooke described Ben Davis, a leading CPUSA official in New York, as "the spirit behind the editorial board." The FBI monitored the newspaper throughout World War II, claiming it had "completely given itself over to the Communist Party line of twisting and distorting facts in order to garner mass support and circulation." The *People's Voice* sold forty to fifty thousand papers a week at its peak.[20]

Even so, most commercial publishers grappled fitfully with a political ideology that touted social equality but also jeopardized a two-party political system that rewarded their editorial support and advocated the destruction of a capitalist economy that generated their profits. They routinely undercut their own progressivism. Publishers hedged their support for radical candidates, viewing an endorsement of a communist as a wasted opportunity to create or secure a political alliance with established power brokers and generous patronage dispensers. The *Afro-American*, for example, never officially endorsed a communist candidate for president, despite the progressive outlook of both its publisher and its managing editor. Similarly, even as an ex-communist editor at the *Defender* complained of the "obnoxious, unwanted presence" of a known communist in the newsroom, William Patterson, a black communist congressional candidate, criticized the paper's publisher for writing that "communists have prayed [*sic*] upon the Negro people." Publishers took their strongest stand against progressive politics when union organizers threatened to diminish their personal profits. They routinely blocked efforts by the communist-influenced American Newspaper Guild to unionize their newsrooms, denounced labor organizers as communists, and urged their employees to recognize the need for racial, rather than class, solidarity.[21]

The *Crisis* surveyed fourteen editors and publishers in 1932 for their views on communism. As a group, they struck an ambivalent tone: They understood why the egalitarianism of communism appealed to African Americans, but they were uncomfortable associating with an ideology contradictory to American ideals. Most believed black support for communism arose more from the United States' failings than the Communist Party's promises. "Is it not paradoxical that Negroes must seek protection under some flag other than the Stars and Stripes, the flag for which they have fought to keep flying in the cause of justice and human liberty?" asked E. Washington Rhodes, publisher of the *Philadelphia Tribune*. P. B. Young of the *Norfolk Journal and Guide*, the most conservative of the major publishers, said his policy was "not to view Communism as a thoroughgoing, death-dealing evil but to regard it as just one of the factors in a growing world-wide ideal to improve the conditions of the under-privileged." He criticized communists for failing to appreciate the full scope of black economic dependence upon white capital. Revolutionary rhetoric, he said, made "it difficult for the best of both races to get together and study and correct problems in an orderly way. Besides, because the Negro is marked racially, he becomes a ready target for anti-Communist venom whenever that develops."[22]

Young sparked a minor flap that exemplified the divide between cautious owners and progressive employees when the *Journal and Guide* engaged in a published back-and-forth with an editor at the *Baltimore Afro-American*. Young lamented the seemingly excessive influence of radical politics on the nation's leading columnists and editorialists. Most opinion writers, the *Journal and Guide* observed, "possess a mental and spiritual obsession of atheism, socialism, communism, bolshevism, political and social idealism and academic radicalism not conformable to anything in practical living, to say nothing of practical journalism." These writers wrote not with objectivity but with "the germs of mental and spiritual obsession," which warped their judgment on the pressing domestic issues most important to African Americans. William N. Jones, the managing editor and a columnist for the *Afro-American*, viewed such an outlook as misguided and narrow-minded. Political successes achieved by socialists and communists in Europe and Asia indicated that one possible new future might be at hand. Journalists had an obligation, Jones argued, to understand and explain what the world might become. While some editors "would content themselves with any status quo," other writers would "hurl themselves against the status quo to advocate a more idealistic state of existence." Jones's criticisms of American capitalism arose not from Soviet propaganda, but from the economic exploitation endured by his grandfather, a sharecropper from South Carolina whose hard work failed to produce a profit. Jones later championed the Communist Party's presidential ticket and then visited the Soviet Union. "There can be no change nor betterment of humanity," he concluded, "without the radical influence."[23]

"Business Propositions" and "Manhood Cooperation"
The Professionalization of Black Journalism

Black reporters' political radicalization coincided with—and intensified—their efforts to gain professional recognition and workplace independence within an expanding, modernizing industry. The Great Depression fully exposed how the commercial black press had evolved into a two-tier industry since World War I, with business-oriented, big-budget publishers in large cities separating themselves from break-even editor-proprietors in small towns. Larger newspapers floundered during the depression's early years, but they possessed the mechanical and personnel assets to survive. Publishers slashed salaries, trimmed news pages, and created new sources of revenue. In Pittsburgh, for example, Vann completed a $104,000 printing plant in late 1929. He filled it with used, but modern, equipment. Despite the paper's indebtedness, the plant helped the *Courier* endure tough economic times by allowing Vann to contract for outside print jobs, reduce production costs, and expand the paper when circulation grew. After several rivals folded, the *Courier* consolidated its dominance among local readers.[24]

Like the *Courier*, other major publishers resumed business expansion in the mid-1930s as potential new competitors appeared. Mechanical modernization occurred so rapidly that one industry insider hesitated to estimate the value of new publishing equipment. Instead, he characterized the plants of the *Defender*, *Courier*, and *Afro-American* as being in the "'big money' class." These newspapers invested hundreds of thousands of dollars in mechanical equipment, which included high-speed rotary presses and photo-engraving plants. In Norfolk, publisher Young claimed the largest black newspapers were "better equipped than was the average large city daily of twenty-five years ago." To make the most of expansion, leading newspapers joined the Audit Bureau of Circulations, an industry organization that verified the accuracy of circulation figures for advertisers. Nine black newspapers became members between 1930 and 1935, including the *Afro-American, Amsterdam News*, and *Courier*. Membership gave these papers a decided advantage over competitors when they solicited advertisers.[25]

As leading publishers saturated local markets, they turned elsewhere for new readers. They opened bureaus, bought out smaller weeklies, or simply sold additional newspapers in other cities. The *Afro-American* started papers in Philadelphia, Washington, D.C., and Newark, New Jersey, and bought the struggling *Richmond Planet*. The *Defender* helped establish the *Louisville Defender* in 1933 and the *Michigan Chronicle* in Detroit three years later. The *Louisville Defender* outlasted three rivals under the leadership of Frank L. Stanley, an English teacher turned editorial writer. Louis E. Martin, a University of Michigan journalism graduate who had worked as a freelance writer in his father's native Cuba, transformed the *Chronicle* into a leading advocate of the labor movement.[26]

Industry growth spurred professionalization and product standardization at the largest newspapers. A younger generation of college-educated, business-minded executives took over as publishers in the 1930s and 1940s. They assumed control of increasingly sophisticated publishing operations during a period of unparalleled expansion. They moved to confine overt political views to editorials and opinion columns, seeing themselves as chief executive officers rather than partisan propagandists like so many of their predecessors. They ceded many editorial duties to their newsroom employees to focus more intently on decisions concerning advertising and administration, circulation and distribution. The net effect of this transition was the amelioration of each newspaper's idiosyncrasies, which imbued the largest newspapers with a more standardized appearance. "The fact is that the Negro press has become of necessity a business proposition first, and an uplift agency, second," observed Roy Wilkins, managing editor of the *Kansas City Call*. Modern publishers were businessmen who often believed they best served the fight for racial justice by informing readers, rather than leading them. As W. E. B. Du Bois observed, "Instead of being prime movers in arousing excitement and directing attention, they publicized excitement and feeling already aroused." These statements by Wilkins and Du Bois explain how business-minded executives could tolerate Marxist radicals in their newsrooms: The expression of political progressivism was just one more article or column to sell to readers.[27]

The new publishers at the nation's five largest black newspapers consisted of second-generation heirs and corporate partnerships. A family trust assumed control of the *Baltimore Afro-American* after Charles Murphy died in 1922. Carl Murphy's brothers appointed him as president and publisher. Known as "Mister Carl" in the newsroom, an industry observer described him as "a studious, cultured man" with horn-rimmed glasses who was "ingenious in his methods of exploitation and an excellent editorial writer." Two physicians, C. B. Powell and P. M. H. Savory, bought the *New York Amsterdam News* in 1935 amid an acrimonious labor dispute. The doctors considered the acquisition a business investment that would help them promote their other ventures. John Sengstacke, Robert Abbott's nephew, became publisher of the *Chicago Defender* in 1940 after his uncle died from kidney disease. Sengstacke had earned a business administration degree from Hampton Institute, where he studied advertising and journalism while editing the student newspaper. A veteran editor described Sengstacke as "a hands-off publisher who rarely voiced any comment or criticism of his editors." Robert Vann's widow, Jesse, succeeded her husband as the *Pittsburgh Courier*'s majority shareholder after he died in 1940 from abdominal cancer. The paper's day-to-day management was handled over the next three decades by three executives—business manager Ira Lewis and newsroom veterans Percival Prattis and Bill Nunn. While the *Courier* maintained a distinct institutional character, no successor branded the newspaper's identity as personally as its founder. P. B. Young Sr. stepped down as editor-in-chief of the *Norfolk Journal and Guide* in 1943, amid lingering health ailments, "with mixed emotions of sorrow and a sense of duty." While Young continued to write editorials, his oldest son, P. B. Jr., took over the editorial department and his youngest son, Thomas W., became president and business manager. Both had earned journalism degrees from Ohio State University. His father proudly called P. B. Young Jr. "'a professional newspaper man.'"[28]

Elsewhere, veteran journalists either launched or overhauled newspapers in cities where they believed stale competitors lacked the business savvy and racial militancy needed to maintain their circulations. William Walker became the managing editor of the nearly defunct *Cleveland Call and Post* and swiftly challenged the city's reigning black newspapers—including the *Cleveland Gazette* and its venerable editor, the uncompromising but intemperate Harry Smith. Within six years, the *Call and Post* sold more papers than all its local rivals combined. Leon Washington Jr. founded the *Los Angeles Sentinel* to compete for the *California Eagle*'s readership, claiming the *Eagle* spoke with a "chirp" when a tiger's growl was needed. Cecil E. Newman emerged as Minnesota's most activist publisher after founding the *Minneapolis Spokesman* and *St. Paul Recorder*. In the South, flagship newspapers in Houston and Atlanta anchored two new publishing chains. Lawyer Carter W. Wesley, who had bought into the *Houston Informer* four years earlier, took over Texas's largest black newspaper in 1931 after its founder quit and started a competing paper. Wesley then merged with his chief rival and began printing localized editions in cities across the state. Meanwhile, publisher William A. Scott II, a hard-charging former Morehouse College running back, transformed his Atlanta weekly into the only sustainable daily newspaper in black publishing. Scott bolstered the *Daily World*'s profits by incorporating a multistate newspaper chain, eventually named the Scott Newspaper Syndicate. Within two years, Scott had founded or partnered with more than fifty newspapers. Radiating from Atlanta, the chain of small-circulation newspapers ranged as far west as Phoenix and as far north as Des Moines but was centered in the South.[29]

Black journalism's surging growth forced the NAACP to acknowledge the industry's expanded reach. NAACP executives and board members had focused their publicity efforts for decades on landing stories in white-owned newspapers. They fitted their news releases to the daily press's editorial demands and production schedules. Roy Wilkins, who quit his journalism career at the *Call* to work full-time for the NAACP, perhaps hoping to leave behind journalism's "business proposition" in favor of direct activism, said that the practice initially made sense because the organization's major task was "the changing of a hostile or indifferent white public opinion." Wilkins, though, altered those policies and "made conscious efforts to cooperate as closely as possible with the Negro press." Black newspapers had become too influential to ignore.[30]

As leading publishers shifted their attention toward managing business operations, journalists increasingly saw themselves as integral partners in the production of race news. Young journalists were better educated and more cosmopolitan than their predecessors. College graduates, once a rarity in black newsrooms, were commonplace by the mid-1930s. One survey found that the *Afro-American*, *Kansas City Call*, and *Houston Informer* identified more than half of their editorial employees as college graduates, while the *Defender* and *Amsterdam News* claimed a third and a quarter, respectively. These reporters also enjoyed greater employment options. The emergence of newspapers with regional and national circulations created opportunities for career diversification, specialization, and promotion. Talented journalists could now move from one newspaper to another in search of a satisfying workplace. Reporter Enoch P. Waters griped for months about the *Journal and Guide*'s low pay and the Youngs's inability to accept criticism. He walked out when the publisher told him he could be replaced by a high school student. Waters then dashed off telegrams to the *Afro-American* and *Defender*. Sengstacke, whom Waters knew as a student at Hampton Institute, hired him that day. The *Afro-American*'s offer arrived later. Newspapers competed as intently for journalists like Waters as they did for news. The best-edited newspapers were also the bestselling, and *Courier* columnist George Schuyler believed poorly written newspapers could not survive. Schuyler told publishers they could ensure their future success only by treating their newsroom employees as valuable assets rather than replaceable parts. Publishers could earn loyalty, cooperation, and efficiency from workers if they increased wages, improved working conditions, and offered job security. The bargain also required a change in attitude. "In place of what is too often an irksome paternalism," Schuyler wrote, "there must be manhood co-operation."[31]

Journalists' emerging sense of professional standing provoked conflict as they argued with publishers about the worth of their contributions to their newspapers' overall success. When employers failed to acknowledge the value of journalistic labor, editorial employees attempted to organize unions. They aimed to raise wages, improve working conditions, and protect themselves from publishers' vindictiveness. Long-simmering resentments erupted at the *Amsterdam News* in 1935, resulting in what one reporter labeled "the first open dispute between Negro workers and a Negro employer." Publisher Sadie Warren-Davis had inherited a controlling interest in the newspaper in 1921 and oversaw its business operations while her husband managed the newsroom. The paper's reporters claimed Warren-Davis treated them like supplicants and cavalierly dismissed their contributions to the publication's profitability. She once threatened wholesale firings after hearing rumors of union organizing. An ill-advised attempt to significantly expand news coverage by doubling the newsstand price to a dime prompted Warren-Davis to cancel vacations in July 1935 as revenue plummeted. Journalists then asked the American Newspaper Guild to negotiate a contract for them. As editorial employees prepared to strike, Warren-Davis fired fifteen workers in October. The two newsroom employees who remained renounced the guild. Eleven weeks of picketing and hectoring followed. On the *Amsterdam News's* front page, Warren-Davis accused the guild of seeking to destroy the newspaper, labeling it "an outlaw dues-collecting organization" whose membership was "made up of white Communist and Socialist writers." Such claims attempted to damn the union twofold—by associating it with the supposedly un-American attributes of radical political ideologies and by implying that a white-led organization would never truly look out for black workers. Strike leaders responded by comparing Warren-Davis to reactionary Southerners who spat "nigger lover" at liberal whites who advocated racial justice. "The *Amsterdam News*, by attacking the unity of black and white newspapermen," the union statement said, "is sacrificing the best interests of our race to its own selfish ends as an employer of labor."[32]

The picketers followed the advice that guild organizers would give to other black journalists attempting to unionize—"capitalize on the vulnerability of the Negro press to certain types of public opinion." Reporters asked other labor unions, civic organizations, and loyal readers to support them. All but five local businesses quit advertising in the *Amsterdam News*, and creditors forced bankruptcy proceedings. In late December, Powell and Savory agreed to buy the paper after reaching a settlement with the guild. The doctors signed a two-year contract that rehired the fired full-time workers, raised wages by 10 percent, and instituted a five-day, forty-hour week with time off for overtime. The victory inaugurated a wave of labor unrest that culminated in 1946 with the American Newspaper Guild successfully negotiating contracts for seven newspapers— *Afro-American, Amsterdam News, Courier, Defender, California Eagle, Los Angeles Sentinel*, and *People's Voice*.[33]

Modernized printing capabilities and professionalized editorial staffs stoked competition and circulation, birthing the modern black newspaper—a segregated business venture of sustained profitability that operated independent of white financing. This business model empowered black journalists by granting them greater authority in shaping news coverage and allowing them to write without white interference. This model elevated publishers' standing as race leaders of national influence and provided them with tangible political power derived from sizable readerships. It enabled journalists to debate the merits of anticapitalism and anticolonialism viewpoints rooted in a Pan-African perspective and encouraged leading publishers to tolerate political views they might personally oppose. This model worked because readers' pennies, nickels, and dimes kept the presses running. From the mid-1930s to just after World War II, black newspapers at least doubled the total number of copies sold each week from less than one million to about two million, with some industry observers touting three million as a credible figure. As newspapers passed from hand to hand, weekly readership could include as many as six million people at a time when the black population totaled slightly less than thirteen million. This spike in circulation transformed a handful of newspapers into a competitive confederation of national publications. Before 1930, only the *Chicago Defender* was truly national. Afterward, the *Pittsburgh Courier* and *Baltimore Afro-American* arose as powerful rivals, with the *New York Amsterdam News* and *Norfolk Journal and Guide* also selling nationally. The combined weekly circulation of just these five publishing companies—there were 169 black newspapers in thirty-six states in 1948—neared nine hundred thousand in the late 1940s. Elsewhere, certain metropolitan newspapers separated themselves from less militant competitors and emerged as dominant regional news sources. Such newspapers included the *Cleveland Call and Post, Houston Informer, Kansas City Call, Los Angeles Sentinel, Louisville Defender, Michigan Chronicle, Oklahoma Black Dispatch,* and *St. Louis Argus.* Syndicates and wire services, most notably the Associated Negro Press, ensured that news from these regional outlets reached a circuitous national readership. Although in the making for a century, it seemed the infrastructure of a transnational communications network for sharing race news among African Americans and other African-descended peoples had suddenly snapped into place.[34]

No More "Preaching and Moaning"
A New Template for Black Newswriting

Two decades of surging radicalism conditioned by a modernist outlook fundamentally altered the tenor of black news reporting. Journalists fitted a militant racial advocacy to commercial appeal by adopting a reporting style that embraced sensationalism, realism, and direct action. While tabloid journalism's influence receded among white newspapers in the 1930s, its popularity expanded among most leading black newspapers. Sensationalism amplified the black press's strengths and ameliorated its weaknesses. Banner headlines, large photographs, and shocking stories captured the attention of newsstand buyers whose weekly purchases were crucial to publishers' profitability since so few national advertisers bought space in black newspapers. Crime-and-scandal stories helped build national circulations because such news held mass appeal, regardless of where it occurred. And despite the hand-wringing, sensational news coverage helped readers make sense of seemingly random, abstract outrages by humanizing the news, which imbued it with a concrete practicality. Personalized news moved readers to contemplate the nation's social inequities and encouraged them to fight racial injustice. Sensationalized coverage of racial outrages implied to readers that their personal experiences with racism also mattered.[35]

Realism aimed to shatter stereotypes and self-deception. It contradicted white caricatures of blackness through specific example and denigrated racial uplift's boosterism by promoting critical scrutiny of black institutions and public figures. Author Richard Wright crafted a Marxist-inspired literary theory in 1937 that demanded truthful depictions of working-class black life, of the "Negro way of life in America." Wright aimed his criticism at authors, poets, and playwrights, but his words also spoke to the influences shaping nonfiction writers—the essayists, reporters, columnists, and editors who wrote for newspapers and magazines. Too many black writers, Wright claimed, were too satisfied with repeating the crowd-pleasing platitudes of racial uplift or showcasing the elegant flourishes that impressed the sophisticates of the white literary world. These writers either became "the voice of the educated Negro pleading with white America for justice" or "a sort of conspicuous ornamentation, the hallmark of 'achievement'" that white society trotted out like "French poodles who do clever tricks." Wright wanted writers to add political purpose to Langston Hughes's call to embrace black culture. This required writers and journalists to grapple with the nationalistic character of black life, which was often expressed through an international perspective sympathetic to the racial oppression of other people of color. For Wright, such portrayals unmasked the revolutionary nature of the freedom struggle. Realism, though, was a constantly compromised ideal in black journalism. While racial uplift encouraged writers to inflate black acceptance of white bourgeois values and aspirations, racial militancy prompted them to exaggerate or distort black accomplishments to more readily dispose of racial stereotypes.[36]

Direct action compelled journalists to not just complain about racial injustices in editorials—Wallace Thurman's "preaching and moaning"—but to investigate and expose wrongdoing. Investigative reporting sometimes meant covertly infiltrating the South like a wartime spy slipping behind enemy lines to sniff out undisclosed facts about racially motivated murders and biased court proceedings. Walter White, whose blonde hair and blue eyes allowed him to pass as white, investigated forty-one lynchings and eight race riots for the NAACP from 1918 to 1928. White southerners who assumed they were talking to a fellow white supremacist candidly revealed why they committed or condoned murder. A Klansman even invited White to join the organization. White published his findings widely. He bolstered his undercover identity with press credentials from daily newspapers like the *Chicago Daily News* and *New York Evening Post*. His articles appeared in the *Crisis* and *Defender*, as well as various white newspapers and magazines. Other black publications covered and commented on his exploits and findings. In contrast, Ted Poston disguised his occupation, not his race, when he went to Decatur, Georgia, for the *Amsterdam News* to cover the 1933 retrial of the Scottsboro case. The assignment required ingenuity and determination. Poston wore old overalls and a greasy cap to court and sat in the balcony with other black spectators, hiding his notes by covering his hands with a ragged overcoat. "To all intents and purposes," he later recalled, "I was just another black boy from the county who had dropped into the courtroom's 'Colored' section to see what all the shooting was about." He relied on the help of a friendly white reporter, Tom Cassidy of the *New York Daily News*, to file his stories. While in the black men's bathroom, Poston left his copy on top of a partition that separated him from the white men's room. Cassidy then picked up Poston's copy and wired it to New York. When Cassidy was unavailable, Poston typed his story at his boardinghouse, sneaked to the train station, and delivered it on the midnight mail car. One night, a group of young toughs grabbed him on the platform and demanded to know if he was the black reporter rumored to be in town. Poston lied. He flashed phony credentials that identified him as a minister. The men let him go.[37]

The *Pittsburgh Courier* and *Baltimore Afro-American* flexed the expanded reporting capabilities of an emerging national black press—and demonstrated the allure of the industry's new newswriting template—when they assigned correspondents in the mid-1930s to cover international events that appealed to progressive black activists. The black press had a rich history of foreign correspondence, but dispatches were typically written by freelancers, missionaries, dignitaries, tourists, and expatriates—not by full-time reporters sent overseas by their employers to cover specific news events. Even so, these reports provided the news and narratives needed to sustain black internationalism by "making it possible," as scholar Lara Putnam observed, "for individual experiences in far-flung locales to add up to cohesive intellectual and cultural movements." Domestically, correspondents' dispatches from abroad challenged white southerners' claims concerning the presumed naturalness of segregation and innate inferiority of African-descended people by examining how racial policies were constructed elsewhere and by promoting black achievement. Internationally, correspondents revealed the limits and lies of the West's rhetoric on democracy and freedom. Foreign correspondents encouraged readers worldwide to see themselves as part of a freedom movement that transcended national borders.[38]

The *Pittsburgh Courier* staked its claim to modern race reportage in 1935–1936 when it climbed to the pinnacle of black journalism while covering the second Italian invasion of Ethiopia. Ethiopia's plight captivated the cultural imagination and political aspirations of African Americans who had long revered the nation for its place in black religious traditions of exodus and its hard-won independence on a continent almost entirely colonized by European powers. Nineteenth-century editors had reinforced this attachment through their "universally positive" coverage of Ethiopia in 1896 when its soldiers defeated Italian troops at the Battle of Adowa. That press coverage, though, was limited to editorials, almanac-style factoids, and short dispatches. The second war aroused African Americans—now more familiarized to the tenets of communism, anticolonialism, and Pan-Africanism—far more than the first. As Mussolini prepared to invade, African Americans volunteered to serve in Ethiopia's military, donated to aid organizations, and staged marches across the United States. "Here, at long last," recalled Roi Ottley, an *Amsterdam News* columnist, "was some sort of tangible idealism—certainly a legitimate issue—around which the black nationalists could rally, and indeed rally a great section of the black population."[39]

The *Courier*'s coverage humbled its rivals, even though black newspapers nationwide stimulated readers' interest by saturating their front pages with war news. The editors' masterstroke was hiring J. A. Rogers to cover the war from Ethiopia and promoting him to readers as a modern foreign correspondent. No other newspaper sent a full-time reporter to the warfront. Shamelessly plugging Rogers's stories as exclusives, editors aggressively capitalized on his reputation as a singular authority on the role of race in world affairs: Only Rogers spoke French, the language of Ethiopia's rulers. Only Rogers was personally acquainted with Emperor Haile Selassie and his advisors. Only Rogers had received assurances of Ethiopia's cooperation. "Mr. J. A. Rogers is the only person, black or white," the *Courier* claimed, "who meets all of the requirements of the situation." After establishing Rogers's credentials, the *Courier*'s editors denigrated the legitimacy of other journalists. They dismissed other papers' dispatches as suspect because their correspondents were freelance writers, not full-time professional journalists. "The others are amateurs, frauds or worse." They were right in at least one instance. The *Defender*'s "Operative 22"—a foreign correspondent supposedly granted anonymity to evade censors—was actually editorial writer Metz T. P. Lochard, who culled information from daily newspapers and wrote his stories from Chicago.[40]

The *Courier*'s editors contended that reports from white newspapers were equally dubious due to racism, distance, and censorship. Ethiopian officials banned white reporters from its front lines, claiming they might be Italian spies or victims of mistaken attacks. White reporters relied mostly on Italian press statements that they could seldom independently verify. Italian censors zealously scrubbed dispatches of criticism. "Whom should *Courier* readers believe?" asked Percival Prattis, a World War I veteran who was Rogers's editor. "The lone typewriter of Rogers pounds out one story—the ETHIOPIAN SIDE. From hundreds of others comes a united chorus—the ITALIAN SIDE." Noting Rogers's exclusive visit to Ethiopia's front and his interview with Selassie, Prattis positioned Rogers's pro-Ethiopian coverage as an objective correction to the preponderance of Italian propaganda. "Our readers deserve and must have the truth!—Regardless of Cost!" the paper declared.[41]

Despite the ballyhoo, Rogers's expertise rested in the particularity of his racial outlook, not the professionalism of his journalistic work. Rogers was more familiar with his own idiosyncratic historical research than the demands of on-the-ground reporting. He quickly frustrated his editor. "His cables bring us very little," Prattis complained, "just the shred of an idea. I have to take that and build it up."

Like white reporters, the tall, light-skinned Rogers also waited far from the front lines for military couriers to deliver him the latest news. "I am fairer than most Ethiopians," he wrote, "and, for that reason, am apt to be mistaken for a European." When Rogers did visit the front, censors initially checked his dispatches just like other correspondents' reports. However, he encountered few hassles. "They soon got to learn that I was entirely in sympathy with Ethiopia," Rogers said, "and sometimes my messages were approved without even being read."[42]

Rogers's enthusiasm for Ethiopia overwhelmed his accuracy. Eager to strengthen Black America's sense of connection to Africa, he ignored and downplayed facts that deviated from his chosen narrative of African redemption. Much of what Rogers—and Prattis—wrote resembled the standard fare of black journalism. Rogers praised the fighting skills of Ethiopia's soldiers and frequently alluded to the nation's stunning victory over Italy in 1896. He outlined Italian atrocities and desertions, countered exaggerated claims of Ethiopian death tolls, and speculated on how Ethiopia could win. But Rogers also treated Ethiopian bravado as fact. He expressed no criticism of Ethiopia's wartime leadership. He speculated the eight-month war would last for years. And long after others had conceded Ethiopia's defeat as inevitable, Rogers described how climate and terrain, diplomatic maneuvering, and Italy's struggling economy could snatch victory from defeat. Five months before Ethiopia lost, Rogers claimed, "Italy's 'war of conquest' is a colossal flop!" Despite the *Courier*'s efforts to portray Rogers as a modern journalist, he was openly racialist in a way that future World War II correspondents would deem unsophisticated and overly acquiescent.[43]

In contrast to Rogers's war dispatches, Langston Hughes illustrated the power of modern race reportage by recasting an international event into a compelling—and realistic—depiction of how racism structured the world. Hughes twinned his distinctive racial outlook in the 1930s with a burgeoning political radicalism born of racism, poverty, and career frustrations. He joined the John Reed Club in New York, contributed regularly to *New Masses*, and wrote a play condemning the injustices of the Scottsboro case. He traveled to the Soviet Union to produce a movie about American racism. He wrote travel stories about life in Soviet-controlled Central Asia for *Izvestia*, an official Soviet newspaper. Inspired by the freedom he enjoyed in the Soviet Union compared to the United States, he penned a poetic tribute to the specter of communist revolution. In 1937, the *Afro-American* asked Hughes to cover the Spanish Civil War. Hughes relished the opportunity to travel abroad at "a good rate of pay" and witness firsthand the showdown between the Republic's Popular Front forces and General Francisco Franco's fascist-backed army. (Hughes bolstered his finances

Langston Hughes (left), correspondent for the *Baltimore Afro-American*, at Fuentes de Ebro in 1937 during the Spanish Civil War. Courtesy of the Harry Randall: Fifteenth International Brigade Films and Photographs, Tamiment Library/Robert F. Wagner Labor Archives, Elmer Holmes Bobst Library, New York University.

by arranging to also write for the *Cleveland Call and Post* and *Globe* magazine.) Spain's war was not the cultural touchstone that the Ethiopian conflict had been, but radicalized African Americans again volunteered for military service, donated financially, and organized support groups. In an editorial explaining why Hughes was covering a European civil war, the *Afro-American*'s editors wrote that Spain was "a battle ground and a country in which all races are fusing under the heat of conflict . . . and colored men from America and other sections of the world, are being hurled into the vortex." For Carl Murphy and his editors, the Spanish Civil War seemed a prelude to a global conflict that could determine the fate of people of color.[44]

Part travel piece, adventure tale, battlefront dispatch, and proletarian propaganda, Hughes's fourteen stories from war-torn Spain situated the *Afro-American*'s readers within a cosmopolitan world where racism was less overt, opportunity was more plentiful, and black travelers hobnobbed with writers and performers, doctors and ministers, social workers and soldiers. Franco, the reactionary rebel general attempting to overthrow the republic's elected leftists, threatened this world's freedoms. Hughes conveyed fascism's perils by describing it in terms familiar to his readers. "Give Franco a hood," he wrote, "and he would be a member of the Ku Klux Klan, a kleagle. Fascism is what the Ku Klux Klan will be when it combines with the Liberty League and starts using machine guns and airplanes instead of a few yards of rope." Highlighting Mussolini's support of Franco, Hughes noted that "colored people from many different countries have sent men, money, and sympathy to Spain in her fight against the forces that have raped Ethiopia, and that clearly hold no good for any poor and defenseless people anywhere." Interviews with African American volunteers fighting for the loyalist cause reinforced the importance of black involvement in world affairs. Hughes, who was grazed by a bullet on the front lines, said his war experiences reaffirmed his decision to pursue the writing life and also transformed his outlook on human affairs. "My interests had broadened from Harlem and the American Negro to include an interest in all colored peoples of the world—in fact, in *all the people* of the world, as I related to them and they to me."[45]

. . .

As the 1940s began, black reporters and publishers peered ahead toward a promising future of expanding professional opportunity, growing profitability, and increasing national influence. And yet, the business model that seemed to ensure continued prosperity carried the seeds of its own destruction. Financial security depended upon discerning the ever-changing interests of a mass readership and maintaining a common understanding of the boundaries of black political discourse, which now included an appreciation, although not necessarily an endorsement, of the politics of anticolonialism, anticapitalism, and Black Nationalism. Success depended upon white ambivalence to race news. It depended upon the continuation of segregation, which journalists sought to dismantle with each edition they published. World War II would jeopardize the precarious success enjoyed by black journalists. For even in wartime, readers would still demand militant news coverage that bluntly criticized the nation's institutions and leaders for advocating racial discrimination. In turn, federal officials and military officers—as they had done during World War I—would again question the loyalty of black journalists and encourage them to moderate and postpone calls for racial reform. Challenged by a seemingly impossible political climate, journalists would attempt to satisfy both supporters and critics by crafting a more coded message of racial militancy that censors could approve and readers could applaud.

CHAPTER 4

The "New Crowd" Goes Global

In the months after Japanese pilots bombed Pearl Harbor and thrust the United States into World War II, 29-year-old publisher John Sengstacke moved to protect the *Chicago Defender* against accusations of wartime disloyalty. He met in private with top federal administrators, hoping to forge a "cooperative relationship" with them. Sengstacke knew these men could cripple the *Defender* by censoring stories, suspending mailing privileges, withholding paper rations, forcing employees into the draft, and charging him with sedition. He intended to forestall such penalties. Again and again, in one office and then another, Sengstacke promised that the *Defender* wanted "to be of every possible cooperation to the government in doing whatever it can to improve and help maintain American morale."[1]

Sengstacke backed his words with action, publishing in September 1942 a massive "Victory Edition" to demonstrate the *Defender*'s loyalty. The edition's editors envisioned an interracial readership. The bulky ninety-four–page paper, which included two magazine supplements, aimed to bolster black support for the war effort, reinforce the need for national unity, and detail black contributions to American society and war mobilization. Leading white liberals and government officials contributed essays. President Franklin D. Roosevelt and Generals Douglas MacArthur and Dwight D. Eisenhower wrote commendatory letters. Sengstacke expected the special edition to show "the Negro's problem is 'a part of' rather than 'apart from' the problem facing America as a democracy."

He wanted to convince government officials that black protest "merely reflects a humiliating feeling of frustration," not a rebuke of the American way. To do so, Sengstacke exaggerated the potency of interracial goodwill and denied the depth of black confliction toward the war effort. His "Victory Edition" ignored African Americans who evaded the draft or registered as conscientious objectors to protest segregation. It never mentioned how some black soldiers and sailors griped about journalists' efforts to undo military segregation and force them into combat for a nation that denied them basic civil liberties. A few *Defender* employees—who "believed in passive support to the war"—refused to work on the edition because of its propagandistic orientation. Sengstacke eventually dismissed them for inefficiency and insubordination.[2]

And yet, Sengstacke never repeated W. E. B. Du Bois's mistaken call to "close ranks" and put off racial justice until after the war. Instead, editorial editor Metz T. P. Lochard, a Haitian who had taught French at Howard and Fisk universities, appropriated the language and symbolism of the Popular Front to characterize the African American struggle as part of a worldwide interracial movement

Chicago Defender publisher John Sengstacke in 1942. Photograph by Jack Delano. Courtesy of the Library of Congress, Prints & Photographs Division, FSA/OWI Collection (LC-USW3-000802-D).

against the forces of fascism. This characterization emphasized the shared concerns of the working class, regardless of race. By broadening the basis of black claims to equality along class lines, Lochard deflected accusations that black newspapers inflamed racial tensions. The edition's lead editorial, for example, opened without reference to race when it claimed "the masses are more enlightened" and "the common man" was no longer content with half-kept promises. When the editorial turned to the fight for racial equality, it reinforced its universality by asserting that the African American "is now ready to join hands with the rest of suffering humanity as a necessary expedient for winning his freedom." Only then did the editorial make its central point about the black man: "He is willing to fight, he is ready to die for a free world, but a free world that will include him long after the roar of cannons and bursting shells shall have subsided." Similarly, Popular Front imagery allowed the *Defender* to appeal to readers' militancy without acknowledging it in text. A full-page drawing on the edition's cover was captioned "All for One—One for All." Readers, though, could decide for themselves what meaning to attach to the glowering, muscular black man poised to defend himself with a bayonet while flanked on his right by white allies and on his left by armed fighters from Asia and the Middle East.[3]

The *Defender*'s "Victory Edition" illustrated how commercial newspaper publishers attempted to reconcile black protest and white scrutiny during World War II by forsaking explicit textual radicalism for a more coded militancy. Reconciliation required compromise. Publishers and journalists appealed to black readers by continuing to denounce segregation in all its forms, earning rebukes from military commanders and cabinet members. Simultaneously, they neutralized government investigators and press critics by encouraging African Americans to fight for their country even though the nation had repeatedly rejected racial reforms after previous wars. They evaded discussing opposition to war participation, avoided direct criticism of American capitalism, and diminished open advocacy of communism. If successful, publishers knew this perplexing negotiation could force the federal government, military, and white media to recognize the potency of black journalism and open access to channels of power. Publishers also hoped to bolster circulation—the basis for their exaggerated claims that they spoke for Black America.

Dispatches from overseas war correspondents exemplified how reporters moderated but maintained their militancy. War correspondents effusively praised the work of black troops in achieving victory, despite the hardships and persistence of American racism. However, they also scrutinized the global nature of white supremacy when they examined and denounced the Western colonial powers' subjugation of people of color. Their criticisms challenged the

Allies' claims of promoting democracy and freedom by linking colonialists' exploitation of conquered populations to fascists' violent repression of dissidents. When war correspondents criticized Western colonialism, they reinforced and broadened an appreciation for black internationalism, a touchstone of black radicalism. They continued a radical critique of the United States' racial practices in wartime by examining them from outside the nation's borders. Correspondents marginalized other aspects of black radicalism, though, when they celebrated the war effort by positing American democracy as a flawed but adequate venue for remedying racial wrongs.

"This Tends to Stifle Patriotism"
Going to War with a Segregated Military

African Americans had little reason to believe the military valued black service in the years before World War II and every reason to question the motives of anyone who urged them to enlist. Despite long-standing complaints, the Army and Navy remained staunchly segregated. The Marine Corps and Army Air Corps (which became the independent Air Force in 1947) excluded all African Americans. Black soldiers and sailors were denied promotions and confined to labor battalions and other support positions. One year before the attack on Pearl Harbor, fewer than nine thousand black servicemen were on active duty. African Americans accounted for no more than 2 percent of personnel in any branch of the Armed Forces. Top military officers promised racial reform to quiet public controversy but seldom followed through on their pledges. Most officers claimed tampering with segregation would lower troop morale, diminish efficiency, and reduce combat readiness. Fraudulent racist beliefs had hardened into institutional knowledge. White officers routinely characterized black recruits as ignorant, lazy, and cowardly. If undertrained and poorly equipped black enlistees performed poorly, white officers blamed the soldiers' abilities rather than the subpar quality of their instruction.[4]

Black journalists mounted an uncoordinated but aggressive campaign for extensive reform within the Armed Forces, anticipating how the looming war could bolster African Americans' claims to citizenship rights. Publisher Robert Vann of the *Pittsburgh Courier* penned an open letter to President Roosevelt in February 1938, asking for increased enlistments, expanded service opportunities in all branches, and creation of a division of black combat troops supervised by black officers. "Even Negro combat troops have been made to feel that they are the domestic servants of the army in peace time," Vann complained. "This tends to stifle patriotism." He was ignored. The *Courier* renewed its campaign two years later when it formed a committee—later reorganized and called the Committee on Participation of Negroes in the National Defense Program—to lobby the Senate Appropriations Committee for inclusion of black troops in all military branches. (The NAACP opposed the campaign since the creation of all-black combat units implied acceptance of segregation.) "The morale of Negro citizens regarding national defense is probably at the lowest ebb in the history of this country," lawyer Charles H. Houston, a committee member, warned senators. "Negroes have absolutely no faith in the leadership of the Army or the Navy."[5]

Military commanders, though, resisted political pressure and stuck to racist traditions, sparking frequent controversy. In October 1940, the *Courier* published a letter signed by nine sailors aboard the USS Philadelphia. The sailors wrote "to discourage any other colored boys who might have planned to join the Navy and make the same mistake we did. All they would become is sea-going bell hops, chambermaids and dishwashers." The sailors complained they could only serve as mess attendants—shining shoes, making beds, and cooking meals. They endured ceaseless provocation and mistreatment and were punished when they retaliated. Nine of the ship's eighteen black sailors were being held in solitary confinement. Rather than forbid racial harassment, Navy officers imprisoned those who signed the letter and discharged them as unfit for service. Secretary of the Navy Frank Knox told Walter White, NAACP executive secretary, that the sailors had violated regulations by publicly stating their criticisms, which demonstrated "by their own actions that they must be classed as malcontents."[6]

Such overt hostility convinced W. E. B. Du Bois to tell his readers in the *New York Amsterdam News* that they had no stake in the outcome of World War II. Du Bois lost his greatest platform for lobbying elite black and white readers in 1934 when he resigned his editorship of the *Crisis*. His thinking on race no longer matched the NAACP's integrationist outlook. Du Bois was becoming a Marxist who favored segregation established according to black demands. He believed the idea of Africa was central to African American identity. The persistence of American racism and its similarities to European colonialism shaped his perspective on international affairs. He had linked American segregation to Nazi anti-Semitism as early as 1933, and he depicted fascism as an incomplete experiment negotiating the middle ground between capitalism and communism. He glossed over Japanese aggression in Asia by comparing it to Europe's injustices in the region and celebrating the rise of a nonwhite military power. Although his direct influence on political events had diminished, Du Bois's increasingly progressive political views reached a wider readership as he wrote weekly columns successively for the *Courier*, *Amsterdam News*, and *Defender*. Just seven months before the United States entered World War II, he claimed, "No outcome of the present war is going to help the American Negro or the Negroes of the world. Their problems after this war will be more difficult than ever."[7]

Onetime radical editor A. Philip Randolph was similarly frustrated when he announced plans in January 1941 to organize a mass march on Washington, D.C., to demand the end of discrimination in the military and industry. With the *Messenger* folded and his journalism days behind him, Randolph spoke as a powerful union leader, the head of the Brotherhood of Sleeping Car Porters. He claimed black citizens "must diplomatically and undiplomatically; ceremoniously and unceremoniously cry out in no uncertain terms our demand for work and our rightful places in every department of the army, navy, and air corps." Randolph recruited supporters for the March on Washington Movement through extensive press coverage. He held briefings for reporters, issued news releases, and wrote numerous guest columns to create publicity and interest. As readers embraced the movement, reporters filed more stories about Randolph's speeches and other public appearances. Stirred by the threat of one hundred thousand or more African Americans marching to the White House, President Roosevelt promised to establish the Fair Employment Practices Committee (FEPC), which was to enforce nondiscrimination in defense employment. Randolph postponed the march but dangled it as a future possibility if the committee proved ineffectual.[8]

Newspaper editors amplified demands for military reform by assigning reporters to investigate the treatment, living conditions, and work details of black troops. The *Baltimore Afro-American*, for example, sent Ollie Stewart in the summer of 1941 on a nationwide inspection of twenty Army training camps. Stewart, a Louisiana minister's son and a graduate of Tennessee State Agricultural and Industrial College, wrote to expose discrimination, correct racial wrongs, and familiarize readers with the day-to-day lives of family and friends serving in the military. At Camp Livingston in Louisiana, Stewart reported that he had "heard no serious complaints," but he also noted that soldiers from the North opposed the base's strict adherence to the rules of southern segregation. While soldiers preferred to have black officers, they figured complaining would achieve nothing. Stewart complimented the camp's efforts to educate and entertain soldiers. "I have seen white and colored meet and salute each other," he wrote. "At other times I have seen them pass without a word or a nod." Stewart's coverage was factual and measured. Elsewhere, he wrote about white officers mistreating black soldiers and the Army's refusal to promote African Americans. He described rundown barracks and inadequate training and recreational buildings and equipment. Calling Alexandria, Louisiana, "a powder keg," he claimed civilian harassment could spark a riot. Such an incident occurred six months later. After investigating reports of racial violence at Fort Bragg, Stewart concluded "the only way a change will come to this part of North Carolina will be for the soldiers first to be sure they are in the right—and then fight for rights."[9]

Army officers tended to view any criticism of their racial practices as unduly hostile and harmful to national security. Under constant scrutiny by black journalists, the War Department scheduled a conference with twenty publishers and editors from twelve news organizations to explain how it operated and to improve its relations with them. Coincidentally, the conference was held the day after Pearl Harbor was bombed. Scrambling to answer Japan's attack, Gen.

Gen. George C. Marshall met with leading black editors the day after the Japanese bombed Pearl Harbor. Among those attending the meeting were, seated left to right, Truman Gibson of the War Department, an unidentified woman, Brigadier General Benjamin Davis, the nation's highest-ranking black officer, Roscoe Dunjee of the Oklahoma *Black Dispatch*, Chester A. Franklin of the *Kansas City Call*, Frank Stanley of the *Louisville Defender*, Percival Prattis of the *Pittsburg Courier*, P. B. Young of the *Norfolk Journal and Guide*; back row, standing, beginning third from the left: Carter Wesley of the *Houston Informer*, Carl Murphy of the *Baltimore Afro-American*, Claude Barnett of the Associated Negro Press, Louis Martin of the *Michigan Chronicle*, and Julius Adams of the *New York Amsterdam News*. Courtesy of the Moorland-Spingarn Research Center, Manuscript Division, Howard University, Washington D.C.

George C. Marshall met briefly with the journalists. He told them the Army was developing black units in every branch. He also announced the possible formation of a black division, as well as three cadet programs at black colleges. He admitted progress was slow, remarking, "And I am not personally satisfied with it either." Marshall spoke the soothing but vague words of the gradualist who claimed to understand demands for change but insisted on waiting for the right time, which most definitely was not during a war. Then Marshall turned the meeting over to subordinate officers and left. Col. Eugene R. Householder was less circumspect in his words. "The Army is not a sociological laboratory," he said. "Experiments, to meet the wishes and demands of the champions of every race and creed for the solution of their problems are a danger to efficiency, discipline, and morale and would result in ultimate defeat." Householder derided "frequently" inaccurate stories. Worse, Brigadier General Benjamin O. Davis Sr.—whose career as the nation's highest-ranking black officer had benefited from strong support from black newspapers—accused publishers of "sowing discontent in the minds of the soldiers." The meeting accentuated what editors and publishers already knew—military commanders would resist change and respond only to pressure.[10]

Officers' complaints failed to silence press criticism. After the Pearl Harbor attack, editorial writers rushed to strike at racial barriers in a moment when calls for patriotism and service were at a premium. They accused segregationists of betraying their country by interfering with the war effort. The *Defender* argued that anyone who insisted on maintaining military segregation "underestimates the gravity of the crisis or sympathizes with the enemy—therefore is a traitor to this country." The *Afro-American* claimed the United States would remain unprepared for war as long as military recruiting stations were closed to black enlistees. "We cannot march against enemy planes and tanks and challenge warships armed only with a whiskbroom and a wide grin." The *New York Amsterdam Star-News* (formerly the *Amsterdam News*) predicted unquestioned triumph if "superficial distinctions based upon skin color" were cast aside and "we throw our full resources into the battle." In Pittsburgh, the *Courier* advised it was "close to treason to hamper total defense by quibbling over the minutiae of racial distinction; to jeopardize national unity by trying to maintain the color bar in the face of stern necessity." The message was consistent—discrimination, not protest, undermined wartime mobilization. Even teenage newsboys understood. A few weeks later, a 14-year-old hawked his papers in Harlem by exclaiming, "Buy a paper! Buy a paper! Read all about it. You're gonna be in uniform soon. You're gonna have a chance to fight for the democracy you ain't never had. Buy a paper!"[11]

"Actions Hinting of Disloyalty"
State Surveillance in Wartime

Fear of spies, sabotage, and sneak attacks—the seething panic of the unknown enemy within—fanned suspicions that dissenters who questioned America's war aims were, at best, unpatriotic and, at worst, seditious and treasonous. The war years witnessed a concerted effort by the federal government to silence, intimidate, and harass its sharpest critics and presumed adversaries. For the nation's commander-in-chief, the expediency of political and military objectives usually trumped ethical concerns about violations of free speech and civil rights. As Attorney General Francis Biddle observed, President Roosevelt believed, "Rights came after victory, not before." Political orientation provided no protection. On the right, prosecutors imprisoned fascist William Dudley Pelley, a conspiratorial isolationist nicknamed the "American Hitler," and officials pressured the Catholic Church to silence the radio broadcasts of Father Charles Coughlin, an anti-Semitic isolationist who recited Nazi propaganda. On the left, the FBI and House Un-American Activities Committee (chaired by Democrat Martin Dies of Texas) intensified surveillance of the Communist Party and its suspected allies after the Soviet Union signed a nonaggression pact in 1939 with Germany. Federal officials also systematically violated the civil liberties of more than 110,000 Japanese citizens and immigrants as they forcibly relocated them from their West Coast homes to desolate concentration camps across the Great Plains. None of them was ever charged with espionage or sedition.[12]

War mobilization caused social and economic upheaval, with white Americans viewing antiracism campaigns as a manipulation of racial tensions at a moment of national vulnerability. More than sixteen million men and women served in the military, with nearly one family in five seeing one or more of their own in uniform. With so many white men in their prime fighting abroad, women and minorities were hired for jobs they would have been denied in peacetime. About 1.5 million African Americans migrated from the South in the 1940s to cities in the North and West. Violence followed as transplanted black families exacerbated housing shortages, moved into white neighborhoods, demanded better schools and public transportation, and took jobs once reserved for white workers. Riots erupted in Detroit, New York, Los Angeles, and elsewhere. Rumors heightened unease. In some places, whites falsely accused blacks of buying ice picks and switchblades to attack them during blackouts. In the South, white women whispered about "Eleanor Clubs," a supposedly clandestine organization of black domestics who vowed to end segregation by refusing to perform manual labor for white employers.[13]

The start of combat operations intensified animosity between military commanders and black journalists. Four months after Pearl Harbor, a black civilian aide to Secretary of War Henry L. Stimson warned the NAACP's Walter White that the War Department was "increasingly hostile" toward black newspapers and civil rights groups. Even sympathetic officers like Brigadier General Frederick H. Osborn, a liberal northerner, conflated black complaints about the military's institutionalized racism with support for Nazi Germany. Osborn accused black newspapers—the *Courier* in particular—of manipulating stories "with adjectives and innuendo, so as to make them inflammatory." Osborn cautioned that "very serious consequences would inevitably develop" if the *Courier* continued to print untrue articles. Percival Prattis, the *Courier's* executive editor, admitted black newspapers tended toward "indiscriminate wording and slanting of stories." However, he argued that such articles came closer to the truth than the military's rationalization of segregation.[14]

Army field officers and military intelligence agents frequently recommended censoring black newspapers and haphazardly but steadfastly barred them from bases, particularly in the South. Sergeant Robert Pitts, a black enlistee who was among the first soldiers trained at Tuskegee Air Field, prepared papers against soldiers considered hostile to the war effort. "In those days anybody reading the *Pittsburgh Courier* was considered suspect," Pitts recalled. "We started a processing dossier on such individuals, and they were transferred elsewhere." Acting Corporal Earl Kennedy, stationed in Stockton, California, saw soldiers berated by sergeants if a black newspaper was found in their footlockers. "The question was asked, 'What are you doing with that inflammatory material in your locker?'" Soldiers complained to the NAACP and publishers when papers were seized. "Forcibly preventing the sale of newspapers," wrote *Defender* columnist S. I. Hayakawa, "is about the most direct abridgement of the freedom of the press that can be imagined, short of shooting the editors or dynamiting the printing plant."[15]

Through threats and investigations, federal agencies once again attempted to intimidate journalists into softening their criticism of American racism. Government investigators were conditioned to treat black newspapers as radical instigators because of their attacks on segregation, ambivalence toward communism, and sympathy for colored populations worldwide, including Japan. Roosevelt asked Attorney General Biddle and Postmaster General Frank Walker during a Cabinet meeting in May 1942 to meet with black editors "to see what could be done about preventing their subversive language." Many officials regarded black journalists as blundering amateurs. Lawrence W. Cramer, executive secretary of the Fair Employment Practices Committee, reportedly claimed black newspapers did not intend to print seditious stories but did so because of "the ignorance of editors and a sort of hysterical competition." The U.S. Post Office investigated whether it should suspend postal privileges for certain newspapers, including the *Courier, Defender, Chicago Bee,* and *Amsterdam-Star News.* The government agencies primarily responsible for managing war news and propaganda—the Office of Censorship, Office of Facts and Figures (OFF), and Office of War Information (OWI)—closely monitored the tone of war coverage in leading newspapers. Censors breezily condemned articles about racial protest as inflammatory and removed them from papers mailed overseas. They also struck references to racial incidents from copy submitted by foreign correspondents writing in the United States. "The enemy not only does not understand it," said Byron Price, director of the Office of Censorship, "but finds it prime ammunition for promotion of his 'divide and conquer' propaganda." In one instance, a *Defender* agent in Cuba returned to Sengstacke all copies of an issue from April 1942 because they were unfit to sell. "The entire paper was cut until only the border remained," Sengstacke complained. "Not a page was readable." Officials from the Navy, FEPC, and Justice Department signaled their support in June 1942 for OWI's policy of giving "unofficial warnings to Negro editors." Milton Starr, an OWI adviser frequently criticized by African Americans for his racial views, claimed the policy "had the desired effect of toning down the Negro press."[16]

FBI agents visited journalists and subscribed to their newspapers, fully intending to impress upon editors the government's vigilance. In 1942 and 1943, FBI Director J. Edgar Hoover ordered an extensive nationwide investigation of racial conditions, which resulted in a classified report that analyzed the content of black newspapers and magazines. Field agents summarized articles that questioned national priorities and identified journalists with alleged affiliations with communists and labor unions. Their conclusions were vague and famil-iar but sounded ominous when couched in the language of law enforcement: "Sources of information have volunteered the opinion that all the Negro press is a strong provocator [*sic*] of discontent among Negroes." *Defender* reporter Enoch Waters believed the FBI held up his credentials as an overseas war correspon-dent for nearly a year to intimidate the newspaper. The delay was supposedly tied to a political donation that Waters made in 1940 to a black communist running for vice president. "It was a warning to the paper," Waters recalled, "that actions hinting of disloyalty during this crucial period could create seri-ous problems for the publisher and for the Negro press generally."[17]

Despite Starr's assertions of compliance, journalists approached the fed-eral government with a mixture of aggression and conciliation. They enjoyed a significantly stronger political position than they had during World War I, and they knew few government officials were willing to jeopardize the desperately needed cooperation of African Americans by waging an overly aggressive campaign against the black press. Sengstacke, for example, arranged a meeting with the attorney general after hearing rumors in mid-June 1942 that officials might attempt to shut down one or more newspapers. As the men talked, Biddle pointed to some newspapers on a conference table and promised to halt their publication if their tone was not moderated. Sengstacke recalled his reply decades later: "You have the power to close us down, so if you want to close us, go ahead and attempt it." Sengstacke tempered his bravado with a compromise. He told Biddle that journalists would write more balanced articles if administration officials responded to interview requests. Biddle offered to call officials and make some appointments. Sengstacke also attempted to cooperate with Archibald MacLeish, the director of the Office of Facts and Figures. While soliciting federal support for his "Victory Edition," Sengstacke offered to have a black publishers' group serve as an advisory committee to MacLeish's agency. "The crisis of the hour," he wrote, "makes it imperative that the relationship between Negro editors and your office be maintained on a high level of cordiality and understanding." MacLeish accepted the aid. However, OFF then merged with OWI. Resentment mounted when Sengstacke's offer encountered delays and indifference from the new department. OWI finally approved the committee seventeen months later.[18]

Meanwhile, other journalists complained publicly about FBI intimidation. Rotund, cigar-chewing columnist Cliff Mackay met twice with agents in the spring of 1942 at the *Atlanta Daily World*. An agent asked during the first interview whether the Communist Party or a news service suspected of circulating Japanese propaganda had attempted to influence the paper's news coverage. Mackay said they had not. The second interview occurred after Mackay angered Hoover by highlighting the agency's poor record of hiring black employees. Knowing Hoover wanted to silence him, Mackay wrote a column that rebuked the FBI for investigating journalists instead of segregationists. "It is they, not Negroes, who now are sabotaging the war effort," he said. "They are blocking the war effort by seeking to create division and disunity at a time when closed ranks should be the order of the day."[19]

Journalists attested daily to their expanded influence by maintaining a strong, visible presence in the nation's capital. Leading publishers organized an industry trade group, the Negro Newspaper Publishers Association (NNPA), in March 1940 to lobby for their common interests. The organization allowed publishers to appeal to federal officials with the full force of their readership behind them, a tactic guaranteed to gain entry (if not results) in President Roosevelt's political world. Publishers also established competitive national news bureaus in Washington, D.C. The NNPA and Associated Negro Press (ANP) sent syndicated stories to subscribers, while the *Defender* and *Courier* staffed their own bureaus. The *Afro-American* covered national politics from the same offices it gathered local news for its Washington edition. The Roosevelt administration acknowledged black journalism's political clout in 1943 when it pressured the all-white White House Correspondents Association to accredit the NNPA's Harry S. McAlpin to attend presidential press conferences.[20]

Black advisers to federal agencies helped journalists gain access to government information by brokering disputes between bureaucrats and reporters. Many advisers had personal relationships with journalists and their supervisors, including former *Amsterdam News* and *New York Post* reporter Ted Poston, former ANP columnist William Pickens, and former *Messenger* editor Chandler Owen. Advisers strove to maintain an imperiled integrity as they advocated for racial reform before their supervisors but championed discriminatory policy to black journalists. If they leaned too much toward advocacy, their tenuous connection to policy-making was undermined. If they shilled too strongly for segregationist plans, they were painted as traitors to their race. Critics faulted Owen and Pickens for underselling discrimination. Other advisers quit to protest policies they could not alter. Former federal judge William Hastie resigned as a civilian aide to the Secretary of War in 1943 when he realized he could not change the military from the inside. Cincinnati lawyer Theodore Berry resigned from OFF because of its reluctance "to frontally attack white racial prejudice through propaganda instead of seeking to mesmerize Negroes with innocuous material." Another adviser worked surreptitiously for racial change. Alfred E. Smith, adviser to the Federal Works Progress Administration, griped to reporters that he could not even write a letter without permission from his supervisors. "His hands are tied and his office is purely one of window dressing," ANP reporter Alvin White observed. And yet, Smith also wrote a popular, anonymously sourced gossip column in the *Defender* under the pseudonym Charley Cherokee. The column traded on scoops Smith picked up as a government insider.[21]

Ted Poston was the most prominent black journalist serving the government. Despite the FBI's objections, he worked for the War Production Board and War Manpower Commission before moving in October 1942 to OWI to head the newly formed—and short-lived—Negro News Desk. Poston's office became a hub of activity, a place where advisers and journalists traded gossip and shared tips, with the loud and garrulous Poston serving as ringmaster. The desk summarized race news from twenty-five black newspapers, prepared press releases for black journalists, and sent information about racial issues to other federal agencies. Poston both hounded and assisted reporters. He called his friend Ellen Tarry, an *Amsterdam News* reporter, after fielding complaints about her articles accusing white naval officers of discriminating against black sailors. Poston told Tarry she was harming the war effort and asked her to tone down her stories. She refused. "You can't muzzle me!" she said. "You wanna bet?" Poston replied. He called her managing editor. The editor persuaded Tarry to make changes. She never felt betrayed, saying Poston "was just doing his job." Another time, Poston wielded the threat of negative news coverage to prod the Navy into reforming its discriminatory policies. Poston claimed in October 1943 that he had been "reliably informed" that editors from several newspapers were planning to campaign for a congressional investigation of the Navy's mistreatment of black sailors. Poston criticized the Navy's public relations efforts for showing only the training of black units, not their participation in combat. Such inattention, he argued, reinforced the belief that black seamen were confined to shore-based labor duties. Poston also noted that naval officers had promised several times to enlist black women and make certain commissions available to black recruits. No action had followed. He urged the Navy to immediately announce the fulfillment of its promises and to publicize the achievements of black sailors. "I know this is going to be tough," he wrote, "but it will be worse if we let the Negro press take the initiative away from us."[22]

White columnists expounded upon military and civilian authorities' complaints about the black press, leading black journalists to characterize press criticism as an extension of government surveillance and harassment. Conservative syndicated columnist Westbrook Pegler accused the *Courier* and *Defender* in April 1942 of combining the worst excesses of Hearst-style sensationalism with the skewed, inflammatory perspective of the Communist Party's *Daily Worker* and Father Coughlin's right-wing *Social Justice*. Pegler knocked the newspapers for featuring undistinguished writing and publishing anonymously sourced gossip and scam advertisements. He essentially reproached them for shoddy journalism. Two months later, Pegler charged black editors with the same shortcomings they typically lobbed at daily newspapers. He claimed white editors handled racial news "with the greatest delicacy," while black editors always sided with their race, "often with injustice to the white man and the truth and to the damage of interracial understanding." Pegler was a formidable opponent. He reached ten million readers through his column and had won a Pulitzer Prize for exposing racketeering in Hollywood labor unions. Another respected critic, liberal southerner Virginius Dabney, editor of the *Richmond Times-Dispatch*, castigated black newspapers and the NAACP for attempting "to force immediate revolutionary

Ted Poston, a reporter for the *New York Amsterdam News* and *New York Post*, served as editor of the Negro News Desk for the Office of War Information during World War II. He discusses a letter from a black editor in 1943 with his assistants, William Clark and Harriette Easterlin. Photograph by Alfred T. Palmer. Courtesy of the Library of Congress, Prints & Photographs Division, FSA/OWI Collection (LC-USE6-D-009072).

revision in customs and practices which have grown up over decades and centuries of usage." Dabney initially complained in his newspaper but later repeated his charges in the prestigious *Atlantic Monthly.* He characterized black activists as war profiteers and accused journalists of "stirring up interracial hate." He claimed "the radical element of the Negro press" so indulged in vilifying white America that riots would break out if whites read those newspapers.[23]

The most damning criticism printed in a major white publication came from a black writer—Warren H. Brown, a race relations adviser for the Council for Democracy, a liberal organization formed to support defense mobilization. Brown's article appeared in the *Saturday Review of Literature* and *Reader's Digest*, the nation's most read magazine. Brown positioned himself as a thoughtful black man who, along with a majority of African Americans, rejected "sensation-mongering Negro leaders." Brown argued that journalists slowed racial progress and emphasized misfortune to incite unrest rather than promote justice. "For giving a dishonest, discreditable picture of American Negro life," Brown wrote, "they are worse than the worst white newspaper. The average Negro newspaper portrays Negro life in burlesque." The criticism was a familiar one lobbed against journalists by middle-class black leaders who favored gradualist reforms that attracted white support. Brown's column, though, served to justify the swell of critical white commentary by suggesting that respectable black society was also repulsed by black journalism. Editors and publishers recognized the threat Brown posed to their credibility and unleashed an avalanche of criticism. They depicted him as the white man's dupe. Louis Martin of the *Michigan Chronicle* referred to Brown as "the long-awaited voice of an Uncle Tom courting affection of his white masters." Martin contended that black journalists spoke for the "insecure black millions" who endured daily discrimination, while Brown, who held a doctorate degree from the New School for Social Research, "numbered among the few who feel safe; and with his hat in his hand, he may be safer still." William Walker of the *Cleveland Call and Post* argued that "appeasement Negroes and Dishwater whites" wanted to destroy the black press because it was "the most formidable weapon" that African Americans possessed in the fight against discrimination and segregation. "Destroy the Negro press," Walker said, "and you will destroy Negro progress."[24]

White journalists' attacks marked an effort to maintain a definition of professionalism that excluded black editors and reporters. White editors accused black journalists of lacking objectivity, an industry doctrine rivaled only by truthfulness as the prime characteristic of the consummate reporter. A belief in objectivity held that professional journalists could and would separate known facts from personal opinion to present readers with an impartial view (often assumed to be the correct view) on a particular subject. Objectivity gradually gained dominance in journalism after the sensationalism of turn-of-the-century yellow journalism, intensive propaganda campaigns of World War I, and tabloid excesses of the 1920s. The ideal of objectivity imbued journalism with a sense of professionalism and rationalism. It promised to give unbiased and verified information to readers. Less noticeably, though, objectivity tended to reinforce the status quo. It achieved impartiality by promoting conventional wisdom and prevailing research. Faith in objectivity encouraged white journalists to judge black journalism on its structure—the one-sidedness of race-angled stories, excessive sensationalism, and a proclivity to exaggerate black achievements and white discrimination—rather than the merits of its underlying belief that African Americans deserved full equality. Within this framework, white journalists could dismiss black reporters as activists unable to impartially judge racial abuse because of their skin color.[25]

Black journalists countered these criticisms by challenging white reporters' faith in objectivity. They questioned whether a racist society could distinguish fact from bias. The *Defender*'s Waters identified objectivity's central flaw when he observed that Chicago's daily newspapers never moved in advance of public opinion on racial justice. White publishers, he said, routinely sacrificed objectivity to maintain circulation. "Faced with an uncomfortable dilemma," he said, "most newspapers chose to express no view contrary to that held by the majority of their advertisers and readers, thus surrendering their editorial independence." Prattis of the *Courier* dismissed objectivity as an "academic curio." He claimed objectivity functioned as "a guilty conscience complex, heeded more often as a space saver than as a builder of character in the newspaper." Prattis harkened back to the journalistic standards of the early 1900s when he claimed all good newspapers took sides and put their resources and intellect behind particular investigations. Forceful newspapers demanded aggressive journalists. Prattis described the black reporter as "a fighting partisan" who battled for full citizenship rights and equal opportunity on behalf of readers who demanded such journalism. "They don't like him tame," Prattis said. "They want him to have an arsenal well-stocked with atomic adjectives and nouns. They expect him to invent similes and metaphors that lay open the foe's weaknesses and to employ cutting irony, sarcasm, and ridicule to confound and embarrass our opponents." Partisanship and cause, though, did not excuse lying or fabrication. Editor P. B. Young Jr. of the *Norfolk Journal and Guide* wrote the "Credo for the Negro Press," a widely endorsed declaration of the press's aims and values. The pledge asserted journalists' commitment to "crusade for all things that are right and just" and to "expose and condemn all things that are unjust." Journalistic crusaders, though, never abandoned "the cardinals of journalism, accuracy, fairness, and objectivity."[26]

"A Wind Is Rising"
Combat, Empire, and Black War Correspondents

Publishers' ceaseless negotiations to maintain their right to publish protest journalism led them to amplify their claims of national allegiance to cloak their writers' most militant observations. Wartime reportage was unabashedly patriotic, despite widespread cynicism among African Americans toward mobilization. The *Courier*'s famed "Double V" campaign illustrated how editors conflated protest with patriotism to fend off state censorship. Editors explained that "Double V" stood for "victory over our enemies at home and victory over our enemies on the battlefields abroad." James G. Thompson, a

26-year-old cafeteria worker at an aircraft manufacturing plant in Wichita, Kansas, coined the expression in January 1942 when he unburdened his uncertainty about looming military service in a letter to the editor published in the *Courier*. "Should I sacrifice my life to live half American?" Thompson asked. "Is the kind of America I know worth defending?" Despite personal confliction, Thompson concluded he was "willing to die for the America I know will someday become a reality." The *Courier*'s publicity-minded editors sniffed a new crusade, but they were so uncertain whether readers would rally to support the war that they launched the campaign without fanfare "to test the response and the popularity of such a slogan." This hesitation to announce the campaign showed that the paper's executives preferred to inform readers rather than lead them. Their concern, though, was unwarranted. Readers sent thousands of telegrams and letters expressing their support.[27]

Implicit in readers' support—but largely excised from the *Courier*'s news coverage—was an understanding that many African Americans were reluctant warriors. While victory abroad represented a concrete military aim, victory at home was an ambiguous bundle of long-standing demands unlikely to be addressed in wartime. Readers often announced their support for "Double V" by emphasizing how racial discrimination undermined the war effort. "The morale of our colored people is alarmingly low and from my point of view, justifiably so," a New York reader wrote. Another reader from Nebraska said, "A few months ago I was ready to fight and die for the U.S.A., but my morale has dropped on reading the way they are treating our boys down South." In contrast, the *Courier*'s editors avoided overtly stating African Americans' ambivalence toward the war effort by substituting Thompson's conflicted patriotism for a spirit of triumphalism. One month into the campaign, reporter Frank E. Bolden knocked critics who accused African Americans of using the war to press for personal freedoms. "We are not trying to take advantage of Uncle Sam while his back is turned," Bolden wrote. "WE ARE FIGHTING TO GET INTO THIS WAR EFFORT." The campaign's propaganda value was attested to by the many white politicians who praised it, even as southern segregationists and military officers accused the *Courier* of inflaming unrest.[28]

Readers used visual cues to imbue the "Double V" campaign with greater militancy than the *Courier*'s editors associated it with in text, which explains the popularity of a slogan that encouraged discriminatory war participation. Scholar Kimberley Phillips argues that newspaper readers countered the government's official depiction of war participation, which avoided showing black troops training for combat or black nurses tending to wounded white soldiers, by submitting personal photographs and snapshots of loved ones performing military duties. The "Double V" campaign was visual as much as it was textual. The pairing of V's became a way to symbolize one's commitment to racial justice. Readers pinned "Double V" buttons to shirts and blouses. They hung "Double V" posters on car windows and store doors. They eyed "Double V" girls, flashed "Double V" hand signs, attended "Double V" dances, and even fashioned a "Double V" hairdo. The *Courier* deployed this symbolism to satisfy two audiences—black readers and white censors. Black readers, though, used the slogan to publicly express their political views, not appease white America. Readers challenged the *Courier's* editors when they believed the paper failed to fulfill their militant ideals. A Cleveland woman chastised the paper in April 1943 after reading an editorial opposing Randolph's March on Washington Movement. "You can't preach 'Double V,'" she wrote, "and expect 'Status Quo.'"[29]

As war mobilization shifted from training to combat, the military and press reached an uneasy accommodation. Military officers made modest changes by mid-1942 to quiet press criticism and ensure a more efficient use of manpower. The Army Air Corps admitted African Americans for the first time, and the Navy and Marine Corps removed racial restrictions on general-service positions. Legislators rewrote the Selective Service Act to include nondiscrimination clauses. The Army's public relations officers formed a special section to serve black journalists. An order issued in late 1943 prohibited field officers from banning black newspapers on military installations. Officials later established a process for deciding which black newspapers to stock at post exchanges. At black newspapers, editors assigned articles that emphasized the work and achievements of black soldiers as well as stories condemning military segregation. The *Afro-American's* Stewart revisited training camps and discovered that some bases had made minor improvements, such as accepting applications for officer appointments and enhancing recreational opportunities. Editors ran more news from Army press releases as the war expanded. Military officials believed they had effectively manipulated and pressured journalists into publishing favorable news. Editors and reporters took credit for convincing the military to improve its treatment of black troops.[30]

More significantly, the War Department reversed the federal government's prior opposition to black war correspondents and issued credentials to black journalists for overseas assignments. During World War I, publishers could neither afford to send reporters overseas nor obtain military accreditation for them. Instead, race-angled news came from soldiers' letters, freelance writers living in Europe, or dignitaries recently returned from abroad. Such dispatches usually offered a constricted, personalized view of the overall war. The writers could not interview officers and usually could not provide firsthand descriptions of combat. The *Defender* sent Roscoe Conkling Simmons to France, but he never left Paris. Simmons occasionally interviewed soldiers on leave before his publisher recalled him in disappointment. A publishers' group covered travel expenses for Ralph W. Tyler, the only accredited black reporter, but his dispatches were heavily censored. With military intelligence officers urging that "special care be exercised in censoring this subject's communications," Tyler's reports about black bravery reached his editors but dispatches critiquing American segregation never left censors' offices.[31]

During World War II, four of the five largest black newspapers—the *Amsterdam News* was the exception—sent accredited reporters into war zones. Correspondents filed copy from Europe, Africa, Asia, and the Pacific. The *Courier* and *Afro-American* offered the most extensive coverage. The *Courier* had eight accredited correspondents. They included anticolonialist George Padmore who lived in London and also wrote for ANP; Roi Ottley, who also spent six months overseas for *PM*, a liberal New York daily; Ollie Harrington, a popular cartoonist who reported from southern Europe; and Edgar Rouzeau, the first black reporter to receive credentials. The *Afro-American* sent seven reporters, including Stewart, who emerged as one of the war's most recognized journalists; Bettye Phillips, the publisher's fast-talking daughter; and sports reporter Art Carter. The *Defender*'s four correspondents included veteran journalist Enoch Waters and company lawyer Ed Toles, who had almost no reporting experience. The *Journal and Guide*'s three reporters included the publisher's son, Thomas W. Young, and John Q. Jordan, who had worked in Norfolk since 1933. The two major news services, ANP and NNPA, agreed to pool reports by their six correspondents. The War Department requested pooling, seeing it as a way to boost troop morale by better ensuring correspondents were available to publicize black soldiers' uncelebrated labor.[32]

Correspondents suffered the same slights and abuses as the troops they covered, but they also enjoyed unusual privileges and latitude as honorary officers backed by powerful newspapers. Rouzeau felt the sting of segregation before his transport ship reached North Africa. He initially shared a stateroom with several white correspondents, and he rebuffed an officer's suggestion that he bunk with a black chaplain and a few other black officers. "I bristled," Rouzeau recalled. "I explained that, as a writer, I had everything in common with the white correspondents; that I had talked the matter over with them and had received assurance from all that my company was not obnoxious." The commanding officer then issued a direct order. Rouzeau faced court-martial if he disobeyed. He moved in with a group of black doctors as the colonel shuffled the living quarters of some white lieutenants to avoid being accused of discrimination.

Enoch Waters, war correspondent for the *Chicago Defender*, interviews soldiers during World War II. Courtesy of the Moorland-Spingarn Research Center, Manuscript Division, Howard University, Washington D.C.

Stewart encountered a similar situation in Oran, a North African city on the Mediterranean Sea. He had boarded with white reporters before, but a colonel bellowed during an air raid, "No black sonofabitch is going to sleep under the same roof with me." Stewart moved to a hotel three blocks from where white correspondents slept. Despite such incidents, Waters believed most officers, even those from the South, bent over backward to help black reporters. "I think they figured we had a lot more influence than we really did," Waters said. "They knew we went down to headquarters a lot." Ottley remarked in his diary that military protocols distinguishing enlisted soldiers from officers (even honorary officers) trumped segregationist practices dividing blacks and whites. The *Journal and Guide*'s Jordan suspected that most officers—as well as white reporters—simply ignored black journalists. Jordan took advantage of their indifference and belief in stereotypes. Even though no black journalist was an accredited photographer, Jordan carried a camera wherever he went. "We weren't supposed to take pictures," he said, "but, being ignorant black reporters, we took our cameras with us. I caught the devil many times, but you see, nobody cared much at first."[33]

The nearly unassailable authority held by military censors in combat zones forced correspondents to measure their words and tone. Several black correspondents claimed that censors cut their copy only a little more than they excised white reporters' dispatches. Even so, the topic of race remained ticklish near the frontlines. Baltimore publisher Carl Murphy claimed censors "cut to ribbons" reports describing a riot between white and black troops in England. News occasionally got out despite censors' objections. One censor refused to approve a story written by the *Defender*'s Deton "Jack" Brooks about a swimming pool in India reserved on alternate days for blacks and whites. Brooks blustered and threatened to contact his newspaper and demand an investigation. The censor relented. The story was published. And the pool was integrated. Field commanders often assisted censors by pressuring reporters to soften criticisms before stories were filed. Jordan covered the Italian bombing runs by Tuskegee-trained pilots in the 99th Fighter Squadron, which was commanded by Col. Benjamin O. Davis Jr., the son of the nation's highest-ranking black officer. "He was so obsessed with doing well that he told me what to print and what not to print," Jordan recalled. "I wasn't supposed to even hint at anything unfavorable. He didn't want me to mention a single casualty. So we had clash after clash." Jordan told Davis he would help make the troops look as good as possible, but he could not pretend they were perfect.[34]

White newspaper readers would have been familiar with the typical dispatches written by black journalists. Several correspondents referred to their stories as "Ernie Pyle stuff," meaning they wrote—like the famed Scripps Howard reporter—about the tension and boredom, joy and sorrow experienced by common soldiers, not about overall strategy or political maneuvering. Since the Army seldom deployed black troops in combat, correspondents usually wrote about the unglamorous work of building roads and airstrips, driving supply trucks, outfitting combat troops, and cooking meals. Reporters often placed themselves in the midst of the action in their stories and concluded their dispatches with a long list of names, letting family and friends stateside know loved ones still lived. "I tried to answer the questions I thought were in the minds of people back home," said Waters, who covered troops in the Pacific. Press critics complained that Pyle and his imitators sacrificed analysis for superficiality. They accused journalists of conveying an overly optimistic view of the war by relying too often on the guy-in-the-trenches and the first-person, eyewitness-to-history forms of narrative. But editors and publishers liked stories that seemed patriotic merely by being written. They also argued that censors scrubbed hard-nosed news that dwelled upon American setbacks, faulty military strategy, or realistic depictions of the war's horrors. Black publishers had an additional justification—the war's day-to-day news was already known by the time their weeklies went to press. The "Ernie Pyle stuff" best suited their purposes.[35]

While most soldiers warmly welcomed correspondents who joined them on the frontlines, others greeted them with genuine disgust. Soldiers took pride in their work and appreciated the recognition offered by news coverage. They used reporters to relay messages home and correct racial grievances within their commands. African Americans, for example, represented 60 percent of the fifteen thousand American soldiers who carved the Ledo Road through the jungles of Burma to supply Chinese allies. Despite their work, no black drivers were included in the first convoy to cross the road. Soldiers complained to the *Courier*'s Frank Bolden, who then flew to headquarters and relayed their concerns. Soon afterward, eleven black soldiers joined the convoy. Elsewhere, though, soldiers griped when reporters appeared. In New Guinea, a soldier stunned Waters when he waved a copy of the *Defender* and criticized an editorial urging the Army to put black troops in combat. Others also complained. "It was the first time in my life," Waters recalled, "I found myself the center of a group protesting the policies of the paper for which I worked." Jordan encountered similar sentiments when he covered the 99th Fighter Squadron in Italy. His mental image of those storied airmen did not mesh with reality. "The guys didn't look at all like the heroic flyers that we had grown used to from the reports in the black papers," he recalled. "They were just a' belly-aching. One guy was carrying on like hell, complaining about flying three missions a day and getting shot at every time." Reporters characterized such complaints as good-natured razzing. To do otherwise jeopardized the patriotic appeal of "Double V"-style reporting.[36]

As they praised black bravery and patriotism, war correspondents expanded African Americans' conception of racial justice by describing how the proponents of white supremacy structured the lives of people of color in Europe, Australia, Asia, and Africa. Fascists were not the only enemy to fight overseas. Journalists witnessed firsthand how the Allied Powers undermined pleas for sacrifice and service in the name of freedom by denying basic human liberties and rights to colonized populations. The war's demands accentuated Western hypocrisy, revealing the privileged nature of Roosevelt's Four Freedoms and the hollowness of Winston Churchill's call for British colonies to share the war's burdens. Writing from foreign shores, black journalists buttressed long-standing arguments that African Americans should play a leading role in mobilizing forces opposed to racism and colonialism—wherever they were located. "A wind *is* rising," Walter White concluded after an overseas tour, "a wind of determination by the have-nots of the world to share the benefits of freedom and prosperity which the haves of the earth have tried to keep exclusively for themselves. That wind blows all over the world."[37]

The war complicated Vincent Tubbs's binary understanding of race before he even left the United States. The *Afro-American* assigned Tubbs, a Morehouse College graduate who had recently joined the paper, to the Pacific Theater. Arriving in California to sail out of San Francisco, the Texas-born Tubbs investigated the confinement of Japanese residents in concentration camps. The flagrant trampling of civil rights stunned him. Tubbs realized "the race problem is not the colored man's concern alone." He depicted the decision to intern Japanese families as a self-interested collusion of nativism and racism coupled with war hysteria and economic insecurity. He bolstered his analysis by observing that similar restrictions did not apply to German and Italian citizens. "Thus the evacuation was conducted on a strictly racial basis," Tubbs concluded, "and therefore must be the concern of all minority groups."[38]

The *Courier*'s Rouzeau arrived in North Africa in the fall of 1942 already convinced the war's most important hidden lesson was "colored people must think globally in terms of freedom and democracy for colored people everywhere." Describing Hitler as "a symbol of his time," Rouzeau believed the aims of the "Double V" campaign, even if fulfilled, would remain "subject to constant threats as long as colored people were exploited in other parts of the world." Born in the British-ruled West Indies, Rouzeau moved to New York City at the height of the New Negro Movement. He lived with other West Indians who condemned Western capitalists for exploiting colonized peoples. Rouzeau was in his late thirties when he went overseas between June 1942 and November 1943 to report on the war from Liberia, Egypt, and Italy. Other excursions took him into neighboring countries and colonies, including India, eastern and western Africa, and the Middle East. His reportage emulated aspects of J. A. Rogers's dispatches from Ethiopia and Langston Hughes's coverage of the Spanish Civil War. Like them, Rouzeau was as much a foreign correspondent and travel writer as a war reporter. He wrote a series, for example, examining the history, economy, geography, and politics of Liberia.[39]

Rouzeau analyzed the international implications of soldiers of color fighting in combat. He condemned the U.S. Army's policy of relegating black soldiers to support duties, believing African Americans would be denied their claim to full citizenship after the war if they did not spill blood for freedom. He warned that British imperialists intended to ban black soldiers from action in

Africa and Asia because they feared their subjects would emulate the troops and either revolt at home or incite unrest in other colonies. "Either way," Rouzeau wrote, "Great Britain is afraid of the consequences and has probably passed on a measure of this fear to white American statesmen." From Cairo, Rouzeau emphasized the contributions of people of color to the war effort by detailing "the complete composite picture of the United Nations at war." Egypt served as a staging ground for campaigns in Africa and the Mediterranean region. Troops from around the world jostled in the city's overcrowded streets. White troops from England, Ireland, France, Belgium, Australia, and South Africa mingled with "big and bearded copper-colored huskies from India, the so-called Cape Colored trooper from South Africa, who resents being called a Negro; the Maoris from New Zealand, East African fighters, West African fighters and, last but not least, the American Brown Buddies." Here, in an Arab nation, soldiers of color prepared to fight and die for the Allied cause. In other dispatches, Rouzeau extolled the fearlessness of Nigerian soldiers, the ferociousness of Indian Sikhs, and the bravery of South African stretcher-bearers, who hurried away wounded white soldiers amid incessant gunfire. Such articles served as roundabout proof of African Americans' fighting abilities and commitment to cause. These dispatches also forged a sense of shared identity among the *Courier*'s readers with colonized peoples in Africa and Asia.[40]

Jack Brooks ostensibly went overseas for the *Defender* to write about the construction of the Ledo Road in Burma and the supplying of combat troops in the region, but he suffused his reporting with the politics of anticolonialism and antiracism. Brooks was a Chicago native who had studied mathematics and international relations at the University of Chicago. He helped shape the *Defender*'s Popular Front-style editorial policy before asking to cover the war in Southeast Asia. He arrived in India in October 1944 and reported from the China-Burma-India Theater for the next year. "I wanted to know what was happening in that section of the world," he said. "I chose the Far East because I saw there, although the war wasn't as big, the social implications of what was happening as far more significant." Brooks repeatedly emphasized the connections between Indians' fight for freedom and African Americans' fight for equality. He wrote in November 1944 about suspicions among Indian nationals that Churchill had convinced Roosevelt to endorse a continuation of the British Empire after the war to advance American imperialistic ambitions in Asia. Brooks interviewed opposition leader Mahatma Gandhi, opening his front-page article by referring to Gandhi's "keen sympathy and understanding of the American Negro's problems." Brooks's reporting helped familiarize the *Defender*'s readers to Gandhi's nonviolent protest tactics. Brooks also interviewed Jawaharlal Nehru, who said he included some African Americans among his "valued friends." "Their problems are obviously very different than ours," Nehru told Brooks, "but inevitably, in the large context of human freedom and equality, there is much in common."[41]

No correspondent denounced colonialism more stridently than George Padmore, the former communist turned Pan-Africanist who lived in London. While other journalists offered readers a tourist's perspective of the world, Padmore never wavered from his role as a critic of capitalism. Billed by the *Courier* as a "reporter, writer, analyst and interpreter all heaped into one," Padmore filed most of his dispatches from London, where his home served as a meeting-place for the opponents of Western empires. Whenever possible, Padmore emphasized the global connections among people of color. He consistently claimed the war undermined British colonialism and readied Africans—as well as other people of color—for postwar independence. Even as he denounced British racism, Padmore observed that Great Britain offered more freedom to blacks than the American South. He credited British officers with improving the morale of African American troops by attempting to "break with Dixie Jim Crow traditions which certain cracker elements are trying to disseminate." Such articles revealed the constructed nature of white supremacy and made Padmore's Pan-Africanist ideology accessible to regular newspaper readers. After African American troops landed in Tripoli, Padmore wrote, "American descendants of Africans have returned to their ancestral homes whence three centuries ago they were taken away as bondmen and with their tears, toil and sweat helped lay the foundation of the now mighty United States." This was black internationalism translated from theory to actuality. For here was a West Indian writing from London describing events in Africa that involved black soldiers born in the United States.[42]

While Padmore explained how the war eroded colonialism, Roi Ottley focused on illustrating how American racism and segregation were distinctive to the United States, crippling racists' contention that inherent black inferiority justified discrimination. The son of a real estate agent, Ottley was born in 1906 and grew up in a comfortable but modest home in Harlem. He joined the *Amsterdam News* in 1930 and worked there as a reporter, editor, and columnist until he was fired in 1937 with other union organizers. He then supervised historical research on African Americans in New York for the Federal Writers' Project (FWP). Ottley established himself as a rising star with *'New World A-Coming': Inside Black America* (1943), a minor literary sensation. Mixing history and current events, politics and personalities, Ottley portrayed Harlem "as a sort of test tube in which the germs of Negro thought and action are isolated, examined, and held up to the full glare to reflect Black America." (He also embroiled himself in a journalistic controversy by using the work of FWP researchers and writers without attributing credit to them.) Ottley then worked as a war correspondent for white and black newspapers. He went overseas in July 1944 on a six-month special assignment for Marshall Field's liberal tabloids, *PM* and the *Chicago Sun*. He left again in February 1945, writing exclusive stories for the *Courier* through 1946. He traveled more than sixty thousand miles and visited twenty-two countries in Europe, Africa, and the Middle East. Despite his segregated readerships, Ottley's style and perspective remained relatively uniform across publishing outlets. Editors' presentation of Ottley varied more than his writing. The *Courier* touted his celebrity and recognition by white writers. *PM* emphasized his blackness, making sure his photo appeared with his stories far more regularly than other correspondents' headshots ran with their dispatches.[43]

Ottley's interracial appeal stemmed from his carefully hedged analysis of race, which spoke a truth both black and white readers could tolerate. Ottley summarized what he learned overseas in *No Green Pastures* (1951), which he described as an "intimately detailed account of racialism abroad." In his book, Ottley judged the severity of racism in different nations, explained the historical forces shaping that racism, and examined how oppressed people responded. He condemned American racism by contrasting it against the relative freedom African Americans experienced in other parts of the world. Travel abroad, he said, allowed an African American to feel like "a whole being" for the first time in his life. "Briefly: in the absence of America's elaborate racial etiquette, he enjoys a self-respect, dignity and personal worth unknown to Negroes in the U.S."[44]

However, Ottley worried that globetrotting writers and journalists—such as Richard Wright, Ollie Stewart, and J. A. Rogers—overestimated the racial progressiveness of Europeans, which caused them to mistakenly diminish the benefits of American citizenship. Europeans viewed black tourists as "glamorous novelties" and "dollar-carrying Americans." Despite knowing and liking African Americans, the citizens of imperialist nations rarely pondered the morality of exploiting colonial populations. "The simple and inescapable conclusion is this," Ottley wrote, "if a country has a Negro population, automatically that country is more or less prejudiced toward a dark skin. This is the logic of colony ownership." With this assertion, Ottley pivoted to praise the United States for offering African Americans more social and economic opportunities than European nations shared with their colonial subjects. That explained why so many dark-skinned foreigners sought admittance to the United States, he said, but comparatively few African Americans desired to leave their homeland.

"America still is the fabulous land of rags to riches, even for Negroes—at least in the eyes of Negroes abroad." Like other war correspondents, Ottley simultaneously criticized and complimented the United States for the obstacles and opportunities it provided black men and women.[45]

. . .

After Japan bombed Pearl Harbor, the military, federal government, and white press openly suspected black journalists of disloyalty. Nearly four years later, after the United States detonated two nuclear bombs over Japan, the leaders of those American institutions had reached an uneasy detente with the commercial black press. They reluctantly accepted black journalists as legitimate political actors. Backed by several million readers, black reporters and publishers were indulged but watched, alternately mollified and intimidated. Toleration, though, came only after journalists tempered and encoded their most radical critiques of American racism. As the anticommunism movement reordered the American political system in the late 1940s and early 1950s, black journalists would encounter urgent demands to renounce the politics of anticolonialism, anticapitalism, and black separatism. Refusal meant losing limited but expanding access to the political establishment and sacrificing potentially lucrative accounts from national advertisers newly interested in the emerging "Negro market." But capitulation threatened to undermine the credibility of commercial black newspapers as disseminators of black opinion, which jeopardized the sizable circulations that secured interviews for reporters and committee appointments for publishers. Complicating matters, white reporters began to encroach upon black journalists' monopoly over race news in the 1950s as expanding civil rights protests gradually seized the nation's attention.

CHAPTER 5

"Questionable Leanings"

The "New Crowd" Driven Out

Frank Marshall Davis, who had recently published his third book of poetry, left Chicago with his wife in December 1948 for a Hawaiian vacation and decided to stay. Davis was a staple in black journalism, working as executive editor and columnist at the Associated Negro Press (ANP). He wrote about music, literature, sports, theater, and politics. During World War II, he increasingly paired his championing of antiracism with zealous advocacy of trade unionism, arguing class inequality reinforced white supremacy. He openly praised the Soviet Union, criticized politicians and journalists who red-baited their adversaries, endorsed the progressive politics of Vice President Henry A. Wallace, encouraged interracial cooperation among unions, and condemned Prime Minister Winston Churchill's defense of Great Britain's colonial empire. In 1946, Davis founded the *Chicago Star*, a labor weekly funded by the American Federation of Labor (AFL) and Congress of Industrial Organizations (CIO). Davis's employer, Claude Barnett, a cosmetics salesman-turned-publisher who frequently solicited Republican patronage to support his news service, tolerated Davis's leftist viewpoints for their news value to his subscribers. "I recall telling him," Barnett later wrote, "we were interested in news about Republicans, Democrats, Socialists, Capitalists, Communists so long as it was news and that we would use news about anarchists, which was the worst word I knew, if it had a news relation to Negroes." Barnett, though, abandoned this pragmatic outlook by early 1947 as mounting animosity toward the Soviet Union—and those harboring sympathy for the political ideology of the United States' cardinal enemy—threatened the viability of his financially tenuous news operation. Barnett, for instance, steered Davis away from asking black educators, activists, and journalists for their views on what Davis characterized as "the rising wave of anti-Communist hysteria and attempts by many leaders in political and industrial circles to indiscriminately condemn militant Negroes and Negro organizations as 'communistic.'" Barnett did not want to provoke anticommunist scrutiny. "There is an apparent attempt to draw a line on Communism," he warned Davis. "If this happens we ought not be involved except as specific cases need to be reported upon."[1]

Davis's self-imposed exile to a distant American territory in the Pacific Ocean—where he could hope to escape anticipated anticommunist persecution while continuing to act upon his political beliefs—symbolized how the Cold War transformed black journalism in the 1950s by marginalizing the progressive political critiques that over three decades had swelled black newspapers' popularity and profitability. Leading black publishers emerged from World War II intent on taking advantage of their hard-won status as political brokers in racial matters. They hoped to grow circulations, attract major corporations as loyal advertisers, and expand into lucrative new ventures. Anticommunists threatened to cripple any publication that tolerated progressive viewpoints, regarding its writers as subversive propagandists whose challenge to the status quo jeopardized national security. To protect their burgeoning businesses, commercial publishers made pragmatic decisions to purge their newsrooms of journalists who had advocated aspects of communism, socialism, and black radicalism. They replaced such writers with younger journalists who reached adulthood during World War II and the "Double V" campaign, which linked racial protest to patriotism. These younger journalists matured politically amid pleas for shared sacrifice and a creeping distrust of leftist politics. Many also aspired to integrate white newsrooms—a remote but suddenly viable prospect for reporters who avoided Popular Front–style politics.

Beyond sidelining progressive journalists like Davis, the Cold War's politics reshaped how commercial publishers and reporters covered the modern Civil Rights Movement. The U.S. Supreme Court outlawed segregated public schools in 1954 and touched off a fifteen-year period of escalating black protest against unrepentant southern white supremacy. As the movement unfolded, editors—who a decade earlier had promoted communists' criticisms of the American political economy and its attendant racism—now blamed Western hypocrisy for transforming communism into an ideology that appealed to people of color elsewhere in the world. Black journalists tapped into Cold War fears when they urged federal officials to strike down segregation to counter Soviet propaganda and win foreign allies in Asia and Africa. Like the "Double V" campaign, Cold War civil rights worked within the prevailing political structure to foster social change. However, commercial black newswriting in the 1950s lacked the radical impulse—whether explicit or implicit—that helped drive the press's tremendous growth during the interwar decades. Readers noticed. Circulations plummeted at national black newspapers as white journalists and broadcasters competed to control coverage of race news. Even so, black journalism maintained a racial perspective that distinguished it from white reportage. A stunted, vulnerable alternative black press reemerged to again promote Marxist solutions to racial discrimination. Commercial black publishers, despite declining profitability, sent reporters into the South to cover trials and demonstrations. Compared to white reporters, black journalists expressed greater skepticism of official explanations for racial wrongs and more aggressively investigated black claims of injustice. While white editors treated African Americans as news subjects, black reporters wrote about them as citizens pushing for social change. Scorned as outsiders and agitators, black reporters endured harassment, threats, and beatings from white supremacists.[2]

"Embarrassing as the Very Devil"
The Red Scare and Newsroom Purges

Commercial black newspapers enjoyed a brief moment of flush times immediately after World War II ended. The U.S. Census Bureau estimated that overall newspaper circulation jumped from under 1.3 million in 1940 to more than 1.8 million in 1945—an increase of about 30 percent. By 1948, independent audits estimated the *Pittsburg Courier* sold 280,000 copies per week, followed by the *Baltimore Afro-American* (235,000), *Chicago Defender* (195,000), *New York Amsterdam News* (105,000), and *Norfolk Journal and Guide* (62,850). Opinion polls indicated that roughly nine out of ten readers believed newspapers accurately portrayed their political views. Readers' allegiance translated into profit, power, and acclaim. Publishers met privately with presidents and cabinet-level officials and received appointments to federal committees. Columnists and editors aired their views on national radio broadcasts, and a few independent stations in major cities aired programs produced by black journalists. The *Washington Post* established the Wendell L. Willkie Awards in 1946 to promote interracial understanding and honor black reporters' best work. Sports writers crusaded to integrate Major League Baseball, which occurred in 1947 when the Brooklyn Dodgers signed first baseman Jackie Robinson. War correspondents drew capacity crowds on publicity tours. When the Korean War broke out in June

1950, the Army swiftly issued press credentials to black reporters, granting them unprecedented access to the frontlines.[3]

Newspapers' impressive circulations tempted white advertising executives who had long refused to partner with black publishers. New tax laws encouraged investments in race-oriented advertising. Congress helped pay for the war by taxing excess profits. Rather than give that money to the government, some companies bought ads in black publications. As wartime rationing gave way to postwar consumption, trade publications implored white businessmen to abandon racist assumptions and reexamine the buying power of the "Negro market." "Business can learn to its profit that Uncle Remus is dead," *Kiplinger Magazine* observed in 1947. Marketing research emphasized Black America's population growth, northward migration, urbanization, and increased buying power. Marketers characterized black consumers as more accessible, more profitable, and largely overlooked. Publishers attempted to capitalize on Madison Avenue's fledgling interest. They formed cooperative companies that solicited national advertisers by touting the combined reach of member publications. Associated Publishers was led by the *Defender* and *Afro-American*, and Interstate United Newspapers represented the *Courier* and *Amsterdam News*, among others.[4]

Improved circulation and advertising opportunities led some editors to risk investing in race magazines—a graveyard for failed titles since the late 1800s. Countering this dismal history, a trade publication claimed in 1946 that black magazines "had finally entered the mass circulation field as we know it today." In Washington, D.C., James and Helen Mason launched *Pulse* "to present some desirable aspects of the Negro in contemporary life that are either unknown or overlooked by other racial groups." Out of Birmingham, Alabama, the ten-cent *NEWSPIC* was touted as "The Complete News-Picture Magazine"—even though it tended to focus on the South. Several other publications were based in New York. *Spotlighter Magazine* ran mostly photos and stories about black celebrities. *Defender* publisher John Sengstacke published *Headlines and Pictures*, a 52-page monthly news magazine cross-promoted in his newspaper chain. *Our World* appeared in April 1946, with publisher John P. Davis billing it as "A Picture Magazine for the Whole Family." Davis was a Harvard-trained journalist and lawyer, former *Crisis* editor, and a founder of the leftist National Negro Congress. *Our World* sold more than 165,000 copies monthly by 1950.[5]

No magazine publisher, though, rivaled the success of John "Johnny" H. Johnson, founder of *Negro Digest* and *Ebony*. Born poor in Arkansas in 1918, Johnson migrated to Chicago with his widowed mother in 1933. During an academic awards banquet, the confident, self-promoting Johnson introduced himself to Harry H. Pace, president of Supreme Liberty Life Insurance Company, one of the nation's largest black-owned businesses. Pace offered him a job. Johnson launched *Negro Digest* in 1942 after borrowing Supreme Liberty's customer list and soliciting prepaid $2 subscriptions for a magazine that did not yet exist. *Negro Digest* summarized and excerpted the top race stories from leading publications. In less than a year, Johnson sold fifty thousand copies a month. Circulation doubled after First Lady Eleanor Roosevelt wrote an essay in October 1943 for the magazine's "If I Were a Negro" feature. Newsstand dealers told Johnson only *Life*, Henry Luce's weekly news picture magazine, rivaled *Negro Digest*'s popularity in black neighborhoods. So, in November 1945, Johnson launched the *Life*-inspired *Ebony*, which became his flagship publication. Monthly circulation reached 250,000 within a half year and rose to 315,000 by 1950. The next year, Johnson folded the declining *Negro Digest* and founded *Jet*, a snappy, pocket-sized weekly digest.[6]

International events, though, soon threatened black publishers' postwar prosperity. American officials had begun backpedaling from the pro-democracy and anti-imperialism rhetoric spouted to mobilize citizens and allies against the fascist powers before World War II even ended. The fault lines of the dawning Cold War had already materialized, and officials willingly sacrificed the United States' political ideals to curry favor with Western colonial powers and maintain strategic footholds, economic and militaristic, in what was labeled the Third World. Confronted by the nuclear menace of Joseph Stalin's Soviet Union, American leaders refused to revert to the isolationism of the interwar years. With the Iron Curtain figuratively dividing Europe into East and West, the underindustrialized nations of Asia and Africa emerged as proxy battlegrounds. Americans' sense of the Cold War as a global ideological confrontation solidified after Mao Zedong's communist forces seized control of China and the North Korean army nearly pushed U.S. troops off the Korean peninsula.[7]

The containment of communism became the nation's No. 1 priority, remaking domestic politics and foreign diplomacy. Throughout the 1950s, any criticism of the American state, any call for liberal reform, had the potential to be regarded as Soviet-inspired propaganda. At home, legislators and administrators battled the Cold War by equating dissidence with disloyalty and recasting once tolerable leftist politics as sinister, fifth-column plotting. White southerners wielded anticommunism sentiment in defense of segregation. Moderate Cold War liberals used red-baiting rhetoric to defuse expansive demands for equality in favor of a narrow definition of civil rights based on existing laws. In Asia, Africa, Latin America, and the Middle East, the United States protected its interests through decidedly undemocratic methods—backroom brokering, propaganda, covert operations, and financial assistance laced with pro-American assumptions. Colonized peoples were deemed a threat to the United States' security when they demanded self-determination and condemned imperial rule. American leaders feared that limitations on access to raw materials, strategic locations, and new markets would benefit the Soviet Union in the zero-sum game of Cold War positioning. Even so, despite American opposition, forty new nations gained independence between 1945 and 1960.[8]

American journalists fired the anticommunism movement and were also scorched by it. Reporters were manipulated and demonized by the likes of Mississippi Senator James Eastland, a segregationist who chaired the Senate Internal Security Subcommittee; J. Edgar Hoover, the director of the FBI who established his reputation as a lawman by deporting suspected leftists after World War I; and Wisconsin Senator Joseph McCarthy, whose name came to define the era's violation of civil liberties. The anticommunists' greatest leverage over those accused of harboring communist sympathies was fear of public exposure and the personal damage that would result—lost income, social and professional blacklisting, and public ridicule. Journalists often collaborated in outing suspected communists, no matter how flimsy the proof, particularly at the Scripps-Howard and Hearst newspaper chains. Hoover fed leaks to friendly reporters and columnists. McCarthy catered to the insatiable news appetite of wire service reporters by being ever ready to level vague but ominous charges, knowing local reporters would do little to follow up his pronouncements. Anticommunists also targeted reporters and editors. Journalism professor Edward Alwood estimates the federal government's primary investigative committees— those headed by Eastland and McCarthy as well as the House Un-American Activities Committee (HUAC)—subpoenaed more than one hundred journalists between 1952 and 1957. Like government employees, union members, and college professors, reporters and editors alternately battled false accusations, dissembled to save careers, defiantly refused to name names, and caved to government pressure. James A. Wechsler, editor of the liberal *New York Post* and a short-time member of the Young Communist League in the mid-1930s, characterized the government's anticommunism hearings as an effort to silence government critics, not root out spies and traitors. "I regard this proceeding," Wechsler told McCarthy, "as the first in a long line of attempts to intimidate editors who do not equate McCarthyism with patriotism."[9]

African Americans were particularly vulnerable to anticommunists' attacks because they had endorsed the Communist Party's antiracism policies and appropriated its techniques to fight for equality. As early as 1946, Pulitzer Prize–winning historian Arthur M. Schlesinger Jr. claimed in *Life* that the Communist Party was trying to win black converts by exploiting a Tennessee race riot and "by sinking tentacles into the National Association for the Advancement of Colored People." Soon afterward, Walter White and Roy Wilkins purged the NAACP's membership rolls, distanced themselves from known leftists, and deemphasized demands for freedom in Asia and Africa. Anticommunists also eyed black journalists—dissident by the very nature of their work—with skepticism and distrust. Few publishers had openly endorsed communism in the 1930s and 1940s, but few had stridently denounced it. They had abided party members and fellow travelers as long as communism advanced their goal of achieving racial justice and, incongruously, bolstered profits. The FBI investigated ANP's Barnett on charges he associated with a known communist, probably a reference to Frank Marshall Davis. Fortunately for Barnett, a cabinet-level administrator intervened on his behalf. "You see," Davis wrote his boss, "how defenseless is an accused person without your connections or record of working with 'safe' groups." Ollie Harrington, a popular cartoonist and former *Courier* war correspondent, lacked Barnett's influential contacts. A friend warned him that federal investigators suspected he was a communist and would call him to testify. Harrington immediately sailed to Paris. Two decades passed before he returned to the United States.[10]

The political pressure applied by anticommunists compelled an ownership change at one of the nation's most radical black newspapers. Despite his paper's circulation success, Adam Clayton Powell Jr. sold his ownership stake in the *People's Voice*—the so-called "Lenox Avenue edition of the *Daily Worker*"—after he was elected in 1946 to the U.S. House of Representatives. His political advisers encouraged him to cut ties with known leftists to bolster his influence in Congress. The paper's treasurer, Max Yergan, a longtime radical best known for working as a YMCA missionary in South Africa, assumed control. Like Powell, Yergan sensed the nation's rising suspicion of communism. He transformed himself into a staunch anticommunist and turned government informant. Yergan fired suspected communists, including general manager Doxey Wilkerson and Marvel Cooke, the assistant managing editor. (Cooke testified before McCarthy's Senate committee in 1953. She declined to answer questions, citing her constitutional right to avoid self-incrimination. She never held another newspaper job, and her husband soon lost his position at a New York brewery.) Yergan hired Wilkerson's successor—Jack Brooks, the *Defender*'s former war correspondent—and initiated a "new, non-sectarian" editorial policy. Wilkerson accused his former employer of "cowering before the witch hunters" and claimed the paper's new editorial perspective would "lead only to the betrayal of the basic interests of the Negro people and the alienation of its progressive white and Negro readers." The *People's Voice* folded in 1948.[11]

At the *Chicago Defender*, Sengstacke aggressively erased signs of his newspaper's wartime advocacy of Popular Front agitation. His actions overlapped with ongoing cost-cutting measures and opposition to newsroom union organizing, allowing the publisher to remove politically tainted employees by claiming to maintain profitability and eliminate insubordination. Editor Ben Burns, a white communist insider, complained that *Pittsburgh Courier* executives and labor leaders like A. Philip Randolph and Willard Townsend "have been spreading the word about the Communism of the *Defender*." Sengstacke fired Burns in the spring of 1946. The byline for John Robert Badger, the pseudonym for communist writer John Pittman, the *Defender*'s foreign affairs columnist, disappeared in November without public explanation. As Pittman observed, "I seem to be embarrassing as the very devil, since my politics are out in the open and well known by all the management crowd." Sengstacke also dismissed longtime editorial editor Metz T. P. Lochard, who helped conceive the paper's progressive outlook and plan the "Victory Edition." W. E. B. Du Bois lost his column a few months after he embraced the controversial Progressive Party, which had sprung up to support Henry Wallace's run in 1948 for president. Wallace campaigned on a platform of ending segregation, supporting unions, and providing universal health care. He also refused to expel communist supporters. Anticolonialist and former communist George Padmore wrote his last column for the *Defender* in June 1949. By then, his once commonplace byline seldom appeared in any black newspapers or magazines. Even though Padmore accused communists of exploiting want and misery in Africa to recruit expendable black revolutionaries to fight imperialist nations, his criticisms seemingly did not offset the political liability of his past party membership.[12]

While Sengstacke overhauled his newspaper, Thomas W. Young defended black journalism and his race by distinguishing the fight for civil rights from the broader aims of black radicals. Young had succeeded his father as president and general manager of the *Norfolk Journal and Guide*, the most conservative of the national newspapers. He testified before HUAC in 1949, touting the loyalty of African Americans against widely publicized remarks made by entertainer Paul Robeson, a leading black radical. Robeson had provoked controversy by reportedly saying black men and women would not fight against the more racially tolerant Soviet Union. (Robeson said he was misquoted.) Young denounced Robeson and praised blacks for their patriotism, citing examples that reached back to the killing of Crispus Attucks by British soldiers before the American Revolution. African Americans demanded racial reform, Young said, but they knew change could be accomplished through "the machinery which we in this country have embraced for the realization of our declared way of life."

Young claimed Robeson's belief in communism had warped his views on race in America. "He does not speak," Young said, "for the common people who read and believe in the Negro newspapers. He does not speak for the masses of the Negro people whom he has so shamelessly deserted." Editorials nationwide mirrored Young's sentiments.[13]

Robeson's continued popularity among African Americans, though, pointed to the public support still enjoyed by radicals. "It is fait accompli," a *Defender* reader wrote, "that a considerable percentage of Afro-Americans are disgusted with the idea of fighting Russia or any other country in the role of second-class citizens." In early 1949, tens of thousands of African Americans attended rallies headlined by Robeson and organized by the Civil Rights Congress. The *Baltimore Afro-American*, in particular, wrote extensively about the organizers' efforts to pass civil rights legislation. *Pittsburgh Courier* columnists J. A. Rogers and Marjorie McKenzie distanced themselves from Robeson's politics but acknowledged that he sounded commonly held frustrations. Rogers suggested that Robeson's loudest critics, including the NAACP's Walter White, should keep quiet. "Negroes are jim crowed through fear and greed," Rogers wrote, "hence they have nothing to lose by keeping the enemy guessing." Unlike Young, Baltimore publisher Carl Murphy refused his invitation from Rep. John S. Wood, a Georgia Democrat, to testify before HUAC. Murphy still regarded communism as a legitimate means for criticizing and eradicating racism. "If anybody asks us," his paper editorialized, "Paul Robeson's eye is on Georgia, not Russia. He is using Communism as a vehicle to get relief from jim crow [*sic*]."[14]

Publisher Charlotta Bass shared Murphy's perspective but was forced to sell the *California Eagle* in 1951 after failing to raise enough money to cover expenses. Bass had embraced communism during World War II, believing its analysis of race pointed "the way to an open door to freedom." Her outspokenness offended advertisers, and Bass subsidized the *Eagle* with donations from "liberal progressive forces in the community." She needed $20,000 to stay afloat when donors stopped giving. Bass claimed that liberals had too few dollars to support all the worthy groups that were attempting to fight racial wrongs while fending off anticommunist witch-hunting. But she also criticized "a disturbing number of former liberals—many of them well-to-do" who had found it "convenient" to abandon political activism to avoid government scrutiny. "They are not to be heard from," Bass said. "They will, of course, find that the path they have chosen will not bring them security." After publishing the *Eagle* for nearly forty years, Bass sold it to Loren Miller, the former *Eagle* reporter-turned-lawyer who helped start the *Los Angeles Sentinel*. In 1952, Bass ran as the Progressive Party's candidate for vice president. She accused black newspapers of conducting a news "blackout" against her during the campaign season.[15]

A flawed indictment likely did more to muffle black radicalism than any other government action. The Justice Department indicted W. E. B. Du Bois in February 1951 for failing to register as a foreign agent for the Peace Information Center (PIC). Du Bois and others had formed the group the previous year to promote peace and publicize nuclear disarmament. Du Bois served as the center's chairman for the six months it existed. The indictment stemmed from PIC's backing of the Stockholm Peace Appeal, an international petition seeking to ban nuclear weapons. Du Bois was disappointed with the limited public support initially offered him after his indictment. He credited black newspapers—perhaps more attuned to mass sentiment and still more independent than other black institutions—for showing "unusual leadership" in defending him. He praised a few journalists by name, including Carl Murphy, J. A. Rogers, and *Courier* editor Percival Prattis. Otherwise, Du Bois believed Black America's business, political, and intellectual elites failed to rally to his cause. "They did not understand the indictment," he wrote, "and assumed that I had let myself be drawn into some treasonable acts or movements in retaliation for continued discrimination in this land, which I had long fought." Du Bois later received extensive support from progressive activists and everyday African Americans. He was ultimately acquitted, but the victory was pyrrhic. The indictment tarnished Du Bois's national reputation and quieted other radicals. "I believe the indictment was sought as the easiest means of intimidating all Negroes," Lochard wrote. "The Justice Department, in this regard, has succeeded pretty well."[16]

Prosecutors achieved more tangible success against Claudia Jones, the *Daily Worker*'s black affairs editor. Jones was jailed four times between 1948 and 1955. A Trinidad native who joined the Communist Party in 1936, Jones challenged what she called the "super-exploitation" of black women by explaining how gender discrimination exacerbated class and racial oppression. She was charged with violating the Alien Registration Act of 1940 (also known as the Smith Act) and the Internal Security Act of 1950 (commonly called the McCarran Act). The Smith Act made it illegal to advocate the violent overthrow of the United States and required alien residents to document their political beliefs. Federal prosecutors embraced the seldom used act to dismantle the Communist Party. The McCarran Act required Communist groups to register with the United States and established a board to investigate individuals suspected of threatening national security. The act denied citizenship to suspected subversives. Jones, who had sought American citizenship for nearly twenty years, argued that her brand of communism advocated the reform of American society, not its overthrow. But her writings and her party membership led to conviction. She dropped her legal challenges after suffering a heart attack and was deported to England in late 1955. "I was a victim of the McCarthyite hysteria against independent political ideas in the USA," Jones said, "a hysteria which penalizes anyone who holds ideas contrary to the official pro-war, pro-reactionary, pro-fascist one of the white ruling class of that country."[17]

While anticommunism marginalized leftist writers, it failed to suppress their politics. Progressive journalists kept writing for either small but influential political journals or a revived but curtailed alternative black press. Du Bois contributed regularly to the *National Guardian*, a weekly founded by Progressive Party supporters. He described the journal as "a few pages of real facts and honestly interpreted truth" that contrasted starkly with the typical daily newspaper, which "calculated to make upon the reader the impression which the owners of this vast economic organization want made on the people of the U.S. and the world." John Pittman wrote columns for the *Daily Worker* and worked to stabilize and enlarge an international communist press. The alternative black press began to reemerge in the 1950s to express viewpoints now curbed by commercial publishers. This press resembled the radical publications of the early 1920s in its militantly progressive perspective, irregular publication, and unreliable finances. Lochard, for example, launched the weekly *Chicago Globe* in April 1950 to espouse the progressive views once endorsed by the *Defender*. However, he struggled to stay solvent during the height of McCarthyism and shuttered his one-man operation before the year ended. The mere presence of such a fleeting, fragile alternative newspaper showed that anticommunism repression had suppressed, not destroyed, black radicals' freedom dreams.[18]

The most prominent black-themed progressive journal was Paul Robeson's *Freedom*, a New York–based monthly that the federal government labeled a communist front. Robeson founded *Freedom* after the State Department stripped him of his passport in August 1950 to prevent him from condemning American racism while traveling in Europe. Given his celebrity, Robeson and his supporters believed commercial black newspapers and magazines failed to provide adequate coverage of the case, although Robeson continued to view the black press as more democratic than the white press. Financed mostly by communists, *Freedom* provided a public forum for defending Robeson's case and airing his political views. Editor Louis Burnham established an editorial policy that endorsed third-party politics, opposed the Korean War, supported the labor movement, denounced racism and colonialism, and promoted world peace. The paper's business manager was George B. Murphy Jr., nephew of the

Afro-American's publisher. *Freedom* helped launch the careers of notable writers. Aspiring playwright Lorraine Hansberry got her first full-time job at *Freedom*, joining as Burnham's chief assistant before becoming an assistant editor. Another future playwright, Alice Childress, introduced a popular column written from the perspective of a maid named Mildred. (She later wrote the column for the *Afro-American*.) The paper, though, was never self-sufficient. The FBI contributed to *Freedom*'s money problems by harassing distributors and subscribers. Dwindling finances led to increasingly erratic publication. *Freedom* folded in the summer of 1955.[19]

Entertainer Paul Robeson, founder of *Freedom*, and Charlotta Bass, publisher of the *California Eagle*, circa 1949. Courtesy of the Los Angeles Daily News Negatives (Collection 1387), UCLA Library Special Collections, Charles E. Young Research Library.

Some progressive journalists managed to keep working in the commercial black press by renouncing their political beliefs. Celebrity and public atonement seemingly saved Langston Hughes's journalism career at the *Chicago Defender*. Hughes began moving away from his scathing criticisms of American society in the 1930s after a national controversy concerning an antireligious poem jeopardized his writing career and curtailed his publishing opportunities. The 1932 poem, "Goodbye Christ," denounced religious hypocrisy and contrasted Christianity negatively with the racial egalitarianism of communism. Hughes publicly apologized for writing the poem in 1940, describing it as a youthful indiscretion stemming from immaturity, not an abiding faith in Marxism. Hughes deployed this defensive tactic again when he testified in 1953 before McCarthy's senate committee. Hughes was subpoenaed to testify about his political views because State Department libraries worldwide held more than two hundred copies of sixteen different books written by him. Most other writers had refused to answer the committee's questions, invoking their constitutional right to avoid self-incrimination. Hughes, though, surprised McCarthy's lead investigator, Roy Cohn, by deciding to tell his story and conceding having made past mistakes. Behind closed doors, the opposing sides agreed to treat Hughes as a cooperating witness. In exchange, Cohn agreed to not recite aloud Hughes's most provocative poems, a tactic reserved for hostile witnesses.[20]

Most of Hughes's testimony repeated other statements he had made over the years, and yet, he managed to widen his separation from the progressive movement. He admitted he had once admired aspects of communism but again denied joining the party. He told the committee he became sympathetic to the Soviet Union's ideology during the early 1930s amid economic depression and flagrant racism. While "there was no abrupt ending" to his affinity for communism, Hughes said, "I would say a complete reorientation of my thinking and emotional feelings occurred roughly 4 or 5 years ago." According to Hughes, the change coincided with a dawning disillusionment with the Soviet Union's foreign policy and its restriction of free speech, as well as "a very distinct step forward in race relations" in the United States. When McCarthy asked if Hughes's earlier radical poems should be placed in government libraries, Hughes sidestepped the implication that those works could be construed as seditious by noting that his use of slang and dialect made them difficult for foreigners to understand. However, the availability of such books, Hughes contended, proved America's belief in free speech. McCarthy pressed him. "Do you feel that those books should be on our shelves throughout the world, with the apparent stamp of approval of the United States Government?" And then Hughes went further than he ever had in distancing himself from his radical past. "I was certainly amazed to hear that they were. I was surprised; and I would certainly say 'No.'" Later on, Cohn picked up McCarthy's line of questioning. "Very frankly," Cohn asked, "you are not particularly proud of them at this state?" Again, Hughes dodged. "They do not represent my current thinking, nor my thinking for the last, say, 6 or 8 years, at any rate." Hughes had not repudiated his most radical poems outright (except the already disowned "Goodbye Christ"), but he had signaled his complete disassociation with progressive politics in favor of a circumscribed focus on racial justice. Hughes would write for the *Defender* until his death in 1967.[21]

With progressive writers sidelined, commercial editors and journalists tended to either ignore radicals or minimize coverage of them. Established columnists occasionally defended progressive activists but only after assuring readers they themselves were not communists. At the *Pittsburgh Courier*, editor Prattis often explained why he opposed communism before observing how anticommunism threatened to erode civil liberties. Prattis also condemned anticommunists' excesses more than he defended their targets, although he wrote columns supporting Du Bois and educator Mary Bethune McLeod. In private, Prattis avoided affiliating and socializing with radicals. He declined, for example, an invitation to join a foundation supporting Du Bois. Prattis worried his participation would taint his reputation. "I can only write, and be effective as long as I can maintain my personal invulnerability," he told Du Bois's wife, Shirley Graham. "If outside, or inside, forces should convince the publisher that positions which I take jeopardize *The Courier*, I would lose my vehicle for expression." As a newsroom executive, Prattis enjoyed more leeway than his beat reporters. Levi Jolley, the *Courier*'s Washington bureau chief, reminded an editor who complained about being scooped on a story about Paul Robeson that, "I was also instructed that persons of questionable leanings (communistic) should not be exploited and played too big."[22]

Prattis further guarded the *Courier*'s flank by printing George Schuyler's frequent tirades against communism, even though his columns occasionally jeopardized the newspaper's relations with leading civil rights activists and seemed to increasingly annoy and puzzle—rather than entertain and provoke—readers. Schuyler saw himself as the black press's lone voice of reason, a courageous journalist willing to withstand ostracism to defeat the worldwide conspiracy of communism. "The failure of the Negro press generally to make any noteworthy attack on communism," he wrote, "is a national scandal and certainly a grave disservice to its readers." Schuyler's strident conservativism and shirt-sleeve patriotism colored memories of his own past. His autobiography never mentioned that he served nine months in a military prison for deserting the

Army in 1918. He depicted his membership in the Socialist Party of America as youthful intellectual exploration rather than a symptom of political radicalism. He claimed to have always viewed communists as a "murderous gang." He was less forgiving of activists and journalists who justified working with communists in the 1930s and 1940s as a way to advance the cause of racial justice. "I scoffed at their excuse that they 'were young at the time' and 'didn't know what they were getting into,'" he said, "despite the fact that they were literate, read the newspapers and magazines and were mostly college graduates who had supposedly been taught to think." Schuyler defended McCarthy even after the senator's national reputation was permanently damaged in the spring of 1954 when Army officials exposed his deceitful and bullying tactics during televised hearings. Schuyler accused liberals, intellectuals, and communist sympathizers of engaging "in a most nefarious conspiracy to ruin the man because he had the courage and tenacity to tackle in a rough and forthright manner a lot of sacred cows of the political and intellectual worlds." Such words propelled Schuyler to prominence in conservative circles, where his warnings about communist infiltration of civil rights organizations reinforced claims made by segregationists. As the Red Scare faded, though, so did the *Courier*'s tolerance for Schuyler's fractious opinions. Prattis told Schuyler in 1960 that the paper's executives wanted him to write less often about communism, suggesting "that the pursuit of this one idea may have become unwittingly an obsession with you." Schuyler fumed. "If we are going to have five or six columnists all saying approximately the same thing on the same themes and without ever questioning anything," he replied, "we might as well do away with columns."[23]

Journalists too young to participate in the Depression-era's leftist agitation escaped the broad criticisms leveled by press critics like Schuyler and could defend colleagues more forthrightly than senior journalists like Prattis. Several months after returning from the Korean War's frontlines, James "Jimmy" Hicks of the *Baltimore Afro-American* testified before a New York administrative board to the loyalty of his friend, Conrad Clark, a federal employee who also wrote for ANP. The U.S. Railroad Retirement Board was investigating whether to fire Clark for belonging to a supposedly subversive organization and marching in a parade to protest racism. Hicks spoke at Clark's hearing, even though associating with a suspected radical could spur inquiries into his own activities. "I had the smug satisfaction of knowing that I was not, had never been a Communist," Hicks wrote, "and of feeling that I would match my loyalty to America against any American in the country today." An Ohio native born in 1915, Hicks dropped out of Akron University to help support his family by working as a bellhop and then as a clerk in Washington, D.C. He later took night courses at Howard University and wrote for the *Cleveland Call and Post*. He enlisted in the Army in 1940. Hicks served three years in the Pacific Theater, becoming a lieutenant who commanded a supply unit. He survived a submarine attack, air raids, gunfire, and three bouts of malaria. He buried friends and wrote letters to their next of kin. Returning stateside, he was promoted to captain and assigned to a Pentagon publicity desk. After he was discharged, Hicks covered veterans' issues for the *Afro-American* and NNPA news service. He argued that the federal government should reward black veterans' sacrifices by dismantling segregation. When discrimination persisted, Hicks pointedly rejected violence as a credible form of protest. "The colored soldier has been cited for everything from rape to bravery," he wrote, "but here are two charges he has stayed away from—cowardice and treason." Hicks had spilled too much of his "blood and sweat and tears" to have his citizenship—or his patriotism—questioned. "If and when they ever start passing out ammunition for the defense of this government against any nation or any group of nations, the line in which you will find the colored veteran and colored soldier will be the one that forms to the right—not to the LEFT!"[24]

"We Don't Like to Cry Wolf"
The Struggles of National Black Newspapers

Circulations melted away in the 1950s at national black newspapers as commercial publishers eroded their editorial militancy by dumping radical journalists; *Ebony* and *Jet* offered colorful, upbeat alternatives to traditional black news coverage; and white editors dabbled in race news and haltingly experimented with newsroom integration. Readership declines deflated publishers' political influence and undermined their posturing as the voice of Black America. By 1955, more than half the *Courier*'s readers were gone from its peak weekly circulation of 358,000 in 1948. The *Afro-American* lost nearly a fifth of its readers after World War II, selling 188,000 papers in 1955. The *Defender, Journal and Guide*, and *Amsterdam News* experienced similar losses. Circulation among regional newspapers was more erratic but generally downward. (Exceptions included the *Cleveland Call and Post* and *Los Angeles Sentinel*, which held steady, and the union-backing *Michigan Chronicle*, which gained readers.) Slumping circulations coincided with a postwar hike in operating and newsprint costs, which fostered a need for expensive, modern mechanical upgrades. Daily newspapers offset their new expenses through steady increases in circulation and advertising revenue. Black weeklies, though, still earned comparatively little revenue from national advertising accounts, despite the ballyhoo about the "Negro market," and circulation losses accelerated if publishers hiked subscription and newsstand prices. Leading black newspapers still catered to large readerships, but their profitability was rapidly eroding. The dilemma prompted retooling and retrenching.[25]

The *Chicago Defender* and *Pittsburgh Courier* moved in strikingly different directions to restore profits. In Chicago, John Sengstacke embarked on an ambitious expansion plan. He hoped to grow the *Defender* out of trouble as his once lucrative national edition bled readers, plummeting from 145,000 copies sold weekly in 1946 to 36,000 copies in 1955. Sengstacke expected to preserve national advertising accounts—the company's largest source of revenue—by establishing or buying local newspapers in major cities. He no longer courted advertisers by pointing to the reach of a single national edition. Instead, he touted how his chain of papers saturated cities with large black markets. In 1951, he founded the Memphis-based *Tri-State Defender*. L. Alex Wilson, a 34-year-old Marine veteran who had reported from the Korean front, served as editor and general manager. Wilson's goal was to make the *Tri-State Defender* the go-to source for black news from the Deep South, directly challenging the supremacy of the Atlanta-based Scott family, which owned influential but conservative papers in Memphis and Birmingham. In 1952, Sengstacke bought the venerable but nearly bankrupt *New York Age*. With this purchase, Sengstacke published a national edition plus put out local newspapers in six cities—Chicago, New York, Detroit, Louisville, Memphis, and Gary, Indiana. He organized those papers into Defender Publications, which he billed as "the first national group of Negro Newspapers to operate through a special coordinated organization to serve advertising agencies, manufacturers and others."[26]

In contrast, the *Courier*'s executives slashed costs, particularly the expenses tied to newsgathering. They hoped to disguise their cutbacks and revive reader interest by redesigning the layout and editorial perspective of their news pages. As early as November 1950, managing editor Bill Nunn warned the paper's Washington bureau of looming layoffs. "We don't like to cry wolf, nor do we want to sound threatening," Nunn wrote, "but it is a definite fact that the *Courier* is facing a financial crisis." The downsized bureau closed a few years later. The *Courier* struggled more than the other national newspapers because Pittsburgh lacked a sizable black community, meaning the *Courier*'s existence as a newspaper of influence depended upon its disappearing national readership. Poor management decisions exacerbated financial troubles. The *Courier* ended its financial year in 1955 with a $127,000 deficit. Prattis warned the paper would close the following year unless the entire operation was overhauled. The company's officers consolidated editions, reduced payroll, and switched from a standard-sized newspaper to a tabloid format. Executives also proposed a new approach to presenting news. "We are going to change," Prattis said, "almost imperceptibly, into a different kind of paper, not depending on news (which the dailies NOW beat us to anyhow), which will have a broader appeal to more people. We feel that is the only way in which we can maintain circulation."[27]

Prattis's proposal to fundamentally alter how the *Courier* covered the news pointed toward black newspapers' existential predicament—newsroom executives clung to reporting conventions that seemed stodgy and dated in an era of increased media competition and mounting racial unrest. The purging of progressivism stripped from black reportage the sense that it offered an expansive, forward-moving response to white supremacy. Instead, stories and columns that once seemed brash and militant now appeared familiar, routine, and even repetitive. "Much of the decline of our press has been its own fault," said Alvin White, a former ANP Washington correspondent and writer for *Our World*. "It is one thing to proclaim the evils that exist, it is another to do something about them." News articles tended to focus on the singular details of a particular event rather than examine broader societal causes and consequences. Countless descriptions of racial abuses—lynchings, cross burnings, riots—blurred into an undifferentiated parade of wrongdoing. Figures in black history were treated as if they were unknown, as if black historians, novelists, and journalists had not spent several decades educating children and adults about their past. Stories that touted racial advancement by profiling African Americans elevated to positions of "first and only" seemed more ambiguous, reflecting tokenism and gradualism as much as achievement and activism. "Negro newspapers, as such, are running out of gas," Prattis warned. "The times, the conditions and the competition have changed."[28]

Black journalism's sense of obsoleteness also played out in foreign affairs news, as shown in particular by diminished coverage of Africa. During World War II, journalists had consistently underscored Africa's demands for equality and explained the steps taken to fulfill those demands. Du Bois complimented black newspapers in 1947 for their "broad and well done" coverage of African affairs. By the mid-1950s, though, coverage of Africa and Asia had shifted from explaining political developments to emphasizing personalities and headline events. These stories stoked a shared sense of racial identity and played up racial pride by reinforcing the sentiment that success against racism—whether in Birmingham, Alabama, or Pretoria, South Africa—enhanced the global standing of all people of color. However, a focus on spirit and spectacle resulted in superficial, erratic, and uneven coverage. Du Bois complained that the American media in general failed to accurately report on events in Africa, particularly in nations and colonies outside of British West Africa. George Padmore, who was privately advising Ghana's future president, Kwame Nkrumah, agreed. "It is a great pity that the Afroamerican newspapers are not giving the struggle the publicity it deserves," he wrote. "Even the *Courier* and *Defender* that at one time carried my despatches [*sic*] are no longer interested. I presume they feel that they have nothing in Africa." Padmore assumed correctly. ANP's Barnett asked forty or so subscribers to evaluate the quality of his service's Africa coverage. "Practically every reply said we were sending too much," he wrote. "They did not use too much and I think they have not awakened even as much as their readers."[29]

Ebony publisher John Johnson achieved unprecedented success in black journalism by purposely setting out to upend the stale conventions of black news reporting. His monthly magazine was slick, shiny, and determinedly cheerful. "*Ebony* will try to mirror the happier side of Negro life—the positive, everyday achievements from Harlem to Hollywood," its editors wrote in the first issue. "But when we talk about race as the No. 1 problem of America, we'll talk turkey." Ben Burns, the former *Defender* editor who served as *Ebony*'s executive editor for nine years, described the magazine's editorial policy as "escaping the negative 'radical' stigma of the Negro press." Johnson eagerly played up his differences with black newspapers, telling *Time*, "The Negro press has depended too much on emotion and racial pride. Negroes have grown out of that." (He later backtracked from the statement.) Newspaper publishers fumed. They dismissed Johnson as a promoter of celebrity fluff. "We can delude ourselves with the opiate of magazines that publish beautiful pictures and Pollyanna articles," said William Walker of the *Cleveland Call and Post*, "but, the more we seek to fool ourselves in this manner, the more difficult we are making our fight for our civil rights." Walker was too harsh. Johnson appealed to a rising middle class by showcasing black celebrity as a balm for everyday worries and promoting capitalism as a venue for righting racial wrongs. Scholar Adam Green argues that *Ebony* depicted racial identity as "a shared life, rather than a common problem." *Ebony* emphasized the wealth and fame acquired despite racism, rather than the poverty and violence that resulted from discrimination. While newspapers often highlighted white America's wrongdoing, *Ebony* introduced a modern twist on racial uplift's emphasis on accomplishment by extolling black glamour. While newspapers focused on politics and protest, *Ebony* examined life in the home and workplace. Johnson's magazine expressed a genuine faith, Green contends, in the "core values presumed to animate national society, particularly the equation of individual ambition and development with civil worth," and embraced "modern ideas of black community" before they were even fully formed. Acceptance of these modern values—with their emphasis on individuality, consumerism, and professionalism—pointed as much toward a new style of reportage as a new understanding of race.[30]

The white press posed a different challenge to black newspapers' future viability by tepidly integrating newsrooms. White news coverage of African Americans remained mostly antagonistic. Harvard University's Nieman Fellows—journalists who received prestigious one-year appointments to study their profession—famously criticized white editors and reporters in 1946 for continuing to trade in stereotypes and inflaming racial prejudices with sensationalistic headlines and misleading stories. "North and South," the fellows wrote, "most newspapers are consistently cruel to the colored man, patronizing him, keeping him in his place, thoughtlessly crucifying him in a thousand big and little ways." New pressures, though, encouraged white editors to contemplate hiring at least a single black reporter. The American Newspaper Guild called for the inclusion of fair employment practices clauses in all contracts as union activism grew among black journalists. White publishers also hired black reporters to assuage guilty liberal consciences, generate positive publicity, and remedy charges of hypocrisy regarding employment practices. Armistead Pride, a Lincoln University journalism professor, figured about eighteen blacks worked in 1953 as editorial employees at white-owned publications. (None held executive positions.) Two years later, *Ebony* estimated thirty-one African Americans covered general reporting assignments for white publications—about double the magazine's count from 1948. "The movement onto general publications is a mere trickle," Pride said, "nothing to become excited over."[31]

The *New York Times* hired its first black reporter in 1945, viewing the appointment as an experiment that would distance the paper from what the NAACP characterized as its "anti-Negro" outlook. Turner Catledge, the paper's assistant managing editor, asked ANP's Claude Barnett to recommend candidates, cautioning that "we should find good general reporters rather than racial advocates." Barnett provided a list of qualified candidates whom he hoped would "create the sort of personal appreciation which will make it easier for others to follow." Instead, the *Times* hired George Streator, a 40-something Nashville native with a master's degree from Western Reserve University and postgraduate work at the University of Chicago and Columbia University. Streator seemed an odd choice given Catledge's emphasis on journalism over agitation. Streator organized a student strike in 1924 at Fisk University, demanding the school's paternalistic white leaders involve students and alumni in their decision making. He allied himself with Du Bois in the early 1930s while working as the business manager and managing editor of the *Crisis*. Then he worked as an organizer for the

Amalgamated Clothing Workers of America and conducted research for other unions. Streator at least sympathized with the Communist Party during this time but claimed to have abandoned leftist circles by the early 1940s. When the war came, Streator joined the federal government as a labor race relations specialist, working at various times for the Office of Production Management, War Manpower Commission, and War Production Board. In late 1944, black leaders in Seattle demanded his removal, saying he had opposed efforts to integrate wartime housing and had "'expressed his lack of confidence in the sympathy and friendliness of any white person or persons.'" The NAACP and National Urban League supported his ouster.[32]

Streator understood he was a token hire for the *Times* and struggled to fulfill Catledge's expectations. He wrote mostly about race news, covering NAACP conventions and controversies, highlighting government efforts to improve housing and employment conditions, and keeping abreast of liberals' bids for interracial cooperation. Streator attempted to cover stories he believed would interest a mostly white readership. He angered Earl Conrad, a white columnist with the *Defender*, when he dismissed an interracial couple's plans to open an integrated church as "only worth two lines in the *Times*." Conrad had arranged a press conference for the couple, and he accused Streator of attempting to demean them with his flip attitude and embarrassing questions. He asked Streator to weigh the story's merits in furthering cooperation between the races. Streator claimed none of that mattered to the *Times*. "I don't think like a Negro," he reportedly replied. "I think like a white man." Regardless, Streator's editors were still dissatisfied. Catledge later claimed Streator "found it almost impossible to be objective when covering stories involving race." Streator once made up quotes and attributed them to A. Philip Randolph because "he was sure he knew what Randolph meant to say, whether or not he said it." Conferences with editors were held, and corrections were written. The final mistake came in July 1949 when an article scrutinizing Texas's commitment to building a quality black university contained "certain regrettable errors and omissions." Streator got the story's tone right but left out important facts. More construction had occurred than he reported, indicating the state was perhaps following through on its promises more than the article implied. Later, though, the law school dean who complained about the story to Streator's editors resigned his post, criticizing the state for failing to do what was necessary to ensure quality education at the university. Suspecting he was on his way out, Streator warned Arthur Gelb, a future managing editor, that the *Times* would not accurately cover African Americans until it hired and trained more black journalists. Streator was fired in 1949.[33]

White editors hired a mix of polished newsroom veterans and inexperienced college graduates. Some black reporters spent their entire careers working for white publications, while others returned to black journalism or left the profession. They typically wrote in restrictive, hostile workplaces. Ted Poston rejoined the *New York Post* after the war. Earl Brown, a New York City councilman, wrote feature stories for *Life* magazine. Author and globetrotting reporter Roi Ottley wrote weekly columns for the *Chicago Tribune*, profiling the careers and good deeds of local African Americans. He also wrote special assignments, which tended to be explanatory studies of urban problems associated with minorities, such as escalating drug usage and inadequate housing. Fletcher Martin, a former city editor for the *Louisville Leader* and *Louisville Defender*, joined the *Chicago Sun-Times* as a staff writer. He was the first African American named a Nieman Fellow. The *Courier*'s Edgar Rouzeau worked briefly for the *New York Herald-Tribune*, but one gossiping reporter heard he was apparently "too much of an introvert and not sufficiently up on what was what." Rouzeau went back into black journalism, editing an Oklahoma paper before joining *Ebony* as an associate editor. The *Herald-Tribune* replaced Rouzeau with Arch Parsons Jr., a New York native who had studied aeronautical engineering at New York University and journalism at the University of Michigan. Parsons led the paper's coverage of the United Nations and organized its Middle East bureau. Benjamin "Ben" Holman, a top student in his journalism school class at the University of Kansas, applied for reporting positions at nearly one hundred daily newspapers before landing a job as a police reporter at the *Chicago Daily News*. On his first day, Holman walked into the bureau shared with competing reporters, and every other journalist stood up and left. "I sat there stunned," he recalled. "I sat at my desk. I didn't know what to do." Holman persevered. His editors stood by him. The *Newark Evening News* hired Luther P. Jackson Jr., whose father was a prominent historian and longtime columnist for the *Norfolk Journal and Guide*, after he graduated with a master's degree in journalism from Columbia University. The manager of the *Baltimore Afro-American*'s New Jersey office knew the young war veteran posed serious competition, telling the publisher, "Jackson's addition to the staff means that he will become the 'Pet' of a large number of our professional and civic leaders and heads of organizations who prefer to give their news first to the white daily, then tell the *AFRO* to copy what it saw in the *News*." By 1957, three black editorial employees worked at the *New York Times*—reporter Layhmond Robinson Jr., news assistant Robert Claybrooks, and copyboy Theodore "Ted" Jones. When Jones interviewed for his job, an assistant managing editor discussed Streator's querulous departure eight years earlier.

For Jones, the message was clear—"The lesson learned: if you hire them, don't let them be rowdy blacks."[34]

The *Washington Post*'s Simeon Booker became the highest-profile reporter to return to black journalism after landing a job with a major metropolitan newspaper. Born in 1918, Booker graduated from Virginia Union University and worked at the *Afro-American* before joining the *Call and Post* in 1944. In Cleveland, Booker won an award for a series on discrimination in public schools. He also earned publisher William Walker's wrath for attempting to unionize the newsroom. Frustrated with the *Call and Post*'s work conditions and editorial quality, Booker applied for and received a Nieman Fellowship. After his year of study, he applied for jobs at forty daily newspapers. Only Phil Graham, the *Post*'s publisher, was interested. He eventually hired Booker as a reporter in 1952. Nearly no one in the newsroom spoke to him. "It was recommended to me that I only use the bathroom on the fourth floor—editorial—so I did," Booker recalled. "I could eat in the cafeteria, and I was thankful for that. But I was always alone." Booker found no relief covering stories in a thoroughly segregated city. Police officers kept him away from fires in white neighborhoods. Interviewees laughed when he introduced himself as a reporter. He could not interview government insiders over lunch because restaurants refused to seat him. He mostly covered crime news. Otherwise, he wrote about racial issues. "It was a real tense situation and had me neurotic," he said. Booker quit in 1954. He moved to Chicago to work for *Ebony* and *Jet*.[35]

In contrast, Carl Rowan of the *Minneapolis Tribune* emerged as one of the most influential black journalists working in white newspapers—but not without struggling to reconcile his professional goals and his belief in racial justice. Rowan grew up poor at the foot of the Cumberland Mountains in McMinnville, Tennessee. A high school valedictorian, he enlisted in the Navy in 1943. Honorably discharged three years later, Rowan soon enrolled in Oberlin College in Ohio. After graduating with a mathematics degree, he joined the *Afro-American* to cover the Midwest from Minnesota. While working, he earned a master's degree in journalism from the University of Minnesota. He decided to apply for a reporting position at Minneapolis's two daily newspapers. The *Tribune* hired him for its copydesk in 1948 and made him a reporter two years later. Rowan wondered what his role should be as a reporter for a white newspaper. He did not want to only cover race news. And yet, he had a personal interest in racial issues. He decided he should be "'just a reporter' and help change America" without violating his professional ethics. He pitched his editors on sending him on a tour of the South, characterizing the resulting series as a black man's view of what it meant to be black in the postwar United States. His editors liked the idea. Rowan flew to Louisville, Kentucky, in January 1951.[36]

The series "How Far From Slavery?" ran over the following two months and established Rowan as a rising star in journalism. A savvy self-promoter always seeking a bigger readership, Rowan condensed his reporting for a high profile picture-story in *Look* and then adapted it for the more personal *South of Freedom*, a book published by Alfred A. Knopf in 1952. In the book, Rowan recounted how he struggled with the dilemma of presenting himself as an objective reporter who also felt the need to right racial wrongs. Weeks into his tour, Rowan made a nighttime visit to an isolated shanty in backcountry Georgia where an over-worked doctor treated a 6-year-old boy ill with pneumonia. Stressed from the pressures of investigating segregation and standing in a place reminiscent of his childhood home, Rowan suddenly felt the full force of what blackness meant in America. "I had begun my journey," he wrote, "feeling that, as a reporter, I could live a black life and write about it as a black man, and then wipe away the effects upon the lives of the people involved. I found that it was not that easy, because the mind is human, and it tried to make human things make sense." Rowan realized he could never separate his identity as a black man from his work as a reporter.[37]

"The Menace Was Obvious"
Reporting the Cold War and Civil Rights

Ideologically constrained and financially strapped, black newspapers confronted formidable challenges as the Civil Rights Movement gained momentum. Anticommunists used Cold War politics to characterize journalists' opposition to segregation as disloyal subversion. To forestall such charges, publishers and journalists depicted racial protest as a patriotic attempt to combat communism by eliminating racism as an exploitable target of Soviet propaganda. As anticommunists acted to neutralize black journalists' militancy, white publishers and editors moved to replace them as the dominant source for race news. America's racial problems emerged as a prominent national story after the Supreme Court ruled in May 1954 that segregated schools violated the U.S. Constitution. News coverage expanded one year later when the justices equivocated on the pace of integration, giving segregationists the latitude they needed to stall. Delay, protest, and violence ensued, compelling white journalists and broadcasters to devote more attention to racial unrest. White journalists enjoyed distinct advantages over their black colleagues: Their editors could assign more reporters to a story and readily cover travel expenses. They had greater access to white-controlled courtrooms, city halls, and police departments. They could report the news almost immediately, either over the airwaves or in multiple daily editions.[38]

Black journalists' coverage of the schools ruling accentuated their newspapers' technological shortcomings and narrowed ideological perspective. Since the major weeklies did not publish national editions on Tuesdays, the *Atlanta Daily World* was one of the few black newspapers to cover the story on the day it happened. The paper's comparatively conservative editorial outlook—forged from publishing amid southern white hostility—led its editors to minimize the significance of the Supreme Court ruling. In a front-page column, managing editor William Gordon claimed black citizens would neither gloat nor brag about the decision. "As in the past, they will exhibit the same loyalty and sanity," Gordon wrote, "and they will work quietly along with their fellow Americans in abiding by what the highest tribunal has handed us." Two days later, the *Los Angeles Sentinel* devoted its entire front page to the story. The *Sentinel* called the ruling "a historic milestone in the struggle for human rights" and characterized it as a Cold War victory that offered "hope to mistreated people everywhere." The *Sentinel*'s editors claimed the decision gave "the lie to the Communist tale that Americans are completely indifferent to aspirations of its minority groups."[39]

The news was five days old by Saturday. The *Afro-American* and *Defender* ran stories about the Supreme Court's ruling on the front page but focused on racial news less publicized in daily newspapers, particularly a decision by the Pullman Company to hire black conductors. The court decision dominated the front page of the *Amsterdam News* and *Courier*. The *Amsterdam News*'s editors referred to the ruling as "the second emancipation," but they cautioned that successful fulfillment meant more work for African Americans. The *Courier*'s editors urged black men and women to keep battling for civil rights by tying the ruling to an ongoing fight over segregated pools in Pittsburgh. Like the *Sentinel*, the *Courier* imbued the ruling with international significance. "This decision ought to stun and silence every Communist traducer behind the Iron Curtain," said publisher Jesse Vann, "and demonstrate to the colored people of Asia and Africa that America has the idealism and moral courage to do what is right, regardless of race, creed or color."[40]

The next year, black journalists' dispatches from the Asian-African Conference in April 1955 provided a fuller display of how they adapted their newswriting to remain consequential despite the Cold War's repressive politics. Held in the sweltering Indonesian provincial capital of Bandung, the conference was a watershed international event—the first major meeting organized by colonies and countries from Asia, Africa, and the Middle East. Sponsors deliberately sidelined European and American officials. The conference's agenda called for the twenty-nine attendees to discuss their mutual problems of colonialism and racism, identify common interests that would allow them to navigate between the Cold War powers, and promote world peace. The small contingent of African American writers that arrived on the island of Java reflected the idiosyncratic nature of black journalism in the mid-1950s. Reporters from national newspapers mixed with leftist writers from small political journals. Celebrities served as special correspondents, and virtual unknowns finagled press credentials. A few reporters wrote for white dailies. Indonesian children swarmed around delegates and reporters alike, indiscriminately asking for autographs, knowing only that these foreign visitors were "colored and important."[41]

Cold War intrigue pervaded the atmosphere, and rumors circulated that the American government or its intermediaries had attempted to influence black correspondents' coverage. Freelancer Eugene Gordon, the communist writer who had worked for the *Boston Post* in the 1920s, was told by a *Chicago Tribune* reporter that his passport had been issued by "mistake." At the other end of the political spectrum, the *Courier* ran articles by Max Yergan, the radical turned anticommunist government informant. Freelance journalist William Worthy, a registered conscientious objector who had spent three years reporting from Europe and Asia, asked to serve as correspondent for the *Afro-American* but was told the State Department had offered to pay expenses for Louis Lautier, the paper's Washington correspondent. "This is a blind for the state department," editor Cliff Mackay told Worthy. "They think Mr. Lautier is safer than a person who has had such a well rounded knowledge of the situation as you have." Worthy was credentialed by Worldover Press, a progressive international news service. The *Minneapolis Tribune* sent Carl Rowan after fielding a telephone call from Allen Dulles, director of the Central Intelligence Agency (CIA). Rowan had just returned from an eight-month speaking tour in India and Southeast Asia sponsored by the State Department. The American consul general in Hong Kong had suggested that Rowan "might be able to do some excellent backstage public relations work for the United States among the delegates and observers."[42]

Black journalists were far less dismissive of the conference than white reporters, although both tailored their coverage to the Cold War's bipolar framework. White journalists judged whether the United States had gained or lost influence in Asia and Africa. They treated delegates' condemnations of racism and colonialism as either communist propaganda or secondary concerns. Black reporters acknowledged the legitimacy of the delegates' anticolonialism statements. ANP columnist Marguerite Cartwright, a widely traveled Hunter College educator, accused white reporters of mischaracterizing the conference.

"Communism is an evil which must be fought," she wrote, "but it was not the man who came to dinner at Bandung. That man might be better described as 'Mr. Get Acquainted.'" Cartwright described the United States' anxiety over the conference's racial outlook as "a sort of collective paranoia and unconscious projection of its own guilt." Rowan, though, ended his trip convinced the Red menace was "greater and more frightening than I imagined." Even so, he still argued that the West must stop pretending Asian hostility sprang from communist plotting rather than "the two most explosive ingredients in the Asian revolution—anti-colonialism and anti-racism."[43]

Regardless of political orientation, black journalists frequently depicted the conference as an event that transformed their views of themselves and the place of African Americans in world affairs. Lautier marveled how his status as a racial minority changed once he reached Honolulu. "As an American moves out into the Pacific," he wrote, "he becomes impressed with the fact that this is not a white man's world." Worthy emphasized the prediction by India's Prime Minister Jawaharlal Nehru that the conference's most important outcome was a long-term, intangible transformation in the mindset of Asian and African peoples. Worthy agreed, concluding "no one with memories of the huge barefoot throngs of cheering, illiterate Indonesians standing outside the conference halls in heat and tropical rains can doubt this intuitive knowledge."[44]

No reporter conveyed this transformational perspective more enthusiastically than Ethel Payne, a 43-year-old Chicagoan on her first overseas assignment as the *Defender*'s national political reporter. For Payne, the conference was not merely a professional obligation. "More important, as a Black American," she wrote, "it meant the emotional experience of interrelating my own ethnic background with those individuals of other 'colored' origins." Payne scored exclusive access to meetings closed to white reporters: She was mistaken as an Arab delegate by Indonesian soldiers guarding the convention. "I never was stopped," she recalled. "I just would go through the lines. They would lift their bayonets." One day, broadcast journalist Chet Huntley, whom Payne characterized as a Cold War warrior who worried she would be fooled by communist propaganda, was stopped by a soldier while Payne kept walking. Huntley argued. Payne smiled and laughed: "So suddenly, just like a big light came over me, for the first time in my life, I realized that I was part of a majority; I was not a minority." Afterward, Payne summarized the conference's main objective as obtaining "the right of self-determination and the privileges that go with freedom of mind and body." Her travels led to a deeper appreciation of America's democratic promise and a stronger will to fight for its fulfillment. She got her chance as racial unrest erupted across the South.[45]

Another major news event five months later, the five-day murder trial of Emmett Till, a 14-year-old Chicago boy killed for allegedly whistling at a white woman, drew unprecedented national scrutiny to the racial wrongs of southern justice. More than fifty reporters and photographers, including a dozen black journalists, covered the court proceedings in Sumner, Mississippi. Media interest stemmed from the decision by Till's mother, Mamie Bradley, to hold an open casket funeral "so all the world can see what they did to my boy." Tens of thousands of people viewed Till's extremely disfigured corpse. *Jet* ran an exclusive close-up—snapped by photographer David Jackson—of his grotesque face. The cutline claimed the image "bares mute evidence of horrible slaying." The issue sold out, and, for the first time, *Jet* printed additional copies. Sociologist Joyce Ladner later claimed the photograph "left an indelible impression on many young Southern blacks who, like my sister and I, became the vanguard of the Southern student movement."[46]

The mere presence of black journalists as working professionals at the murder trial undermined the code of white supremacy that assured the defendants' freedom, despite their apparent guilt. Unlike in earlier decades, black reporters covered the trial without posing as white men or disguising themselves. They wore suits and ties or dresses, openly took notes, and discreetly questioned white officials and citizens. They sat at a segregated press table. Ostracized to a corner of the courtroom, *Jet*'s Simeon Booker said black journalists served as "the antagonistic Exhibit A of Northern Negro reporters who were capitalizing on low-rating the South." Inside the courtroom, reporters were harassed and insulted. Each day, Sheriff H. C. Strider walked past their table and asked, "How you niggers doing this morning? Are you niggers all right?" Ernest C. Withers, a Memphis-based freelance photographer, always responded with a sardonic reply, "We're in good shape. You looking out for us just fine."[47]

More sinister threats occurred outside the courthouse. When *Ebony*'s Cloyte Murdock interviewed Till's great uncle on his front porch, white men armed with shotguns slowly rolled by in a pickup truck. "The menace was obvious," she recalled, "the message clear." Unknown callers rang the motel room occupied by James Hicks, writing for the *Afro-American* and NNPA, in the all-black town of Mound Bayou. After one caller promised to come by later, Hicks borrowed a .38-caliber pistol and clutched it when someone knocked first on his door and then on Booker's door. Neither reporter answered. Another day, a jittery deputy waved a gun at Hicks and arrested him on the fabricated charge of passing a stopped school bus. Instead of taking him to the courthouse, the deputy veered into another building. Sensing trouble, three white reporters followed, including Hicks's friend Murray Kempton, a *New York Post* columnist. Soon a local reporter arrived with Strider, warning the sheriff that he was "getting ready to give this town the biggest black eye it ever has had." After meeting in private, Strider returned with a justice of the peace, who declared court open and dismissed the charge as a favor to Hicks. A local reporter later told Murray the sheriff had intended to beat Hicks.[48]

Black reporters strengthened the case against the alleged murderers by participating in what Booker characterized as "Mississippi's first major interracial manhunt." During the trial, T. R. M. Howard, a Mound Bayou surgeon and Mississippi's leading civil rights activist, learned from a field hand that five or so other black workers might have witnessed Till's kidnapping and heard his screams as he was beaten to death in a barn. Prosecutors did not know about these witnesses. Howard asked Hicks, Booker, Murdock, and the *Tri-State Defender*'s L. Alex Wilson to help find the men and persuade them to testify. He then asked three white reporters—one from the *Memphis Press-Scimitar* and two from the *Jackson Daily News*—to tell the authorities that new witnesses would soon turn themselves in. That night, though, the white reporters and law officers joined the search. Riding with the officers, the black reporters convinced three witnesses to take the stand. Later on, Wilson and Hicks searched on their own for two other witnesses rumored to have cleaned the murder scene after Till was killed. Both reporters tracked down sources who claimed the men were locked up under false names to prevent them from testifying. Prosecutors refused to pursue the matter. After the trial ended, Wilson found one of the missing witnesses. A contact lured the man into a meeting with Wilson who convinced him to go to Chicago. A *Defender* lawyer deposed the man for two days. The interview ran in the paper. The man, whose family still lived in Mississippi, denied seeing anything.[49]

Fearing deadly repercussions, Hicks saved his juiciest bombshells until he returned to Harlem. "I have never been under the kind of pressure the story produced, even at Korea's most crucial moments," the military veteran and one-time war correspondent told his editors. "I'm not proud of it, but I will admit that at times I was just plain scared." And yet, about a month later, Hicks returned to Mississippi to cover a grand jury's refusal to indict on kidnapping charges the two men accused of killing Till. Hicks's wife and mother urged him to stay home. But Hicks believed Till's murder was just the first in a series of racial incidents sure to rock the South as integration accelerated. "And every such incident should, and must be covered by the colored press," Hicks wrote. "Who is better qualified to do this than a colored reporter?"[50]

As the white media's interest in race news grew, the 381-day boycott of public bus service in Montgomery, Alabama, illustrated why hundreds of thousands

of African Americans kept reading black newspapers. The boycott drew peri-
odic national interest throughout 1956 as white journalists reported on lawsuits, arrests, threats of violence, and significant developments in negotiations
between the boycott's leaders and city officials. Boycott news percolated in
the back pages of the *New York Times*, occasionally bubbling into a more prominent placement. The Reverend Ralph Abernathy, a boycott organizer, credited
national press coverage with unifying the boycotters and raising their morale.
Such publicity increased organizers' political clout when they discussed a settlement with city leaders. Most daily newspapers and broadcast outlets, though,
gave the story little more than a passing mention. White reporters turned elsewhere for news when negotiations stalled. "A story with no new developments
is no story at all," Abernathy said. "And when our struggle was not being carried
on the Associated Press wires, the nation forgot about us."[51]

Black newspapers provided more consistent, more detailed coverage. They
ran regular updates, solicited donations, and covered lecture tours by the boycott's leaders. Photographs inspired African Americans nationwide. Snapshots
of a mild-mannered Rosa Parks, an energetic Martin Luther King Jr., and well-
dressed church crowds depicted a familiar world that suggested any reader
was capable of similar actions. Black reporters frequently scooped their white
competitors. Emory Overton Jackson, a tireless NAACP activist who edited
the *Birmingham World*, a feisty newspaper with the Scott Newspaper Syndicate,
reported inside information after attending early sessions of the Montgomery
Improvement Association, which was organized to guide the boycott. (Jackson
also offered his advice.) Black reporters corrected false statements. The *Minneapolis Tribune*'s Rowan secured an enduring footnote in history after noticing a
discrepancy overlooked by white reporters. When the Associated Press reported
that the boycott had abruptly and unexpectedly ended, Rowan, who had just
returned from Montgomery, phoned King to confirm the story. King told him
the boycott was still on. Rowan's call gave the boycott's leaders enough time to
discredit the ruse before it disrupted the protest.[52]

Black reporters more fully depicted the pain and jubilation of protest. Both
Hicks and Payne profiled Jeannetta Reese, a woman ostracized by boycotters
after she claimed a lawyer with the Montgomery Improvement Association
never had permission to use her name in an antisegregation lawsuit. Their
stories examined how Montgomery's surprisingly unified and vigorous protest exposed an older generation's willingness to relent to white demands,
whether from fear or for favor. Calling Reese "the white man's masterpiece,"
Hicks emphasized her personal confliction, her desire to live freely and her
need to avoid trouble and please whites. Payne depicted Reese's plight as a

cautionary tale for other African Americans who might betray their race's cause. Similarly, the *Tri-State Defender*'s Wilson and photographer Withers rushed to gauge the degree of success actually achieved by boarding a bus at 6:30 a.m. the day after the boycott ended. They wanted to test whether drivers would adhere to the court ruling forbidding segregation. "It was an inspiring and exhilarating experience," Wilson wrote, "to observe true, Christian democracy function deep in the heart of bias-ridden Alabama and deep in the heart of Dixie."[53]

Black journalists portrayed King's use of passive resistance as a potentially dynamic way for other African Americans to strike against southern segregation. Just a few weeks after the boycott began, the *World*'s Jackson wrote that King seemingly wanted "to find a suitable adaptation of the Gandhi philosophy and method and apply it to the Montgomery problem." Within a few months, newspapers were filled with news and commentary about "Alabama's Gandhi." A *Courier* writer explained how Mahatma Gandhi's Hindu beliefs shaped King's conception of nonviolence. Then the writer connected the practice of nonviolence to the teachings of Christianity. William Worthy, who advised King on passive resistance, assured the *Afro-American*'s readers that no one visiting Montgomery "could ever be the same after seeing the mystic force of nonviolence erode the vainly guarded dikes of southern tribalism." The *Defender* ran Payne's extended interview with King on the front page, allowing him to explain his intentions to a large readership before he was recognized as a national leader. Although space existed for disagreement, as the *Courier*'s Prattis showed the following year, nonviolence was almost universally endorsed by journalists. Passive resistance was a pliable tactic that seemed sufficiently militant to northern reporters and suitably accommodating to southern publishers. One year after the boycott started, Jackson described King as the "chief architect" of an expanded freedom fight that regarded nonviolence as its guiding philosophy and impulse.[54]

Despite printing news unavailable elsewhere, black newspapers continued to struggle financially. The *Defender* and *Courier* again illustrated the extremes taken to halt circulation losses. Sengstacke decided to double-down on expansion after his buying spree failed to preserve his most valuable national advertising accounts. While celebrating the *Defender*'s golden anniversary, Sengstacke announced plans to transform his flagship newspaper into a daily. He had contemplated the move for ten years. The changeover cost more than $1 million, including money spent to build a new printing plant, buy modern production equipment, and hire more editorial and mechanical employees. Sengstacke believed a five-day-a-week newspaper could allow a more economical use of his equipment and boost circulation by expanding news coverage for "readership appeal beyond the limits of race or partisanship." Within two years, daily circulation rose from under 20,000 to nearly 30,000. Satisfyingly, the weekly national edition maintained its circulation. At the *Courier*, though, declining profitability eroded reporting capabilities. Reporter Phyl Garland chafed when "the paper could not afford to send its writers out to cover what were to emerge as some of the biggest stories of the century." Prattis, for example, dismissed as "a substantial expense" the suggestion that he assign a reporter to tour the South and write an overview of southern race relations—an increasingly common newspaper practice. When the *Courier* did send reporters into the South, Prattis complained their coverage was not only late compared to the dailies but also undistinguished.[55]

White journalists and broadcasters effectively replaced black reporters as the dominant disseminator of race news in September 1957 when Arkansas Governor Orval Faubus refused to integrate Central High School in Little Rock. Faubus's belligerence drew international condemnation and forced President Dwight D. Eisenhower to mobilize an Army division and federalize the Arkansas National Guard. The standoff mesmerized the nation for two months. For the first time, television cameras played a significant role in capturing the drama of racial unrest. The decade had opened with just 7 percent of the nation's homes having a television. Seven years later, though, 82 percent of households owned a TV set. Intimate and visual, television footage of hostile white crowds jeering black children gripped viewers—black and white—across the nation. Leading news outlets dispatched teams of reporters for saturation coverage. Race news reporting was permanently altered. After Little Rock, the national white media turned a sharper critical eye upon the South. Editors assigned reporters, photographers, and cameramen to what they called the "race beat." These new "race reporters" traveled from one hotspot to the next. Their crisis-oriented stories and images focused public opinion on southern racism, often compelling federal officials and politicians to take action. In *The Race Beat* (2006), veteran journalists Gene Roberts and Hank Klibanoff described race reporters as "the witnesses, transmitters, and agents of change" needed to dismantle American discrimination.[56]

Black journalists reported the Arkansas crisis just as they had countless other racial controversies, but they encountered new challenges in Little Rock. Editors wrote blistering editorials. "There is no other way to evaluate the present situation," the *Afro-American* declared, "than to recognize the unvarnished truth that Arkansas has declared war on the United States." Reporters attended press conferences, scored scoops, and wrote compelling stories. They noted the presence of black soldiers among mobilized troops and praised the fortitude of the nine students. They enjoyed unusually intimate access to a key figure—Daisy Bates, a NAACP activist who served as the students' spokeswoman and also published the *Arkansas State Press* with her husband L. C. The Bates's home functioned as a strategy center and press bureau. Activists and reporters ate and slept there, sharing advice and information.[57]

The crisis' speed and scope, though, overwhelmed the resources of struggling black newspapers. Television's expanded role amplified the slowness of weekly reporting. White journalists still focused mostly on political negotiations and violent clashes, but demands for saturation coverage compelled them to examine angles once exclusive to black newspapers. The *New York Post*, for example, ran an eleven-part series, written by Ted Poston, profiling the students. (The *Defender* reprinted the series a few weeks later.) An Arkansas National Guard commander barred black reporters from standing near school grounds. He claimed he was protecting them from physical attacks. Moses Newson of the *Afro-American* complained no one was harassing him when four guardsmen escorted him to his car. Guardsmen also booted reporters from the *Defender* and *Amsterdam News*. Sengstacke wired Faubus to protest this interference with press freedom, saying the governor, if necessary, should assign guardsmen to protect black reporters.[58]

Military strong-arming failed to protect black journalists from violence. On a late September Sunday, Bates said in a radio interview that the students would not attempt to enroll the following day. She hoped to discourage protesters from lining up outside the school. Privately, she told several black reporters to be ready to go the next morning. Heeding Bates's tip, Wilson drove to Central High with three other reporters—Hicks, Newson, and Earl Davy, a photographer for the *Arkansas State Press*. Wilson parked a couple of blocks away. Bystanders glared at the reporters as they neared the school. "Here come the niggers," one yelled. Angry men blocked the sidewalk. Wilson and Hicks explained they were journalists. A policeman told them to leave. As they turned back, the crowd surged and attacked. The reporters ran. Someone kicked Newson. A one-armed man slugged Hicks in the head. Another man tripped Davy. Others kicked him and smashed his camera. Wilson halted a moment. He thought of Elizabeth Eckford, a student who had withstood insults and jeers weeks earlier before being turned away from the school. He thought back to his days as a Marine in World War II and as a correspondent covering the Korean War. "I decided not to run," he recalled. "If I were to be beaten, I'd take it walking if I could—not running." His calm enraged the mob. A man struck him in his right side. Someone hit him in the jaw. Another man jumped on his back and choked him. Wilson shook him off. "Run, damn you, run," the man yelled. Wilson bent down. He picked up his hat, re-creased it, and walked away. His body buckled as he was struck again. Wilson staggered to his car. The mob turned back. Photographs of Wilson's beating landed on the front page of newspapers nationwide. "Yes, I was abused—a victim of misguided violence—but I am not bitter," he wrote. "If my effort to help bring human dignity in its fullest sense to the oppressed minority here is successful, then the welfare of all will be enhanced."[59]

At Little Rock, segregationists also intimidated black journalists through economic sanction. A delegate for a group of "Southern Christian women" urged Daisy Bates to persuade the students to withdraw from Central High. The woman promised future cooperation on integration in exchange for more time. Daisy and L. C. saw the request as a familiar, do-nothing dodge. They refused to help. "You'll be destroyed—you, your newspaper, your reputation," Daisy recalled the woman saying. "Everything!" Soon after the visit, the *State Press*'s financial troubles worsened. Utility companies, real estate ventures, and small local businesses stopped advertising in the paper. A supportive grocer was told his store would be bombed if he advertised with the Bates. Circulation agents were warned not to distribute the paper. "Being a friend of the Bates's in Little Rock is a risky enterprise," L. C. said. The paper survived on donations and NAACP advertising but ceased publishing in November 1959. "Our friends all over the country have kept us going since 1957," Daisy told *Jet*, "but we couldn't expect the American people to keep up their support forever."[60]

· · ·

Ultimately, purged radicalism and expanding competition constrained the influence of commercial black newspapers more than physical assaults and advertising boycotts. One of the most damning critiques concerning the black press's curtailed progressiveness came in 1957 from Howard University sociologist E. Franklin Frazier. He ridiculed commercial publishers for lopping off their most radical political aspirations and reinforcing the middle class's false sense of achievement. In *Black Bourgeoisie*, Frazier accused well-to-do African Americans of abandoning black cultural traditions and embracing consumer capitalism in hopes of gaining white society's acceptance. Frazier claimed the rejection of black values, coupled with the persistence of racial exclusion, fostered feelings of inferiority among professionals and business owners. To compensate, they flaunted their wealth at debutante balls where they paraded before photographers' cameras. Frazier blistered publishers and journalists, particularly John Johnson of *Ebony*, for serving as the "mouthpiece" of this intellectually stunted middle class. He accused publishers of celebrating a "make-believe" high society that deluded wealthy African Americans into thinking they had achieved notable success, even though racism powered the free-market economy. Journalists promoted this illusion by reveling in the acquisition of wealth, inflating the importance of minor accomplishments, and equating recognition by the rich and powerful with actual achievement. Frazier concluded that journalists had a shallow understanding of the economic and social forces that shaped the world. He blamed their ignorance on "the inferior, segregated Negro schools" and a mindset "restricted by the social and mental isolation of the Negro world." Since reporters lacked a robust worldview, they heedlessly shored the self-deception that inhibited the middle class's political awakening. While Frazier scored some telling insights, he opened himself to criticism through his selective mining of newspapers and magazines and his overstated smearing of journalists. His ire was focused mostly on *Ebony*, the nation's most popular black publication, which also happened to be a lifestyle magazine more than a protest publication. More broadly, Frazier denounced a self-censoring, self-congratulatory commercial press for the seeming triviality of day-to-day journalism. Despite his argument's flaws, Frazier's criticisms found receptive readers and pointed toward a cause for the declining national relevance of leading black newspapers.[61]

The anticommunism movement splintered the black press in the 1950s, dividing it once again into distinctive commercial and alternative presses. Black print culture still nurtured a permeability that promoted interaction between these two print platforms, but the boundaries were less porous. An era had ended. The demands placed on journalists and the expectations of their readers had changed. Writers who aspired to a lifetime career in journalism more often worked exclusively in the commercial black press, especially as employment opportunities gradually opened in the white press for reporters who satisfied its standards of professionalism. With its progressive impulse diminished, commercial black journalism often seemed a rehashing of stories that readers had already learned about from daily newspapers and network television. As the decade closed, readers quit buying commercial black newspapers for their coverage of national and international affairs. Instead, they bought them to learn about local news and community events that white editors continued to ignore and to read commentary interpreting national and international news from a black perspective. For the progressive outlook once offered by commercial newspapers, readers in the 1960s increasingly turned to the editors, activists, and writers of a resurgent alternative black press that embraced the language and politics of the Black Power Movement.

CHAPTER 6

Black Power Assaults the Black Newspaper

A 23-year-old Black Power activist known for exclaiming, "Burn, baby, burn," H. Rap Brown fed a relentless media frenzy in the summer of 1967 by provocatively welcoming the riots that scorched black neighborhoods in Detroit, Milwaukee, Newark, and elsewhere. Brown was virtually unknown when he was elected in May to lead a radicalized Student Nonviolent Coordinating Committee (SNCC). Just three months later, his name, words, and photograph appeared in newspapers and on television sets nationwide. By then, Brown awaited trial on charges of arson and inciting a riot in a troubled city on Maryland's Eastern Shore. Rioters had torched nearly twenty buildings, shot and wounded a police officer, and struck Brown in the head with a shotgun pellet after he told about four hundred people to "burn this town down if this town don't turn around." As white commentators and columnists attempted to comprehend the country's escalating racial turmoil, they depicted Brown as a publicity-hungry hothead whose recklessness symbolized the new direction of black protest. Brown both beckoned and belittled this news coverage. Journalists transformed Brown—to the dismay of established civil rights leaders—into a national spokesman for Black America. And yet, Brown distrusted the white reporters and broadcasters who stoked his celebrity. "I'm a crazy, dangerous nigger, who hates white folks, according to the media," he wrote in his autobiography. "The news media is one of the greatest enemies to Black people. It is controlled by the ruling classes and is used to articulate their point of view." Other militants agreed with Brown's accusations. They often regarded the commercial black press with similar suspicion.[1]

Amid August's upheaval, Brown accused commercial black publishers of abandoning their industry's long tradition of strident racial protest. Too often, he claimed, black journalists replicated "the same distortions and falsehoods" traded in the white media. He wondered why editors refused to condemn America's imperialistic involvement in the Vietnam War as their nineteenth-century predecessors had denounced the invasion of Cuba and the Philippines during the Spanish-American War. "Indeed," Brown wrote, "the earlier black press often fitted a proper description of what an informed, militant, struggling medium should be: it ferreted out wrong, exposed corruption, pressed for reform and revolution, and was quick to point out traitors amid the race." Echoing sociologist E. Franklin Frazier's decade-old criticisms, Brown argued that commercial newspapers were too concerned with bolstering advertising revenue and appeasing a middle class that hoped to assimilate into white society by celebrating wealth and applying skin whiteners and hair straighteners. He grouped modern commercial black publishers with moderate abolitionist editors who hoped to end slavery through moral persuasion. He linked alternative black editors—at publications such as SNCC's newsletter and the Nation of Islam's *Muhammad Speaks*—to those abolitionists who contended that only force could compel emancipation.[2]

Brown was just one of the many impatient student protesters, Popular Front progressives, community organizers, and armed activists who revitalized the alternative black press in the 1960s to steer racial protest toward an unprecedented militancy. These alternative writers and editors produced idiosyncratic publications that included college newspapers, mimeographed newsletters, leftist political journals, and organizational papers for Black Nationalist groups. They founded their own publications to ensure the unfettered expression of viewpoints they believed commercial black publishers and white journalists ignored, marginalized, and demonized. While radical writers' political agendas often clashed, their overall editorial outlook recalled the urgent immediacy and global perspective of the New Negro Movement after World War I. Frustrated by white southerners' violent obstructionism to the Civil Rights Movement, they questioned the value of integration, endorsed armed self-defense, stoked a singular appreciation of black culture, and embraced a Marxist critique of American capitalism and empire. Their language and tone was brazen and outrageous, calibrated to engage black youths and enrage white authorities. In doing so, they aimed to define the meaning of Black Power. As the Civil Rights Movement expanded northward and urban uprisings raged in the nation's largest cities, newly minted militants revamped the editorial mission of existing publications and launched scores of new newspapers in American inner cities. The FBI closely monitored these journalists, particularly those writing for the Black Panther Party. Law enforcement operatives even sabotaged the printing and distribution of newspapers. And yet, the militancy of the alternative press's writers percolated throughout Black America by the late 1960s, with two publications, *Muhammad Speaks* and the *Black Panther*, rivaling and exceeding the readership of the nation's leading commercial black newspapers.[3]

Commercial black publishers still boasted the largest concentration of black readers in the nation, but they alienated many young African Americans by attempting to moderate racial militancy and denouncing the Black Power Movement. Leading publishers had morphed into establishmentarian dissidents in the 1950s after purging their newspapers of progressive journalists. Government authorities regarded them as legitimate political actors entitled—within proscribed limits—to voice contrary opinions on public affairs. Publishers achieved this qualified insider status by accepting the Cold War's binary framework and seeking to reform American society through nonviolent political compromise. In the early 1960s, publishers attempted to guide young protesters, describing the hundreds of sit-ins across the South as a justified, if potentially dangerous, politicization of nonviolence. They later wavered between validating and disavowing black anger. Publishers challenged white journalists' characterizations of urban riots by acknowledging the legitimacy of African American frustrations and blaming police brutality for sparking violence. But they also attempted to strip the "Black Power" slogan of its provocative overtones of suspended violence by assigning it a narrow political meaning. By the late 1960s, leading publishers openly condemned Black Power militants. They feared the provocativeness of Black Power rhetoric would destroy hard-won gains in voting rights, political representation, and legal protection. An editor with the *Baltimore Afro-American* defended the newspaper against Brown's criticisms by drawing "a very clear distinction between constructive militancy and destructive stupidity." As establishmentarian dissidents, commercial publishers enjoyed expanded access to political power, even as the readership that had established their national influence melted away under intensifying technological and competitive pressures. Unwilling to embrace the era's militancy, they remained relevant by supplying local news to large communities whose daily affairs were still mostly ignored by the white media. "In earlier years," *Afro-American* publisher John Murphy said in 1970, "black newspapers were spearheads of protest. Today, we're much more informational."[4]

"Lead Us Together . . . or Step Aside"
A New Alternative Black Press

The alternative black press was just one component of a flowering underground press that emerged in the early 1960s as American youths and other dissidents expressed dissatisfaction with the status quo. The introduction of photo-offset printing eliminated mechanical costs as a publication barrier. Any amateur with a typewriter, scissors, glue, and a little money could become a newspaper owner. Inspired by the early successes of African Americans' collective action for racial justice, alternative editors believed their printed words could galvanize sympathetic readers, recruit newcomers to their causes, and inaugurate substantial societal reform. Their publications popped up here and there until nearly every major city and college campus claimed at least one alternative paper. These editors distrusted authority. They opposed the Vietnam War and supported African Americans' fight for civil rights. They endorsed leftist politics that criticized the nation's political economy and promoted a cultural revolution that celebrated open sexuality, recreational drug use, rock 'n' roll, and an irreverent youth culture. They were partisan, profane, polemic, and sometimes pointlessly contrarian. Their readership and political vibrancy peaked in the late 1960s and early 1970s as racial unrest rippled across the nation, the draft forced young men onto the unwinnable battlefields of Vietnam, and women, gays and lesbians, Latinos and Native Americans, and other oppressed groups demanded their civil liberties and social acceptance. The most radical editors prepped for worldwide revolution.[5]

Like the broader underground press, the alternative black press took shape in the early 1960s as diverse interests built support for nonconventional political views. Editors endorsed the right to carry guns for protection, defended the need for direct-action protest, advocated Marxist-oriented progressivism, and touted black separatism. Robert Williams, the NAACP chapter president in Monroe, North Carolina, who was issued an undesirable discharge from the Marines for challenging racial discrimination, emerged as a pioneering alternative editor when he turned to self-publishing to promote armed self-defense as a legitimate tactic for combatting racial injustice. Williams protested in May 1959 when a racially motivated jury acquitted a white man who had attempted to rape a black woman. Williams declared he would "meet violence with violence, lynching with lynching." His comments ignited a national controversy widely covered by black and white newspapers. NAACP Executive Secretary Roy Wilkins suspended Williams from his chapter presidency, claiming his views undermined the organization's credibility and effectiveness. Williams circumvented his suspension by publishing the *Crusader*, a short-lived mimeographed newsletter. Williams used the newsletter to publicize his fight for equality in Monroe and to highlight protests and demonstrations that occurred in small towns across the South. Too often, he claimed, white reporters ignored localized activism. "The real Afro-American struggle," Williams wrote, "was merely a disjointed network of pockets of resistance and the shameful thing about it was that Negroes were relying upon the white man's inaccurate reports as their sources of information about these isolated struggles." The *Crusader*'s popularity attracted new members to Monroe's NAACP chapter.[6]

Nine months after Williams's suspension and about one hundred miles away, four college freshmen triggered student protests across the South after they sat down at a segregated lunch counter in downtown Greensboro, North Carolina, and refused to get up. The sit-ins marked a bold, confrontational adaptation of Martin Luther King Jr.'s conception of nonviolence. Instead of boycotting segregated businesses until they integrated—as citizens in Montgomery, Alabama, had done—the students entered stores and stayed until they were served or arrested. Their actions visibly and forcibly disrupted the flow of everyday life in southern cities. The widespread popularity of sit-ins forced black leaders, including publishers and columnists, to demand integration more aggressively or risk losing credibility with readers. Within two years, student protests spurred more than two hundred cities in the upper South to desegregate public services. Demonstrators, though, experienced far fewer successes in the Deep South.[7]

National publishers supported the students' protests but lectured young activists on the need for proper leadership and organization. Editorials defending the students skimmed over the implicit aggressiveness of their actions by emphasizing the peacefulness and legality of their protests. Publishers still urged restraint. The *Afro-American*'s editors advised students to consult a local lawyer, align themselves with a civil rights organization, and review their plans with city and police officials. Their advice was sound, but it stripped students of leadership responsibilities and diminished the spontaneity and urgency of their actions. Publishers could issue parental-style endorsements because they linked student demonstrations to past examples of mass protest championed in their newspapers. The *Chicago Defender*, for example, compared the sit-ins to A. Philip Randolph's March on Washington Movement and the bus boycott in Montgomery. The citing of historical precedent emphasized continuity and hid from publishers the sit-in movement's significance as a pivotal moment in accelerating youth militancy. Publishers saw the sit-ins as a threat only to southern white supremacists, not as an opening salvo rebuking establishmentarian black leadership.[8]

Lutrelle "Lu" Palmer, editor of the Memphis-based *Tri-State Defender*, was one of the first journalists to recognize the new uncompromising determination that infused student demonstrations. Palmer wrote a five-part series, "The New Face of Young Negro America," in March 1960 that explained why college students had become such ardent protesters so quickly. He interviewed students in Alabama, Tennessee, Virginia, North Carolina, and elsewhere. "At every stop we made," Palmer wrote, "we stood in awe as young people explained why they were all of sudden in such hot pursuit against the screaming devils of prejudice." Palmer connected students' growing unrest to the accretion of past injustices, King's effective use of nonviolence, and the success of African independence movements. He debunked speculation that adults controlled the students, noting that young adults could afford to sacrifice more because they had less to lose than parents concerned with protecting jobs and families. Palmer also witnessed how heavy-handed southern justice redoubled students' commitment to racial justice. Palmer was one of five black reporters and photographers arrested and convicted of disorderly conduct in Memphis while covering a sit-down demonstration at a segregated public library. Despite the humiliation of arrest and being confined in an overcrowded prison cell, Palmer "was proud to lift my voice with those of the college men who sang out clearly and lustily the words of such stirring songs as 'America the Beautiful,' 'Lift Every Voice and Sing,' 'Nobody Knows the Trouble I've Seen.'" After being bailed out, Palmer saw "even greater determination on the part of the students to continue their protest until victory was won."[9]

Students' resoluteness clashed with a commercial publisher's caution in Atlanta. C. M. Scott of the *Daily World* had found favor with white civic leaders and achieved societal standing and financial stability over the decades by supporting gradual integration and endorsing negotiation over protest. His outlook was shared by most of Atlanta's black business and professional class. The publisher claimed to "understand the impatience of youth" when students attending Atlanta's six black colleges picketed downtown businesses and organized sit-ins. He approved of their nonviolent tactics and acknowledged the legitimacy of their demands. Scott balked, though, at direct protest, arguing it only created hostility and slowed reform. "Wise, mature counsel, combined with youthful energy and enthusiasm," Scott's newspaper editorialized, "can carry the march toward full freedom and citizenship farther with more permanent results and with less racial ill-will being generated." Scott's conservative outlook shaped the *Daily World*'s news coverage. Reporters' stories were mostly procedural. They identified who was arrested and listed the charges. They covered courtroom hearings. However, they seldom wrote about the students' concerns and aspirations. Julian Bond, a Morehouse College student, attributed the *Daily World*'s disinterested coverage to financial concerns, not philosophical differences. Bond claimed an A&P store had yanked its advertising from Scott's paper after students picketed it.[10]

Student activists bypassed the *Daily World*'s indifference in July 1960 by launching a rival newspaper, the *Atlanta Inquirer*. Editors M. Carl Holman, an English professor at Clark College, and J. Lowell Ware, who owned a printing press, described the paper as "the brain child of a group of young men who felt a void existed in the reporting of news in the Atlanta Negro community." The staff's pluck won it admiration and sales. "When people say a story should be suppressed 'for the good of the community,'" Holman said, "what they usually mean is peace at any price. We just don't believe in that." Another writer pointedly told Atlanta's black leaders to "either join hands and lead us together down the path of freedom or step aside." The editors refused advertising from segregated businesses. Reporters maneuvered a leading hospital into accepting all emergency room patients, regardless of their color. They also exposed Jim Crow practices at the Lockheed Aircraft Corp. plant in Marietta, Georgia, which violated a federal order prohibiting discrimination in government contract work. Staff reporter Charlayne Hunter, who integrated the University of Georgia and later wrote for the *New Yorker* and *New York Times*, said she "began applying my developing journalistic skills to social issues" at the *Inquirer*. Within a few years, the *Inquirer* was a modest financial success. The paper expanded from its emphasis on racial protests and politics into the broader coverage typical of commercial newspapers. By 1963, even early opponents advertised in it. Circulation topped 24,000 weekly in 1965, which compared favorably to the 30,000 copies the *World* sold daily. Success was not welcomed by all. Ware believed that the *Inquirer*'s advocacy mellowed as it matured. He left in 1966 to start the *Atlanta Voice*.[11]

Meanwhile, in New York, editors once affiliated with Paul Robeson's leftist *Freedom* published a new journal that showcased black progressive thinking on contemporary politics and culture. *Freedomways* boasted an eclectic mix of contributions from acclaimed scholars, writers, and activists, pushing its cultural influence far beyond its small monthly circulation, which started at 2,000 and rose to about 15,000. The journal was edited by Shirley Graham, the Communist Party member who helped radicalize her husband, W. E. B. Du Bois, and Esther Cooper Jackson, an activist and former social worker married to a prominent Communist Party official. The editors called their journal "a quarterly review of the Negro freedom movement." Writers' contributions in early issues bore the hallmarks of the Old Left's influence. The editors dedicated their inaugural issue to "the world's workers, whose ranks are larger than all the military armies put together, and who today march in PEACE and FRIENDSHIP." Graham and Jackson nurtured a Pan-African perspective by "examining experiences and strengthening the relationship among peoples of African descent in this country, in Latin America, and wherever there are communities of such people anywhere in the world." John Pittman, the communist editor who wrote a foreign affairs column for the *Chicago Defender* during World War II, explained how socialism aided African independence. Eugene Gordon, onetime reporter for the *Boston Post* and *Moscow Daily News*, reflected on the far-reaching legacy of the 1955 Asian-African Conference in Bandung, Indonesia. Up-and-coming writer Julian Mayfield praised Premier Fidel Castro for attempting to eliminate racism in Cuba, concluding that "necessary social change need not wait on the patient education and persuasion of the bigot and the reactionary." Historian John Henrik Clarke explained how the death of Congo Prime Minister Patrice Lumumba, whose 1961 assassination occurred amid allegations of American and Belgian complicity, served to "rekindle the flame of Afro-American nationalism." Clarke warned that Black Nationalists recognized Pan-Africanism as a powerful instrument that could unite African-descended people around the world. With that realization, Clarke argued, black men and women had turned away from "a leadership that was begging and pleading to a more dynamic leadership that is insisting and demanding."[12]

The Nation of Islam was among the Black Nationalist groups that Clarke identified as a revolutionary force in the United States. The sect advocated a theology that promoted black separatism, self-help, and righteous living. It also characterized whites as "devils." Its leader, Elijah Muhammad, and his adviser, Malcolm X, initially publicized the group's teachings in commercial black newspapers and white media. The *Pittsburgh Courier*'s bleak finances and the Nation of Islam's desire to recruit followers entangled the two institutions in a perplexing relationship. In the spring of 1956, the *Courier* introduced its readers to the Black Muslims' worldview and activities in a fawning, two-part story. Two months later, the paper began running a regular column, "Mr. Muhammad Speaks," which was reputedly written by Muhammad but was typically penned by Malcolm X. The *Courier*'s editors figured to sell as many as 25,000 additional papers nationwide to new Muslim readers. The Muslims hoped to win converts. They also expected no editorial interference. The arrangement was destined to fail. Malcolm X soon complained that *Courier* editors wanted to "censor" his copy because they feared angering prominent black and white leaders. Publisher W. Beverly Carter Jr. characterized column changes as routine editing done "in the best journalistic fashion." Privately, though, Carter confided to longtime editor

Percival Prattis that he saw "no justification for our using something that we can anticipate as being antagonistic to an already existing segment of our readers and supporters." The *Courier's* executives soon found themselves caught in a trap of their own making. Muhammad told Black Muslims to boycott the paper whenever he decided its editors had slighted him. One week, 5,800 Muslims canceled their subscriptions after their leader concluded the *Courier* had "lost interest in their business." The paper's circulation director responded by urging company executives to "treat this account as a *preferred customer*."[13]

Despite a regular column and frequent articles in black newspapers, the Nation of Islam remained relatively obscure until mid-July 1959 when independent WNTA-TV, Channel 13, in New York aired a provocative television newscast. Malcolm X, who managed the sect's publicity, granted interviews by Muhammad and himself to Louis Lomax, a veteran black reporter working as a commentator for Channel 13. (The religious leaders refused to take questions from Mike Wallace, the white anchorman for the station's evening news broadcast.) The five-part series, "The Hate that Hate Produced," provoked immediate controversy. Wallace introduced the program as "a story of the rise of black racism," a compelling reversal of the typical civil rights story reported from the South. Few viewers had heard of the Nation of Islam and fewer had seen footage of its worship services or rallies. Viewers' fascination prompted the station to re-air the program the following week. Malcolm X described the report as purposely sensationalistic, saying, "Every phrase was edited to increase the shock mood." However, he also credited the program with catapulting the Nation of Islam into the national consciousness.[14]

Other news outlets—black and white—followed up with their own stories, and the ensuing press coverage elevated the sect's influence far beyond its membership. Controversy provoked the *Courier's* new board chairman, an assimilationist Chicago cosmetics manufacturer, to dump Muhammad's column. Other black publishers, though, rushed to capitalize on the sect's newfound fame and eagerly aligned themselves with the Nation of Islam. The *Los Angeles Herald Dispatch* picked up Muhammad's column and soon operated as a sect affiliate. Other newspapers, including the *New York Amsterdam News* and *Milwaukee Defender*, continued to run occasional columns and news articles. Stories also appeared in national publications, including the *New York Times*, *Time*, and *Newsweek*. As white readers learned more about Black Muslims, the FBI moved to discredit the group. Federal agents fed negative information to journalists, and unfriendly stories later appeared in *Time*, *U.S. News & World*, *Saturday Evening Post*, and other publications labeled "friendly" by the bureau's agents. Scholar Jane Rhodes argues that the FBI's wide-ranging media campaign backfired because "the adverse publicity actually heightened black interest in the organization and helped increase its membership."[15]

Black journalists' coverage of the Nation of Islam illustrated why black newspapers still mattered in the early 1960s, despite the white press's success in controlling how the Civil Rights Movement was covered. Both black and white journalists typically wrote about Black Muslims when they were arrested or appeared in court. However, when white reporters wrote about the sect's beliefs, they portrayed its followers as extremists who threatened racial progress. In contrast, commercial black editors and columnists tended to depict the Nation of Islam's ideology as understandable, if wrongheaded, given America's history of racism. Black writers frequently compared Black Muslims to race-baiting white southern politicians and white supremacist groups—not to justify or discredit the sect's beliefs but to deflate white America's outrage by emphasizing the nation's long-standing tolerance of racial hatred. Retired baseball star Jackie Robinson criticized the House Un-American Activities Committee in his *Amsterdam News* column for wanting to investigate the Nation of Islam. Committee members never uttered "a mumbling word," Robinson observed, about the Ku Klux Klan or White Citizens Councils. Even as book reviewer J. Saunders Redding criticized Black Muslims for race hatred, he traced aspects of their views to Richard Wright's Bigger Thomas, the ill-fated, fictional antihero defeated by racism in *Native Son* (1940), and Marcus Garvey's back-to-Africa movement. By opposing but defending Black Muslims' teachings, Robinson and Saunders simultaneously marginalized the sect as a source of legitimate race leadership and undermined its use as propaganda by segregation's defenders.[16]

The Nation of Islam exploited its notoriety in 1961 by founding *Muhammad Speaks* to assert control over how its beliefs were presented to the general public. Malcolm X wanted the monthly tabloid, which became a weekly two years later, to serve as a concentrated news source for information about the sect's teachings, beliefs, and views on world events. While the white media had extended the group's influence, Malcolm X believed only an independent black publication could accurately portray black viewpoints. "The Negro press is our only medium," he said, "for voicing the true plight of our oppressed people in the world." The paper's editorial staff consisted mostly of non-Muslim, leftist writers and editors. Freelancer Louis Lomax helped put out the first few issues. Dan Burley, a seasoned journalist who had worked for the *Chicago Defender*, *Amsterdam News*, *Ebony*, and other black publications, succeeded Malcolm X as editor. Burley recruited other journalists from commercial newspapers and magazines. Veteran journalist Richard Durham, a former *Defender* reporter and radio broadcaster, joined the staff and was later named editor. These journalists transformed *Muhammad Speaks* into one of the nation's most popular black publications.[17]

By 1963, the escalation of black militancy and white violence was inescapable. *Time* described the year "as the time when the U.S. Negro's revolution for equality exploded on all fronts." More than 1,400 separate demonstrations occurred that summer—an unprecedented wave of protest. Police squared off against picketers protesting job discrimination in Philadelphia and New York. Militants booed Mayor Richard J. Daley in Chicago and jeered moderate black leaders during a rally. Police beat sit-in protesters in Mississippi and used tear gas against demonstrators in Florida. Martin Luther King Jr. and the Southern Christian Leadership Conference (SCLC) encouraged children and teenagers to march in the streets of Birmingham, Alabama. Photographers and cameramen captured police commissioner Eugene "Bull" Conner blasting those kids with fire hoses and siccing attack dogs on them. International condemnation by Cold War allies and adversaries alike led President John F. Kennedy to propose civil rights legislation. That fall, four schoolgirls died when white supremacists bombed Birmingham's 16th Street Baptist Church. Then Kennedy was assassinated. Growing discontent led African Americans to question the leadership of civil rights organizations and commercial black newspapers, prompting many to explore the words and aims of black militants.[18]

As unrest spread, alternative editors radicalized. The New York–based *Liberator* reflected this rising anger as Daniel H. Watts, an architect turned activist-publisher, built a national circulation by promoting armed self-defense as the only responsible option for securing full equality. The *Liberator* began as a newsletter for supporters of African independence but soon morphed into a militant monthly that juxtaposed Africa's independence movements with the black freedom struggle in the United States. Watts believed his journal could serve as "a bridge for unity between the two movements which must eventually become one." When moderates began 1963 by celebrating the hundredth anniversary of the Emancipation Proclamation, Watts questioned the claims of progress repeated in polite speeches. "Racism and jim crow [*sic*] are such basic ingredients of the American way of life," he wrote, "that they will not be eliminated without major surgery." His statement explained his opposition to nonviolence and negotiation: Reform was impossible. Only radical change could eradicate racism. In August, Watts dismissed the March on Washington for Jobs and Freedom as a co-opted display of integrationist unity "more concerned about keeping the demonstration orderly and controlled than making it a demonstration of the uncompromising militant mood of the people." He encouraged his readers to disrupt the march, confident others would abandon the doctrine of nonviolence if provoked. Watts later pointed to the 16th Street Baptist Church bombing to explain the difference between King's "dream" of integration and the "reality" of violent white supremacy. He criticized King "for continuing to preach a policy of nonviolence and love in spite of the daily toll of humiliation, blood and life which this policy has cost his people."[19]

"It Is Virtually Impossible to Provide Adequate Coverage of the National Scene"
The Commercial Black Press Retrenches

Commercial publishers struggled in the mid-1960s to reconcile an increasingly polarized readership. They urged African Americans to seek reform within a flawed but more accessible political system while acknowledging the legitimacy of deepening frustrations with discrimination, violence, and obstructionism. Pressed by President Lyndon B. Johnson, Congress passed the Civil Rights Act of 1964 over the opposition of Republican presidential candidate Barry Goldwater and a lengthy filibuster by southern senators. The act outlawed segregation and other forms of racial discrimination. The following year, Johnson signed into law the Voting Rights Act, which prohibited disenfranchisement measures, such as literacy tests and poll taxes, used in southern states to prevent black men and women from casting ballots. Publishers applauded the landmark legislation but cautioned that the laws marked a moment of transition in civil rights activism, not a conclusion. The laws would be successful only if African Americans transformed printed words into actual practice. "There must be a high resolve by all Negroes," wrote William Walker, longtime publisher of the *Cleveland Call and Post*, "that they will make full use of all civil rights as they are achieved. Unless we do this, we will lose the support of many of our white friends and supporters, without whose help the civil rights we now enjoy would not be possible." The *Baltimore Afro-American* also touted the importance of voting but cautioned that "the glaring need for stern enforcement" must be remedied before protest could move from the streets into courtrooms.[20]

The euphoria over significant legislative successes was short-lived. Just two weeks after the Civil Rights Act became law, a white police officer shot and killed a black teenager in New York City. Infuriated rioters burned buildings and looted stores. One person was killed, and more than one hundred were injured. Hundreds more were arrested. Commercial editors and columnists blamed the Harlem uprising on unjustified police brutality, but they also criticized black citizens for expressing their legitimate frustrations through destruction instead of political action. Leading publishers did not welcome violence.

As rioting raged, the *New York Amsterdam News*'s editors urged readers "to do everything within your power to bring an end to the riots in our Negro communities, which are hurting us all." They attempted to restore calm by arguing that rioting solved none of Harlem's problems and only reinforced its enemies' preconceptions. The editors paired their efforts to curb ongoing violence with aggressive political demands. They proposed the creation of a civilian review board to investigate charges of police brutality and encouraged the promotion of black officers to supervisory positions. Only a sincere attempt at reform, they argued, could "restore the confidence of our community in its Police Department." The *Chicago Defender*'s editors warned that urban uprisings would spread unless the federal government attempted to resolve the inner-city's joblessness, dilapidated housing, and slum conditions. "America's social order must undergo drastic revisions," they stated, "if it is to meet the challenge of the new Negro." Such efforts required an expensive and substantive commitment. *Defender* columnist Chuck Stone argued that white officials and commentators preferred "a superficial analysis" of rioting because blaming militants and communists for plotting fiery insurrections allowed them to propose "equally superficial remedies." Later that summer, riots flared in Philadelphia and Rochester, New York. Similar uprisings happened each summer for the rest of the decade.[21]

As racial upheaval gripped the nation, commercial publishers worried about losing access to influential lawmakers and important federal agencies. Their collapsing circulations jeopardized their reputations as well-regarded opinion-shapers. Presidential contenders, though, recognized the value of continuing to acknowledge and accommodate commercial black journalists. Kennedy and Johnson knew Democratic-leaning black voters were crucial to their electoral ambitions. Both presidents curried favor with the commercial black press. Each met with delegations of publishers to discuss civil rights. Each appointed journalists and publishers to government boards and offices. Kennedy placed *Defender* publisher John Sengstacke on the President's Committee on Equal Opportunity in the Armed Forces, which was formed to study ways to accelerate racial integration and curb discrimination occurring just outside of military bases. Louis Martin, the founding editor of the *Michigan Chronicle* and a longtime political operative, became the deputy chairman of the Democratic National Committee. He represented publishers' interests when political patronage was distributed. Bureaucrats also continued to find value in the black press. The State Department, for example, named journalist Carl Rowan a deputy assistant director. Rowan immediately broadened the agency's racial perspective by culling briefing materials from black publications, observing that the frustrations of African diplomats "often are reflected in the pages of these publications long before they come to the official attention of anyone in Government." He later served as the director of the U.S. Information Agency and encouraged Johnson to expand the American propaganda campaign against North Vietnam.[22]

No newspaper publisher, though, garnered the special presidential attention lavished on the publisher of *Jet* and *Ebony*. John Johnson's publishing company easily boasted the nation's largest black readership, and his pliable politics posed fewer obstacles to politicians who wanted to gain black voters without upsetting white constituents. Both Kennedy and Johnson complained to the publisher about criticism dished in *Jet*. Each time, Johnson agreed with the president's criticism and promised fairer coverage in the future. The presidents rewarded his amenability. Johnson claimed Kennedy offered him a government post. Instead, he asked for help lining up new advertisers. Soon afterward, the Ford Motor Company began advertising with Johnson Publications. Later, Kennedy asked Johnson to attend the Ivory Coast's independence celebration as an official delegate. After President Johnson berated publisher Johnson for thirty minutes, the publisher conceded that some of "our people were Kennedy people who resented the fact that Kennedy was dead and that somebody was trying to take his place." The duo then held up a copy of *Jet* (which the president had brought with him) and posed for a photograph. President Johnson appointed the publisher to a presidential commission that examined ways to fix the Selective Service System and eliminate discrimination in the military draft. The publisher later spiked an opinion poll—even though it had already been promoted—after *Ebony* readers indicated they strongly favored Democratic presidential hopeful Robert F. Kennedy over the incumbent Johnson.[23]

Photo ops and presidential appointments, though, did nothing to halt the plummeting circulations that forced national newspapers to retrench. Like metropolitan publishers, black publishers saw climbing production costs erode their profitability. Like white newspaper executives, they watched helplessly as the national television networks lured away readers, advertisers, and even a few reporters. Black-oriented radio also emerged as a formidable competitor, jumping from forty-three stations located largely in the South in 1956 to 108 stations nationwide in 1968. While dedicated to playing music, radio stations also functioned as electronic community bulletin boards. Deejays could announce news immediately and increase turnout for live protests. They also aired public affairs programming.[24]

As newspapers' profits dwindled, the mechanics of national distribution cost too much to maintain. "We can't afford field men any longer," said John Jordan, managing editor of the *Norfolk Journal and Guide*, "and transportation is too complicated and expensive. It is virtually impossible to provide adequate coverage of the national scene anyway." No national newspaper escaped the industry's plight. The 74-year-old Claude Barnett retired and shuttered his news service, the Associated Negro Press, when he failed to find a buyer. The *New York Amsterdam News* focused more intently on Harlem. The *Baltimore Afro-American*'s front page retained a national perspective—partly because the federal government was part of its local coverage—but its readership was concentrated in cities with individualized local editions—Baltimore, Richmond, Newark, and Washington, D.C. At the *Chicago Defender*, Sengstacke conceded his inability to grow a national readership when he transformed his flagship newspaper into a daily. The diminished relevance of commercial black newspapers was fully realized in October 1966 when the *Defender* bought the nearly bankrupt *Pittsburgh Courier*.[25]

Despite such setbacks, black newspapers remained relevant to readers because their editors and reporters still printed news unavailable elsewhere. White editors refused to print photographs of black brides and obituaries for domestics and laborers. They never wrote up black charity galas, sorority fund-raisers, church events, and school award ceremonies. "If you only read the regular press," said Lee Blackwell, the *Defender*'s managing editor, "you'd think Negroes never were born, never got married, and didn't die." Blackwell's boss characterized such editorial decision making as "censorship by omission." For Sengstacke, purposeful exclusion of African Americans in most sections of daily newspapers exposed white journalists' interest in racial justice as a fraud designed to boost circulation through tokenism. While black editors neglected expensive investigations and in-depth reporting, they compensated by keeping readers updated on prolonged protests and providing space for coverage of speeches and rallies and diverse commentary. The *Amsterdam News*, for example, boasted a heavy-hitting columnist lineup in the mid-1960s that included six leading activists—Martin Luther King Jr., Roy Wilkins, A. Philip Randolph, Whitney Young, James Farmer, and Dorothy Height. Editor James Hicks joked that he got so mad when his celebrity columnists turned in their copy late that he dressed down his staff writers.[26]

News coverage of the murder of Malcolm X by three armed assailants in February 1965 showed that commercial black newspapers still provided reporting and commentary unavailable in the white media but also illustrated why readers appreciated the distinctive outlook of an uncompromising alternative black press. Leading newspapers offered extensive coverage of the controversial but popular leader who had renounced the Nation of Islam. Editors devoted entire pages to recounting his accomplishments and confrontations, printing numerous photographs from his life and funeral. However, with limited national reporting capabilities, they relied heavily on wire stories—typically the less expensive United Press International (UPI)—that updated the ongoing criminal investigation and collected statements from world leaders. Thanks to their close proximity to officials and events, the *Defender* and *Amsterdam News* played up local angles. The *Defender* reported statements from the Nation of Islam's headquarters in Chicago. Its journalists quoted anonymous sources concerned that Muhammad, the sect's leader, faced threats of retaliation. Reporters also talked with a former member who explained that Malcolm X had left the group after he "was able to see and understand all that the true teachings have to offer" while discussing the Quran with imams in Mecca. As Harlem's hometown newspaper, the *Amsterdam News* commissioned guest columnists who discussed Malcolm's national significance and conducted man-on-the-street interviews to gauge local reaction to his death.[27]

National commercial editors, though, equivocated when they opined upon Malcolm's political views and legacy. They offered measured assessments, attempting to distance themselves from his advocacy of armed self-defense without overtly criticizing a well-liked slain leader. Editors repeatedly alluded to the adage that those who live by the sword die by the sword, but they stopped short of saying Malcolm X's life fulfilled the bromide. The *Afro-American* argued that Malcolm X had performed a useful service by prodding "some people into seeing how reasonable and acceptable are the demands of the Roy Wilkinses, the Whitney Youngs and the Martin Luther Kings." The *Defender* shifted its criticisms from Malcolm X's personal shortcomings to the United States' inherent racism. Its editors characterized "Malcolmism" as "an off-shoot of that theology of intolerance and racial hate" that also sustained the Ku Klux Klan and claimed Black Nationalism was "indigenous to a soil that produces in abundance the bitter fruits of racism." "To conclude that Malcolm X was sick," the editors wrote, "is an admission that leads to the same diagnosis of the American society. For pathologically sick men are the logical consequences of a sick society." The *Norfolk Journal and Guide* asserted that Malcolm X's death vindicated the tactic of nonviolence, observing that he had "preached violence and hatred" in most of his public statements. "If his death helps to eliminate hatred and violence from the struggle for justice and equality, Malcolm X will have made a significant contribution to the progress of mankind."[28]

In contrast, alternative editors covered Malcolm X's death with the depth of sorrow and anger befitting a militant eulogized as "our own black shining Prince!" *Liberator* publisher Daniel Watts accused the white press, which "made millions promoting, distorting and sensationalizing his views," of "gloating over" Malcolm's death. Watts warned that the black freedom struggle was "doomed to the garbage heap of the graveyard that is America" if so-called "responsible" civil rights leaders failed to heed Malcolm's message. Meanwhile, Eldridge Cleaver, an inmate in California's Folsom State Prison, "existed in a dazed state" after learning of Malcolm's death. Black Muslims had inspired Cleaver to alter his life's path. He praised the Nation of Islam for "building solidarity and black awareness" but disagreed with the sect's overt antagonism toward white men and women. He had secretly used the prison hospital's mimeograph machine to copy Muhammad's banned newspaper column and Malcolm's speeches, which he then distributed to other inmates. "The truth which Malcolm uttered," Cleaver later wrote, "had vanquished the whole passle [*sic*] of so-called Negro leaders and spokesmen who trifle and compromise with the truth in order to curry favor with the white power structure." Cleaver credited Malcolm X's example with steering him toward his involvement with the Black Panther Party for Self Defense, where he edited the *Black Panther*, which became the nation's most influential alternative black newspaper.[29]

"The Alternative to the 'Government Approved' Stories"
Black Power and Black Panthers

The year after Malcolm X's murder, commercial black publishers attempted to neutralize the violent undertones in the powerful but ambiguous "Black Power" slogan that intrigued white journalists. Stokely Carmichael, a Howard University graduate who had led a successful voter registration drive in rural Alabama before being elected SNCC chairman, popularized the phrase in June 1966 when he led chants of "Black Power" as he, King, and thousands of other marchers tramped through Mississippi in honor of James Meredith, who had been shot just thirty miles into his ill-fated publicity-raising journey. Within weeks, the rallying cry had commandeered white reporters' attention and transformed Carmichael into a national spokesman on civil rights. Despite reporters' repeated questioning, the cagey Carmichael refused to clarify what he meant by Black Power. His open-ended statements played upon white racial phobias. *Afro-American* columnist Ralph Matthews contended that white journalists inflated Carmichael's relevance to replace Malcolm X as the incendiary black bogeyman in their journalistic narratives. "They wanted somebody with a switch blade tongue like Malcolm," Matthews wrote. "Stokely was their boy." Martin Luther King shared Matthews's perspective. "In every drama," he wrote, "there has to be an antagonist and a protagonist, and if the antagonist is not there the press will find and build one." If not for sensationalistic news coverage, King claimed, the debate about Black Power might have been "little more than a healthy internal difference of opinion."[30]

Leading black publishers moved to define Black Power as the effective use of the voting rights available to all citizens in a representative democracy. At the *Amsterdam News*, publisher C. B. Powell and editor James Hicks described Black Power as "all acts of self-defense by black men to force white city, state and Federal governments to comply with the civil rights laws guaranteed by the Federal Government and the Constitution of the United States." The *Afro-American's* editors conflated Black Power with political representation and electoral campaigning. "There is nothing wrong with 'power,'" they wrote. "In American democracy, the majority rules. Majority is the equivalent of power and everybody, colored or white, seeks it." They warned against armed self-defense, which could easily "lead to an underground movement and violence without restraint." *Defender* publisher Sengstacke and his editors rejected black separatism and emphasized cooperation with liberal whites. For them, Black Power was the "development of a black power structure that will command attention and compel action in areas where progress is now at snail's pace or where the Negro has to depend on the shifting attitudes of the white folk for resolution of critical issues."[31]

Few commercial publishers pushed as relentlessly as William Walker of the *Call and Post* to shift black anger into political channels. A Republican insider who had served on Cleveland's City Council, Walker frequently invoked abolitionist Frederick Douglass, supported measures to grow the black business sector, and called for pragmatic, interracial leadership to avoid racial clashes. Walker doubted that African Americans would benefit much from integration if they did not first pursue gains in voting, employment, and education. While applauding demonstrators' enthusiasm in Birmingham and elsewhere, he argued that "real victories are won and made secure at the conference table." As protests multiplied, Walker lamented the emergence of militant leaders who favored confrontation over negotiation. He dismissed them as "hot heads" and "publicity seekers." He compared Black Power's advocates to enslaved rebels like Nat Turner and Denmark Vesey, noting that their famous insurrections, while often celebrated, had failed to achieve change and ended with their executions. Walker called Black Power an "unfortunate cliché" that posed "a potent stumbling block in our path to full civil rights." He worried that riots destroyed black unity by fostering hatred between "the Negro middle-class and the ghetto people." In place of violence and destruction, Walker urged African Americans to rally around politicians like Carl Stokes, who became the first black mayor of a major city when he was elected in 1967 to Cleveland's top office. "I still say," Walker wrote, "that the most powerful weapon we have and can use is that pencil in the voting booth on election day, and the dollars we spend every day for the things we need and the things we want."[32]

William Walker, publisher of the *Cleveland Call and Post*, at his office desk. Courtesy of the Moorland-Spingarn Research Center, Manuscript Division, Howard University, Washington D.C.

Efforts to moderate the meaning of Black Power frequently proved futile in the political and cultural foment that propelled the rise of the Black Panther Party and its bellicose articulation of black militancy. Cofounded in 1966 in Oakland, California, by Bobby Seale and Huey Newton, the Black Panthers simultaneously courted and baited journalists with their provocative language and menacing demeanor. Armed and attired in fatigues, members intention-ally displayed themselves as freedom fighters staging a revolution against an imperialist American state that abused its police powers. The Panthers gained national attention in May 1967 when they rallied outside the California State Assembly, conspicuously but legally displaying their rifles and handguns, to pro-test a gun-control bill that aimed to stop them from monitoring police actions while armed. The rally received international news coverage, and reporters clamored for statements from party members. Members had already published the first issue of the *Black Panther Intercommunal News Service* (commonly called the *Black Panther*), which began as a four-page monthly newsletter, to protest the death of Denzil Dowell, a party member shot in the back by a police officer. The publicity surrounding the Sacramento protest, Seale said, convinced him and Newton to continue publishing their own newspaper to raise money and explain their political views directly to the people they wanted to recruit. Like *Muhammad Speaks*, early issues of the *Black Panther* focused on defining the party's ideology and sharing party business. David Hilliard, the party's chief of staff, carried papers to rallies, hangouts, and workplaces, hoping to start conversations. "Find out what's really going on in this country," he told strangers as he handed them a copy. "Open up your mind! Stop being one of the living dead. See what's really happening." In-house advertisements written by Newton described the paper as "the alternative to the 'government approved' stories presented in the mass media and the product of an effort to present the facts not stories as dictated by the oppressor, but as seen from the other end of a gun." The *Black Panther* became a weekly newspaper in January 1968 and eventually expanded to thirty-two pages.[33]

The *Black Panther*'s content evolved with its production standards—its visual militancy reinforced its textual aggression. The newspaper's design was as inflammatory as its spokesmen. The paper popularized the party's caricature of police officers as pigs. Headlines warned of "Pig Lies," "Pig Conspiracy," and "Pig Plans for Genocide against the Black Panther Party." Emory Douglas, an artist who learned printing in juvenile detention, designed and laid out the paper. His artwork frequently depicted police officers as anthropomorphic pigs slaughtered by black avengers. In a feature captioned, "WE HAVE TO BEGIN TO DRAW PICTURES THAT WILL MAKE PEOPLE GO OUT AND KILL PIGS," Douglas included sketches of a black inmate choking a pig jailer, women seducing and stabbing a pig policeman, armed men storming a government building, a black soldier shooting a white officer in the head, and a revolutionary bombing a factory. Editors framed columns and statements by party officials, particularly Newton, as revolutionary manifestos, with rules and belief statements numbered, titled, and officially issued, as if by formal decree. Iconic photographs and drawings portrayed party members as colonial freedom fighters, their hard stares paired with raised rifles. Writers tackled issues concerning the black inner city. They condemned police brutality, a biased criminal justice system, substandard housing, and inadequate healthcare. They encouraged readers to form self-defense leagues and printed articles that illustrated how to properly load and shoot various firearms. Writers embraced Marxist thought and regularly linked the African American fight for racial justice to revolutionary causes around the world. They celebrated communist leaders—including Cuba's Castro, China's Chairman Mao Zedong, North Korea's Premier Kim Il-sung, and North Vietnam's President Ho Chi Minh—as champions of the people. Cleaver and Byron Booth, another Panther member, traveled to North Korea in 1969 to attend a communist journalists' conference that denounced

American imperialism and militarism. The Panthers not only condemned American military involvement in Vietnam but sided with the North Vietnamese government.[34]

While widely accused of inciting racial violence, the *Black Panther* mostly inspired readers to raise their social consciousness, not to aim and fire a gun. For teenagers and young adults, browsing the newspaper marked a political awakening. Living in Minneapolis, future party member Craig L. Rice felt isolated from the Black Power Movement until the *Black Panther* roused "the sense of wrong, the thirst for justice I already felt burning in my soul." The paper's content radicalized him. "The centuries of degrading images that Black people had endured," Rice recalled, "the images of us as weak and subservient, the images of us 'getting along to get along'—went away. Instead images of power and pride radiated from the pages." Colette Gaiter, then a teenager attending a predominantly white high school in Washington, D.C., expressed similar sentiments. Douglas's drawings, she recalled, "visualized ideas that I did not know how to express. I was coming into my political consciousness and awareness of the world." Flores Alexander Forbes, a 16-year-old high school dropout, stayed up late when his older brother Fred returned home on weekends and holidays from the University of California, Los Angeles, with copies of the *Black Panther* tucked among his textbooks. "I must have read Fred's two or three issues ten or twenty times," Forbes recalled. "I was obsessed with something for the first time in my life besides girls and getting high." Forbes compared his dawning militancy to the experience of religious conversion. Both brothers joined the Panthers. The newspaper appealed to young black men and women because its editors and reporters, designers and distributors—whom Seale described as "lumpen proletarian brothers and sisters"—reflected their anger and urgency with a vibrancy unrestrained by the commercial black press's steadfast commitment to journalistic objectivity and legislative reform. By 1970, the Black Panthers claimed to distribute more than 110,000 copies each week—trailing the *Baltimore Afro-American* by about 10,000 copies but exceeding the circulations of the *Chicago Defender, Pittsburgh Courier,* and *New York Amsterdam News.*[35]

Commercial publishers almost universally condemned the Black Panther Party and other militant activists, their stark consistency revealing how the factors of age and class shaped African Americans' response to the Black Power Movement. Youthful radicalism contradicted the life lessons learned by commercial publishers who had led their newspapers since at least the mid-1950s—when their industry had abandoned its tolerance for communist sympathizing. Their commitment to nonviolence and negotiation had advanced the civil rights cause and safeguarded profitable business relationships. Militants' reckless language and radical politics, publishers believed, threatened to thoughtlessly unravel momentous achievements and derail future gains. John Dunjee, the publisher (and nephew of the founder) of the *Black Dispatch* in Oklahoma City, dismissed the Black Panthers as "false prophets and instant saviors of the black race." *Journal and Guide* managing editor John Jordan contrasted the venerable NAACP with upstart militant organizations, calling it "a perennial warrior for equality, not a flash in the pan pugilist." When the *Defender* offered cash prizes for the best suggestions to prevent summertime riots, editors warned readers to avoid "the professional haters who conceal their basic hatred by assuming the mantle of fighters of freedom." Many publishers, including 71-year-old William Walker, lamented young militants' reliance on vulgarity and disregard for proper manners to shock complacent Americans. Walker urged them to get haircuts. "A bushy head of hair that looks like it needs combing," he wrote, "a beard that has no purpose in improving the wearer's appearance, or some makeshift copies of imagined African tribal garb, do not contribute in the least to the solutions of the many complex social, economic, and political problems Negroes face."[36]

Most commercial publishers insisted Black Power activists were bogus leaders without a following, and they lobbied white journalists to ignore them. "Let's stop giving birth to Negro leaders," Louisville publisher Frank Stanley told journalists at the National Press Club. "No one Negro, not even Dr. Martin Luther King or Roy Wilkins or Whitney Young, speaks for the entire American Negro population. It is unrealistic to assume such and it is ridiculous to print it." Other publishers simply ignored the militants. Mildred Brown, who had founded the *Omaha Star* with her husband in the mid-1930s, enjoyed friendly relations with local Black Power activists who respected her decades-long fight against discrimination, but she seldom assigned coverage of their protests and demands. She refused, for example, to publish a photograph snapped by a *Star* staffer that showed a Black Panther member protecting her newspaper's offices during a riot, fearing the image would encourage other black Nebraskans to arm themselves with rifles. The leading exception to commercial publishers' opposition was family physician Carlton Goodlett, who owned the *San Francisco Sun-Reporter* and covered the Black Panther Party as local news. While Goodlett distanced himself from the group's most provocative remarks, he asserted the legitimacy of their perspective and criticized their harassment by law enforcement officers.[37]

Leading black publishers still rejected the Nation of Islam's separatist beliefs, but the sect's leaders no longer relied upon the commercial press, either black or white, to attract new members. Commercial black publishers devoted significantly fewer column inches to Black Muslims in the late 1960s than they did to the Black Panthers. National news coverage of the sect had become more perfunctory after Malcolm X's murder, with reporters writing mostly about lawsuits and court cases, studies and speeches, and boxer Muhammad Ali's trials and tribulations. By then, *Muhammad Speaks* had evolved into a wide-ranging weekly newspaper that printed Elijah Muhammad's teachings and reported on world events from a Black Nationalist perspective. While former *Ebony* writer John Woodford regarded the Nation of Islam's theology with "a sort of scoffing amazement," he joined *Muhammad Speaks*'s staff because he admired its aggressive news coverage. Woodford believed the paper "was presenting more stories about issues and events that concerned African Americans and Africans than any other publication, and that it was doing so in a more forthright, more 'together' way." Avid readers of commercial black newspapers saw familiar names in *Muhammad Speaks*. The newspaper carried bylines by celebrated writers like Langston Hughes, James Baldwin, and Julian Mayfield. It also subscribed to small news services, such as Associated Negro Press International, a successor to Claude Barnett's Associated Negro Press, and Howard News Service, a syndicate operated from the United Nations by Charles P. Howard Sr., a onetime member of the Progressive Party.[38]

However, *Muhammad Speaks*'s similarity with commercial black newspapers ended there. Editors' searing headlines, sometimes graphic photographs, accusatory editorial cartoons, and adamant opposition to Western imperialism in Africa and Asia contrasted sharply with the more neutral display of journalistic objectivity found in commercial black newspapers. Woodford sent correspondents to the Soviet Union, Cuba, North Vietnam, and various African nations. He frequently published articles written by African scholars and journalists who reveled in revealing the hypocrisy deployed by American officials in defense of the United States' imperialistic foreign policy. "We never supposed that the nations we supported were chock full of selfless, flawless peasant heroes and heroines," Woodford said. "We supported their right to get Uncle Sam & Co. off their backs." Unlike black journalists during World War II, *Muhammad Speaks*'s reporters did not couch their demands for racial reform during the Vietnam War in patriotic appeals. They challenged the fairness of the draft, offered sympathetic coverage of trials against conscientious objectors, highlighted the disproportionate number of fatalities among black soldiers, and asked why African Americans should participate in the killing of another group of oppressed people of color. While Elijah Muhammad's intermediaries occasionally reminded Woodford that the Nation of Islam did not participate in the white man's politics, the juxtaposition of Muhammad's teachings with critical international news coverage established a charged editorial perspective that portrayed a world aflame in its fight against white supremacy. By 1970, the secretive group claimed an unaudited weekly circulation of more than 400,000.[39]

The Black Power Movement's growing popularity and notoriety led law enforcement agencies to disrupt the production and distribution of publications associated with organizations that FBI Director J. Edgar Hoover deemed "black hate groups." Cities and towns passed ordinances to restrict street sales. Police officers arrested individuals hawking *Muhammad Speaks* or the *Black Panther* on misdemeanor charges, such as loitering, blocking traffic, and disturbing the peace. Prosecutors subpoenaed editors, knowing court appearances and legal fees could force them to miss deadlines. The Panthers suspected someone intentionally lit a fire in a San Francisco building in early 1970 with the intent of burning all of their unsold back issues. They accused the firefighters who responded to the blaze of knowingly soaking and destroying salvageable copies. "The black press has always been a potential danger to the ameriKKKan 'front' and as that 'front' wears more thin," wrote Judi Douglas, a Panther editor, "it is only natural that those who have been hidden behind it for so long would become more fanatical in trying to preserve the fading facade." Hoover clearly recognized the central importance of Black Power newspapers in recruiting members and bolstering organizational finances. He used the Counterintelligence Program (commonly known as COINTELPRO), a covert operation that often illegally spied on radical dissidents, to issue orders and solicit advice on how to disrupt publication and distribution. Bureau agents contacted a transportation carrier to ensure the Panthers were charged the maximum allowable fee for shipping their newspapers from the West Coast to New York, a change that likely increased distribution costs by several thousand dollars. (The Panthers suspected airlines also quietly cooperated with the FBI to lose or damage shipments.) Hoover told agents in Chicago, San Francisco, and New York to "create friction" by encouraging the Nation of Islam to retaliate against the Black Panther Party for luring away readers and shrinking *Muhammad Speaks*'s profitability. Agents intended to foster widespread dissension among Black Muslims in New York by circulating an unsigned illustrated pamphlet that accused the sect's leaders of living lavish lifestyles funded by money collected from newspaper sales. They expected their campaign to succeed because members were asked to purchase 150 copies of *Muhammad Speaks* each week and then resell them, a time-consuming endeavor that netted a personal profit of $6. No manner of harassment was deemed too petty. Agents moved to complicate a writer's personal life by anonymously revealing to her landlord in San Francisco that she belonged to the Black Panthers. They wanted her evicted. In Newark, New

Jersey, agents asked to revisit the rejected idea of spraying newspaper bundles with skatole, a foul-smelling compound found in feces.[40]

Elsewhere, other alternative publications explored the merits of the Black Power Movement's intellectual and artistic endeavors, establishing the boundaries and expanding the influence of what came to be known as the Black Arts Movement. National political journals like *Freedomways*, *Liberator*, and *Negro Digest*—and also smaller but inspired literary and student publications, including *Soulbook*, *Black Dialogue*, *Umbra*, and the *Journal of Black Poetry*—promoted the movement by publishing young authors, artists, and poets, as well as critics who deconstructed and explained the meaning of their works. Scholar James Edward Smethurst contends that these publications served as the foundation for this burgeoning literary movement by building "a national community in which ideology and aesthetics were debated and a wide range of approaches to African American artistic style and subject displayed." Black cultural nationalism challenged the centrality of nonviolence and integration—of white appeasement—to the Civil Rights Movement and instead emphasized racial pride, autonomy, and artistic innovation. Poet Amiri Baraka (né LeRoi Jones) acknowledged the importance of print in advancing Black Power's cultural sensibilities when he outlined while teaching at San Francisco State College how to promote black militancy through a range of media platforms, from community bulletin boards to newsletters to newspapers. "The political liberation of the Black Man," wrote poet Larry Neal, who joined the *Liberator*'s editorial board in 1965, "is directly tied to his cultural liberation. Any black organization that overlooks this point, will find themselves sorely out of step with the needs of the people."[41]

Negro Digest's emergence as a leading patron of the Black Arts Movement marked a surprising but explainable toleration of racial militancy by the commercial press's most successful publisher. John Johnson, who had shuttered *Negro Digest* ten years earlier, relaunched the monthly magazine in 1961. He named Hoyt W. Fuller as his managing editor, putting him in charge of editorial decisions. Fuller was a former *Detroit Tribune* and *Michigan Chronicle* reporter who had worked at *Ebony* for three years as an associate editor. He quit *Ebony* in 1957, claiming the nation's most popular black publication "did not seem to be moving in any direction that it seemed important for me to go." Doubting any publisher would come up with cash for overseas travel, Fuller paid his own way to Africa to gain insights for future articles, essays, and fiction. His journey, Fuller later said, "fulfilled my desire for rootedness." He eventually returned to the United States as a keen supporter of Africa's various independence movements and its leftist governments. At *Negro Digest*, Fuller published an eclectic selection of reprinted articles discussing racial politics and culture and profiling prominent African Americans. Even though no editorials appeared, Fuller displayed a sympathetic curiosity for black radicalism and Pan-Africanism that could seem incongruous with other stories that stuck to Johnson Publications's long-standing celebration of integration and black entrepreneurialism. The same magazine that reprinted Johnson's speech praising the National Urban League for encouraging interracial cooperation and ran his advertising manager's sales pitch touting black purchasing power, also featured a cover story by Elijah Muhammad explaining Black Muslims' beliefs and an essay by Senegalese poet and politician Leopold Senghor on the meaning of the Negritude movement among French-speaking black men and women. As the black freedom movement radicalized in the mid-1960s, Fuller regarded black militancy as a credible political response to racism and increasingly provided young black artists with a national forum for reaching a general-circulation readership. Johnson, ever the savvy salesman, seemingly tolerated *Negro Digest*'s evolution, despite his personal discomfort with Black Power, sensing an opportunity to quietly capitalize on shifting cultural terrain without hurting his primary publications. Fuller completed the magazine's transformation in 1970 when *Negro Digest* was renamed *Black World*. The name change, Fuller noted, reflected the magazine's dual commitment to covering both Africa and the United States. "*Black World* will routinely publish articles," he wrote, "which will probe and report the condition of peoples and their struggles throughout the Black World." However, when *Black World*'s circulation plummeted from 100,000 subscribers to 15,000, Johnson moved quickly to cut his losses. He suspended publication in 1976.[42]

Police surveillance and harassment failed to stop aspiring radical editors in the late 1960s and early 1970s from revamping the editorial missions of existing publications and launching scores of new newspapers in inner cities and on college campuses. The alternative black press as a print platform flourished, even though most individual publications struggled to pay writers and cover other operating expenses. SNCC's *The Movement* shifted from covering the group's involvement in registering black voters in Alabama and aiding striking farmworkers in California—activities supported by liberal white readers—to criticizing the Vietnam War, opposing the draft, and endorsing Carmichael's conception of Black Power. Its editors reprinted speeches by Malcolm X and essays by anticolonialist psychiatrist Frantz Fanon. New publications emulated the *Black Panther*'s spirit of confrontational provocation and Marxist politics. Deeming the Congress of Racial Equality (CORE) insufficiently militant, Robert L. Lucas, a former postal worker who had headed the group's Chicago chapter, founded the Black Liberation Alliance. In the pages of the *Black Liberator*, Lucas pledged to "expose the systematic oppression of the black masses in America and the genocidal programs initiated against black people." In St. Petersburg, Florida, Army veteran Joseph Waller founded the Junta of Militant Organizations to organize revolutionary change. Waller characterized the United States as an imperial power that had colonized African Americans. In the group's paper, the *Burning Spear*, Waller wrote, "Black people have no responsibility—morally or legally—to perpetuate, sustain or protect this country which is actively oppressing us." Two months after riots erupted in Detroit, five residents published the *Inner City Voice*, telling readers that because the paper was "not controlled by white liberals or Uncle Toms with a little cash, we do not have to sacrifice any principles to satisfy their anti-black demands." At Kansas University, the Black Student Union published the first issue of *Harambee* after the state's attorney general declared the newspaper offensive but not obscene. Editor Monty Beckwith accused administrators and professors of perpetuating racial oppression. Similarly, the Black Student Movement (BSM) at the University of North Carolina-Chapel Hill launched *Black Ink*, which identified its editor-in-chief, Cureton Johnson, by the acronym "H.N.I.C.," which stood for Head Nigger in Charge. "If at all possible," the editors wrote, "the BSM's new newspaper would be printed black letters on black background."[43]

· · ·

As the 1960s ended, black journalists peered ahead to an uncertain future. Commercial publishers had finally secured legal recognition of the citizenship rights that they and their forebears had ceaselessly campaigned for. To achieve success, though, they had transformed themselves into establishmentarian dissidents who defended the American way by characterizing the Civil Rights Movement as an attempt to prove to a skeptical world that the United States would fulfill its democratic ideals. This decision provoked conflict with the black radicals who defined the Black Power Movement. The ensuing disputes weakened the commercial black press's claims to leadership as technological change and increased competition continued to erode weekly newspapers' profitability. Media critics questioned whether commercial black newspapers could remain viable—politically and economically—in a nation that had declared the end of de jure racial segregation.

Alternative black journalists also faced a precarious future. They remained relevant only as long as the social turmoil that fueled the Black Power Movement compelled readers to browse their publications. Their livelihoods depended upon financial supporters for whom mass communications was a secondary concern—a means for converting others to their political beliefs rather than a business enterprise that defined their purpose. By around 1975, as black militancy receded from national attention and shifted in new directions, progressive journalists saw most of the leading alternative publications downsize or fold.

Increasingly then, black journalists in general viewed the white media as the most viable venue for advancing their careers. As white-owned news outlets hired more black journalists, those reporters fought to dismantle the barriers of institutionalized racism and expand the presence of black-oriented perspectives in mainstream news coverage. Their struggle was daunting.

CHAPTER 7

Into the White Newsroom

When Ted Poston rejoined the *New York Post* soon after World War II ended, his peers lauded him as a trailblazer—a journalist talented enough to write for a major metropolitan newspaper and resilient enough to withstand the daily slights that came with being the only black reporter in a white newsroom. By the 1960s, though, Poston wondered whether he should have done more to expose how his editors' blindness to their racial biases shaped news coverage and hiring decisions. While African Americans had once applauded the liberal *Post* for simply writing about them, Poston warned of a "growing resentment in the community against the *Post* for what many regard as a patronizing attitude towards the Negro and an effort to segregate him from the rest of the larger community as something different and bizarre." His editors ignored him. Poston also chafed at the restrictions that limited his professional ambitions—unwritten rules that prohibited his promotion, constricted his reporting, and limited how many other black journalists could work with him. "I was the *Post*'s alibi Negro for 25 years," Poston concluded. Ultimately, the white media's dismal coverage of the destructive uprisings that engulfed the nation's black inner cities proved the veracity of Poston's criticisms.[1]

A watershed presidential commission spotlighted the civic cost of American journalism's institutionalized racism in February 1968 when it condemned news coverage of the previous summer's urban uprisings. The National Advisory Commission on Civil Disorders, commonly known as the Kerner Commission, accused editors and reporters of inaccuracy and indifference. In print and on air, reporters exaggerated the breadth and destructiveness of the uprisings. Journalists, particularly on television, fostered fear and misunderstanding by characterizing unrest as race riots that pitted blacks against whites, even though nearly all deaths, injuries, and property destruction occurred in black neighborhoods. Reporters did not robustly investigate rioters' frustrations with police brutality, slum conditions, and economic inequality. "The media report and write from the standpoint of a white man's world," the commission stated. "The ills of the ghetto, the difficulties of life there, the Negro's burning sense of grievance, are seldom conveyed." While the commission credited journalists with generally avoiding sensationalism and acknowledging their flaws, its members urgently warned "much more must be done, and it must be done soon." Two months later, Martin Luther King Jr. was assassinated in Memphis, and riots erupted in more than one hundred cities.[2]

The commission's findings prompted public hand-wringing among white editors who moved grudgingly in the 1970s to repair their reputations and flawed news coverage mostly by heeding the recommendation to hire more black journalists. The moment marked a significant transition in the history of black journalism: The black press lost its near exclusive access to black journalists, and the white press began to reluctantly reconsider how it wrote about African Americans and other minorities. The Kerner Commission had described the news profession as "shockingly backward in seeking out, hiring, training, and promoting Negroes." Publicly shamed, white editors intensified recruiting efforts, established minority training programs, and pledged greater racial sensitivity in future news coverage. Their efforts, though, mostly failed, with editors' rather singular focus on black employment encapsulating their narrow understanding of how racism structured both the workplace and its product. Even as they hired more black reporters, white editors denied or shifted blame for the news industry's racism. They clung to idealistic visions of the doctrine of objectivity. "Negro activities are covered without regard to race," said the editor of the *Rockford* (Ill.) *Register Republic*. "If they make news they are covered." Like the generals and admirals who led the military during World War II, white editors claimed they could only be as progressive as society at large allowed them to be. Again and again, editors blamed black journalists for employment discrimination: Too few black reporters satisfied the white media's professional standards. Many white editors scrutinized black journalists' articles more skeptically than they did their papers' overall coverage of racial issues.[3]

Black journalists exploited new but limited employment opportunities to force white editors and producers to recast how they framed racial news, a push that eventually led to fairer but imperfect coverage of minority concerns. Reporters acted to fortify their job security and also attempted to overhaul how the news industry conceptualized the role of race and racism in American society. Black news consumers often reinforced journalists' efforts by also demanding fairness in content and employment, particularly in television. However, newsroom activism in the 1970s produced more heartache than headway. Reporters safeguarded their professional rights by demanding affirmative action hiring, filing employment discrimination complaints and lawsuits, challenging government subpoenas, and forming advocacy organizations. "But, beyond all that," observed Lerone Bennett, *Ebony*'s senior editor, "there is a need for white-oriented media to integrate their vision, their control, and their management. In other words, we face the need, not for just a new reporter here, or a new story there, but for fundamental change in the spirit permeating white-oriented media. We face the need for white-oriented media to transcend the limitations of whiteness." That did not happen, leading to frequent newsroom arguments, which encouraged skepticism among African Americans who doubted the credibility of black reporters beholden to white editors. Even so, as the 1980s approached, black journalists had forced white news executives to acknowledge that no newspaper or television station could deliver on its promise of complete news coverage without including African Americans and other minorities.[4]

"A Bill Is Coming In"
The White Press Frames Race News

White newspapers steadily expanded coverage of black activists' efforts to desegregate southern institutions after the *Brown v. Board of Education* decision, but their editors remained oblivious to how deeply they misunderstood the nature of black protest and American racism. In the 1950s, most white editors and reporters had worked with negligible awareness of black journalists and their publications, viewing them as partisan advocates who wrote for small weeklies and a specialized readership. They mostly accepted the racial stereotypes that permeated the outlook of all American institutions. "I feel the profession, more than any other," said reporter Simeon Booker, who had quit the *Washington Post* in 1954 because of discrimination, "represents the hypocrisy in America to Negroes and corrodes, in too many cases, the faith of those of my people who wish only a fair shake." As the Civil Rights Movement unfolded in the early 1960s, white editors and reporters dismissed charges of bias, seeing themselves as objective professionals who accurately represented the contrasting perspectives of white segregationists and black integrationists. They published the news from the South—the speeches, marches, sit-ins, and violence—but seldom paused to consider how their own newspapers had institutionalized racism. Black journalists had few opportunities to unmask the white press's racial bias from within the industry. The American Newspaper Guild estimated in 1964 that only forty-five blacks worked as reporters, copyreaders, photographers, or deskmen at large daily newspapers. The U.S. Census Bureau figured African Americans occupied just one hundred of the fifty thousand newsroom positions at such papers. Token employment practices ensured black silence and protected white news executives against allegations of racism.[5]

Without black insiders to challenge their perspective, white journalists regularly critiqued their coverage of the "Negro revolution" by examining whether they upheld technocratic professional standards instead of asking if they owed a moral obligation to advance inclusion within a democratic nation. The central debate about civil rights coverage in *Editor & Publisher*, the newspaper industry's leading trade publication, revolved around geography rather than justice. Southern editors routinely accused northern reporters covering racial protests of engaging in sensationalism and ignoring discrimination in their own circulation areas. These charges challenged the neutrality of national race reporters and their editors, pressuring them to adopt a rigid understanding of journalistic objectivity. In turn, northern editors defended their work but wondered whether they made news—instead of covering it—when they assigned reporters to write about protests. They also debated who qualified as a legitimate black spokesman. Such discussions implicitly undermined the legitimacy of black protest by displaying an inherent distrust of the words spoken by ordinary black men and women and conflating diverse political perspectives to create a monolithic black community. *Editor & Publisher*—like the daily newspapers it covered—mostly ignored the black journalists who warned of African Americans' growing unrest.[6]

Few publications scrutinized white journalists' framing of racial protest as intently as *Negro Digest*, where Managing Editor Hoyt W. Fuller commissioned (and reprinted) writers who critiqued the language adopted by white journalists. Writers in 1964 tackled the white press's popular use of *Negro revolution* as the favored umbrella term for linking the disparate protests erupting across the South. Psychologist Kenneth B. Clark contended that the term mischaracterized the movement's actions and aims. Unlike revolutionaries, black protesters mostly refrained from the violence historically associated with revolutions since the late 1700s. Unlike revolutionaries, protesters did not seek to radically transform America's political economy. Clark observed that the black man demanded inclusion within the existing order, not its destruction. "He is accepting of the

American system," Clark wrote. "He is identifying with the American ideology and is insisting that the American protestations of democracy be taken literally, seriously, and be inclusive of him." The term *revolution*—and its implication of destructive violence—undermined the Civil Rights Movement by discouraging white cooperation. Poet Calvin C. Hernton argued that the term also misled African Americans. He described the misapplication of revolution as a purposeful manipulation of language to prevent substantial social change. "If Negroes can be made to *think* they are being revolutionary," Hernton wrote, "they will become satisfied with what they are getting or will become illusioned as to the exact nature of what it takes to really make them free, and what it is really like to *be* free." Revolution was misused to encourage the acceptance of token integration. The commonplace counterweight to *Negro revolution* was *white backlash*, a term used to blame black militants for a decline in white support for equality. Fuller called the term "a particularly insidious canard," contending substantial white support had never existed for black freedom. He wondered whether white journalists used the concept "to blackmail Negroes into submission."[7]

A few high-profile black freelance writers hired by white magazines and journals ensured that white readers were not completely blindsided by the rising tide of black militancy. Writers like James Baldwin, Louis Lomax, and William Worthy wrote for interracial readerships in the early 1960s, their commentary informed by their familiarity with black print culture, particularly its alternative publications. Their articles appeared mostly in literary magazines of politics and opinion (as well as some more mainstream publications), including *Harper's*, *New Republic*, *The Nation*, *Commentary*, *Saturday Review*, and *Esquire*. They foretold the Civil Rights Movement's turn toward unrest a few years before riots erupted in hundreds of cities. They warned that young African Americans were fed up with white opposition to equality and black leaders' willingness to compromise. Their insights revealed why daily newspapers desperately needed to integrate their newsrooms.

Approaching forty, Baldwin was an acclaimed essayist and novelist who had returned to the United States in 1957, after living for nine years in France, to play a more active role in the black freedom movement. He would emerge as one of the signature literary voices of his generation. Baldwin wrote urgent, uncompromising essays that spoke knowingly about the incessant insurgency of black youths, world significance of African independence, and separatist teachings of Black Muslims, who invited him to edit *Muhammad Speaks*. His 1961 *Harper's* profile of Martin Luther King cautioned that disaffected young African Americans "have begun a revolution in the consciousness of this country which will inexorably destroy nearly all that we now think of as concrete and indisputable." In the *New York Times Magazine*, he observed that white indifference to black concerns had prompted many African Americans to question the value of integration, especially if it meant sacrificing a newly appreciated African heritage. "Any effort, from here on out, to keep the Negro in his 'place,'" Baldwin wrote, "can only have the most extreme and unlucky repercussions." The following year, he published two essays—one in the *New Yorker* and the other in *Progressive*—which became the bulk of his critically acclaimed and best-selling *The Fire Next Time* (1963). "A bill is coming in," he warned, "that I fear America is not prepared to pay."[8]

Neither Lomax nor Worthy enjoyed Baldwin's literary prestige, but both also astutely navigated the conventions of the commercial black press, alternative black press, and white media to create a body of reportage that transcended the editorial restrictions of their outlets. Lomax was a controversial reporter, author, and broadcaster who began his journalism career at the *Baltimore Afro-American*, then joined the *Chicago American*, an afternoon daily, and won accolades for his documentary about the Nation of Islam, "The Hate That Hate Produced." He wrote books concerning African independence, Black Muslims, and the shifting dynamics of the freedom movement. After studying student demonstrations in twenty-six southern cities, Lomax concluded that young activists realized older black leaders in education and business might undermine the fight for integration because their livelihoods depended upon pleasing the white officials who paid their wages. "But the students told me," he wrote in *Harper's*, "they are not prejudiced—they are willing to stand up to their enemies, Negro and white alike." Lomax's straight talk earned him celebrity and enmity. White reporters soon quoted him and Baldwin as authorities on race in America. Black reporters regularly covered their speeches and criticisms of prominent race leaders. Such news coverage frustrated top civil rights officials who considered the writers' remarks ill-timed and overly provocative. "Baldwin and Lomax are excellent writers," said Whitney Young Jr., executive director of the National Urban League, "but they are responsible to nobody but themselves. They are responsible to no organization so they can make statements that get front page space."[9]

More than other writers, Worthy linked African American militancy to the colonial revolutions in Asia and Africa. A roving foreign correspondent, Worthy was a pacifist who helped organize an all-black political party and barred whites from a committee organized to defend him against government prosecution. And yet, he enjoyed the respect of national news outlets, thanks to the early patronage of legendary newsman Edward R. Murrow, his opposition to the State Department's efforts to restrict journalists' foreign travels in the mid-1950s, and his unrivaled access to international leaders who challenged America's foreign policy interests. Worthy's most high-profile pieces on black radicalism appeared in *Esquire*, a men's magazine celebrated for its quality journalism. His articles examined how American hypocrisy in its dealings with African and Asian nations inspired black militants to embrace aggression. Worthy's first *Esquire* article was a dispassionate explanation of the Nation of Islam aimed at a white readership. Worthy neither shied away from the sect's excesses nor sensationalized them. He noted that Black Muslims "believe in discrimination against whites," but refuted a government report that characterized them as a national security threat. He compared the sect to Marcus Garvey's Back to Africa movement. He explained how its appeal was broader than most observers realized by noting that the group's definition of black identity included "all of the darker peoples of Asia, Africa, and the Middle East." As a black writer for a white magazine, Worthy provided his readers with the context they needed to understand—without necessarily agreeing with—black militancy.[10]

Even the most progressive daily newspapers—those that assigned "race reporters" to cover racial unrest in the South—struggled to contextualize the freedom movement in the mid-1960s as protests moved beyond Dixie and turned destructive. A content analysis of four leading newspapers—the *New York Times, Chicago Tribune, Boston Globe,* and *Atlanta Constitution*—found that their editors significantly expanded coverage of civil rights protests in the 1960s but still underplayed one of the decade's defining stories. National race reporters moved from one southern protest to the next, reporting on one crisis after another. Their coverage pitted snarling southern racists against nonviolent, conscientious objectors. They tended to emphasize white southerners' staunch opposition to integration rather than fully explain why black men and women protested. Their editors continued to mostly ignore African Americans within their own circulation areas. "Despite the admittedly fine job many Northern papers have done on the racial struggle in the South," the *Post*'s Poston told colleagues, "few of them have met their responsibilities to those of their readers who are hemmed in, hopeless, and sometimes helpless in their own back yards." The focus on distant crisis deluded many white journalists and their readers into believing that the black freedom struggle was isolated and contained—a distinctively southern problem. A 1967 Gallup poll confirmed the prevalence of this perspective, finding only one white American in one hundred believed black men and women were badly treated, with 75 percent of them believing blacks and whites were treated about the same. The explosion of urban riots frightened and baffled the oblivious.[11]

Bewildered white journalists responded to urban uprisings by adopting a new narrative for the Civil Rights Movement that reflected their alarm, as well as their readers' fears. Sympathetic national news coverage, which had emphasized the wrongness of segregation, vanished as public opinion polls showed that a majority of whites were fed up and wanted more repressive measures taken to control black behavior. The new framing characterized black protest as extremist, unexplainable, and self-defeating. White reporters emphasized the aggressiveness of northern black militants and the threat they posed to the status quo. Activist Stokely Carmichael sensed white reporters' consternation when he held a press conference to discuss the new militancy of the Student Nonviolent Coordinating Committee (SNCC). "What I do remember clearly," he recalled, "is how little they seemed to understand, as though they were stuck in 1960 with the student sit-ins and we were speaking in unknown tongues." The white reporters who had supplanted black journalists as chroniclers of the black freedom fight characterized Black Power activists as a foreign threat— "apparently from outer space," Carmichael observed—rather than an evolution in the movement's character.[12]

Once welcomed by black men and women who wanted to expose the injustices they endured, white journalists now suffered physical assaults by angry African Americans disgusted with the white press's neglect and distortion of their lives. Protesters hurled rocks, fired bullets, and pummeled reporters and photographers, broadcasters and cameramen. A New York reporter warned his colleagues "to drive through 'rebel-held' territory at normal speeds" to avoid attracting unwanted attention. In Los Angeles, a television technician was beaten, stripped, and left for dead, and a wire-service reporter was hit by a brick while telephoning in his story. "I felt like Custer must have felt at Little Big Horn," an AP staffer recalled. The *Detroit Free Press* received clearance from the city police commissioner and U.S. Army to enter a "sniper zone" in an armored car borrowed from its manufacturer. Militants stormed a press briefing during the National Conference on Black Power in Newark, New Jersey, and chased white reporters from the room. "It was horrible, just horrible," a UPI photographer said, "an absolute war zone, worse than front line duty."[13]

Such violence unnerved veteran race reporters who thought they understood African Americans and their concerns. *Newsweek* reporter Karl Fleming, for example, had covered nonviolent marches and sit-ins across the South. Black families had welcomed him into their homes and churches. He had shared their distrust of racist cops and blanched when protesters were beaten. Segregationists had stalked and harassed him. Then Fleming transferred to California and covered the uprising in Watts, where he encountered hostility for the first time from angry African Americans instead of white segregationists. That working-class black neighborhood in Los Angeles burned for six days in August 1965 after a traffic stop for drunk driving escalated into a riot. Thirty-four people died. Fires gutted more than one thousand buildings. The National Guard was mobilized. Authorities arrested nearly four thousand people. Eight months later, Fleming attended a rally where Carmichael pointed him out to the crowd and accused him of feeding off of black misery. Later, an assailant attacked Fleming from behind, apparently hitting him over the head with a board and kicking him after he fell. Fleming fractured his skull and jaw. "To blacks in the South, I was one of the good guys, someone to trust and shelter," he recalled. "To blacks in Watts, I was just another faceless exploitive whitey, someone to hate, and hurt."[14]

The new journalistic plotline disturbed civil rights activists who had worked closely with white reporters in the South. They sensed a widening gulf between their outlook and the views of previously supportive news outlets. "This new phase," SNCC's Julian Bond recalled, "was characterized by much greater press suspicion of what appeared to be ever more radical black demands for the restructuring of America's economic, political, and social system." Ralph Abernathy, the Alabama minister with the Southern Christian Leadership Conference (SCLC), believed the movement's shift northward challenged notions of moral superiority held by white publishers and journalists. "When you attacked Mississippi, New Yorkers and San Franciscans felt good about themselves," Abernathy said. "When you attacked Chicago, everybody felt uncomfortable. So the press backed off, and when we went back down South, they never quite rejoined us, not with their previous enthusiasm."[15]

"Everybody Has a Point of View"
Black Reporters in White Newsrooms

Black Power militancy compelled white editors to hire more black journalists. As riots exploded in their hometowns, northern editors realized black residents regarded white reporters with suspicion and hostility. These editors slowly began to hire black journalists to help them explain the reasons for black anger and understand the turn toward Black Power. These editors pointed to black journalists working in predominantly white newsrooms as proof of the media's racial tolerance, despite persistent workplace discrimination, while Black Power activists often accused those reporters of betraying racial progress to satisfy the editorial aims of their employers.

Urban uprisings presented both opportunity and dilemma for black journalists seeking work in the white media. Robert C. Maynard, a Nieman Fellow who wrote for the *Washington Post*, credited the rebellions with spurring some white editors to move beyond token racial hiring. Others finally opened their newsrooms to one or two black journalists. In particular, Maynard cited the Watts riot as a moment of transition because attacks on white journalists forced them to retreat from scenes of violence and looting in black neighborhoods. Since the *Los Angeles Times* had no black reporters on its staff, for example, editors could not obtain an eyewitness account of rioting. Forced by necessity, editors asked 24-year-old office messenger Robert Richardson to phone in reports from the riot's frontlines. An editor's note accompanied his story, touting the authenticity of Richardson's first front-page report by identifying him as "a Negro" who had observed rioters for nearly eight hours. Maynard noted that such coverage—repeated in many other cities—was inherently flawed. Editors would ask a copy aide, librarian's assistant, or circulation truck driver to blend in with the crowd and report what they saw "so that others could write a story they had not in most instances witnessed and whose causes they could only dimly perceive." The following year, the *Times* hired its first black reporter. Other major metropolitan papers did so as well. White editors expected black journalists to report almost exclusively on riots and other racial issues. Ted Poston joked with the handful of other black reporters working for New York's dailies in the late 1960s that they covered the "RUINS beat," an acronym for "Riots, Urban affairs, Indians, and Niggers."[16]

President Lyndon Johnson formed the Kerner Commission in 1967 to figure out why racial uprisings had occurred in inner-city neighborhoods and how to prevent future destruction. The following year, the commission, chaired by Illinois Governor Otto Kerner, concluded that America was "moving toward two societies, one black, one white—separate and unequal." Its members attributed the riots to pervasive discrimination and segregation, which resulted in crushing poverty and negligible opportunities for improved social standing. They held white Americans directly responsible for sustaining an oppressive environment that incited disorder: "White institutions created it, white institutions maintain it, and white society condones it." While the media "made a real effort to give a balanced, factual account" of the riots, the commission found that coverage did not accurately represent the "scale and character" of the violence. More significantly, journalists also failed to "report adequately on the causes and consequences of civil disorders and the underlying problems of race relations." The commission proposed several recommendations to eliminate the media's racial bias: Assign permanent reporters to cover urban and racial matters. Integrate African Americans into all aspects of news content. Recruit and promote black journalists. Coordinate more effectively with police to improve riot coverage. Adopt "stringent internal staff guidelines" for reporting on race and riots. Establish a private Institute of Urban Communications to train journalists, support research, improve press-police relations, and study news coverage. "Along with the country as a whole," the commission wrote, "the press has too long basked in a white world, looking out of it, if at all, with white men's eyes and a white perspective. That is no longer good enough."[17]

Most editors considered the call for a substantive overhaul of race coverage unwarranted. They acknowledged the need to make changes but believed their industry generally provided adequate coverage of African Americans. Critics who claimed otherwise, executives contended, were probably too invested in maintaining or dismantling segregation to be objective. Ongoing reforms, they claimed, were already correcting most of the commission's criticisms. Journalists had drafted guidelines for covering racial issues and riots three years earlier during a conference at the University of Missouri. Journalism schools and professional development seminars trained reporters in urban communications. Nearly fifteen years of protests, followed by several years of riots, had led many newspapers to expand their coverage of race news. Many editors worried public sentiment to reform quickly would undermine, rather than improve, news coverage. "A metropolitan newspaper does not change in character every time a new social or political issue rises to the surface of public consciousness," said *Chicago Sun-Times* Editor Emmett Dedmon. "What a good newspaper does, rather, is to continue to function in its role as a newspaper and do the best possible job it can of informing the people." At the *New York Times*, Managing Editor Clifton Daniels worried he assigned too many column inches of newsprint to African Americans. "The problem," he said, "is to give appropriate attention to Negro activities without violating our well-established standards of news judgment—in other words, not to be condescending and give Negro news prominence simply because it relates to Negroes." For many editors, the government's report was essentially nonnews. Sterling Noel, executive editor of the *Baltimore News American*, spoke more bluntly than most, but his strong words seemed to capture his peers' general outlook. "The concern of the Kerner Commission in this area is understandable," Noel said, "but obviously grows out of ignorance of media attitudes and aims."[18]

No one, though, argued that daily newspapers offered fair employment opportunities to black journalists. Instead, they made excuses. The Kerner Commission estimated fewer than 5 percent of newsroom editorial workers were black, and less than 1 percent were editors and supervisors. (African Americans made up about 11 percent of the United States' population in 1970.) White editors countered criticisms that hiring disparities proved institutionalized racism by explaining their struggles to recruit and retain black journalists who fulfilled their professional standards. Cy King, executive editor of the *Buffalo Courier-Express*, asked seventeen journalism schools for employee recommendations but received no hiring leads. "We do not have Negro staff members," King said, "only because they are not available." Such explanations emphasized that too many African Americans simply favored more lucrative career opportunities. Even communications majors preferred to work in the better-paying fields of advertising and public relations. With too few journalism graduates to fill openings, many metropolitan newspapers established high school and college internship programs to increase the pool of potential candidates. Others contacted historically black universities and black community leaders for referrals and advertised openings in black newspapers. Some claimed to lower their hiring standards and extend probationary periods to assist underqualified applicants.[19]

Such uncoordinated and inconsistent recruitment efforts reflected white editors' unwillingness to truly hold themselves responsible for a prolonged and unbroken history of discrimination and racism. Norman Isaacs, the editor of the *Louisville Courier-Journal* and a promoter of newsroom integration, was one of the few executives to admit he had unwittingly held black job candidates to a higher standard. "Yet while I took many a long shot on white reporters, deskmen and photographers," he recalled, "I somehow always thought it necessary to exercise the greatest of care when it came to hiring minority staffers." The Kerner Commission dismissed the editors' excuses. "But this rings hollow," the report stated, "from an industry where, only yesterday, jobs were scarce and promotion unthinkable for a man whose skin was black." The commission urged white editors to forgo traditional recruitment methods and make "a commitment to seek out young Negro men and women, inspire them to become—and then train them as—journalists." No such coordinated effort emerged due to lack of interest. The American Society of Newspaper Editors (ASNE), for example, waited until three years after the commission released its report to form a committee, led by Isaacs, to study minority employment. Two years later, the group disbanded it. Isaacs achieved no meaningful inroads. "Although whites who bring blacks into formerly all-white workplaces talk a lot about integration," said Roger Wilkins, the nephew of the NAACP's Roy Wilkins and an editorial writer for the *Washington Post*, "they seem at bottom to want the *appearance* of change without its substance."[20]

Editors' responses to the Kerner Commission revealed the unwelcoming, distrustful professional atmosphere encountered by black journalists working at daily newspapers, which prompted them to intensify their demands for workplace equality. Coworkers and supervisors doubted black reporters' qualifications and rejected their assertions that story angles or coverage decisions failed to adequately represent the black community's perspective. White executives and black reporters routinely accused one another of failing to present the news objectively. Too often, contended Fred Friendly, a renowned CBS News executive and Columbia University professor, black journalists' reports on racial issues devolved into "cheerleading and evangelicalism." Austin Scott, a black reporter for the Associated Press in New York, claimed white executives held such opinions because "they did not know enough about black communities to find what was going on in the streets of America believable." Scott's editors regularly rewrote his reports from uprisings in Harlem, Rochester, and elsewhere because they distrusted what he told them. "I soon learned there was no such thing as objective reporting," Scott later said. "Everybody has a point of view. If someone tells you that you're objective, they are probably saying that you have met their biases in terms of what you are reporting." To counter white editors' prejudices, Scott focused his riot reporting on "what black people were feeling," rather than talk to police captains or politicians. "Nobody was going to cover the streets," he said, "if I didn't do it." Such feuds with white editors over the framing of news stories betrayed the limits of token integration. William Raspberry, a *Washington Post* columnist, said black reporters' initial gratitude for being hired by daily newspapers evaporated as they realized the racial assumptions and professional restrictions imposed upon them by white supervisors. Many reporters had hoped their employment "represented an opportunity for black influence on what is communicated, to whom, and how." That influence, though, was limited without black leadership. "What has now become clear," Raspberry wrote, "is that when it is white editors who make the assignments, and white editors who judge the results of those assignments, it almost does not matter what color the reporters happen to be."[21]

Raspberry successfully negotiated the pairing of white journalism conventions with black perspective by writing about African Americans and their concerns in columns that explained racial problems and controversies but avoided condemnation and outrage. Guided by a philosophy of "naive optimism," he tended to let his interviewees outline his perspective, leading readers toward his personal conclusions but seldom explicitly stating them. Raspberry had worked during college at the *Indianapolis Reporter*, a black weekly, and then served as a military public information officer. He joined the *Post* in 1962 as a teletypist, was made a reporter soon after the Watts riot, and in 1966 began writing a local affairs column called "Potomac Watch." "I don't see myself as a crusader," he said three years later. "What the column can do is provide graphic illustrations of the nature of the problem, and people brighter than I can figure out the solutions." Raspberry emphasized the need for practical, small-measure reforms that alleviated everyday racial discrimination and promised increased economic opportunity. In regular column topics, he supported fair housing practices and job training programs, defended the rights and character of welfare recipients, and described how crime and addiction to drugs and alcohol undermined the stability of black communities. He criticized police departments for using excessive force and discriminating against black officers. He challenged the expansion of police powers. He tracked how President Richard M. Nixon wooed racist voters. Raspberry wrote from the perspective of the black middle class, urging politeness in dialogue and respect for others. He advocated moderation at the peak moment of the Black Power Movement's popularity, expecting to be called an "Uncle Tom" or a "sellout." "Beyond that," Raspberry wrote, "it has reached the point that any Negro who starts to make it in the system is not proof that the system is negotiable by blacks but merely proof that the Negro, when successful, is to that degree no longer black."[22]

The white media's long history of racism ensured that black reporters writing for daily newspapers encountered skepticism and outrage from African Americans who had learned through experience to distrust the white press. Many activists expected sympathetic coverage from black journalists, even though those reporters were beholden to the doctrine of objectivity and the revisions of white editors. Civil rights leaders bristled when they were publicly criticized—or at least perceived themselves to be rebuked. The Reverend Jesse Jackson, president of Operation PUSH, repeatedly clashed with journalists in Chicago who covered his feud with the SCLC's Abernathy and the operations of the social justice organization he led. Jackson's supporters allegedly threatened to physically assault offending reporters. They picketed the home of one reporter. They made phone calls to supervising editors and publishers. Vernon Jarrett, who became the *Chicago Tribune*'s first black columnist in 1970, said Jackson, whom he accused of building a "Messiah Machine," unfairly tainted the credibility of black reporters by tying them to their employers' discrimination. "I vowed many years ago," Jarrett wrote, "that as a journalist my first obligation is to the masses rather than to their messiahs."[23]

Black Power activists, in particular, stood ready to denounce black reporters in the white press as "ghetto sniffers" who traded upon their skin color to gain favor with white employers. A headline in the *Black Panther* referred to Raspberry as "A Tool in the Hands of the Oppressors" after he criticized the group's tactics. "This lackey is an enemy of the people," the article concluded, "and should be dealt with accordingly. LET IT BE DONE." Similarly, Paul Delaney of the *New York Times* was accused of writing "the most scurrilous, vicious and completely truth-less and unethical article I have seen or read" by Charles Moreland, editor of *Muhammad Speaks*. Delaney, who had once worked for the *Atlanta Daily World*, wrote a handful of articles about the Nation of Islam in 1972 and 1973. He covered dissidents' criticisms of Elijah Muhammad's leadership and spending habits, law enforcement officials' concerns about escalating violence among Black Muslims, and allegations that the Nation of Islam sanctioned the slaying of seven members of a rival Muslim group in Washington, D.C. Delaney culminated his reporting with a critical examination of the sect's future viability given its shaky finances, lack of managerial expertise, Muhammad's age, a relaxing of its moral philosophy, and some members' involvement in extortion, robbery, and murder. The Nation of Islam initially scheduled a press conference to rebut the article but then canceled it, claiming it "would only serve to dignify the cheap remarks of The *Times* and Mr. Paul Delaney."[24]

Even a writer with William Worthy's reputation for racial protest and progressive politics drew scrutiny and criticism from black readers. Worthy argued in *Esquire* in 1967 that White America's conception of the Black Power Movement was too narrowly focused on urban inner cities. "But Negroes increasingly see Black Power as not confined to ghetto rebellions," he wrote, "but rather as a part of a general fight of the oppressed against the oppressor all over the world." Worthy explained how the militancy of Stokely Carmichael and Floyd McKissick, of the Congress of Racial Equality (CORE), was inspired by the communist revolutionary ideologies of North Vietnam's Ho Chi Minh and Cuba's Fidel Castro. He examined how the suspected involvement of the CIA in the murder of deposed Congo premier Patrice Lumumba and rumors concerning the government's role in Malcolm X's assassination "made Negroes aware of the global character of the fight against black men." He warned that Black Power advocates—informed by revolutionaries abroad and harassed by state authorities at home—might "move into the underground stage of activity with outside forces challenging U.S. power."[25]

Militants and moderates alike accused Worthy of betraying his race. Militants claimed he had exposed their secrets to a white audience—even though most of what he reported was readily verified by browsing alternative black publications. Moderates accused him of playing to racial stereotypes and needlessly heightening white anxiety by attributing legitimacy to the spokesmen of Black Power—even though his reporting conveyed greater nuance and understanding than coverage by white journalists. Both militants and moderates berated Worthy for sensationalized headlines and promotions written by white copyeditors. Worthy, though, maintained his belief that the journalist's role was to inform the entire public, not just segments of it. He rebuked white editors for distorting his work but rejected black demands that he alter his reporting for a white audience. "It is an unworkable and undesirable concept of halfway censorship-by-boycott," he said, "to which no self-respecting reporter can subscribe."[26]

C. Sumner "Chuck" Stone was one of the few black reporters writing for daily newspapers who could match Worthy's radical credentials as well as his demands for editorial independence. Like Worthy, he refused to temper his racial perspective to win over a white readership. Billed as "the angry young man of the Negro Press," Stone wrote for the *New York Age* and the *Washington Afro-American* before joining the *Chicago Daily Defender* in 1963 as its editor-in-chief. He provoked controversy by frequently criticizing establishmentarian leaders, regardless of their race. Stone was fired two years later amid long-running criticism of Mayor Richard J. Daley and the mayor's enduring support for a public schools superintendent who maintained racial segregation. Stone then worked as a legislative aide for Rep. Adam Clayton Powell, an iconic politician who represented Harlem in Congress, and helped organize the National Conference on Black Power, a four-day event held in July 1967 in Newark, New Jersey, that attracted more than one thousand participants. In 1969, Stone accused *Washington Post* publisher Katherine Graham and her editors of playing "the role of the white plantation master, alone deciding what its editorial satrapy construed to be best for D.C. blacks, singularly deciding whom it should anoint as the 'Negro leaders,' how fast the black community should and could achieve liberation, who its allies should be and what strategies the black community should adopt." (The *Post* cut Stone's criticisms of Raspberry, whom he called "a reprehensible Uncle Tom, an inelegant apologist and a depressingly mediocre writer, he is that Black surrogate of white racism with whom the Black community must and will have its day of reckoning.") The tabloid-sized *Philadelphia Daily News*, which billed itself "the People Paper," hired Stone in 1972, telling readers, "Maybe you won't always agree with him. But you'll never find him dull."[27]

Stone strove to transform white readers' narrow understanding of racial issues by introducing them to a robust defense of Black Power ideology. In his first column, titled "My Black Perspective," Stone explained that his—and other African Africans'—one-dimensional belief in integration had crumbled in the 1960s as the nation refused to embrace civil rights reform. Afterward, they adopted a "multi-dimensional" perspective that accepted other tactics and goals. "Sociologically, that's healthy," he wrote. "Historically, that's America. Politically, it's mature." Stone often commended black public figures typically denounced by white columnists. Angela Davis, a Marxist scholar and activist cleared of gun charges related to a bloody prisoners' escape attempt from a California courtroom, was "a tough, valiant and brilliant young black woman." Powell, his former employer and a frequent target of ridicule for the personal scandals and legal problems that led to his removal from Congress, was "a black titan fighting for the black masses with the sword of nationhood in one hand and the shield of religion in the other." Stone praised Kwame Nkrumah, independent Ghana's founding prime minister, and his socialist policies for making "a white-oriented world of power-hungry nations recognize that black men could be independent and could achieve statesmanship in foreign policies between nations." He characterized Paul Robeson, whose continued support for communism made him a public pariah, as a "proud black revolutionary" who was "fiercely denouncing racism while most black artists were nursemaiding accommodation." Such commentary irked many readers. Stone received enough mail criticizing his columns that *Daily News* editor Rolfe Neill penned an editorial defending him just two months after he was hired. "To the Stone haters," Neill wrote, "it seems simply not to have occurred that it may be they who tell lies, hate the working class, are racists and lack respect for America. How can they be so sure they're right and he's wrong?" Other readers, though, appreciated a columnist in a white newspaper voicing their concerns and beliefs. Disenfranchised inmates in the State Correctional Institution outside of Wilkes-Barre considered Stone a respected and honest broker, and they asked him in July 1972 to serve as a mediator in their dispute with the prison's administration. Stone's assistance was praised by both parties and illustrated the rise of the activist journalist.[28]

"Black Reporters Must Become Revolutionaries"
Activism in the White Newsroom

Black reporters' workplace activism occurred as part of a larger trend toward newsroom democratization in the 1970s that one press critic described as employees' efforts "to impress their professional beliefs and occupational misgivings upon management." Journalists' activism was informed by the Civil Rights Movement, antiwar protests, campus uprisings, women's equality, and militancy among other minority groups. Their actions contested conservative law-and-order campaigns that defended the status quo in the workplace by equating employer concessions with capitulation to agitators and the erosion of institutional authority. Regardless of race, gender, or sexual orientation, editorial employees demanded more involvement in establishing coverage priorities and making staff assignments and hiring decisions. For black journalists, the ensuing clashes with management defined their efforts to end token employment practices and compel total integration. They pressed their demands by filing lawsuits, lodging complaints, asserting their right to report freely without government interference, and establishing support networks.[29]

Ironically, well-intentioned but ambiguous minority recruitment and hiring practices frequently turned liberal publishers and editors into targets of discrimination lawsuits. At the *New York Post*, editors pursued minority hiring more vigorously after the Kerner Commission released its report. From 1968 to 1970, the *Post* offered tryouts to nine probationary minority reporters and hired two of them. An aging, hard-drinking Ted Poston mentored them and covertly helped one prepare discrimination charges. Poston told William Artis, a 28-year-old graduate of Ohio State University who had worked at the *Buffalo Evening News*, that the *Post* would not hire him because it already employed three black reporters. (The paper briefly had five black reporters on staff but two took jobs elsewhere.) Artis filed a complaint with the New York State Division of Human Rights when he was dismissed after six weeks. He accused the *Post* of capping its minority hires with an unwritten quota. Poston helped Artis obtain supporting statements from other black reporters. The *Post* denied the charge. Publisher Dorothy Schiff said she had brought in Artis and others specifically to expand the paper's roster of black writers. Schiff also observed that the *Post* employed more black reporters percentagewise than either the *New York Times* or *New York Daily News*. A human rights commissioner ordered Artis reinstated on a technicality—he had not served his full three-month tryout. The *Post* gave him another tryout and again dismissed him. The *Post* was ultimately cleared of wrongdoing by the State Supreme Court. Similar disputes played out across the nation.[30]

As Artis battled for his job, Earl Caldwell fought to protect his journalistic integrity at the *New York Times* after the Justice Department subpoenaed his unpublished notes on the Black Panther Party. Caldwell had joined the *Times* in 1967 and quickly proved himself covering that summer's riots. He was the only reporter present at the Lorraine Motel in Memphis in April 1968 when Martin Luther King was assassinated. Later that year, an editor told him to try to contact Eldridge Cleaver, the Black Panthers's minister of information. "When I linked up with the Panthers late in 1968 on the West Coast, they called me a cop," Caldwell recalled. "I had to be a cop, they reasoned: The *New York Times* was not about to send a black reporter 3,000 miles just to cover them." Caldwell provided the *Times*'s readers with angles on the Panthers seldom described elsewhere. Unlike most other reporters, he delved behind the party's rhetoric and posturing to explain why its strident nationalism appealed to young black men. He covered the Panthers's shootouts and trials, but he also wrote about a free breakfast program that fed schoolchildren. He explained a shift in party ideology in 1969 that led members to tone down their heated language, cooperate with white radicals, and embrace Marxism. Caldwell met with Cleaver the morning before the party leader fled the country while on bail for an attempted murder charge. After he wrote about the Panthers transporting guns, agents from the FBI asked for additional details. Caldwell told them that everything he knew had appeared in the newspaper. Then agents asked him to spy for them. Caldwell refused. "I could be physically harmed if I presented myself as a reporter to the Panthers," he said, "and then ran around being some kind of spy for the FBI."[31]

Since Caldwell refused to cooperate, he was subpoenaed and ordered to testify before a grand jury—an unprecedented expansion of subpoena powers against the press that posed particular concerns to black journalists. Caldwell's subpoena was part of a comprehensive campaign against media independence orchestrated by the Nixon administration. The Justice Department issued many subpoenas in early 1970 against reporters who had interviewed Black Panthers and antiwar protesters. Several leading news organizations complied with the court orders, but others challenged them. Caldwell decided to fight his subpoena, which was issued against him, not the *Times*. Before he was subpoenaed, Caldwell destroyed two years' worth of notes, tapes, and documents, ruining his plans to write a book. Then he refused to testify, claiming his reputation as a trustworthy journalist would be destroyed if he answered questions in a secret legal proceeding. A lower court judge granted Caldwell a partial victory. The judge ruled Caldwell had to testify before a grand jury like every other citizen, but he did not have to divulge confidential information. Against the advice of the *Times*'s lawyers, Caldwell still refused to testify. Although the paper's executives were sympathetic, Caldwell said "the *Times* sort of cut me loose at that point."[32]

Other black journalists supported Caldwell, worrying that testifying in secret would destroy their credibility with African American citizens who distrusted a prejudiced justice system. In an advertisement that ran in the *New York Amsterdam News*, about seventy journalists promised to not spy on their communities for the government. They pledged to protect their confidential sources, "using every means at our disposal." They characterized subpoenas like the one issued against Caldwell as "attempts by law enforcement agencies to exploit our blackness." The journalists argued that such subpoenas threatened their ability to do their jobs more than they disrupted white reporters' work. They knew editors were more likely to assign them to cover Black Power groups and other racial news. They also knew they were more likely to ask for such assignments "out of a sense of responsibility to bring about a greater understanding and clarity of the dynamics and nuances of the black revolution." Since they lived and worked in black communities, the journalists could not afford to appear compromised, either professionally or personally. "Any appearance of such a 'deal' between the police and black journalists," they argued, "kills the credibility and trust black reporters have built up over the years." Black journalists emphasized their commitment to their professional principles by supporting Caldwell's legal defense. Black Perspective, an advocacy group formed by black reporters in 1967, cooperated with the NAACP Legal Defense and Education Fund to provide Caldwell with his own lawyer.[33]

Caldwell ultimately lost his lawsuit—and his unrivaled access to the Black Panthers. An appeals court sided with him, saying he did not have to testify because the government had not shown a strong need for his testimony. But in 1972, the U.S. Supreme Court ruled 5–4 against Caldwell and two other reporters with similar cases. Even so, Caldwell never testified—the grand jury and its subpoena had lapsed. He also never again reported in depth on the Black Panther Party, recalling that "by then, the Panthers that I knew were either in jail, out of the country, or in the graveyard."[34]

Public awareness of black journalists' professional struggles peaked in early 1972 after a series of controversies in Washington, D.C., focused press criticism on the role of minorities in white newsrooms. The first incident involved charges of employment discrimination against *Newsweek*, the most racially progressive of the nation's major newsweeklies. In December 1971, *Newsweek* editor Osborn Elliott fired reporter Samuel F. Yette, a four-year employee who worked in the Washington bureau. Elliott said the dismissal was based "purely on professional grounds." Yette promptly filed a discrimination complaint with the Washington, D.C., Commission on Human Relations. Yette acknowledged long-standing tensions with his employer. (He later said editors sent him to King's funeral, not to cover the ceremony, but to argue against his widow, Coretta Scott King, being named his successor at the Southern Christian Leadership Conference.) Yette attributed his firing to the militancy of his recently published book, *The Choice: The Issue of Black Survival in America*. In the book, Yette argued that the Nixon administration had used the social protests of the 1960s as an excuse to violate constitutional rights and create a police state that targeted black militants for "selective genocide." According to Yette, his bureau chief asked him to tone down his criticisms. "I do not mean to be pejorative or vindictive when I say this," Yette told *Jet*, "but had I been a nigger instead of Black, a spy instead of a reporter, a tool instead of a man, I could have stayed at *Newsweek* indefinitely."[35]

Yette's discrimination complaints prompted the Congressional Black Caucus to hold a two-day hearing in March 1972 on the relationship between the mass media and African Americans. Chaired by Rep. William L. Clay, a Missouri Democrat, the Caucus intended to investigate white editors' "failure to properly interpret the Black movement and the issues affecting the Black community, their unwillingness to adequately increase minority employment on their staffs, and the insidious method of firing a number of highly competent Black journalists." About two dozen witnesses testified, including black journalists who worked for black and white newspapers and magazines, as well as television. Clay concluded that African Americans in general and black journalists in particular were "grossly excluded, distorted, mishandled and exploited by the white-controlled news media." The Caucus urged Nixon to appoint black representatives to the Federal Communications Commission (FCC), asked media companies to promote African Americans into management, and encouraged watchdog groups to monitor media fairness and file lawsuits against discriminatory news outlets. Later that year, Nixon appointed the first African American—Benjamin Hooks, a Memphis lawyer and Baptist minister—to a five-year term on the FCC.[36]

Then in April, seven black reporters on the metro desk at the *Washington Post* filed discrimination charges with the U.S. Equal Employment Opportunity Commission (EEOC). It was the first complaint lodged by a group of black journalists with the federal agency. The reporters alleged they were denied "an equal opportunity with respect to job assignments, promotional opportunities, including promotions to management positions and other terms and conditions of employment." The *Post*'s parent company also owned *Newsweek*. The paper's lawyer defended the *Post* by pointing to its affirmative action program and noting that it employed twenty-one black reporters, editors, and photographers—more than any other white-owned newspaper. None of those journalists, though, covered foreign or national news, and none were included in top editorial management.[37]

Discrimination complaints, lawsuits, and the congressional hearing reflected a growing recognition by many black reporters that they could counter media bias, which was disguised by the supposed racial blindness of journalistic objectivity, only by pairing factual reporting with an overriding commitment to racial justice. While offensive to most newspaper editors, so-called "activist journalism" was informed by the popularity of New Journalism, a style of reportage embraced by leading magazines that infused traditional reporting with literary techniques to convey the counterculture's skepticism of institutional authority. Activist journalists were also empowered by the protest mission of the black press and the editorial acuity of the leftist alternative press. "For too long black people have been subjected to exhortations of whites who in the name of 'objectivity' have imposed their subjective views on the world about us," said Tony Brown, director of Howard University's newly opened School of Communications. "There is another witness with important evidence—the black man with a black viewpoint."[38]

Supporters of activist journalism advocated reporting that acknowledged racial identity as a central determinant in the framing of news articles. Its practitioners believed that white editors would not admit their biases without counter-reporting written from a black perspective. They claimed black journalists needed a firm awareness of their racial identity to prevent their work from being used to reinforce stereotypes or harass activists. They also said a strong sense of self helped sustain them through the hardships of challenging white supervisors. Lutrelle Palmer, a *Chicago Daily News* columnist and radio commentator who once worked for the *Chicago Defender*, warned Howard's student journalists that "if I had not established in my present job that I was a black man first and a newspaperman second, I would've gone crazy. I would have lost my sense of identity." While radical black writers had articulated political alternatives to the inherent racism of the capitalistic American nation-state, activist journalists demanded social equality within existing institutions—namely the white media. Activist journalists encouraged African Americans to pursue careers in the white media in hopes of increasing the news industry's racial awareness and sensitivity. "Black reporters must become revolutionaries—agents of changes rather than agents; part of the solution," said Charlayne Hunter, the onetime *Atlanta Inquirer* reporter who had joined the *New York Times*. "And it can be done, while maintaining a sense of fairness—some prefer objectivity—and ethical correctness, as well."[39]

Black journalists who challenged white editors' claims to objectivity often found their voices marginalized within their newsrooms. Reporter Austin Scott resigned from the Associated Press in early 1972 after working there for eleven years. While grateful for the "exceptional treatment" he received, Scott told general manager Wes Gallagher that he quit because the wire service refused to extend the courtesies he received to its eighteen other black reporters. Scott considered himself a token on the editorial staff, his mere presence justifying editors' decisions to ignore his requests to reorient the framing of racial news, hire more black reporters, and promote them to prominent beats and supervisory positions. Scott figured his resignation would "help stop the pretense that we have done what we should, or help us to move faster." Scott joined the *Washington Post* just as the EEOC complaint was filed there. Similarly, Palmer resigned from the *Daily News* in January 1973, telling his employer "the white establishment press and the honest views of a black journalist are totally incompatible." Palmer had feuded frequently over editing in his stories. He quit after managing editor Don Gormley spiked a column demanding community control measures to ensure police officers were held accountable for shootings. Gormley reportedly told Palmer that his views went beyond what his mostly white readership could accept. Four months later, Palmer launched the *Black X-Press*, a weekly newspaper "planned and geared to elevate information, awareness, interest and involvement levels of Black people."[40]

Black consumers bolstered activist journalists' mission by pressuring news organizations, particularly television broadcasters, to commit themselves to fairer representation of African Americans in media employment and news coverage. A coalition of Harlem churches and political organizations formed Black Citizens for a Fair Media soon after the Congressional Black Caucus hearing. The coalition's leaders promised to negotiate with television news executives for improvements but warned they would challenge FCC license renewals and launch boycotts and pickets if their demands were ignored. "When they're going to be up in the offices negotiating in their way," said 17-year-old Al Sharpton, "we'll be down on the street or in the lobby negotiating our way." Watchdog groups also pressured local stations to increase minority involvement in Kansas City, Houston, Cincinnati, Philadelphia, San Francisco, and elsewhere. FCC commissioners met privately with more than twenty citizens groups the following year, marking the first time the agency listened to black consumers' demands. In early 1973, consumer activism helped save *Black Journal*, a groundbreaking public affairs program that provided a forum for black viewpoints on public television. The Corporation for Public Broadcasting (CPB) intended to eliminate the program but instead cut its budget from $900,000 to $350,000. More than one hundred protesters picketed outside the CPB meeting held on budget matters. "The picketing culminated it," said executive producer Tony Brown. "This proves that cohesiveness among Black people is our salvation." *Black Journal*, though, faced repeated threats to its survival.[41]

Activist journalists and consumers continued to value black newspapers and magazines because those publications reaffirmed and promoted their critique of the white mass media. Thomas A. Johnson, a *New York Times* foreign correspondent, argued that black journalists in white newsrooms benefited from "the strongest possible black media." Its presence spoke to the diverse perspectives and needs of African Americans. Its independence allowed its editors and reporters to expose the biases of white objectivity and provided a sympathetic forum where black journalists could fully air their concerns about discrimination in white newsrooms. While both commercial black newspapers and alternative black publications declined in influence and reach in the 1970s, each continued to publish, despite persistent predictions of their imminent demise. *Ebony* and *Jet* enjoyed unprecedented popularity. A slew of new niche magazines—*Black Enterprise*, *Essence*, and *Black Sports*, among others—revealed a vast demand for a variety of news written from a black perspective. "Black America's media needs go far beyond the now and again special of *Newsweek*, *CBS*, or the *New York Times*, good though they generally are," Johnson wrote. "This is an abiding and permanent need and it will also require a media of abiding and permanent interest."[42]

By the mid-1970s, black journalists feared white editors' commitment to integration had irrevocably waned, compelling them to cooperate more closely to win workplace equality. As early as 1972, *Washington Post* staffer Dorothy Gilliam had observed that "the bloom is off when it comes to hiring and promoting nonwhite reporters." With the threat of riots fading and the presence of black reporters seeming to prove inclusion, Roger Wilkins argued that white editors were overtaken by "a new generation of racial attitudes and fantasies." The white press had ignored African Americans before the protests, legislation, and violence of the 1960s, viewing black concerns as inconsequential to the nation's wellbeing. As the turmoil receded, yet another journalistic narrative emerged to distort the nation's racial problems. White news executives believed, Wilkins wrote, "America has broken the back of its racial problem. That being so, there is little more to do and the insights of blacks are unnecessary. The circle is thus closed—from silence to silence."[43]

Black journalists countered by forming a national organization that publicized the white media's institutional racism. They hoped their advocacy would expand career opportunities and promote improved coverage of racial issues. Representatives from journalists' associations in Philadelphia, Chicago, San Francisco, and Washington, D.C., met in December 1975 to organize the National Association of Black Journalists (NABJ). They struggled to unite. Professional divisions sparked disputes. Big-city reporters questioned the credentials of small-town journalists. Writers in the black press wondered if their concerns would be ignored. Some members debated who qualified for membership. Others worried the organization would devolve into a social club where journalists networked but accomplished no significant change in their industry. Guided by the vision of Chuck Stone, NABJ's first president, the group quickly established a twofold purpose—to improve the white media's coverage of race and racism and to provide professional development opportunities for aspiring young journalists and veteran reporters seeking promotion. NABJ also extended the reach of activist journalism when its officers spoke directly on controversial issues. During its first national convention, one month before the 1976 presidential election, the group released a press statement criticizing Republican President Gerald Ford and Democratic challenger Jimmy Carter for "assiduously bypassing black voters." NABJ also chastised Carter for declining to speak to its members during its convention in Houston and then scheduling to meet privately with handpicked black journalists in Maryland. "NABJ does not pretend to speak for all black journalists," the statement read. "But we do reflect the concerns of all black people who would like to believe that candidates who say they care for them, really do!"[44]

· · ·

Newsroom integration recast the history of black journalism, shifting the locus of black journalists' writing and activism from black newspapers into the white media. In the early 1960s, press critics wondered if national black news-papers could regain the peak circulations they had reached after World War II. By the 1970s, they asked how long those newspapers could survive in an era of integration. The splintering of black print culture over Black Power politics had further sapped the profitability of commercial newspapers and eroded their capacity to adequately report on far-flung protests and controversial politics. As more white editors cautiously hired black reporters, black publishers griped about being reduced to training schools for white newspapers. Many black reporters, they contended, hoped to leave quickly for better pay and better career opportunities at daily papers.

While black reporters had secured a tenuous toehold in white newsrooms as the 1980s approached, an uncertain future awaited them in their chosen profes-sion. Ten years after the Kerner Commission's report, a survey by the American Society of Newspaper Editors (ASNE) estimated that minority journalists made up just 4 percent of the editorial workforce at daily newspapers. Black journalists accounted for about half of those 1,700 journalists, or 2 percent of all editorial employees. Only four African Americans held top management positions—in Philadelphia, Akron, Portland, and Niagara Falls. About 68 percent of daily newspapers still employed no minority journalists, compared to 80 percent in 1968. At the time, minorities made up 17 percent of the nation's popula-tion. White editors rehashed old arguments to defend their poor hiring records: Qualified minority applicants were hard to find. Integration smacked of social engineering and progressive politics. Minority journalists could not remain objective when covering racial issues. The ASNE's Committee on Minorities challenged editors' stale excuses when it concluded "the newspapers that have the best minority employment record are those papers that have tried the hard-est—have set an objective and then done their utmost to reach it." The *Washington*

Post, for example, significantly improved minority representation in its newsroom after the EEOC complaint filed in 1972. The *Post* more than doubled its number of minority editorial employees, raising the total to thirty-five, and it promoted four to editorships.[45]

Many black journalists, though, continued to press for workplace rights through the courts. Black and women journalists filed a discrimination lawsuit at the Associated Press after failing to negotiate an affirmative action hiring plan with management. (AP president and general manager Keith Fuller urged employees to recognize management's need "to preserve the high caliber of our news service by retaining the right to hire and promote the most qualified persons without regard to what could be irrelevant or reverse discriminatory factors.") The *New York Times* experienced similar turmoil. Nineteen black editorial employees joined an affirmative-action lawsuit filed four years earlier by the paper's noneditorial minority employees. "Blacks at the *Times* have a sense of doom," said Paul Delaney, who had risen to assistant national news editor. "There is a feeling that they are not going to get good assignments, they are not going to advance, and that their editors think poorly of them."[46]

Two journalists—a married couple—pressed white editors to embrace meaningful integration. Robert Maynard, an associate editor at the *Washington Post*, and Nancy Hicks, a *New York Times* reporter, resigned their positions in 1977 to found the Institute for Journalism Education (known today as the Maynard Institute for Journalism Education) in Oakland, California. The institute promoted newsroom integration and trained minority journalists. The couple believed integration involved much more than just jobs. "As much as I might be concerned about the effects of segregation and bigotry in the news on blacks," Maynard said during a conference at the University of Michigan, "I am even more concerned about its effects on the whole of our society." Maynard wanted white editors to quit approaching integration from a position of fear—employing black reporters only because they did not know what was happening in black communities and might be scooped by the competition—and hire minority journalists so their news pages could represent the nation in its full complexity.[47]

Maynard and Hicks lobbied the ASNE to establish an industrywide minority hiring goal that would attempt to match the percentage of minority journalists (not just African Americans) working for daily newspapers to the percentage of minorities within the total population by the year 2000. The initiative received strong support from Richard Smyser, the editor of the *Oak Ridger* in Oak Ridge, Tennessee, who chaired the ASNE's Committee on Minorities, and was approved by the organization in 1978. The final agreement, though, provided uninterested editors plenty of opportunities to ignore the affirmative action initiative. It established a goal but did not mandate how individual newspapers should pursue it. No penalties punished those who ignored the measure. Success depended on the good faith of many. Ultimately, the ASNE failed to meet its goal. Minority journalists accounted for just 11 percent of newsroom employees in 1997 when they made up 26 percent of the total population. Despite its eventual failure, the initiative marked a significant symbolic turning point. The daily press had formally committed itself to integration and acknowledged the enduring presence of African Americans in its newsrooms. "Integration of the press is no longer a protest issue," Maynard said, "it's a matter of process." Black journalists had forged the inroads required to broaden future minority involvement in American journalism. Never again could white publishers and editors completely ignore black communities and refuse to hire any black reporters. Despite the obstacles of institutionalized racism, issues of interest to African Americans were a regular, if an inconsistent and frequently misconstrued, aspect of news coverage.[48]

White editors' refusal to fully commit to integration established news trends that persisted for several decades. Limited employment and promotion opportunities for black journalists meant African American communities still received inadequate and biased news coverage. "We seem to be in the age of the cross-over reporter," said the *Post*'s Dorothy Gilliam, "where the black reporter is often told to cover stories of the white communities, but the cruel joke is that nobody is still paying attention to the black community." Journalism professor Carolyn Martindale analyzed the content of the *New York Times*, *Chicago Tribune*, *Boston Globe*, and *Atlanta Constitution* from 1972 to 1980 and found that all four newspapers had mostly maintained ongoing coverage of African Americans despite the decline in civil rights protests. Each newspaper also provided more realistic coverage of everyday life. Other elements of news coverage, though, remained problematic. The newspapers too frequently discussed African Americans in stereotypical language, needed to better explain inner city concerns, and often substituted national coverage in place of in-depth local reporting on black communities.[49]

Such voids ensured black media remained relevant in the decades to come. Black newspapers continued to publish, even as their readership shrunk. An increasingly fragmented media marketplace provided opportunities for the development of new black-themed publications, radio and television programs, cable channels, and, eventually, internet websites. These outlets maintained financial viability by thoughtfully exploring black perspectives on domestic and foreign affairs, as well as sports, entertainment, and lifestyles. By working for the black press and the not-so-white media, black journalists pushed for racial justice into the twenty-first century.

Epilogue

A Crusade into the Digital Age

> "I SHALL CRUSADE for all things that are right and just and I
> will, with equal fervor, expose and condemn all things that are
> unjust. I shall be a CRUSADER but will not permit my fervor nor
> the rightness of my cause to provoke the abandonment of the
> cardinals of journalism, accuracy, fairness, and objectivity."

The opening paragraph of the "Credo for the Negro Press," penned in 1945 by
the *Norfolk Journal and Guide*'s P. B. Young Jr., perfectly captured the essential
perspective of black newswriting by joining two seemingly irreconcilable com-
mitments—advancing crusades against racial injustice while maintaining journalistic objectivity. Commercial black journalists accomplished this task by
broadening the professional meaning of objectivity. Their conception of fair
news coverage rejected white society's straitlaced acceptance of a segregated
and discriminatory status quo in favor of reporting that invigorated the United
States' democratic impulse. Black journalists believed they could challenge the
racism ingrained within America's flawed institutions because they intended
to witness the fulfillment of the nation's highest ideals, as expounded in its
founding document, the Declaration of Independence. Thus, dissident journalism accused and condemned but also aspired. It pursued a better tomorrow by
searching for uplifting and expansive alternatives to an exclusionary and racist
political economy that debased African American life.[1]

The progressiveness of commercial black newswriting in the twentieth
century shifted with prevailing political currents, first enlarging and then con-
tracting the parameters of black political discourse, amid constant pressure
from impatient black radicals, suspicious government agents, and reproachful
white journalists. Black newswriting grew increasingly progressive from 1900

to 1945—a period that also witnessed record circulations and the emergence of national newspapers. During these decades, black journalists reported how President Woodrow Wilson's ambition of making the world safe for democracy was greeted in the United States with an eruption of racial violence and rioting. They reported how the Great Depression exposed the uncertainty of promised prosperity, particularly for already impoverished African Americans. They reported how democratic nations reaffirmed their claims to colonial empires in Africa, Asia, and the Middle East and how fascist dictators secured power by demonizing racial and ethnic minority groups. News coverage of one incident of racial abuse after another gradually revealed a mosaic of modern state authority rooted in white supremacy. This seemingly ceaseless cavalcade of racial injustice impelled many commercial black journalists to use the humdrum of routine news reporting and opinion writing to scrutinize the very structure of American society—its cultural sensibilities, economic orientation, and political foundation. They drew inspiration and insight from more radical writers within black print culture—the communists and socialists, Black Nationalists and Pan-Africanists, literary authors and artists who also unmasked the nation's hypocrisy and disputed its legitimacy. Fairly well-defined political distinctions between the alternative and commercial black presses blurred and diminished between the world wars as journalists and other writers advanced this leftward turn.

The commercial black press's pronounced progressiveness, though, imperiled its survival as the actual war against fascism morphed in the late 1940s into an ideological contest against communism. Throughout the first half of the twentieth century, the prospect of American bloodshed on foreign battlefields had guaranteed increased vigilance of black journalists' words by zealous military censors and cautious federal bureaucrats. However, such state scrutiny was tempered by the urgent need to fully and effectively mobilize all of the nation's resources to defeat a warring enemy. Progressive newswriting persisted, thanks, in part, to the black press's patriotic exhortations. Commercial black journalists condemned racism but praised the war effort. That tactic no longer worked in ideological warfare because the act of dissent itself became the enemy. Anticommunists and segregationists claimed hostile words about the United States betrayed the presence of insidious fifth columnists advancing the interests of the Soviet Union. Commercial publishers and journalists pragmatically protected their professional livelihoods by retreating from their more radical suggestions. In essence, black journalists again redefined the meaning of objectivity in the 1950s and 1960s. This time they excluded the discourse of radical black politics. In doing so, they diluted the impact of commercial black newswriting by stimulating the reestablishment of an alternative black press. Black newswriting remained meaningful (regardless of the staggering circulation declines experienced by national newspapers), but the renewed bifurcation of black journalism undermined the legitimacy of black radicalism just as protests across the South fused into the modern Civil Rights Movement. By condemning the Black Power Movement, commercial publishers overwhelmingly sacrificed radicals' loftier aims of full social and economic equality for the more immediate and practical gains of desegregating public places and securing voting rights. The publishers' gravitas, burnished by decades of editorial crusading, amplified the rightfulness of their narrowed perspective, no matter the angry denunciations penned by youthful alternative editors.

Debates about the meaning of objectivity extended into white-led newsrooms in the 1970s as black journalists integrated daily newspapers. White editors expected black reporters to establish contacts in—and provide details about—African American communities. However, they did not intend for those reporters to challenge how management framed stories about race relations, either locally or nationally. But black reporters drew upon experiences and perspectives informed by black print culture and professional training to defy an understanding of objectivity that readily advanced a narrative of racial enlightenment amid entrenched discrimination and inequality. Black reporters saw a societal retreat from earlier civil rights gains where supervisors saw continued racial progress. White editors disputed black reporters' conclusions because they doubted a perspective that was neither voiced by traditional institutional authorities nor recognized by a white readership. These editorial conflicts undermined the sense of mutual trust needed to effectively report the news. Newsroom inclusion failed to achieve full equality, either in terms of employment for black journalists or in coverage of African Americans and their concerns.

The failure of the American mass media to resolutely integrate newsgathering practices in the final decades of the twentieth century led to an intensified scrutiny of racial bias in print and electronic news that continues today. Media studies scholars explain how the societal stigma now associated with overt racism birthed a "modern racism" that cloaked the privileges of whiteness and distorted white understanding of racial issues. Content analyses of news coverage outline the industry's chronic reliance on racial stereotypes, persistent marginalization of minority perspectives, and frequent exaggeration of the nation's success in achieving racial inclusion. Daily newspapers generally provide fairer coverage than television stations because the printed (and digital) page allows reporters to include more context and nuance in their stories. Minority journalists, though, feature more prominently on local television stations. The Federal Communications Commission prohibited hiring discrimination by broadcasters in 1969 and even mandated that television stations' employees reflect the diversity of their communities. Regardless, many African Americans regard mainstream journalism as prejudicial. News coverage of one racially charged incident after another reaffirms their skepticism of the American media. Critical news consumers condemn the media's tendency to criminalize black youths suspected of wrongdoing, seeing consistency over time when they compare the inimical characterizations of the five teenagers wrongfully convicted of raping a white woman in Central Park in 1989 to the negative press depictions of Trayvon Martin, an unarmed black teenager who was fatally shot in Florida in 2012. They criticize journalistic assertions of black wantonness amid destruction when they examine news coverage about the riots that erupted in Los Angeles in 1992 after the acquittal of the four police officers who beat unarmed motorist Rodney King and the hardships endured by survivors after Hurricane Katrina flooded New Orleans in 2005.[2]

Media critics contend racial bias persists, regardless of the presence of black journalists who provide mainstream news organizations with the "illusion of inclusion," because African Americans remain underrepresented as reporters and editors and are pressured to accept institutional norms that uphold a doctrine of objectivity defined in the age of segregation. One study suggests substantive improvement in how particular minority communities are covered will not occur until each newspaper hires a "critical mass of minority journalists." Individual black journalists can improve their publications' coverage of race through the stories they write themselves, but the presence of their bylines seldom reorient how a white-dominated newsroom frames racial events. Unfortunately, the collapse of newspaper circulations and advertising revenue, which was brought on by the rise of digital media and accelerated after the financial crisis of 2008, has significantly shrunk employment opportunities. The American Society of News Editors estimated newspaper newsrooms employed about 33,000 workers in 2014—a loss of 20,000 jobs over two decades. African Americans accounted for just 5.7 percent of newsroom employees at a time when they made up 13 percent of the United States' population. Two years later, only nine African Americans worked as top editors at daily newspapers. Writer and journalist Joshunda Sanders concludes that mainstream media organizations will continue to shed profits and jobs as long as they "resist telling new narratives about significant social, gender, racial, and economic shifts in America."[3]

Inadequate and flawed coverage of minority concerns elsewhere ensures the continued presence of an expansive black media in the early-twenty-first century, but corporate consolidation and digital transformation mean profitability remains elusive for print publications. The National Newspaper Publishers Association (NNPA), a trade group for the black press, estimates that more than twenty million readers each week browse at least one of more than two hundred black newspapers. Venerable papers, including those that once circulated nationally, have weathered a half-century's worth of skepticism about their future viability. They survive because their journalists continue to provide historical context, community access, and political perspective often lacking elsewhere. Even so, black newspapers struggle to negotiate the same unforgiving economic trends and digital competition from the internet and social media that have so diminished newspapers and magazines with larger readerships and more secure finances. Johnson Publishing, for example, transitioned *Jet* magazine to an online-only publication in 2014 and then sold both *Ebony* and *Jet* in 2016 to a Texas-based private equity firm. Newspaper circulations continue to fall, excepting occasional spikes here and there, and online advertising revenue has failed to offset the loss of more lucrative print advertising. According to audited circulation figures, the *Afro-American* sold about 10,300 copies each week in Baltimore and Washington, D.C., in 2015, while the *Amsterdam News* sold about 8,300 copies across New York. The *Chicago Defender* sold about 4,500 copies. Sengstacke Enterprises sold the *Defender* in 2003. Real Times Media, a Detroit-based multimedia company, owns the *Defender* and also publishes the *Atlanta Daily World*, *Michigan Chronicle*, *New Pittsburgh Courier*, and *Tri-State Defender*.[4]

Even though digital media jeopardizes the long-term viability of legacy print publications, it has also made diverse African American perspectives more readily available to the reading public. Journalists now share their role as the gatekeeper of news with social media users. Technology has removed the barriers to publication, allowing anyone with access to a public computer connected to the internet to post tweets, update blogs, and criticize unfolding news coverage. Anyone with a smartphone can broadcast live video and generate coverage of otherwise unnoticed events. According to the Pew Research Center, African Americans are twice as likely to read posts about racial issues on social media, particularly on Twitter, as white users. In 1942, the "Double V" slogan blossomed into a mass movement only after the *Pittsburgh Courier* published the letter written by cafeteria worker James G. Thompson, quietly gauged reader interest, and then built a publicity campaign around Thompson's message. In contrast, today's Black Lives Matter movement emerged as activists savvy with social media protested the indifference of mainstream news organizations and criminal justice institutions to police shootings of young black men. As activists networked with one another, protests around the nation coalesced into a coherent movement. Mass media responded by covering, rather than shaping, the burgeoning movement.[5]

Hashtag activism, though, does not eliminate the need for crusading black journalism in digital spaces. While digital media is new, the opportunities and obstacles it poses to black print culture are familiar. Black news consumers' posts about race tend to peak after major events, such as the protests that erupted in April 2015 in Baltimore when Freddie Gray died while in police custody or the mass shooting in June 2015 at Emanuel African Methodist Episcopal Church in Charleston, South Carolina. Digital-based writers, journalists, scholars, and activists provide the information, context, and analysis that inform social media reaction. Their expertise shapes public commentary. Unlimited digital space provides for tremendous diversity in views and content. Readers can print editorials from the *Los Angeles Sentinel*, watch the weekly "Left of Black" webcasts hosted by Duke University professor Mark Anthony Neal, and follow the Twitter feed of feminist scholar and writer Brittney Cooper of Rutgers University. They can save magazine articles by Ta-Nehisi Coates of *The Atlantic*, receive weekly emails summarizing leftist commentary from Black Agenda Report, and track racial justice issues at Colorlines, a news site produced by Race Forward, which seeks to develop solutions and leaders that promote racial equity. The economic collapse of journalism, though, leaves many writers writing for free or minimal pay and with little job security. Without advertising or sponsorship, many bloggers must post continuously to prevent readers from leaving for a new website or Twitter feed or Facebook page. Longevity is the exception. And yet, similar challenges failed to unnerve Ida B. Wells or John Mitchell Jr., Hubert Harrison or Robert Abbott, Percival Prattis or Charlotta Bass, Marvel Cooke or Langston Hughes, James Hicks or Ethel Payne, Charlayne Hunter-Gault or Chuck Stone. Black journalists' fight for racial justice marches on.[6]

Notes

Introduction

1. Baker and Cooke, "Bronx Slave Market," 330. Also see Gore, *Radicalism at the Crossroads*, 106–112; Harris, "Marvel Cooke," 91–126; and Streitmatter, *Raising Her Voice*, 84–94.

2. Cooke, *Interviews with Marvel Cooke*, interview by Kathleen Currie, Women in Journalism Oral History Project, October 31, 1989, 79, 83.

3. Muhammad, "Interview with Payne," 7. Also see Streitmatter, *Raising Her Voice*, 118–128.

4. Payne, "Spectrum" transcript, CBS Radio Network, October 24, 1972, box 43, folder 9, *Payne Papers*, Library of Congress, Washington, D.C.

5. La Brie, "The Black Press: An Outlet for Black Poets and Black Fiction Writers?" in *Perspectives of the Black Press*, 53–65. Regarding the study of print culture, see Darnton, "What Is the History of Books?" 65–83; and Wiegand, "Introduction: Theoretical Foundations for Analyzing Print Culture as Agency and Practice in a Diverse Modern America," in Danky and Wiegand, *Print Culture in a Diverse America*, 1–16.

6. Wilkins, "Negro Press," 362. Regarding *Freedom's Journal*, see James, *Struggles of John Brown Russwurm*.

7. "Appreciating the Newspaper," *Pittsburgh Courier*, April 12, 1930.

8. "Editorial Policy," *Black Panther*, September 27, 1970; and "Owing to the High Cost of Manhood," October 18, 1917, box 5, folder 50, *Harrison Papers*, Columbia University.

9. Regarding the federal government's efforts to censor black newspapers in wartime, see Finkle, *Forum of Protest*; Jordan, *Black Newspapers and America's War for Democracy*; Kornweibel, *Investigate Everything*; and Washburn, *Question of Sedition*.

10. Dabney, "Nearer and Nearer the Precipice," 94; Hanchard, "Afro-Modernity," 247; and Sancton, "Negro Press," 558. Gonzalez and Torres contend "newspapers, radio, and television played a pivotal role in perpetuating racist views among the general population" in *News for All the People*, 2.

11. Harrison, "Two Negro Radicalisms," in *Harrison Reader*, 102–105; and Singh, *Black Is a Country*, 69.

12. My characterization of commercial publishers as "establishmentarian dissidents" was inspired by the discussion of political protest in Vladimir Putin's Russia in Dobson, *Dictator's Learning Curve*.

13. Washburn, "Dozen Best," supports my description of the historiography of the black press. Biographies frequently referenced in this book include Buni, *Robert L. Vann*; Farrar, *Baltimore Afro-American*; Hogan, *Black National News Service*; Perry, *Hubert Harrison*; and Suggs, *P.B. Young*. For the wartime interaction of the black press and federal government, see Finkle, *Forum of Protest*; Jordan, *Black Newspapers and America's War for Democracy*; Kornweibel, *Investigate Everything*; and Washburn, *Question of Sedition*. Notable reference works include Pride and Wilson, *History of the Black Press*; Suggs, *Black Press in the South* and *Black Press in the Middle West*; Wolseley, *Black Press, U.S.A.*; and Washburn, *African American Newspaper*.

14. See Singh, *Black Is a Country*; Mullen, *Popular Fronts*; Plummer, *Rising Wind*; and Von Eschen, *Race against Empire*.

Chapter 1. "Negro Subversion"

1. See, generally, Jordan, *Black Newspapers and America's War for Democracy*; and Kornweibel, *Investigate Everything*.

2. Col. M. Churchill to Chief of Staff, War Department, July 2, 1918, *Federal Surveillance of Afro-Americans*, microfilm, reel 19, 732; and Jordan, *Black Newspapers and America's War for Democracy*, 122–133.

3. Maj. J. E. Spingarn to Churchill, June 22, 1918, and Churchill to Chief of Staff, July 2, 1918, *Federal Surveillance of Afro-Americans*, reel 19, 732, 734; and "Editors Discuss War Problems with Scott," *Baltimore Afro-American*, July 5, 1918.

4. Thornbrough, "American Negro Newspapers, 1880–1914," 468. For a brief introduction to black print culture from the Civil War to World War II, see James P. Danky, "Reading, Writing, and Resisting: African American Print Culture," in Kaestle and Radway, *Print in Motion*, Vol. 4, 339–358.

5. Ayers, *Promise of the New South*, 132–159.

6. Brown, "Negro Character as Seen by White Authors," 179–203; and "Education by the Press," *Norfolk Journal and Guide*, July 20, 1935.

7. "Negro Tramps about Washington," *New York Times*, March 4, 1880.

8. "Lynch Law in Cuthbert," *Macon Telegraph and Messenger*, August 11, 1885; "Work for Judge Lynch," *Wheeling Register*, February 8, 1886; and "Lynching a Negro Brute," *St. Louis Post-Dispatch*, April 7, 1882. Also see Wasserman, *How the Media Packaged Lynching*.

9. Wells, *Crusade for Justice*, 69; and Richard Yarborough, "Violence, Manhood, and Black Heroism," in Cecelski and Tyson, *Democracy Betrayed*, 228.

10. Jackson, "Popular Media," in *Black American Reference Book*, 849–852.

11. Biographical sketches of nineteenth-century editors are found in Penn, *Afro-American Press and Its Editors*; and Suggs, *Black Press in the South* and *Black Press in the Middle West*. For fuller discussions of the editors mentioned, see Alexander, *Race Man*; Bay, *To Tell the Truth Freely*; Chase, "Shelling the Citadel of Race Prejudice," 371–391; Gatewood, "Edward E. Cooper," 269–275, 324; and Thornbrough, *T. Thomas Fortune*.

12. Fortune quoted in Penn, *Afro-American Press and Its Editors*, 483; and Alexander, *Race Man*, 41–42.

13. Baker, *Following the Color Line*, 110–111; U.S. Department of Commerce, *Negro Population in the United States*, 404; and Hershaw, "Negro Press in America," 67.

14. Trachtenberg, *Incorporation of America*; and Ohmann, *Selling Culture*.

15. Starr, *Creation of the Media*, 252; and Ohmann, *Selling Culture*, 29.

16. Schudson, *Discovering the News*, 71. Also see Campbell, *Year That Defined American Journalism*, 1–16; Daly, *Covering America*, 112–182; and Spencer, *Yellow Journalism*, 77–94.

17. Ohmann, *Selling Culture*, 220, 258, 264–265; and Starr, *Creation of the Media*, 233–266.

18. Johnson, *Negro Americans, What Now?*, 26; and Gore, *Negro Journalism*, 14–15.

19. Pride, "Negro Newspapers," 181; and Julius Eric Thompson, "Mississippi," in Suggs, *Black Press in the South*, 178.

20. "Constitution and By-Laws of the Niagara Movement," July 12–13, 1905, University of Massachusetts Amherst, http://scua.library.umass.edu/digital/niagara.htm (accessed September 22, 2016); Harlan, *Booker T. Washington*, 32–62; and Lewis, *Du Bois: Biography of a Race*, 297–342. Also see Fox, *Guardian of Boston*. Concerning Washington's press relations, see Meier, "Booker T. Washington and the Negro Press," 67–90; Harlan, "Booker T. Washington and the Politics of Accommodation," in Franklin and Meier, *Black Leaders of the Twentieth Century*, 1–18, and "Secret Life of Booker T. Washington," 393–416.

21. Henderson, "Need of a Monthly Magazine," 41; "*The Voice of the Negro* for 1904," advertisement, *Voice of the Negro*, January 1904; and Hopkins, "Heroes and Heroines in Black," in *Daughter of the Revolution*, 290. Also see Bullock, *Afro-American Periodical Press*.

22. Lewis, *Du Bois: Biography of a Race*, 325–328, 337–338, 409–413, 474; and "The Crisis," *Crisis* 1 (November 1910): 10.

23. Du Bois, "The Talented Tenth," in *Negro Problem*, 34.

24. "Our Baby Pictures," *Crisis* 8 (October 1914): 298–300.

25. "The Truth," *Crisis* 5 (December 1912): 76; "The Manufacture of Prejudice," *Crisis* 2 (May 1911): 35–37; and "The Manufacture of Prejudice," *Crisis* 5 (February 1913): 195–196.

26. "Divine Right," *Crisis* 3 (March 1912): 197.

27. "From White Folk," *Crisis* 5 (April 1913): 301; Ovington to Du Bois, April 11, 1914, in Aptheker, *Correspondence of W.E.B. Du Bois*, Vol. 1, 192; and "The Gall of Bitterness," *Crisis* 3 (February 1912): 153.

28. Ottley, *Lonely Warrior*. Also see Juliet E. K. Walker, "The Promised Land: The Chicago *Defender* and the Black Press in Illinois: 1862–1970," in Suggs, *Black Press in the Middle West*, 9–50.

29. "In Journalism; Eight Pages for the *Defender*," *Chicago Defender*, September 12, 1914; and "*Defender* Leads in Number of Big Departments," *Defender*, April 17, 1915. Also see Albert Kreiling, "The Commercialization of the Black Press and the Rise of Race News in Chicago," in Solomon and McChesney, *Ruthless Criticism*, 176–203.

30. "Enough Said," *Defender*, September 9, 1916.

31. "Editor's Mail," *Defender*, October 19, 1918. Grossman's *Land of Hope* remains the definitive account of the *Defender*'s role in promoting black migration in the late 1910s, particularly pages 74–88.

32. Grossman, *Land of Hope*, 74, 79.

33. Baker, "Gathering Clouds along the Color Line," 235.

34. Buni, *Robert L. Vann*, 42–54; and Farrar, *Baltimore Afro-American*, 1–8.

35. T. R. Poston, "The Inside Story," *Amsterdam News*, December 22, 1934; and Suggs, *P.B. Young*, 9–29.

36. George Everett Slavens, "Missouri," in Suggs, *Black Press in the South*, 215–217; "Chester Arthur Franklin Biography," Black Archives of Mid-America, http://www.blackarchives.org/node/104 (accessed January 20, 2016); and Thompson, "The Little Caesar of Civil Rights" (PhD diss.), 35, 48–49, 52.

37. Bass, *Forty Years*, 27–32, 35–36.

38. Wilson, "War Message to Congress," April 2, 1917, in Link, *Papers of Woodrow Wilson*, Vol. 41, 523, 525; and "The U.S. Only Poses," *Cleveland Gazette*, May 19, 1917. Regarding the significance of civic obligation during World War I, see Capozzola, *Uncle Sam Wants You*.

39. See, generally, Ellis, *Race, War, and Surveillance*; Kornweibel, *Investigate Everything*; and Lentz-Smith, *Freedom Struggles*.

40. Quoted in Rudwick, *Race Riot at East St. Louis*, 64.

41. Bay, *To Tell the Truth Freely*, 300–301; and "East St. Louis Aftermath," *Defender*, July 28, 1917.

42. "Riot a National Disgrace," *St. Louis Argus*, July 6, 1917; "The Mob vs. the Law," *Argus*, July 13, 1917; and "Negroes Again Insulted," *Argus*, September 14, 1917.

43. "Roosevelt," *Crisis* 14 (August 1917): 164; "The East St. Louis Riots," *Journal and Guide*, July 7, 1917; "The Right of Free Speech," *Journal and Guide*, August 18, 1917; and Ellis, *Race, War, and Surveillance*, 45.

44. "Houston Incident Closed—Not Forgotten," *Afro-American*, December 15, 1917; and "In the Enemy's Camp," *Defender*, September 1, 1917.

45. Quoted in Kornweibel, *Investigate Everything*, 127; Stone, *Perilous Times*, 136–220; and Ellis, *Race, War, and Surveillance*, 65–69, 101–120.

46. Kornweibel, *Investigate Everything*, 118–131; and Loving to Chief, Military Intelligence Branch, May 10, 1918, *Federal Surveillance of Afro-Americans*, reel 19, 611.

47. Abbott to Loving, May 11, 1918, R. H. Van Deman to Loving, May 13, 1918, and Mitchell to Loving, May 25, 1918, *Federal Surveillance of Afro-Americans*, reel 19, 612–613, 689, 698.

48. Quoted in Kornweibel, *Investigate Everything*, 171, 170–175.

49. "Close Ranks," *Crisis* 16 (July 1918): 111; Lewis, *Du Bois: Biography of a Race*, 552–554; Kornweibel, *Investigate Everything*, 132–148; and "A Philosophy in Time of War," *Crisis* 16 (August 1918): 164.

50. Spingarn to Churchill, June 22, 1918, *Federal Surveillance of Afro-Americans*, reel 19, 735, 733–735; and Jordan, *Black Newspapers and America's War for Democracy*, 126.

51. Wilson, "A Statement on Lynchings and Mob Violence," July 26, 1918, in Link, *Papers of Woodrow Wilson*, Vol. 49, 97, 98; Jordan, *Black Newspapers and America's War for Democracy*, 126–130; and Ellis, *Race, War, and Surveillance*, 151.

Chapter 2. Enter the "New Crowd" Journalists

1. Thurman, "Editorial," *Harlem* 1 (November 1928), in Huggins, *Voices from the Harlem Renaissance*, 73, 74.

2. Gordon, "The Negro Press," 252; and "The Negro Grows Up," *Baltimore Afro-American*, June 22, 1929.

3. Wilson, "An Address to a Joint Session of Congress," January 8, 1918, in Link, *Papers of Woodrow Wilson*, Vol. 45, 537. See Kornweibel, *Seeing Red*. For a sociological analysis of the causes and effects of the 1919 riots, see Voogd, *Race Riots and Resistance*.

4. Chicago Commission on Race Relations, *Negro in Chicago*, 650–651.

5. Marks, *Farewell—We're Good and Gone*, 122.

6. Harrison, "As the Currents Flow," in *Harrison Reader*, 98; and "'If We Must Die,'" *Messenger*, September 1919, 4.

7. Harrison, "The Liberty League of Negro-Americans," and "The East St. Louis Horror," in *Harrison Reader*, 87, 94–95. See, generally, Perry, *Hubert Harrison*.

8. Harrison, "Two Negro Radicalisms," in *Harrison Reader*, 102–105; and "The New Policies for the New Negro," *The Voice*, September 4, 1917, box 5, folder 35, *Harrison Papers*, Columbia University.

9. Quoted in Jordan, *Black Newspapers and America's War for Democracy*, 123; "Hear Our Grievances," in Aptheker, *Documentary History of the Negro People*, 217; Perry, *Hubert Harrison*, 366–395; Ellis, *Race, War, and Surveillance*, 123; and Harrison, "The Descent of Dr. Du Bois," in *Harrison Reader*, 172.

10. Randolph, "A New Crowd—A New Negro," 27; and Owen, "Failure of Negro Leaders," 23. Also see Kornweibel, *No Crystal Stair*; and Anderson, *A. Philip Randolph*, 83–150.

11. Randolph, "A New Crowd—A New Negro," 26–27; Owen quoted in Harrison, "Patronize Your Own," in *Harrison Reader*, 110; and Editors, "The Cause of and Remedy for Race Riots," *Messenger*, September 1919, 15, 21.

12. Makalani, *In the Cause of Freedom*, 45–69; Solomon, *Cry Was Unity*, 5–17; editorial quoted in Ellis, *Race, War, and Surveillance*, 106–107; "Government of the Negro: By Whom and for Whom?" and "The African Blood Brotherhood," *Crusader*, August 1919, 4, and June 1920, 7. Also see Kornweibel, *Seeing Red*, 132–154.

13. Garvey, "The Negro's Greatest Enemy," in Wintz, *African American Political Thought*, 171, 173; and quoted in Stein, *World of Marcus Garvey*, 37.

14. Hahn, *Political Worlds of Slavery and Freedom*, 118; Crowder, *John Edward Bruce*, 164, 166; and Seraile, *Bruce Grit*, 156–158.

15. Grant, *Negro with a Hat*, 135; A Bermudian, "A Message from Barbadoes [*sic*]," *Negro World*, April 2, 1921; and Hahn, *Political Worlds of Slavery and Freedom*, 115–164.

16. "The African Blood Brotherhood," *Crusader*, June 1920, 22; Briggs to Theodore Draper, March 17, 1958, *Theodore Draper Papers*, Hoover Institution Archives, box 31, http://www.marxisthistory.org/history/usa/groups/abb/1958/0317-briggs-todraper.pdf (accessed January 18, 2016); and Makalani, *In the Cause of Freedom*, 178. A federal informant helped Briggs prepare and distribute the Crusader News Service. See *Federal Surveillance of Afro-Americans*, reel 3, 232–340.

17. Randolph, "A New Crowd—A New Negro," 27; "Roscoe Conklin [*sic*] Simmons," *Messenger*, October 1919, 26; and Calvin, "Who's Who," 611.

18. Johnson, "African Colonization Schemes," *New York Age*, August 12, 1922, in Wilson, *Selected Writings of James Weldon Johnson*, Vol. 1, 130, 132.

19. See Grant, *Negro with a Hat*, and Stein, *World of Marcus Garvey*.

20. "A Lunatic or a Traitor," *Crisis* (May 1924): 8; "Brundage 'Sinks' Black Star Line," *Defender*, October 4, 1919; Stein, *World of Marcus Garvey*, 79, 80; and "Garvey Pleads for Fairer Estimate of His 'Movement,'" *Washington Bee*, November 5, 1921. Also see Ottley, *Lonely Warrior*, 212–218.

21. *Chicago Broad Ax*, October 11, 1919; "Can Garvey Win in Africa," *Afro-American*, September 10, 1920; and "Marcus Garvey," *Amsterdam News*, June 27, 1923.

22. See Crowder, *John Edward Bruce*; and Seraile, *Bruce Grit*.

23. Hauke, *Ted Poston*, 15–18, 29–33.

24. Floyd J. Calvin, "Calvin Gives *Courier* Readers 'Intimate Story' of Man Who Will Give Them the Truth about War," *Pittsburgh Courier*, November 23, 1935; and Ottley, *New World A-Coming*, 102–103.

25. Rogers, "Your History," *Courier*, November 10, December 1, and December 15, 1934. For Rogers's thinking on race, see Pinckney, *Out There*, 13–53.

26. Peter W. Clark, "History Teacher Acclaims 'Your History' Feature as One of Finest Things in *Courier*," *Courier*, January 19, 1935; and Hattie Edwards, "Your History," *Courier*, February 2, 1935.

27. Locke, *New Negro*, xxv, 48; and Carroll, *Word, Image, and the New Negro*, 3. Also see Hutchinson, *Harlem Renaissance in Black and White*; and Lewis, *When Harlem Was in Vogue*.

28. Hughes, *I Wonder as I Wander*, 3, 5. Bontemps quoted in Washington, *Ideologies of African American Literature*, 15.

29. Du Bois, "Criteria of Negro Art," in Ervin, *African American Literary Criticism*, 42; and Hutchinson, *Harlem Renaissance in Black and White*, 152–153, with Johnson quoted on 176.

30. "Book Chat," review of *Home to Harlem*, by Claude McKay, *Courier*, March 17, 1928; Jones, "More 'Nigger Heaven,'" review of *Home to Harlem*, *Chicago Defender*, March 17, 1928; and Matthews, "In Darker Baltimore," *Afro-American*, July 7, 1928.

31. McKay, "A Negro Writer to His Critics," in Gates and Jarrett, *New Negro*, 390, 391.

32. Thurman, "Negro Artists and the Negro," in *Collected Writings of Wallace Thurman*, 197; and Hughes, *Big Sea*, 233–234.

33. Bowser, "Dirt for Art's Sake," review of *Home to Harlem*, *Amsterdam News*, March 21, 1928; and Thurman, "Negro Artists and the Negro," 195.

34. Bessie, *Jazz Journalism*, 25; Young, "The Thoroughfare," *Norfolk Journal and Guide*, July 23, 1927; Miller, "Black 'Yellow' Journalism," *New York Amsterdam News*, July 18, 1928; "Appreciating the Negro Newspaper," reprinted in *Journal and Guide*, April 19, 1930; T. G. Bramlette, letter to the editor, *Afro-American*, April 13, 1929; and Matthews, *Afro-American*, July 7, 1928.

35. Schuyler, *Black and Conservative*, 113–114, 134–136. Also see Williams, *George S. Schuyler*. Schuyler downplayed his early radicalism in his autobiography. For a scholarly correction, see the introduction by Leak in *Rac(e)ing to the Right*.

36. Schuyler, "Views and Reviews," *Courier*, January 4, 1930, and July 9, 1927; Schuyler, "Thrusts and Lunges," *Courier*, September 12, 1925, and January 31, 1925; and "'Exert Entire Effort in Elevating Status,' Declares Schuyler," *Courier*, December 6, 1930.

37. Farrar, *Baltimore Afro-American*, 44; "The Passing of John Mitchell Jr.," *Messenger*, November 1922, 528–529; Calvin, "Mirrors of Harlem," 610; and Gottlieb et al., *Next Los Angeles*, 52.

38. Juliet E. K. Walker, "The Promised Land: The Chicago *Defender* and the Black Press in Illinois: 1862–1970," in Suggs, *Black Press in the Middle West*, 31–35; and Davis, *Livin' the Blues*, 108–109.

Chapter 3. Popular Fronts and Modern Presses

1. Mockler, *Haile Selassie's War*, 53–55; Margolick, *Beyond Glory*, 82–86; and "Sport: Misfortunes of a Monster," *Time*, October 5, 1931. In *Black Metropolis*, 403, Drake and Cayton examined every issue of the *Defender* between 1933 and 1938 to determine which personalities garnered the most front-page headlines and/or photographs. Three people involved with the Second Italo-Ethiopian War ranked in the top ten. Joe Louis received the most mentions, receiving nearly 3.5 times as many prominent displays as the second most popular personality, Ethiopian Emperor Haile Selassie.

2. "*Defender* Big Extra First on Streets," and "Editor Abbott Hears Fight at His Home," *Chicago Defender*, June 29, 1935.

3. Nunn, "'Bill' Nunn Writes His Story 10,000 Feet in the Air," and "Speed Cameras, Airplanes and Clicking Wires Aid *Courier* Men, Who 'Stand By' All Night, Make Special 'Fight Extra' Greatest of Year," *Pittsburgh Courier*, June 29, 1935.

4. Prattis and Barnett, February 5, 1936, and February 13, 1936, and "Publisher's Statement Ending December 31, 1935, for the *Pittsburgh Courier*," box 138, folder 9, *Barnett Papers*, microfilm; and Buni, *Robert L. Vann*, 251–252, 257.

5. The intellectual framework of this chapter was influenced by Singh, *Black Is a Country*, especially 58–70, with quote on 69; and Mullen, "Turning White Space into Black Space: The *Chicago Defender* and the Creation of the Cultural Front," in *Popular Fronts*, 44–74.

6. Buni, *Robert L. Vann*, 193–194.

7. See Sitkoff, *New Deal for Blacks*; and Katznelson, *Fear Itself*.

8. "Education: Smart Pickaninnies," *Time*, April 1, 1940. Regarding the state of race relations, see Myrdal, *American Dilemma*.

9. High, "Black Omens," 6, 64.

10. "Newshawks Do Most Stories on White Assignments," *Ebony*, April 1948, 59; and Johnston, "Pioneering Black Newsman," 34.

11. Regarding African Americans and communism in the 1920s and 1930s, see Gore, *Radicalism at the Crossroads*; Kelley, "Africa's Sons with Banner Red," in *Race Rebels*, 103–122; Kelley, *Hammer and Hoe*; Makalani, *In the Cause of Freedom*; Naison, *Communists in Harlem*; Smethurst, *New Red Negro*, 16–42; and Solomon, *Cry Was Unity*.

12. Wright, *Black Boy*, 374; "Eugene Gordon: Autobiographical Notes," box 1, folder 2, *Gordon Papers*, New York Public Library; and "Negro Editors on Communism: A Symposium of the American Negro Press," *Crisis* 41 (April 1932): 117.

13. Mullen, *Popular Fronts*, 47; and Walker, "The Negro Press in America," undated speech delivered to John Reed Club, box 197-6, folder 31, *Walker Papers*, Howard University.

14. "Mr. Public Safety," *Ebony*, January 1956, 51. Regarding the *Chicago Whip*'s campaign, see Reed, *Depression Comes to the South Side*, 66–76.

15. Rampersad, *Ralph Ellison*, 94–100; and Burns, *Nitty Gritty*, 56.

16. For biographical information about Padmore, see Hooker, *Black Revolutionary*; Ottley, *No Green Pastures*, 62–69; and W. Randy Dixon, "Calling: George Padmore, London Reporter," *Defender*, July 31, 1943.

17. Quoted in Hooker, *Black Revolutionary*, 54; Padmore, "Ethiopia and World Politics," 157, and "Second World War and the Darker Races," 327.

18. "Is the *Spokesman* Red?" *San Francisco Spokesman*, March 29, 1935.

19. Pittman and Burns, October 22, 1942, November 6, 1942, and undated, box 2, folder 7A, *Pittman Papers*, New York University; and Badger, "World View," *Defender*, December 19, 1942, and August 28, 1943.

20. Hamilton, *Adam Clayton Powell*, 105; Cooke, *Interviews with Marvel Cooke*, interview by Kathleen Currie, Women in Journalism Oral History Project, November 1, 1989, 98; and Hill, *FBI's RACON*, 178.

21. Farrar, *Baltimore Afro-American*, 150; Mullen, *Popular Fronts*, 55; and Patterson to Sengstacke, undated, box 80, folder 47, *Abbott-Sengstacke Papers*, Chicago Public Library.

22. "Negro Editors on Communism," *Crisis*, 117, 118.

23. "Another Newspaper Hyper-critic," and "Worries of a Columnist," *Norfolk Journal and Guide*, October 25, 1930, and November 22, 1930; and Jones, "Day By Day," *Baltimore Afro-American*, November 15, 1930, and November 29, 1930.

24. Buni, *Robert L. Vann*, 172, 222–223.

25. Fleming, "Emancipation of the Negro Press," 216; Young, "Negro Press—Today and Tomorrow," 204; and Murdock, "Some Business Aspects of Leading Negro Newspapers" (MBA), 75.

26. Murphy, et al., "*Afro*," 44–46, 50; "AFRO Family Increases," *Afro-American*, May 21, 1938; and "AFRO Chain Has Many Birthdays," *Afro-American*, September 19, 1942. Also see Pride and Wilson, *History of the Black Press*, 145, 146–147; and Martin, "Blood, Sweat, and Ink," 37–39.

27. Wilkins, "Negro Press," 362; and Du Bois, "The American Negro Press," reprint from the *Chicago Defender*, 1943, box 144, folder 4, *Barnett Papers*. Brief descriptions of the generational transition among publishers are found in Bardolph, *Negro Vanguard*, 338–339; and Finkle, *Forum of Protest*, 59–60.

28. Pride and Wilson, *History of the Black Press*, 134; Sale, "*Amsterdam News*"; Burns, *Nitty Gritty*, 93; Buni, *Robert L. Vann*, 325; Young, "No Crusades, Please!" 69–71; and Suggs, *P.B. Young*, 99, 131.

29. See "Cleveland's *Call and Post*," *Crisis* 45 (December 1938): 404; Kenneth C. Field, "Leon H. Washington Jr., Story Tells *Sentinel* 'Growing Pains,'" *Los Angeles Sentinel*, June 25, 1959; Leipold, *Cecil E. Newman*; George McElroy, "The Black Press in Houston: Some Notes," in La Brie, *Perspectives of the Black Press*, 80–81; and Davis, *Livin' the Blues*, 182–188.

30. Wilkins to Claude Barnett, July 28, 1939, box 374, folder 9, *Barnett Papers*.

31. Murdock, "Some Business Aspects of Leading Negro Newspapers," (MBA) 36–37; Waters, *American Diary*, 11–112; and Schuyler, "Views and Reviews," *Courier*, December 14, 1935. Regarding professionalization and journalism, see Dooley, *Taking Their Place*, 1–44; and John Soloski, "News Reporting and Professionalism: Some Constraints on the Reporting of the News," in Berkowitz, *Social Meanings of News*, 138–154.

32. Ottley, *New World A-Coming*, 281; "An Explanation," *Amsterdam News*, October 19, 1935; and Chase, "*Amsterdam News* Is Winning," 567.

33. "Contents of American Newspaper Guild Contracts Covering Negro Weekly and Semi-Weekly Newspapers," October 15, 1946, box 20, folder 41, *Newspaper Guild of New York Records*, New York University; and "Ousted Scribes Win First Tilt in Paper Fight," *Defender*, November 9, 1935.

34. Oak, *Negro Newspaper*, 66–67; Burma, "Analysis of the Present Negro Press," 172; and Murray, *Negro Handbook*, 316. Circulation and readership are notoriously hard to estimate. Publishers often inflated their circulation figures to win advertisers and unsettle rivals. Reference publications, such as *N. W. Ayer & Son's Directory of*

Newspapers and Periodicals, Editor & Publisher International Year Book, and *Negro Handbook*, employed a haphazard methodology in tracking the existence and circulation of black newspapers. Although hard data is scarce, a single edition of a black newspaper was believed to be read on average by more people than a typical daily newspaper. Scholars have attributed increased readership to the race-specific content and weekly format of black newspapers, as well as the larger family size and lower income of black families compared to white families. Consuelo C. Young estimated that seventeen people read a single copy of the *Chicago Defender*, about four times the number of readers for a daily newspaper, in "A Study of Reader Attitudes," 148–152. Joan Shelley Rubin examines the biases of early readership studies in "Making Meaning: Analysis and Affect in the Study and Practice of Reading," in Kaestle and Radway, *Print in Motion*, Vol. 4, 511–527.

35. See James E. Murphy, "Tabloids as an Urban Response," in Covert and Stevens, *Mass Media Between the Wars*, 55–69. My thinking on the conventions of reportage was influenced by Schudson, "The Politics of Narrative Form," 99, 106–108, and Richard L. Kaplan, "From Partisanship to Professionalism," in Kaestle and Radway, *Print in Motion*, Vol. 4, 133–136.

36. Wright, "Blueprint for Negro Writing," in Gates and McKay, *Norton Anthology of African American Literature*, 1380, 1383.

37. White, "I Investigate Lynchings," 77–84; Poston, "My Most Humiliating Jim Crow Experience," 55–56; and Hauke, *Ted Poston*, 57–59.

38. Putnam, *Radical Moves*, 5. Regarding black foreign correspondence, also see Broussard, *African American Foreign Correspondents*; Plummer, *Rising Wind*; and Von Eschen, *Race against Empire*.

39. Quirin, "African American Perceptions of the Battle of Adwa," in *Proceedings of the XVth International Conference of Ethiopian Studies*, 344; and Ottley, *New World A-Coming*, 105. Regarding African American activism in support of Ethiopia, see Corbould, *Becoming African Americans*, 196–213.

40. "Monkey See, Monkey Do," *Courier*, November 30, 1935. Ottley names Lochard as Operative 22 in *Lonely Warrior*, 347–349.

41. Prattis, "Rogers Alone Giving Real Facts on War, Belief," *Courier*, March 14, 1936; and Rogers, "J.A. Rogers Off to War Zone," *Courier*, October 26, 1935.

42. Prattis to Barnett, January 7, 1936, box 138, folder 9, *Barnett Papers*; and Rogers, "Correspondents Barred from Ethiopian Front," *Courier*, January 25, 1936, and "Spies Thwarted by Wily Censors," *Courier*, May 2, 1936.

43. Rogers, "Enemy Bombers Unable to Find Selassie Troops," *Courier*, December 21, 1935.

44. Rampersad, *Life of Langston Hughes*, Vol. 1, 214–220, 251–254; Hughes, *I Wonder as I Wander*, 315, 400; and "Our Stake in Spain," *Afro-American*, October 30, 1937. Regarding African American support for Spain's Popular Front government, see Kelley, "This Ain't Ethiopia, but It'll Do," in *Race Rebels*, 123–160.

45. Hughes, "Soldiers from Many Lands United in Spanish Fight," *Afro-American*, December 18, 1937; "Hughes Finds Moors Being Used as Pawns by Fascists in Spain,"

Afro-American, October 30, 1937; and Hughes, *I Wonder as I Wander*, 400. Also see Michael Thurston, "'Bombed in Spain': Langston Hughes, the Black Press, and the Spanish Civil War," in Vogel, *Black Press*, 140–159.

Chapter 4. The "New Crowd" Goes Global

1. Sengstacke, "Report to the Board of Directors of the Robert S. Abbott Publishing Company," June 1942 and July 1942, box 50, folder 11, and Sengstacke to Ulric Bell, April 11, 1942, box 58, folder 1, *Abbott-Sengstacke Papers*, Chicago Public Library.

2. Ibid.; and Charles P. Browning to George J. Bott, March 31, 1943, box 58, folder 2, *Abbott-Sengstacke Papers*, Chicago Public Library.

3. "A New Jerusalem," *Defender*, September 26, 1942. See Mullen, "Turning White Space into Black Space," in *Popular Fronts*, 44–74.

4. Mershon and Schlossman, *Foxholes and Color Lines*, 1–24.

5. Vann, *Pittsburgh Courier*, February 19, 1938; and Houston, "*Courier*'s Appeal to U.S. Senate," *Courier*, May 18, 1940. A full account of the Committee on Participation of Negroes in the National Defense Program is found in Finkle, *Forum of Protest*, 129–147.

6. "Mess Attendants Write: 'Don't Join the Navy,'" *Courier*, October 5, 1940; and Knox to White, December 18, 1940, *Papers of the NAACP*, microfilm, part 9, series B, reel 27, 1017–1018.

7. Lewis, *W.E.B. Du Bois: Fight for Equality*, 388–421, 462–470; and Du Bois, "As the Crow Flies," *New York Amsterdam News*, May 31, 1941.

8. "10,000 Should March on D.C. Says Randolph," *Baltimore Afro-American*, January 25, 1941. Also see Anderson, *A. Philip Randolph*, 246–261.

9. Stewart, "Camp Livingston Has Backwoods Army," *Afro-American*, July 19, 1941; "Powder Keg at 2 Army Camps," *Afro-American*, July 26, 1941; and "Why Fort Bragg Is as Sore as a Boil," *Afro-American*, August 30, 1941.

10. Marshall, "Remarks: Conference of Negro Newspaper Representatives," December 8, 1941, box 312, folder 5, *Barnett Papers*; Lee, *United States Army in World War II*, 141–144; and Washburn, *Question of Sedition*, 57–59.

11. "Discrimination vs. Unity," *Defender*, December 20, 1941; "Mr. President, Count on Us," *Afro-American*, December 13, 1941; "An Editorial," *New York Amsterdam Star-News*, December 13, 1941; "No Time for Quibbling," *Courier*, December 20, 1941; and Hedgeman, "Role of the Negro Woman," 467.

12. Biddle, *In Brief Authority*, 226; and Stone, *Perilous Times*, 235–310. Also see Winfield, *FDR and the News Media*, 155–214.

13. Kennedy, *Freedom from Fear*, 636–637.

14. Truman K. Gibson Jr. to White, April 6, 1942; Osborn to White, April 3, 1942; White to Prattis and William H. Hastie, April 1, 1942; Prattis to White, April 4, 1942, and April 14, 1942, *NAACP Papers*, part 9, series A, reel 13, 411, 414–415, 417, 425–426.

15. Lee, *United States Army in World War II*, 383–387; Motley, *Invisible Soldier*, 204, 243; and Hayakawa, "Second Thoughts," *Defender*, August 7, 1943.

16. Washburn, *Question of Sedition*, 81; Starr to Barry Bingham, June 30, 1942, *Office of War Information*, microfilm, part 1, reel 8, 480; Sengstacke to Price, June 3, 1942, box 58, folder 1, *Abbott-Sengstacke Papers*, Chicago Public Library; Howard Gould, "Censor Bars All Negro News to Foreign Nations," *Defender*, December 12, 1942; and "Denies Bar on All Race News in U.S.," *Defender*, January 16, 1943. Washburn cites Biddle's private notes for the quote from the Cabinet meeting.

17. Hill, *FBI's RACON*, 419; and Waters, *American Diary*, 371.

18. Quoted in Washburn, *Question of Sedition*, 90; Sengstacke and MacLeish, June 8, 1942, and June 12, 1942, *Office of War Information*, part 1, reel 1, 910–911. Washburn interviewed Sengstacke in 1983.

19. Cliff Mackay, "The Globe Trotter: Now Just Who Is Subversive?" *Atlanta Daily World*, July 5, 1942.

20. See Hogan, *Black National News Service*, 96–97; and Johnson, "Washington News Beat," 126–127. On the fight for press credentials, see Ritchie, *Reporting from Washington*, 28–46. Reporters did not gain access to the congressional press galleries until 1947.

21. Berry to Walter White, September 17, 1942, *Office of War Information*, part 1, reel 8, 538–539; and White to Barnett, undated 1941, box 140, folder 6, *Barnett Papers*.

22. Terry quoted in Hauke, *Ted Poston*, 102; and Poston to George Lyon, October 23, 1943, *Office of War Information*, part 1, reel 8, 179–182.

23. Pegler, "Fair Enough," *Los Angeles Times*, April 29, 1942, and June 18, 1942; Farr, *Fair Enough*, 169; "The Negroes and the War," *Richmond Times-Dispatch*, April 26, 1942; and Dabney, "Nearer and Nearer the Precipice," 96, 97.

24. Brown, "Negro Looks at the Negro Press," 5–6; Martin, "Fallacies of Brown's Blast at Press Exposed," *Afro-American*, January 9, 1943; and Walker, "Is the Negro Press Friend or Foe of Negro Progress," speech delivered January 10, 1943, St. James Literary Forum, box 197-6, folder 25, *Walker Papers*, Howard University. Finkle examines the criticisms of Pegler, Dabney, Brown, and others in *Forum of Protest*, 62–81.

25. Regarding the evolution of journalistic objectivity, see Schudson, *Discovering the News*; Ward, *Invention of Journalism Ethics*; and Frus, *Politics and Poetics*, 100–114. In *Making News*, Tuchman examines how the production of news reproduces the status quo.

26. Waters, *American Diary*, 87, 221; Prattis, "Role of the Negro Press in Race Relations," 276; and "Credo for the Negro Press," *Norfolk Journal and Guide*, March 3, 1945.

27. "The *Courier*'s Double 'V' for a Double Victory Campaign Gets Country-wide Support," *Courier*, February 14, 1942; and Thompson, "Should I Sacrifice to Live 'Half-American?'" *Courier*, January 31, 1942. Also see Washburn, "Pittsburgh *Courier*'s Double V Campaign," 73–86.

28. "Victory at Home, Victory Abroad Sweeps the Nation," *Courier*, March 21, 1942; "Nationwide Support Grows for 'Double V,'" *Courier*, March 14, 1942; and Bolden, "We Want Full Participating Rights in War to Save Democracy," *Courier*, March 7, 1942.

29. Jean M. Murrell, "You Can't Preach 'Double V' and Expect 'Status Quo,'" *Courier*, April 3, 1943. Also see Phillips, *War! What Is It Good For?* 20–63.

30. Mershon and Schlossman, *Foxholes and Color Lines*, 51; Gibson to White, November 9, 1943, *NAACP Papers*, part 9, series A, reel 13, 817; and "Race Newspapers Okeh on Army List," *Atlanta Daily World*, August 22, 1944.

31. Brig. Gen. M. Churchill to Assistant Chief of Staff, October 22, 1918, *Federal Surveillance of Afro-Americans*, reel 19, 493; Ottley, *Lonely Warrior*, 152; and Hamilton, *Journalism's Roving Eye*, 335.

32. Stevens, *Back of the Foxhole*; Hamilton, *Journalism's Roving Eye*, 331–349; and "Newspaper Publishers to 'Pool' Reporters," *Amsterdam News*, September 18, 1943. Hamilton and Broussard examined the coverage of the *Norfolk Journal and Guide*'s three war correspondents in "Covering a Two-Front War," 33–54. In this article, they stress the "urgency in conducting research on the foreign correspondence of outside-the-mainstream voices" (49).

33. Rouzeau, "My Most Humiliating Jim Crow Experience," 64–65; Huddle, *Roi Ottley's World War II*, 60; and Stevens, *Back of the Foxhole*, 13, 15.

34. Murphy, "The Week," *Afro-American*, November 20, 1943; Stevens, *Back of the Foxhole*, 15; and Terry, *Missing Pages*, 80.

35. Stevens, *Back of the Foxhole*, 11; Waters, *American Diary*, 385; and Hamilton, *Journalism's Roving Eye*, 312–317.

36. Stevens, *Back of the Foxhole*, 54–55; Waters, *American Diary*, 389; and Terry, *Missing Pages*, 80. Troop resentment against the press campaign to put them in combat began while units were still training in the United States. Some soldiers complained that middle-class leaders wanted to rush them into combat before they were adequately trained. See Jefferson, *Fighting for Hope*, 149–150.

37. White, *Rising Wind*, 155. Also see Singh, *Black Is a Country*, 117.

38. Tubbs, "How Japs Were Chased Out of Their West Coast Homes," *Afro-American*, April 24, 1943, and "How Japs Were Forced Out of Their West Coast Homes," *Afro-American*, May 1, 1943.

39. "Hitler Is Only a Symbol of World Exploitation'—Rouzeau," *Courier*, May 23, 1942; "Edgar Rouzeau, Ace Newsman, Buried Wednesday," *Amsterdam News*, August 16, 1958; and "Flying Scribe," *Negro Digest*, April 1943, 54.

40. "Black Troops May Not See Action in Present World Conflict—Rouzeau," *Courier*, March 21, 1942; and Rouzeau, "Black Troops Facing Rommel," *Courier*, September 26, 1942.

41. Stevens, *Back of the Foxhole*, 55; Brooks, "U.S. Ignores Atlantic Charter, India Fears," *Defender*, November 11, 1944; "*Defender* Reporter Visits Gandhi," *Defender*, June 16, 1945; and "India's Nehru Sends Freedom Message to American Negroes," *Defender*, July 21, 1945.

42. W. Randy Dixon, "Calling: George Padmore, London Reporter," *Defender*, July 31, 1943; Padmore, "London Hospitality Is Rebuke to South, Says *Defender* Writer," *Defender*, August 22, 1942; and "'Negroes in Forefront of African Invasion'—Padmore," *Courier*, November 21, 1942.

43. Ottley, *New World A-Coming*, v. For Ottley's biography, see Huddle, *Roi Ottley's World War II*, 1–32.

44. Ottley, *No Green Pastures*, vii, 2.
45. Ibid., 5, 7, 12.

Chapter 5. "Questionable Leanings"

1. Barnett to Corienne R. Morrow, March 29, 1954, box 109, folder 1, and Barnett and Davis, undated, box 108, folder 6, *Barnett Papers*. For Davis's politics, see Davis, *Writings of Frank Marshall Davis*; and Mullen, *Popular Fronts*, 190–191.
2. The study of Cold War foreign policy and domestic civil rights is a rapidly expanding field. It includes Anderson, *Eyes off the Prize*; Borstelmann, *Cold War and the Color Line*; Dudziak, *Cold War, Civil Rights*; Meriwether, *Proudly We Can Be Africans*; Plummer, *Rising Wind*; Singh, *Black Is a Country*, 101–133; and Von Eschen, *Race against Empire*. Borstelmann and Dudziak explain how American officials attempted to manage and minimize racial activists. Plummer, Singh, and Von Eschen examine how black radicals provoked change.
3. Finkle, *Forum of Protest*, 53; and Murray, *Negro Handbook, 1949*, 316. Regarding radio and race, see Barlow, *Voice Over*, and Savage, *Broadcasting Freedom*. Polls gauging the popularity of the black press include "Citizens Endorse Crusade of the Negro Press," *Courier*, January 23, 1943; "*Defender* Poll: Readers Back Crusading Policy of Negro Press," *Defender*, February 24, 1945; and Lee, "*Negro Digest* Poll," 54. *Negro Digest* polls are dubious. Wallace Lee was actually editor Ben Burns, who confessed in his autobiography that, "My sample polling to reflect national opinion was usually no more than a dozen acquaintances, but my margin of error was probably no greater than those of so-called scientific polls." See Burns, *Nitty Gritty*, 32–33.
4. "14 Million Negro Customers," *Kiplinger Magazine*, April 1947, 21. Also see "Negro Markets," *Tide*, March 15, 1946, 86, 88; "The Negro Market: An Appraisal," *Tide*, March 7, 1947, 15–18; and Chambers, *Madison Avenue and the Color Line*.
5. Miles, "Negro Magazines Come of Age," 12, 21; S. W. Garlington, "Popular Negro Magazines Offer Broad Opportunities in Reading," *Amsterdam News*, July 15, 1944; and *N. W. Ayer & Son's Directory of Newspapers and Periodicals, 1950* (Philadelphia: N. W. Ayer & Son, 1950), 1338, 1339.
6. See Johnson, *Succeeding against the Odds*.
7. For informative essays analyzing American policy toward the Third World during the Cold War, see Statler and Johns, *Eisenhower Administration*.
8. See Kenneth A. Osgood, "Words and Deeds: Race, Colonialism, and Eisenhower's Propaganda War in the Third World," in Statler and Johns, *Eisenhower Administration*, 3–25.
9. Alwood, *Dark Days in the Newsroom*, 3–4, 6; and Wechsler, *Age of Suspicion*, 284. Regarding the abuses of McCarthyism, see Schrecker, *Many Are the Crimes*; Stone, *Perilous Times*, 235–310; and Caute, *Great Fear*. Regarding the interaction between anticommunists and journalists, also see Halberstam, *Powers That Be*, 193–201; and Davies, *Postwar Decline of American Newspapers*, 31–48.

10. Schlesinger, "U.S. Communist Party," 90; Barnett and Davis, February 20, 1949, and March 2, 1949, box 136, folder 3, *Barnett Papers*; and Harrington, "Why I Left America," in *Why I Left America*, 96–109.

11. "Powell Breaks Ties with Harlem Paper," *New York Times*, December 25, 1946; Testimony of Marvel Cooke, September 8, 1953, U.S. Senate, Hearings before the Permanent Subcommittee on Investigations of the Committee on Government Operations, 4–9; and "Harlem Paper Held Aiding Negroes' Foes: Plays 'Uncle Tom' Role, Red Critics Says," *New York Times*, December 19, 1947. Also see Anthony, *Max Yergan*, 228–231. Powell's separation from the *People's Voice* was so total that the paper did not merit inclusion in the index of his autobiography, *Adam by Adam*. Paul Robeson Jr. notes in his book that his parents' FBI files confirmed rumors that Yergan informed for the FBI. See *Paul Robeson*, 129.

12. Burns to Pittman, undated and April 5, 1946, box 2, folder 7A, and Pittman to Eugene Holmes, May 8, 1946, box 1, folder 26, *Pittman Papers*, New York University; Mullen, *Popular Fronts*, 182–183; and Lewis, *W.E.B. Du Bois: Fight for Equality*, 538–539. Du Bois also irritated Sengstacke by calling the publisher's preferred candidate, Republican Thomas E. Dewey, "a complete opportunist politician," in "The Winds of Time," *Chicago Defender*, January 3, 1948. Padmore outlined his views on communism in *Pan-Africanism or Communism?*

13. Testimony of Young, July 13, 1949, U.S. House of Representatives, Hearings before the Committee on Un-American Activities, 454, 455.

14. McKinley Sims, "Afro-Americans Disgusted," letter to the editor, *Defender*, July 9, 1949; Rogers, "Rogers Says," *Pittsburgh Courier*, May 7, 1949; and "Where Real Probe Is Needed," *Afro-American*, July 23, 1949.

15. Gottlieb et al., *Next Los Angeles*, 54; "*California Eagle* Needs $20,000 to Remain Alive," *Atlanta Daily World*, May 24, 1950; Bass, *Forty Years*, 177; and "Mrs. Bass Charges 'Blackout' by Press," *Defender*, November 1, 1952.

16. Horne, *Black and Red*, 125–136, 151–182; Du Bois, *Autobiography of W.E.B. Du Bois*, 11, 362–363, 370; and Lochard to Du Bois, December 17, 1951, *Papers of W.E.B. Du Bois*, microfilm, reel 66, 1068.

17. Jones, "End to the Neglect of the Problems!" 52; and Boyce Davies, *Left of Karl Marx*, 134–165, with quote on 143.

18. Du Bois, "On the Collection of Honest News," *National Guardian*, January 29, 1953, in *Newspaper Columns by W.E.B. Du Bois*, Vol. 2, 907–908.

19. Lamphere, "Paul Robeson, *Freedom* Newspaper" (PhD diss.). Concerning the political radicalism of Childress and Hansberry, see Mary Helen Washington, "Alice Childress, Lorraine Hansberry and Claudia Jones: Black Women Write the Popular Front," in Mullen and Smethurst, *Left of the Color Line*, 184–204.

20. Hughes, "'Goodbye Christ' Withdrawn," *Afro-American*, January 11, 1941; Rampersad, *Life of Langston Hughes*, Vol. 2, 3–5, 209–222; and testimony of Hughes, March 26, 1953, U.S. Senate, Hearings before the Permanent Subcommittee on Investigations of the Committee on Government Operations, 74.

21. Ibid., 74, 75, 79, 80.

22. Prattis to Graham Du Bois, October 14, 1952, *Papers of W.E.B. Du Bois*, reel 68, 840–841; and Jolley to George F. Brown, July 3, 1956, box 190-1, folder 8, *Pittsburgh Courier Washington Bureau Papers*, Howard University. Regarding Prattis's columns, see "The Horizon," October 18, 1952, and October 31, 1953.

23. Schuyler, "Views and Reviews," *Courier*, August 22, 1953, July 7, 1956, and "The Lynching of McCarthy," November 6, 1954; Schuyler, *Black and Conservative*, 98, 332–333; and Prattis and Schuyler, July 8, 1960, and July 13, 1960, *Prattis Papers*, Howard University.

24. Hicks, "Hicks Attends First 'Loyalty' Hearing in N.Y.," *Afro-American*, March 31, 1951, "Veterans Whirl," April 17, 1948, and "I Am an American Too," May 26, 1951.

25. "The Negro Press, 1955," *Time*, November 7, 1955. Regarding postwar business trends in the newspaper industry, see Davies, *Postwar Decline of American Newspapers*, 1–14.

26. "Systematic Future Development of the Robert S. Abbott Publishing Company," May 4, 1958, box 46, folder 1, *Abbott-Sengstacke Papers*, Chicago Public Library; and "Unveil New *Defender* Family of 7 Papers," *Defender*, December 13, 1952. Also see Klibanoff, "L. Alex Wilson."

27. Nunn to Stanley Roberts, November 7, 1950, box 190-3, folder 29, *Courier Washington Bureau Papers*, Howard University; "*Pittsburgh Courier* Board of Directors Minutes," October 30, 1956, box 129, folder 2, *Abbott-Sengstacke Papers*, Chicago Public Library; and Prattis to Barnett, June 28, 1956, and April 30, 1956, box 139, folder 2, *Barnett Papers*.

28. Poston, "Negro Press," 16; and White to Barnett, June 18, 1953, box 141, folder 5, and Prattis to Barnett, April 30, 1956, box 139, folder 2, *Barnett Papers*.

29. Du Bois to Padmore, January 27, 1955, *Du Bois Papers*, reel 71, 643; Padmore to Du Bois, December 3, 1954, in Aptheker, *Correspondence of W.E.B. Du Bois*, Vol. 3, 374; and Barnett to Marguerite Cartwright, May 22, 1956, box 135, folder 9, *Barnett Papers*. My characterization of journalists' framing of news from Africa during the 1950s complements Meriwether's analysis in *Proudly We Can Be Africans*.

30. "Backstage," *Ebony*, November 1945, 2; Burns, *Nitty Gritty*, 94; "The Negro Press, 1955," *Time*, November 7, 1955; Walker, "The Negro Press: Its Importance, Its Mission," speech delivered March 16, 1959, North Carolina College at Durham, box 197-6, folder 33, *Walker Papers*, Howard University; and Green, *Selling the Race*, 142–143.

31. Svirsky, *Your Newspaper*, 23; "ANG Opens Drive to Place Negroes on Daily Papers," *Amsterdam News*, June 29, 1946; Pride to Frank Stanley, October 2, 1953, box 8, folder "Negro Press," *Stanley Papers*, University of Louisville; and "Negroes on White Newspapers," *Ebony*, November 1955, 77–82. Also see "Negro Newsmen on White Dailies," *Ebony*, April 1948, 56–60, and "The Black Newshawks," *Our World*, March 1952, 46–49.

32. Catledge and Barnett, May 18, and May 22, 1945, box 142, folder 4, *Barnett Papers*; "George Streator, Newsman, Was 53," *New York Times*, July 29, 1955; Streator, "Senator on the Warpath," *New York Star & Amsterdam News*, January 25, 1941; and Ernest E.

Johnson, "West Coast Demands Recall of WPB's George Streator," *Courier*, December 2, 1944. For Streator's relationship with Du Bois, see Lewis, *Du Bois: Fight for Equality*, 139–142, 318, 336–337.

33. Conrad, "Yesterday and Today," *Defender*, January 26, 1946; Tifft and Jones, *Trust*, 276–277; Catledge, *My Life and the* Times, 218; Streator, "Negro University in Texas Dragging," *New York Times*, July 24, 1949; "University Status in Texas Clarified," *New York Times*, August 14, 1949; and Gelb, *City Room*, 107–108.

34. "Nieman Notes: Fletcher P. Martin," *Nieman Reports* 60 (Spring 2006): 92–93; Alvin White to Claude Barnett, undated, 1949, box 141, folder 4, *Barnett Papers*; "Tulsa Editor Joins *Ebony* in Chicago," Associated Negro Press, February 4, 1952; Adam Bernstein, "Longtime Reporter Arch Parsons," *Washington Post*, January 18, 2001; Newkirk, *Within the Veil*, 60–61; Samuel A. Haynes to Carl Murphy, August 5, 1951, box 50, folder Haynes, *Afro-American Papers*, Howard University; and Jones, "I Was Going to Be a Timesman."

35. Wil Haygood, "The Man from *Jet*," *Washington Post*, July 15, 2007. Also see Angela Terrell, "Simeon Booker: Of Survival and Facts of Life," *Post*, March 28, 1974.

36. Rowan, *Breaking Barriers*, 98.

37. Rowan, *South of Freedom*, 139.

38. Regarding press coverage of the Civil Rights Movement, see Roberts and Klibanoff, *Race Beat*.

39. Gordon, "Reviewing the News," *Atlanta Daily World*, May 18, 1954; and "Equality in Our Time," *Los Angeles Sentinel*, May 20, 1954.

40. "The Second Emancipation," *New York Amsterdam News*, May 22, 1954; and "Decision Means as Much to America as It Does to Negroes . . . Mrs. Vann," *Courier*, May 22, 1954.

41. Wright, *Color Curtain*, in *Black Power*, 537.

42. Gordon, "Seven Years since Bandung," 301; Mackay to Worthy, February 15, 1955, box 98, folder Bill Worthy, *Afro-American Papers*, Howard University; and Rowan, *Breaking Barriers*, 128–129. The U.S. consul general in Hong Kong is quoted in Cary Fraser, "An American Dilemma: Race and Realpolitik in the American Response to the Bandung Conference, 1955," in Plummer, *Window on Freedom*, 123–124.

43. "Communism Was No Issue at Bandung," *Courier*, May 28, 1955; Cartwright, "Bandung: For the Record," *Amsterdam News*, June 4, 1955; and Rowan, *Pitiful and the Proud*, 417–418.

44. Lautier, "Travelers to East Learn Our World Is Non-White," *Afro-American*, April 30, 1955; and Worthy, "The Asian-African Conference: Bandung in Retrospect," *Afro-American*, June 11, 1955.

45. Payne, "Reflections from a Mountain Top," TMs, 1, box 41, folder 2, *Payne Papers*, Library of Congress; Payne, *Interviews with Ethel Payne*, interview by Kathleen Currie, Women in Journalism Oral History Project, September 22, 1987, 66–67; and "National Grapevine: Return of the Native," *Defender*, June 4, 1955. Also see Morris, *Eye on the Struggle*, 152–168.

46. "Sheriff Hints Mother Doesn't Know Her Child," *Jet*, September 22, 1955, 10; "Nation Horrified by Murder of Kidnaped [*sic*] Chicago Youth," *Jet*, September 15, 1955, 9; and Ladner quoted in Feldstein, *Motherhood in Black and White*, 109. A thorough overview of the press's role in the trial is found in Roberts and Klibanoff, *Race Beat*, 86–108. Also see Booker, *Shocking the Conscience*, 63–83.

47. Booker, "1956: A Negro Reporter at the Till Trial"; and Terry, *Missing Pages*, 139. Booker's article was originally published in January 1956.

48. Murdock Larsson, "Land of the Till Murder Revisited," 54, 56; Terry, *Missing Pages*, 144–146; and Hicks, "Unbelievable! Inside Story of Miss. Trial," *Afro-American*, October 29, 1955.

49. Booker, "1956: A Negro Reporter at the Till Trial"; Roberts and Klibanoff, *Race Beat*, 99–100; Wilson, "*Defender* Tracks Down Mystery Till 'Witnesses,'" and "Here Is What 'Too Tight' Said," *Defender*, October 8, 1955.

50. Hicks to Carl Murphy, Art Carter, Cliff Mackay, September 27, 1955, box 50, folder Hicks, *Afro-American Papers*, Howard University; and Hicks, "Why Hicks Just Had to Go Back to Mississippi," *Afro-American*, November 26, 1955. Hicks's letter to his editors was published on October 8, 1955.

51. Abernathy, *And the Walls Came Tumbling Down*, 154–155. Also see Roberts and Klibanoff, *Race Beat*, 109–112.

52. Roberts and Klibanoff, *Race Beat*, 120–121. Compare Rowan's account of his phone call about the bus boycott in *Breaking Barriers*, 140, to Donald T. Ferron, "Notes of the Executive Board," January 23, 1956, in Carson, *Papers of Martin Luther King*, Vol. 3, 102. Rowan portrayed his call as an objective reporter's attempt to disprove seemingly false information, but King characterized Rowan as personally attached to the story. King said the story "disturbed" Rowan because "he didn't want a compromise."

53. Hicks, "The Most Pathetic Woman in Alabama," *Amsterdam News*, March 10, 1956; Payne, "Boycotters Won't Talk To or Visit 'Aunt Tom,'" *Defender*, March 7, 1956; and Wilson, "*Defender* Writer Tells of Ride with History," *Defender*, December 24, 1956.

54. Garrow, *Bearing the Cross*, 32; Al Sweeney, "'Not Worried' Says Alabama's Gandhi," *Afro-American*, March 3, 1956; Harold L. Keith, "Are Gandhi's Principles at Work in Montgomery?" *Courier*, March 10, 1956; Worthy, "Tale of Two Cities: One Has Got to Go," *Afro-American*, March 24, 1956; Payne, "Rev. King's Own Story," *Defender*, March 31, 1956; and Jackson, "The Tip Off," *Atlanta Daily World*, December 9, 1956.

55. "Systematic Future Development of the Robert S. Abbott Publishing Company," *Abbott-Sengstacke Papers*, Chicago Public Library; "Announce *Defender* Daily at 50th Anniversary Chicago Salute," *Defender*, December 10, 1955; Garland, "Staying with the Black Press," in La Brie, *Perspectives of the Black Press*, 177; and Prattis to W. Beverly Carter, September 13, 1956, box 144-3, folder 14, *Prattis Papers*, Howard University.

56. Bogart, *Age of Television*, 10; and Roberts and Klibanoff, *Race Beat*, 196.

57. "We Are at 'War,'" *Afro-American*, September 1957.

58. Hicks, "'We Were Kicked, Beaten,'" *Amsterdam News*, September 28, 1957; Newson, "AFRO Man Ousted; Other Writers Stay," *Afro-American*, September 21, 1957; and "Protests Ban on Newsmen," *Defender*, September 12, 1957.

59. Hicks, "We Were Kicked, Beaten," *Amsterdam News*, September 28, 1957; and Wilson, "*Defender* Reporter Beaten by Mob, Tells His Story," *Defender*, October 5, 1957. Also see Klibanoff, "L. Alex Wilson."

60. Bates, *Long Shadow of Little Rock*, 170–178; "Bates Tells Why Ark. Paper Folded," *Defender*, December 2, 1959; and "Paper in Red, Bateses Give Up in Little Rock," *Jet*, November 26, 1959, 49.

61. Frazier, *Black Bourgeoisie*, 174–194.

Chapter 6. Black Power Assaults the Black Newspaper

1. Ben A. Franklin, "S.N.C.C. Chief Shot in Cambridge, Md.," *New York Times*, July 27, 1967; and Brown, *Die Nigger Die*, 120.

2. Brown, "More Douglass, Less Garrison," letter to the editor, *Baltimore Afro-American*, August 26, 1967.

3. See Jane Rhodes, "The Black Press and Radical Print Culture," in Nord, Rubin, and Schudson, *Enduring Book*, Vol. 5, 286–303. Regarding the rise of black militancy in the 1960s, see Branch, *At Canaan's Edge*; Joseph, *Waiting 'Til the Midnight Hour*; and Sugrue, *Sweet Land of Liberty*.

4. "Perils of Rap Brown," *Afro-American*, September 2, 1967; and Palmer, "Black Press in Transition," 33–34.

5. McMillian, *Smoking Typewriters*, 1–12. Also see Glessing, *Underground Press in America*; Leamer, *Paper Revolutionaries*; and Wachsberger, *Voices from the Underground*, Vol. 1.

6. Williams, *Negroes with Guns*, 63, 66; and Tyson, *Radio Free Dixie*, 192–198.

7. Sitkoff, *Struggle for Black Equality*, 73.

8. "They Can't Lose," *Afro-American*, March 5, 1960; and "The New South in Action," *Defender*, February 16, 1960.

9. Palmer, "Bare 'New Face of Young Negro America,'" *Defender*, March 26, 1960; and "Editor Tells of Jail Experience," *Defender*, March 21, 1960.

10. "The Sit-Downs Hit Here," *Atlanta Daily World*, March 16, 1960; "Students Deserve a Sympathetic Hearing," *Daily World*, May 6, 1960; and interview with Julian Bond, November 1 and 22, 1999, interview R-0345, Southern Oral History Program Collection (#4007), University of North Carolina at Chapel Hill.

11. Alton Hornsby Jr., "Georgia," in Suggs, *Black Press in the South*, 138, 139; "The Press: Loud Voice in Atlanta," *Time*, June 30, 1961; and Hunter-Gault, "I Remember," 7.

12. "Hail Workers of All Lands on This May Day," and "It's a Journal!" *Freedomways* 1 (Spring 1961): 9; Cooper Jackson, *Freedomways Reader*, xxii; Mayfield, "Cuban Challenge," 188; and Clarke, "New Afro-American Nationalism," 286, 295. Smethurst examines the influence of the "Old Left" on *Freedomways* and the *Liberator* in *Black Arts Movement*, 23–56.

13. Carter to Malcolm X, November 28, 1956, box 144-9, folder 9; Carter to Prattis, June 12, 1957, box 144-3, folder 15; and Nunn to Prattis, April 28, 1958, and Sylvestre C. Watkins to Carter, May 6, 1958, box 144-10, folder 19, *Prattis Papers*, Howard University.

14. Malcolm X, *Autobiography of Malcolm X*, 242. Wallace conceded in a memoir that, "Without Louis Lomax or another black reporter, we wouldn't have gotten the story." See Wallace, *Between You and Me*, 88.

15. Rhodes, "Black Press and Radical Print Culture," 295; and Turner, *Islam in the African-American Experience*, 196–199.

16. Robinson, "Home Plate: The Right to Hate," *Amsterdam News*, August 25, 1962; and Redding, "Behind the Black Muslims," review of *The Black Muslims in America*, by C. Eric Lincoln, *Afro-American*, June 17, 1961.

17. Rhodes, "Black Press and Radical Print Culture," 295–296; and Turner, *Islam in the African-American Experience*, 199.

18. "Races: The Revolution," *Time*, June 7, 1963; and Sugrue, *Sweet Land of Liberty*, 286–312.

19. *Liberator*, January 1963, 2; "Let Us March ON Washington," *Liberator*, August 1963, 2; and Watts, "Dream and Reality," 2. For an overview, see Tinson, "Voice of the Black Protest Movement," 3–15.

20. Walker, "Down the Big Road," *Cleveland Call and Post*, October 17, 1964; and "The Cry for Justice," *Afro-American*, July 17, 1965.

21. Matthews, "Thinking Out Loud! Has Press Seized Upon Stokely as Replacement for Malcolm X?" *Afro-American*, July 23, 1966; "Come On Harlem—Let's Play It Smart!" and "Harlem's Plea," *Amsterdam News*, July 25, 1964; "The Expected Happened," *Defender*, July 29, 1964; and Stone, "A Stone's Throw: Advice to White Leaders on Responsible Negro Leadership," *Defender*, July 28, 1964.

22. "Publishers Visit President Kennedy," *Daily World*, January 27, 1962; "Publishers Have Frank and Open Discussion with Pres. Johnson," *Daily World*, February 2, 1964; and Rowan to Roger Tubby, February 3, 1961, subgroup 3, series 3, box 1, *Rowan Papers*, Oberlin College.

23. Johnson, *Succeeding against the Odds*, 270–272, 281–283; and John Woodford, "Messaging the Blackman," in Wachsberger, *Voices from the Underground*, Vol. 1, 82.

24. Davies, *Postwar Decline of American Newspapers*, 128–136; and Stephen Walsh, "Black-Oriented Radio and the Civil Rights Movement," in Ward, *Media, Culture, and the Modern African American Freedom Struggle*, 67–81.

25. Palmer, "Black Press in Transition," 32; and Reid, "Associated Negro Press Closes," 23–25. Washburn identifies the sale of the *Courier* as the end of black newspapers' prominence in *African American Newspaper*, 5.

26. "A Victim of Negro Progress," *Newsweek*, August 26, 1963, 51; Sengstacke, "Censorship by Omission," March 14, 1962, box 24, folder 29, *Abbott-Sengstacke Papers*, Chicago Public Library; and Hicks, "Meet the Family (Part II)," *Amsterdam News*, April 3, 1965.

27. "Cuts Tie with Black Muslims," February 24, 1965, *Defender.*

28. "Malcolm X, *Defender*, February 23, 1965; "Malcolm X," *Afro-American*, March 6, 1965; and "Those Who Live by the Sword," *Norfolk Journal and Guide*, February 27, 1965.

29. Davis, "Our Own Black Shining Prince," 7; "Malcolm X, The Unfulfilled Promise," *Liberator*, March 1965, 3; Cleaver, *Soul on Ice*, 53, 60, and *Soul on Fire*, 74.

30. Matthews, "Thinking Out Loud!" *Afro-American*, July 23, 1966; and King, *Where Do We Go from Here?* 32–33.

31. Powell and Hicks, "Black Power Is Self Defense," *Amsterdam News*, July 23, 1966; "Black Power," *Afro-American*, July 16, 1966; and "Racial Solidarity," *Defender*, June 30, 1966.

32. Walker, "Down the Big Road," *Call and Post*, June 29 and July 6, 1963, June 25, September 3, and October 22, 1966, and July 1, 1967.

33. Seale, *Seize the Time*, 177–180; Hilliard and Cole, *This Side of Glory*, 149; *Black Panther*, March 22, 1970; and Christian A. Davenport, "Reading the 'Voice of the Vanguard': A Content Analysis of the *Black Panther Intercommunal News Service*, 1969–1973," in Jones, *Black Panther Party Reconsidered*, 197. Also see Rhodes, "*Black Panther* Newspaper," 151–158.

34. *Black Panther*, August 2 and 30, 1969, August 29, 1970, and November 21, 1970. Regarding *Black Panther*, see JoNina M. Abron, "'Raising the Consciousness of the People': *The Black Panther Intercommunal News Service*, 1967–1980," in Wachsberger, *Voices from the Underground*, Vol. 1, 343–360; Durant, *Black Panther*; and Hilliard, *Black Panther Intercommunal News Service*. Rhodes analyzes press depictions of the Black Panther Party in *Framing the Black Panthers*. I read copies of the *Black Panther* in the *Guthrie Papers*, Duke University. The collection holds copies of the *Black Panther* from 1969 to 1971.

35. Hilliard, *Black Panther Intercommunal News Service*, xvii; Colette Gaiter, "What Revolution Looks Like: The Work of Black Panther Artist Emory Douglas," in Durant, *Black Panther*, 94; Forbes, *Will You Die with Me?* 19–20; Seale, *Seize the Time*, 179; and Palmer, "Black Press in Transition," 35. The *Black Panther*'s circulation was unaudited.

36. Thornton and Cassidy, "Black Newspapers in 1968," 10, 11; Hanson, "An Evaluative Assertion Analysis of the Black Press" (PhD diss.); "$500 for Peace," *Defender*, April 22, 1967; and Walker, "Down the Big Road," *Call and Post*, December 2, 1967.

37. Stanley, "Reporting about Extremism," speech delivered February 15, 1967, National Press Club, Washington D.C., *Stanley Papers*, University of Louisville; Forss, *Black Print with a White Carnation*, 148, 154–155; and Rhodes, *Framing the Black Panthers*, 85–87, 147–149.

38. Woodford, "Messaging the Blackman," 82, 84.

39. Ibid., 86.

40. *Black Panther*, January 31 and August 8, 1970; and Memo, G. C. Moore to W. C. Sullivan, October 16, 1969; Airtel, FBI Director to SAC [Special Agent in Charge], Chicago, New York, San Francisco, June 29, 1970, Memo, SAC, New York, to FBI Director, February 27, 1968, Memo, FBI Director to SAC, San Francisco, September 24, 1969; and Airtel, SAC, Newark, to FBI Director, June 3, 1970, *COINTELPRO*, Archives Unbound.

41. Smethurst, *Black Arts Movement*, 92; Jones, "Communications Project," 53–57; and Neal, "Black Arts Movement," 26. Also see Ongiri, *Spectacular Blackness*, 88–123.

42. Smethurst, *Black Arts Movement*, 207–208; Fuller, *Journey to Africa*, 17–18, 81; Fuller, "Editor's Notes," 4; and Johnson, *Succeeding against the Odds*, 288–289.

43. "Editorial Policy," *Black Liberator*, June 1969; "What JOMO Believes," *Burning Spear*, June 15–29, 1970; Heard, "*Inner City Voice*," 30; *Black Ink*, November 1969; and "Harambee Near Publication," *Lawrence* (Kans.) *Journal-World*, February 26, 1970.

Chapter 7. Into the White Newsroom

1. Poston to Paul Sann, July 17, 1962, in Poston, *First Draft of History*, 170; and Hauke, *Ted Poston*, 181.

2. United States, *Report of the National Advisory Commission on Civil Disorders*, 203.

3. Ibid., 211; and Noall, "Report on Rioting," 18.

4. Bennett, "The White Media," in Daly, *Media and the Cities*, 9.

5. Booker, *Black Man's America*, 145; and Fisher and Lowenstein, "Introduction and Guidelines," in *Race and the News Media*, 8, 71, 76–77. Also see Mellinger, *Chasing Newsroom Diversity*, 19–45, and Martindale, *White Press and Black America*, 53–71.

6. My characterization of how journalists critiqued their coverage of race news comes from my examination of *Editor & Publisher* from the mid-1950s through the 1960s. Also see Davies, *Postwar Decline of American Newspapers*, 63–76. Roberts and Klibanoff illustrate in *Race Beat* how the standard journalistic narrative concerning news coverage of the Civil Rights Movement continues to shape history. They present a sympathetic account of a particular set of journalists—white reporters covering race news for national news outlets. These objective reporters are contrasted with well-intentioned liberal white southern journalists who favored gradual desegregation, reactionary white southern editors who aimed to halt integration, and brave but partisan black reporters relegated to the movement's sidelines. In this framing, black journalists are attributed minor relevance because they work for slow-paced weeklies, are unable to breach the color line when on assignment, and violate the professional dictate of objectivity. Their courage is praised, but their work is mostly ignored after the Little Rock crisis in 1957. With black journalists marginalized, the authors emphasize geographical difference as the main fault line in news perspective rather than racial difference. This emphasis exaggerates the racial progressiveness of national race reporters by having them serve as a counterpoint to intolerance rather than full equality. When examining the totality of media coverage, scholars are more critical of how journalists framed 1960s social movements for public consumption. For examples, see Gitlin, *Whole World Is Watching*; Lentz, *Symbols, the News Magazines*; and Rhodes, *Framing the Black Panthers*.

7. Clark, "Crisis in the Civil Rights Crisis," 18; Hernton, "Is There *Really* a Negro Revolution?" 18; and Fuller, "Myth of the White Backlash," 12.

8. Baldwin, "The Dangerous Road before Martin Luther King," "East River, Downtown: Postscript to a Letter from Harlem," and "The Fire Next Time," in Baldwin, *Collected Essays*, 186, 345, 656.

9. Lomax, "Negro Revolt against 'The Negro Leaders,'" 48; and Friedman, "Negro Leader Looks at the Press," 38.

10. Worthy, "Angriest Negroes," 102. Regarding Worthy's militancy, see Joseph, *Waiting 'Til the Midnight Hour*.

11. Poston, "The American Negro and Newspaper Myths," in Fisher and Lowenstein, *Race and the News Media*, 71; Martindale, *White Press and Black America*, 59, 79–101; and Lyle, Introduction, in *Black American and the Press*, ix–xviii.

12. Erskine, "The Polls: Demonstrations and Race Riots," 655–677; Rhodes, *Framing the Black Panthers*, 62–68; and Carmichael, *Ready for Revolution*, 487–488.

13. "Some Helpful Hints for Riot Reporters," *Editor & Publisher*, July 22, 1967, 12; "Beatings and Sniper Shots Mark Coverage of Rioting," *Editor & Publisher*, August 21, 1965, 10, 11; "Editors Give Views on Riot Coverage," *Editor & Publisher*, August 5, 1967, 11; and "'Black Power' Fury Scares Cameramen," *Editor & Publisher*, July 29, 1967, 9.

14. Fleming, *Son of the Rough South*, 20.

15. Bond, "The Media and the Movement: Looking Back from the Southern Front," in Ward, *Media, Culture*, 17; and Abernathy, *And the Walls Came Tumbling Down*, 496.

16. Maynard, "This Far by Fear" (opening remarks at Kerner Plus 10: Conference on Minorities and the Media); Richardson, "'Get Whitey,' Scream Blood-Hungry Mobs," *Los Angeles Times*, August 14, 1965; and Hauke, *Ted Poston*, 171.

17. United States, *Report*, 1, 9, 201, 213.

18. Noall, "Report on Rioting," 18, 40.

19. United States, *Report*, 211; Klein, "Survey Shows News Media Working on Racial Tension," 40; Noall, "Report on Rioting," 18; and Mellinger, *Chasing Newsroom Diversity*, 52–62.

20. Isaacs quoted in Mellinger, *Chasing Newsroom Diversity*, 59; United States, *Report*, 211, 212; and Wilkins, *A Man's Life*, 330.

21. Friendly quoted in Steve Kline, "Black Executives on White Newspapers," in Tinney and Rector, *Issues and Trends*, 130; Terry, *Missing Pages*, 252, 253; and Raspberry, "Ultimate Compliment," *Washington Post*, March 27, 1972.

22. McCullough, "Not All Racial News Is Black and White," 17; and Raspberry, "Militants, Moderates Disagree—But Civilly," *Washington Post*, November 20, 1967.

23. Jarrett, "'Messiah Machine': Don't Get in Its Way," and "Jesse Picks Strange Forum to Air Attack," *Chicago Tribune*, January 9, 1972, and March 25, 1973.

24. "William Raspberry: A Tool in the Hands of the Oppressors," *Black Panther*, February 27, 1971; Moreland to Chuck Stone, January 25, 1974, box 16, folder, general correspondence, 1963–1987, *Stone Papers*, Duke University; Delaney, "Black Muslim Group in Trouble from Financial Problems and Some Crime," *New York Times*, December 6, 1973; and C. Gerald Fraser, "Financial Ills Denied by Black Muslims," *New York Times*, December 11, 1973.

25. Worthy, "American Negro Is Dead," 126, 168.

26. Worthy, "Negro Reporter's Dilemmas," 62.

27. Brown, "Negro Press," 34; Stone, letter to the editor, *Washington Post*, December 29, 1969; Stone to Graham, November 21, 1969, box 32, folder 2, black press, 1964–1983, *Stone Papers*, Duke University; and *Philadelphia Daily News*, in-house advertisement, March 9, 1972.

28. Stone, "Page 10," *Daily News*, March 20, April 6, May 2, and June 5, 1972, and April 9, 1974; Neill, "The Editor Talks with You," *Daily News*, May 8, 1972; and Stone, "Jail Cools after Newsman's Visit," *Daily News*, June 27, 1972. Stone's *Daily News* columns are collected in his papers at Duke University.

29. Diamond, "'Reporter Power' Takes Root," 12. MacLean explores the connections between the Civil Rights Movement and workplace equality in *Freedom Is Not Enough*.

30. Hauke, *Ted Poston*, 181–182; and Nissenson, *Lady Upstairs*, 350–352.

31. Caldwell, "Ask Me. I Know I Was the Test Case," 4; and Terry, *Missing Pages*, 273.

32. "The Nixon Administration and the News Media," *Congressional Quarterly Weekly Report*, January 1, 1972, 3–7; and Terry, *Missing Pages*, 278.

33. "Message to the Black Community . . . From Black Journalists," *New York Amsterdam News*, February 21, 1970.

34. Terry, *Missing Pages*, 282.

35. Kirk Scharfenberg, "Bias by *Newsweek* in Firing Charged," *Washington Post*, January 6, 1972; Fleming, *Yes We Did?* 82; Yette, *The Choice*, 15; and "*Newsweek* Fires Yette; He Charges Discrimination," *Jet*, January 20, 1972, 9. The D.C. commission sided with Yette, but an appeals court sided with *Newsweek*. The U.S. Supreme Court let stand the appeals court decision.

36. "Black Caucus to Explore Relationship of Mass Media and Black Community," *Jet*, January 27, 1972, 44; and Nan Robertson, "Blacks in House Denounce F.C.C.," *New York Times*, March 9, 1972.

37. "Black Reporters Charge *Washington Post* Is Biased," *Jet*, April 13, 1972; and Bart Barnes, "Black *Post* Writers Claim Hiring Bias," *Washington Post*, March 24, 1972.

38. Hollie I. West, "Howard's 'Black Journalism,'" *Washington Post*, January 30, 1972. For more on New Journalism, see Weingarten, *The Gang That Wouldn't Write Straight*.

39. West, "Black Newsmen Voice Frustration," *Post*, March 5, 1972; and Hunter, "Black Reporter Must Be Revolutionary," *Amsterdam News*, June 19, 1971.

40. Nicholas von Hoffman, "The Black News Issue," *Post*, March 24, 1972; "Lu Palmer in CSU Speech," *Chicago Defender*, April 9, 1973; "Publications," *Black World*, July 1973, 90; and Armistead S. Pride, "The News That Was," in La Brie, *Perspectives of the Black Press*, 42.

41. Michael T. Kaufman, "Black Groups Open a Campaign against 'Racism' in Media Here," *New York Times*, April 6, 1972; Paul Delaney, "Blacks Complain of Media to FCC," *New York Times*, March 19, 1973; and "Group Decides to Fund TV's *Black Journal* Show," *Jet*, February 22, 1973, 18. See MacDonald, *Blacks and White TV*, 204–214.

42. Johnson, "A Graduate of the Black Press Looks Back," in La Brie, *Perspectives of the Black Press*, 187, 188.

43. Gilliam, "What Do Black Journalists Want?" 47; and Wilkins, "Further MORE," 27.

44. Dawkins, *Black Journalists*, 24, 34–35.

45. "Kerner Plus Ten," *Problems of Journalism: Proceedings of the 1978 Convention*, 293–296; and Kotz, "Minority Struggle," 27.

46. Kotz, "Minority Struggle," 24–25.

47. Maynard, "This Far by Fear," 2.

48. Kotz, "Minority Struggle," 23; and Mellinger, *Chasing Newsroom Diversity*, 74–82.

49. "Professionalism on Both Sides of the Desk" (discussion panel at *Kerner Plus 10: Conference on Minorities and the Media*), 18; and Martindale, *White Press and Black America*, 106–108.

Epilogue

1. My discussion of objectivity as a contested arena for ideological debate is informed by Hall, *Silver Linings*.

2. Entman explains "modern racism" in "Modern Racism and the Images of Blacks" and with Rojecki in *Black Image in the White Mind*. Campbell outlines the myths of marginalization, difference, and assimilation in *Race, Myth, and the News*. Also see Campbell et al., *Race and News*; and Wilson et al., *Racism, Sexism, and the Media*. For a fuller discussion of integrating broadcast news from the 1960s to the 1990s, see Gonzalez and Torres, *News for All the People*, 301–338.

3. Pew Research Center, "State of the Media," 17, 82; and Sanders, *How Racism and Sexism Killed Traditional Media*, xxiii. Wilson discusses the "illusion of inclusion" in *Black Journalists in Paradox*, 137–158. He heard the phrase applied to journalism when U.S. District Judge Alcee Hastings spoke in 1986 to the National Association of Black Journalists. Nishikawa et al., argue for a "critical mass of minority journalists" in "Interviewing the Interviewers," 255.

4. Ibid., 82; Robert Channick, "Johnson Publishing Sells *Ebony*, *Jet* Magazines to Texas Firm," *Chicago Tribune*, June 15, 2016; and Bill Shea, "Hiram Jackson's Goal: Update Real Times to Modern Times," *Crain's Detroit Business*, October 14, 2013. Also see Cheryl D. Jenkins, "Newsroom Diversity and Representations of Race," in Campbell et al., *Race and News*, 22–42.

5. Pew Research Center, "Social Media Conversations about Race," 2, 3. Also see Cobb, "Matter of Black Lives."

6. Ibid., 9. Also see McChesney, *Digital Disconnect*, 172–215.

Bibliography

Archives and Manuscript Collections

Chicago Public Library, Vivian G. Harsh Research Collection
  Abbott-Sengstacke Family Papers
Columbia University, Rare Book and Manuscript Library, New York
  Hubert H. Harrison Papers
Duke University, David M. Rubenstein Rare Book & Manuscript Library, Durham, N.C.
  Chuck Stone Papers
  Milo Guthrie Papers
Howard University, Moorland-Spingarn Research Center, Washington, D.C.
  Baltimore Afro-American Papers
  Percival L. Prattis Papers
  Pittsburgh Courier Washington Bureau Papers
  William O. Walker Papers
Library of Congress, Washington, D.C.
  Ethel L. Payne Papers
New York Public Library, Schomburg Center for Research in Black Culture
  Eugene Gordon Papers
New York University, Tamiment Library, Robert F. Wagner Labor Archives
  John Pittman Papers
  Newspaper Guild of New York Records
Oberlin College, Oberlin College Archives
  Carl T. Rowan Papers

University of Louisville, University Archives and Records Center
Frank L. Stanley Sr. Papers

Published or Microfilmed Archives and Manuscript Collections

Aptheker, Herbert, ed. *The Correspondence of W.E.B. Du Bois*. Vol. 1, *Selections, 1877–1934*. Amherst: University of Massachusetts Press, 1973.

———. *The Correspondence of W.E.B. Du Bois*. Vol. 3, *Selections, 1944–1963*. Amherst: University of Massachusetts Press, 1978.

Carson, Clayborne, ed. *The Papers of Martin Luther King, Jr.* Vol. 3, *Birth of a New Age, December 1955-December 1956*. Berkeley: University of California Press, 2005.

Claude A. Barnett Papers: The Associated Negro Press, 1918–1967. Frederick, Md.: University Publications of America, 1986.

COINTELPRO: The Counterintelligence Program of the Federal Bureau of Investigation, Black Nationalist Hate Groups. Accessed through Archives Unbound. Web database.

Federal Surveillance of Afro-Americans, 1917–1925: The First World War, the Red Scare, and the Garvey Movement. Frederick, Md.: University Publications of America, 1986.

Link, Arthur S., ed. *The Papers of Woodrow Wilson*. Vol. 41, *January 24–April 6, 1917*. Princeton, N.J.: Princeton University Press.

———. *The Papers of Woodrow Wilson*. Vol. 45, *November 11, 1917–January 15, 1918*. Princeton, N.J.: Princeton University Press.

———. *The Papers of Woodrow Wilson*. Vol. 49, *July 18–September 13, 1918*. Princeton, N.J.: Princeton University Press.

Papers of the NAACP. Part 9, *Discrimination in the U.S. Armed Forces, 1918–1955*. Frederick, Md.: University Publications of America, 1989.

The Papers of W.E.B. Du Bois. New York: Microfilming Corporation of America, 1981.

Records of the Office of War Information, Part 1. Frederick, Md.: University Publications of America, 1986.

Internet Sources

The Black Archives of Mid-America. Kansas City, Mo., http://www.blackarchives.org.

Early American Marxism. Tim Davenport, ed., Corvallis, Ore., http://www.marxist history.org.

Niagara Movement. Special Collections and University Archives, W.E.B. Du Bois Library, University of Massachusetts Amherst, http://scua.library.umass.edu/digital/niagara.htm.

Pew Research Center. "Social Media Conversations about Race." August 2016, http://www.pewinternet.org/2016/08/15/social-media-conversations-about-race/.

———. "State of the Media, 2016." June 2016, http://www.journalism.org/2016/06/15/state-of-the-news-media-2016/.

Southern Oral History Program Collection. Southern Historical Collection, Wilson Library, University of North Carolina at Chapel Hill, http://www.lib.unc.edu/dc/sohp/.

Women in Journalism Oral History Project. Washington Press Club Foundation, Washington, D.C., http://wpcf.org/women-in-journalism/.

Government Publications

Chicago Commission on Race Relations. *The Negro in Chicago: A Study of Race Relations and a Race Riot.* Chicago: University of Chicago Press, 1922.

United States. *Report of the National Advisory Commission on Civil Disorders.* Washington, D.C.: U.S. Government Printing Office, 1968.

U.S. Department of Commerce. *Negro Population in the United States, 1790–1915.* Washington, D.C.: Government Printing Office, 1918; New York: Arno Press, 1968.

U.S. House of Representatives. Hearings before the Committee on Un-American Activities. *Hearings Regarding Communist Infiltration of Minority Groups,* Part 1. 81st Cong., 1st sess., July 13–14, and 18, 1949.

U.S. Senate. Hearings before the Permanent Subcommittee on Investigations of the Committee on Government Operations. *Communist Infiltration among Army Civilian Workers.* 83rd Cong., 1st sess., September 8 and 11, 1953.

———. Hearings before the Permanent Subcommittee on Investigations of the Committee on Government Operations. *State Department Information Program—Information Centers.* 83rd Cong., 1st sess., March 24–26, 1953.

Published Conference Proceedings

Kerner Plus 10: Conference on Minorities and the Media, University of Michigan, Ann Arbor, April 22, 1977. Ann Arbor: Howard R. March Center for the Study of Journalistic Performance, University of Michigan, 1977.

"Kerner Plus Ten." In *Problems of Journalism: Proceedings of the 1978 Convention in Washington, D.C., April 9–12,* American Society of Newspaper Editors, 292–307. Easton, Penn.: American Society of Newspaper Editors, 1978.

Quirin, James. "African American Perceptions of the Battle of Adwa, 1896–1914." In *Proceedings of the XVth International Conference of Ethiopian Studies,* Hamburg, Germany, July 20–25, 2003, edited by Siegbert Uhlig, 342–347. Wiesbaden, Germany: Otto Harrassowitz, 2006.

Newspapers and Magazines

Atlanta Daily World
Baltimore Afro-American
The Black Panther
Chicago Defender
Chicago Tribune
Cleveland Call and Post
Cleveland Gazette
Crain's Detroit Business

Crisis
Crusader
Ebony
Freedomways
Jet
Kiplinger Magazine
Liberator
Los Angeles Sentinel
Los Angeles Times
Macon (Georgia) *Telegraph and Messenger*
Messenger
Muhammad Speaks
Negro Digest (Black World)
Negro World
Newsweek
New York Age
New York Amsterdam News (*New York Amsterdam Star-News*)
New York Times
Norfolk Journal and Guide
Our World
Pittsburgh Courier
Richmond Times-Dispatch
San Francisco Spokesman
St. Louis Argus
St. Louis Post-Dispatch
Tide
Time
The Voice
Voice of the Negro
Washington Bee
Washington Post
Wheeling (West Virginia) *Register*

Books

Abernathy, Ralph David. *And the Walls Came Tumbling Down, An Autobiography*. New York: Harper and Row, 1989.

Alexander, Ann Field. *Race Man: The Rise and Fall of the "Fighting Editor," John Mitchell Jr.* Charlottesville: University of Virginia Press, 2002.

Alwood, Edward. *Dark Days in the Newsroom: McCarthyism Aimed at the Press*. Philadelphia: Temple University Press, 2007.

Anderson, Carol. *Eyes off the Prize: The United Nations and the African American Struggle for Human Rights, 1944–1955*. New York: Cambridge University Press, 2003.

Anderson, Jervis. *A. Philip Randolph: A Biographical Portrait*. New York: Harcourt Brace Jovanovich, 1973.

Anthony, David Henry, III. *Max Yergan: Race Man, Internationalist, Cold Warrior*. New York: New York University Press, 2006.

Aptheker, Herbert, ed. *A Documentary History of the Negro People in the United States, 1910–1932*. Secaucus, N.J.: Citadel Press, 1973.

Ayers, Edward L. *The Promise of the New South*. New York: Oxford University Press, 1992.

Baker, Ray Stannard. *Following the Color Line: An Account of Negro Citizenship in the American Democracy*. New York: Doubleday, Page, 1908.

Baldwin, James. *Baldwin, Collected Essays*. New York: Library of America, 1998.

Bardolph, Richard. *The Negro Vanguard*. New York: Alfred A. Knopf, 1959; New York: Vintage Books, 1961.

Barlow, William. *Voice Over: The Making of Black Radio*. Philadelphia: Temple University Press, 1999.

Bass, Charlotta A. *Forty Years: Memoirs from the Pages of a Newspaper*. Los Angeles: Charlotta A. Bass, 1960.

Bates, Daisy. *The Long Shadow of Little Rock*. New York: David McKay, 1962.

Bay, Mia. *To Tell the Truth Freely: The Life of Ida B. Wells*. New York: Hill and Wang, 2009.

Berkowitz, Dan, ed. *Social Meanings of News*. Thousand Oaks, Calif.: SAGE Publications, 1997.

Bessie, Simon Michael. *Jazz Journalism: The Story of the Tabloid Newspapers*. New York: E. P. Dutton, 1938; New York: Russell and Russell, 1969.

Biddle, Francis. *In Brief Authority*. Garden City, N.Y.: Doubleday, 1962.

Bogart, Leo. *The Age of Television*. New York: Frederick Ungar Publishing, 1958; New York: Frederick Ungar Publishing, 1972.

Booker, Simeon. *Black Man's America*. Englewood Cliffs, N.J.: Prentice-Hall, 1964.

———. *Shocking the Conscience: A Reporter's Account of the Civil Rights Movement*. Jackson: University Press of Mississippi, 2013.

Borstelmann, Thomas. *The Cold War and the Color Line: American Race Relations in the Global Arena*. Cambridge: Harvard University Press, 2001.

Boyce Davies, Carole. *Left of Karl Marx: The Political Life of Black Communist Claudia Jones*. Durham, N.C.: Duke University Press, 2007.

Branch, Taylor. *At Canaan's Edge: America in the King Years, 1965–68*. New York: Simon and Schuster, 2006.

Broussard, Jinx Coleman. *African American Foreign Correspondents, A History*. Baton Rouge: Louisiana State University Press, 2013.

Brown, H. Rap. *Die Nigger Die*. New York: Dial Press, 1969; Chicago: Lawrence Hill Books, 2002.

Bullock, Penelope L. *The Afro-American Periodical Press, 1838–1909*. Baton Rouge: Louisiana State University Press, 1981.

Buni, Andrew. *Robert L. Vann of the* Pittsburgh Courier: *Politics and Black Journalism*. Pittsburgh: University of Pittsburgh Press, 1974.

Burns, Ben. *Nitty Gritty: A White Editor in Black Journalism.* Jackson: University Press of Mississippi, 1996.

Campbell, Christopher P. *Race, Myth, and the News.* Thousand Oaks, Calif.: SAGE Publications, 1995.

Campbell, Christopher P., Kim M. LeDuff, Cheryl D. Jenkins, and Rockell A. Brown. *Race and News: Critical Perspectives.* New York: Routledge, 2012.

Campbell, W. Joseph. *The Year That Defined American Journalism: 1897 and the Clash of Paradigms.* New York: Routledge, 2006.

Capozzola, Christopher. *Uncle Sam Wants You: World War I and the Making of the Modern American Citizen.* New York: Oxford University Press, 2008.

Carmichael, Stokely. *Ready for Revolution: The Life and Struggles of Stokely Carmichael (Kwame Ture).* New York: Scribner, 2003.

Carroll, Anne Elizabeth. *Word, Image, and the New Negro: Representation and Identity in the Harlem Renaissance.* Bloomington: Indiana University Press, 2005.

Catledge, Turner. *My Life and the* Times. New York: Harper and Row, 1971.

Caute, David. *The Great Fear: The Anti-Communist Purge under Truman and Eisenhower.* New York: Simon and Schuster, 1978.

Cecelski, David S., and Timothy B. Tyson, eds. *Democracy Betrayed: The Wilmington Race Riot of 1898 and Its Legacy.* Chapel Hill: University of North Carolina Press, 1998.

Chambers, Jason. *Madison Avenue and the Color Line: African Americans in the Advertising Industry.* Philadelphia: University of Pennsylvania Press, 2008.

Cleaver, Eldridge. *Soul on Fire.* Waco, Tex.: Word Books, 1978.

———. *Soul on Ice.* New York: McGraw-Hill, 1968.

Cooper Jackson, Esther, ed. *Freedomways Reader: Prophets in Their Own Country.* Boulder, Colo.: Westview Press, 2000.

Corbould, Clare. *Becoming African Americans: Black Public Life in Harlem, 1919–1939.* Cambridge: Harvard University Press, 2009.

Covert, Catherine L., and John D. Stevens, eds. *Mass Media between the Wars: Perceptions of Cultural Tension, 1918–1941.* Syracuse, N.Y.: Syracuse University Press, 1984.

Crowder, Ralph L. *John Edward Bruce: Politician, Journalist, and Self-Trained Historian.* New York: New York University Press, 2004.

Daly, Charles U., ed. *The Media and the Cities.* Chicago: University of Chicago Center for Public Policy, 1968.

Daly, Christopher B. *Covering America: A Narrative History of a Nation's Journalism.* Amherst: University of Massachusetts Press, 2012.

Danky, James P., and Wayne A. Wiegand, eds. *Print Culture in a Diverse America.* Urbana: University of Illinois Press, 1998.

Davies, David R. *The Postwar Decline of American Newspapers, 1945–1965.* Westport, Conn.: Praeger Publishers, 2006.

Davis, Frank Marshall. *Livin' the Blues: Memoirs of a Black Journalist and Poet.* Edited by John Edgar Tidwell. Madison: University of Wisconsin Press, 1992.

———. *Writings of Frank Marshall Davis*. Edited by John Edgar Tidwell. Jackson: University Press of Mississippi, 2007.

Dawkins, Wayne. *Black Journalists: The NABJ Story*, 2d ed. Merrillville, Ind.: August Press, 1997.

Dobson, William J. *The Dictator's Learning Curve: Inside the Global Battle for Democracy*. New York: Random House, 2012.

Dooley, Patricia L. *Taking Their Place: Journalists and the Making of an Occupation*. Westport, Conn.: Greenwood Press, 1997.

Drake, St. Clair, and Horace R. Cayton. *Black Metropolis: A Study of Negro Life in a Northern City*. New York: Harcourt, Brace, 1945; Chicago: University of Chicago Press, 1993.

Du Bois, W. E. B. *The Autobiography of W.E.B. Du Bois*. New York: International Publisher, 1968.

———. *Newspaper Columns by W.E.B. Du Bois*. Vol. 2, *1945–1961*. Edited by Herbert Aptheker. White Plains, N.Y.: Kraus-Thomson Organization, 1986.

———. "The Talented Tenth." In *The Negro Problem*, 31–76. New York: James Pott, 1903.

Dudziak, Mary L. *Cold War, Civil Rights: Race and the Image of American Democracy*. Princeton, N.J.: Princeton University Press, 2000.

Durant, Sam, ed. *Black Panther: The Revolutionary Art of Emory Douglas*. New York: Rizzoli, 2007.

Ellis, Mark. *Race, War, and Surveillance: African Americans and the United States*. Bloomington: Indiana University Press, 2001.

Entman, Robert M., and Andrew Rojecki. *The Black Image in the White Mind: Media and Race in America*. Chicago: University of Chicago Press, 2000.

Ervin, Hazel Arnett, ed. *African American Literary Criticism, 1773–2000*. New York: Twayne Publishers, 1999.

Farr, Finis. *Fair Enough: The Life of Westbrook Pegler*. New Rochelle, N.Y.: Arlington House Publishers, 1975.

Farrar, Hayward. *The Baltimore* Afro-American, *1892–1950*. Westport, Conn.: Greenwood Press, 1998.

Feldstein, Ruth. *Motherhood in Black and White: Race and Sex in American Liberalism, 1930–1965*. Ithaca, N.Y.: Cornell University Press, 2000.

Finkle, Lee. *Forum of Protest: The Black Press during World War II*. Cranbury, N.J.: Associated University Presses, 1975.

Fisher, Paul L., and Ralph L. Lowenstein, eds. *Race and the News Media*. New York: Frederick A. Praeger, 1967.

Fleming, Cynthia Griggs. *Yes We Did? From King's Dream to Obama's Promise*. Lexington: University Press of Kentucky, 2009.

Fleming, Karl. *Son of the Rough South, An Uncivil Memoir*. New York: PublicAffairs, 2005.

Forbes, Flores Alexander. *Will You Die With Me? My Life and the Black Panther Party*. New York: Washington Square Press, 2007.

Forss, Amy Helene. *Black Print with a White Carnation: Mildred Brown and the* Omaha Star *Newspaper, 1938–1989*. Lincoln: University of Nebraska Press, 2014.

Fox, Stephen R. *The Guardian of Boston: William Monroe Trotter*. New York: Atheneum, 1970.

Franklin, John Hope, and August Meier, eds. *Black Leaders of the Twentieth Century*. Urbana: University of Illinois Press, 1982.

Frazier, E. Franklin. *Black Bourgeoisie*. Glencoe, Ill.: The Free Press, 1957.

Frus, Phyllis. *The Politics and Poetics of Journalistic Narrative: The Timely and Timeless*. New York: Cambridge University Press, 1994.

Fuller, Hoyt W. *Journey to Africa*. Chicago: Third World Press, 1991; Third World Press, 1971.

Garrow, David J. *Bearing the Cross: Martin Luther King, Jr., and the Southern Christian Leadership Conference*. New York: HarperCollins Publishers, 1986; New York: Perennial Classics, 1999.

Gates, Henry Louis, Jr., and Gene Andrew Jarrett, eds. *The New Negro: Readings on Race, Representation, and African American Culture, 1892–1938*. Princeton, N.J.: Princeton University Press, 2007.

Gates, Henry Louis, Jr., and Nellie Y. McKay, eds. *The Norton Anthology of African American Literature*. New York: W. W. Norton, 1997.

Gelb, Arthur. *City Room*. New York: Putnam, 2003.

Gitlin, Todd. *The Whole World Is Watching: Mass Media in the Making and Unmaking of the New Left*. Berkeley: University of California Press, 1980.

Glessing, Robert J. *The Underground Press in America*. Bloomington: Indiana University Press, 1970.

Gonzalez, Juan, and Joseph Torres. *News for All the People: The Epic Story of Race and the American Media*. London: Verso, 2011.

Gore, Dayo F. *Radicalism at the Crossroads: African American Women Activists in the Cold War*. New York: New York University Press, 2011.

Gore, George W., Jr. *Negro Journalism: An Essay on the History and Present Conditions of the Negro Press*. Greencastle, Ind.: Journalism Press, 1922.

Gottlieb, Robert, Mark Vallianatos, Regina M. Freer, and Peter Dreier. *The Next Los Angeles: The Struggle for a Livable City*. Berkeley: University of California Press, 2005.

Grant, Colin. *Negro with a Hat: The Rise and Fall of Marcus Garvey*. New York: Oxford University Press, 2008.

Green, Adam. *Selling the Race: Culture, Community, and Black Chicago, 1940–1955*. Chicago: University of Chicago Press, 2007.

Grossman, James R. *Land of Hope: Chicago, Black Southerners, and the Great Migration*. Chicago: University of Chicago Press, 1989.

Hahn, Steven. *The Political Worlds of Slavery and Freedom*. Cambridge: Harvard University Press, 2009.

Halberstam, David. *The Powers That Be*. New York: Alfred A. Knopf, 1979.

Hall, Stuart. "The Whites of Their Eyes: Racist Ideologies and the Media." In *Silver Linings: Some Strategies for the Eighties*. Edited by George Bridges and Rosalind Brunt, 28–52. London: Lawrence and Wishart, 1981.

Hamilton, Charles V. *Adam Clayton Powell, Jr.: The Political Biography of an American Dilemma*. New York: Atheneum, 1991.

Hamilton, John Maxwell. *Journalism's Roving Eye: A History of American Foreign Reporting*. Baton Rouge: Louisiana State University Press, 2009.

Harlan, Louis R. *Booker T. Washington: The Wizard of Tuskegee, 1901–1915*. New York: Oxford University Press, 1983.

Harrington, Oliver W. *Why I Left America and Other Essays*. Jackson: University Press of Mississippi, 1993.

Harrison, Hubert. *A Hubert Harrison Reader*. Edited by Jeffrey B. Perry. Middletown, Conn.: Wesleyan University Press, 2001.

Hauke, Kathleen A. *Ted Poston: Pioneer American Journalist*. Athens: University of Georgia Press, 1999.

Hill, Robert A., ed. *The FBI's RACON: Racial Conditions in the United States during World War II*. Boston: Northeastern University Press, 1995.

Hilliard, David, ed. *The Black Panther Intercommunal News Service*. New York: Atria Books, 2007.

Hilliard, David, and Lewis Cole. *This Side of Glory: The Autobiography of David Hilliard and the Story of the Black Panther Party*. Boston: Little, Brown, 1993.

Hogan, Lawrence D. *A Black National News Service: The Associated Negro Press and Claude Barnett, 1919–1945*. Rutherford, N.J.: Fairleigh Dickinson University Press, 1984.

Hooker, James R. *Black Revolutionary: George Padmore's Path from Communism to Pan-Africanism*. New York: Frederick A. Praeger, 1967.

Hopkins, Pauline E. *Daughter of the Revolution: The Major Nonfiction Work of Pauline E. Hopkins*. Edited by Ira Dworkin. New Brunswick, N.J.: Rutgers University Press, 2007.

Horne, Gerald. *Black and Red: W.E.B. Du Bois and the Afro-American Response to the Cold War, 1944–1963*. Albany: State University of New York Press, 1986.

Huddle, Mark A., ed. *Roi Ottley's World War II: The Lost Diary of an African American Journalist*. Lawrence: University Press of Kansas, 2011.

Huggins, Nathan Irvin, ed. *Voices from the Harlem Renaissance*. New York: Oxford University Press, 1976.

Hughes, Langston. *The Big Sea*. New York: Alfred A. Knopf, 1940.

———. *I Wonder as I Wander, An Autobiographical Journey*. New York: Rinehart, 1956; New York: Thunder's Mouth Press, 1991.

Hutchinson, George. *The Harlem Renaissance in Black and White*. Cambridge: Harvard University Press, Belknap Press, 1997; Cambridge: Harvard University Press, 1995.

Jackson, Luther P., Jr. "The Popular Media: Part I—The Mission of Black Newsmen." In *The Black American Reference Book*. Edited by Mabel M. Smythe, 846–874. Englewood Cliffs, N.J.: Prentice-Hall, 1976.

James, Winston, ed. *The Struggles of John Brown Russwurm: The Life and Writings of a Pan-Africanist Pioneer, 1799–1851*. New York: New York University Press, 2010.

Jefferson, Robert F. *Fighting for Hope: African American Troops of the 93rd Infantry Division in World War II and Postwar America*. Baltimore: John Hopkins University Press, 2008.

Johnson, James Weldon. *Negro Americans, What Now?* New York: Viking Press, 1934.

Johnson, John H., with Lerone Bennett Jr. *Succeeding against the Odds.* New York: Warner Books, 1989.

Jones, Charles E., ed. *The Black Panther Party Reconsidered.* Baltimore: Black Classic Press, 1998.

Jordan, William G. *Black Newspapers and America's War for Democracy, 1914–1920.* Chapel Hill: University of North Carolina, 2001.

Joseph, Peniel E. *Waiting 'Til the Midnight Hour: A Narrative History of Black Power in America.* New York: Henry Holt, 2006.

Kaestle, Carl F., and Janice A. Radway, eds. *Print in Motion: The Expansion of Publishing and Reading in the United States, 1880–1940.* Vol. 4, *A History of the Book in America.* Chapel Hill: University of North Carolina Press, 2009.

Katznelson, Ira. *Fear Itself: The New Deal and the Origins of Our Times.* New York: Liveright Publishing, 2013.

Kelley, Robin D. G. *Hammer and Hoe: Alabama Communists during the Great Depression.* Chapel Hill: University of North Carolina Press, 1990.

———. *Race Rebels: Culture, Politics, and the Black Working Class.* New York: The Free Press, 1994.

Kennedy, David M. *Freedom from Fear: The American People in Depression and War, 1929–1945.* New York: Oxford University Press, 1999.

King, Martin Luther, Jr. *Where Do We Go from Here? Chaos or Community?* New York: Harper and Row, 1967; Boston: Beacon Press, 2010.

Kornweibel, Theodore, Jr. *Investigate Everything: Federal Efforts to Compel Black Loyalty during World War I.* Bloomington: Indiana University Press, 2002.

———. *No Crystal Stair: Black Life and the* Messenger, *1917–1928.* Westport, Conn.: Greenwood Press, 1975.

———. *Seeing Red: Federal Campaigns Against Black Militancy, 1919–1925.* Bloomington: Indiana University Press, 1998.

La Brie, Henry G., III, ed. *Perspectives of the Black Press: 1974.* Kennebunkport, Maine: Mercer House Press, 1974.

Leamer, Laurence. *The Paper Revolutionaries: The Rise of the Underground Press.* New York: Simon and Schuster, 1972.

Lee, Ulysses. *United States Army in World War II, Special Studies: The Employment of Negro Troops.* Washington D.C.: Office of the Chief of Military History, United States Army, 1966.

Leipold, L. E. *Cecil E. Newman, Newspaper Publisher.* Minneapolis: T. S. Denison, 1969.

Lentz, Richard. *Symbols, the News Magazines, and Martin Luther King.* Baton Rouge: Louisiana State University Press, 1990.

Lentz-Smith, Adriane. *Freedom Struggles: African Americans and World War I.* Cambridge: Harvard University Press, 2009.

Lewis, David Levering. *W.E.B. Du Bois: Biography of a Race, 1868–1919.* New York: Henry Holt, 1993.

——. *W.E.B. Du Bois: The Fight for Equality and the American Century, 1919–1963*. New York: Henry Holt, 2000.

——. *When Harlem Was in Vogue*. New York: Knopf, 1981; Knopf, 1984.

Locke, Alain, ed. *The New Negro*. New York: Touchstone, 1997; New York: Albert and Charles Boni, 1925.

Lyle, Jack, ed. *The Black American and the Press*. Los Angeles: Ward Ritchie Press, 1968.

MacDonald, J. Fred. *Blacks and White TV: Afro-Americans in Television since 1948*. Chicago: Nelson-Hall, 1983.

MacLean, Nancy. *Freedom Is Not Enough: The Opening of the American Workplace*. Cambridge: Harvard University Press, 2006.

Makalani, Minkah. *In the Cause of Freedom: Radical Black Internationalism from Harlem to London, 1917–1939*. Chapel Hill: University of North Carolina Press, 2011.

Malcolm X. *The Autobiography of Malcolm X*. New York: Random House, 1964; New York: Ballantine Books, 1999.

Margolick, David. *Beyond Glory: Joe Louis vs. Max Schmeling, and a World on the Brink*. New York: Alfred A. Knopf, 2005.

Marks, Carole. *Farewell—We're Good and Gone: The Great Black Migration*. Bloomington: Indiana University Press, 1989.

Martindale, Carolyn. *The White Press and Black America*. Westport, Conn.: Greenwood Press, 1986.

McChesney, Robert W. *Digital Disconnect: How Capitalism Is Turning the Internet against Democracy*. New York: New Press, 2013.

McMillian, John. *Smoking Typewriters: The Sixties Underground Press and the Rise of Alternative Media in America*. New York: Oxford University Press, 2011.

Mellinger, Gwyneth. *Chasing Newsroom Diversity: From Jim Crow to Affirmative Action*. Urbana: University of Illinois Press, 2013.

Meriwether, James H. *Proudly We Can Be Africans: Black Americans and Africa, 1935–1961*. Chapel Hill: University of North Carolina Press, 2002.

Mershon, Sherie, and Steven Schlossman. *Foxholes and Color Lines: Desegregating the U.S. Armed Forces*. Baltimore: John Hopkins University Press, 1998.

Mockler, Anthony. *Haile Selassie's War*. London: Oxford University Press, 1984; New York: Olive Branch Press, 2003.

Morris, James McGrath. *Eye on the Struggle: Ethel Payne, the First Lady of the Black Press*. New York: Amistad, 2015.

Motley, Mary Penick, ed. *The Invisible Soldier: The Experience of the Black Soldier, World War II*. Detroit: Wayne State University Press, 1975.

Mullen, Bill V. *Popular Fronts: Chicago and African-American Cultural Politics, 1935–46*. Urbana: University of Illinois Press, 1999.

Mullen, Bill V., and James Smethurst, eds. *Left of the Color Line: Race, Radicalism, and Twentieth-Century Literature of the United States*. Chapel Hill: University of North Carolina Press, 2003.

Murray, Florence, ed. *The Negro Handbook, 1949*. New York: McMillan, 1949.

Myrdal, Gunnar. *American Dilemma: The Negro Problem and Modern Democracy*. New York: Harper and Brothers, 1944.

Naison, Mark. *Communists in Harlem during the Depression*. Urbana: University of Illinois Press, 1983.

Newkirk, Pamela. *Within the Veil: Black Journalists, White Media*. New York: New York University Press, 2000.

Nissenson, Marilyn. *The Lady Upstairs: Dorothy Schiff and the* New York Post. New York: St. Martins, 2007.

Nord, David Paul, Joan Shelley Rubin, and Michael Schudson, eds. *The Enduring Book: Print Culture in Postwar America*. Vol. 5, *A History of the Book in America*. Chapel Hill: University of North Carolina Press, 2009.

Oak, Vishnu V. *The Negro Newspaper*. Yellow Springs, Ohio: Antioch Press, 1948.

Ohmann, Richard. *Selling Culture: Magazines, Markets, and Class at the Turn of the Century*. London: Verso, 1996.

Ongiri, Amy Abugo. *Spectacular Blackness: The Cultural Politics of the Black Power Movement and the Search for a Black Aesthetic*. Charlottesville: University of Virginia Press, 2010.

Ottley, Roi. *The Lonely Warrior: The Life and Times of Robert S. Abbott*. Chicago: H. Regnery, 1955.

———. *'New World A-Coming': Inside Black America*. Boston: Houghton Mifflin Co., 1943.

———. *No Green Pastures*. New York: Scribner, 1951.

Padmore, George. *Pan-Africanism or Communism? The Coming Struggle for Africa*. New York: Roy Publishers, 1956.

Penn, Garland I. *The Afro-American Press and Its Editors*. Springfield, Mass.: Willey, 1891. Reprint, New York: Arno Press, 1969.

Perry, Jeffrey B. *Hubert Harrison: The Voice of Harlem Radicalism, 1883–1918*. New York: Columbia University Press, 2009.

Phillips, Kimberley L. *War! What Is It Good For?: Black Freedom Struggles and the U.S. Military from World War II to Iraq*. Chapel Hill: University of North Carolina Press, 2012.

Pinckney, Darryl. *Out There: Mavericks of Black Literature*. New York: BasicCivitas Books, 2002.

Plummer, Brenda Gayle. *Rising Wind: Black Americans and U.S. Foreign Affairs, 1935–1960*. Chapel Hill: University of North Carolina, 1996.

———, ed. *Window on Freedom: Race, Civil Rights, and Foreign Affairs, 1945–1988*. Chapel Hill: University of North Carolina Press, 2004.

Poston, Ted. *A First Draft of History*. Edited by Kathleen A. Hauke. Athens: University of Georgia Press, 2000.

Powell, Adam Clayton. *Adam by Adam*. New York: Dial Press, 1971.

Pride, Armistead S., and Clint C. Wilson II. *A History of the Black Press*. Washington, D.C.: Howard University, 1997.

Putnam, Lara. *Radical Moves: Caribbean Migrants and the Politics of Race in the Jazz Age*. Chapel Hill: University of North Carolina Press, 2013.

Rampersad, Arnold. *The Life of Langston Hughes*. Vol. 1, *I, Too, Sing America, 1902–1941*. New York: Oxford University Press, 1986.

——. *The Life of Langston Hughes*. Vol. 2, *I Dream a World, 1941–1967*. New York: Oxford University Press, 1988.

——. *Ralph Ellison: A Biography*. New York: Alfred A. Knopf, 2007.

Reed, Christopher Robert. *The Depression Comes to the South Side: Protest and Politics in the Black Metropolis, 1930–1933*. Bloomington: Indiana University Press, 2011.

Rhodes, Jane. *Framing the Black Panthers: The Spectacular Rise of a Black Power Icon*. New York: New Press, 2007.

Ritchie, Donald A. *Reporting from Washington: The History of the Washington Press Corps*. New York: Oxford University Press, 2005.

Roberts, Gene, and Hank Klibanoff. *The Race Beat: The Press, the Civil Rights Struggle, and the Awakening of a Nation*. New York: Alfred A. Knopf, 2006.

Robeson, Paul, Jr. *Paul Robeson: Quest for Freedom, 1939–1976*. Hoboken, N.J.: John Wiley and Sons, 2010.

Rowan, Carl T. *Breaking Barriers: A Memoir*. Boston: Little, Brown, 1991.

——. *The Pitiful and the Proud*. New York: Random House, 1956.

——. *South of Freedom*. New York: Alfred A. Knopf, 1952; Baton Rouge: Louisiana State University Press, 1997.

Rudwick, Elliott M. *Race Riot at East St. Louis, July 2, 1917*. Carbondale: Southern Illinois University Press, 1964.

Sanders, Joshunda. *How Racism and Sexism Killed Traditional Media*. Santa Barbara, Calif.: Praeger, 2015.

Savage, Barbara Dianne. *Broadcasting Freedom: Radio, War, and the Politics of Race, 1938–1948*. Chapel Hill: University of North Carolina Press, 1999.

Schrecker, Ellen. *Many Are the Crimes: McCarthyism in America*. Boston: Little, Brown, 1998.

Schudson, Michael. *Discovering the News: A Social History of American Newspapers*. New York: Basic Books, 1978.

Schuyler, George S. *Black and Conservative: The Autobiography of George S. Schuyler*. New Rochelle, N.Y.: Arlington House Publishers, 1966.

——. *Rac(e)ing to the Right: Selected Essays of George S. Schuyler*. Edited by Jeffrey B. Leak. Knoxville: University of Tennessee Press, 2001.

Seale, Bobby. *Seize the Time: The Story of the Black Panther Party and Huey P. Newton*. New York: Random House, 1970.

Seraile, William. *Bruce Grit: The Black Nationalist Writings of John Edward Bruce*. Knoxville: University of Tennessee Press, 2003.

Singh, Nikhal Pal. *Black Is a Country: Race and the Unfinished Struggle for Democracy*. Cambridge: Harvard University Press, 2004.

Sitkoff, Harvard. *A New Deal for Blacks: The Emergence of Civil Rights as a National Issue*. New York: Oxford University Press, 1978.

——. *The Struggle for Black Equality, 1954–1992*, rev. ed. New York: Hill and Wang, 1993.

Smethurst, James Edward. *The Black Arts Movement: Literary Nationalism in the 1960s and 1970s*. Chapel Hill: University of North Carolina Press, 2005.

———. *The New Red Negro: The Literary Left and African American Poetry, 1930–1946*. New York: Oxford University Press, 1999.

Solomon, Mark. *The Cry Was Unity: Communists and African Americans, 1917–36*. Jackson: University Press of Mississippi, 1998.

Solomon, William S., and Robert W. McChesney, eds. *Ruthless Criticism: New Perspectives in U.S. Communication History*. Minneapolis: University of Minnesota Press, 1993.

Spencer, David R. *Yellow Journalism: The Press and America's Emergence as a World Power*. Evanston, Ill.: Northwestern University Press, 2007.

Starr, Paul. *The Creation of the Media: Political Origins of Modern Communications*. New York: Basic Books, 2004.

Statler, Kathryn C., and Andrew L. Johns, eds. *The Eisenhower Administration, the Third World, and the Globalization of the Cold War*. Lanham, Md.: Rowman and Littlefield, 2006.

Stein, Judith. *The World of Marcus Garvey: Race and Class in Modern Society*. Baton Rouge: Louisiana State University Press, 1986.

Stevens, John D. *From the Back of the Foxhole: Black Correspondents in World War II*. Lexington, Ky.: Association for Education in Journalism, 1973.

Stone, Geoffrey R. *Perilous Times: Free Speech in Wartime, From the Sedition Act of 1798 to the War on Terrorism*. New York: W. W. Norton, 2004.

Streitmatter, Rodger. *Raising Her Voice: African-American Women Journalists Who Changed History*. Lexington: University Press of Kentucky, 1994.

Suggs, Henry Lewis, ed. *The Black Press in the Middle West, 1865–1985*. Westport, Conn.: Greenwood Press, 1996.

———. *The Black Press in the South, 1865–1979*. Westport, Conn.: Greenwood Press, 1983.

———. *P.B. Young, Newspaperman: Race, Politics, and Journalism in the New South, 1910–1962*. Charlottesville: University Press of Virginia, 1988.

Sugrue, Thomas J. *Sweet Land of Liberty: The Forgotten Struggle for Civil Rights in the North*. New York: Random House, 2008.

Svirsky, Leon, ed. *Your Newspaper: Blueprint for a Better Press*. New York: MacMillan, 1949.

Terry, Wallace. *Missing Pages: Black Journalists of Modern America, An Oral History*. New York: Carroll and Graf Publishers, 2007.

Thornbrough, Emma Lou. *T. Thomas Fortune, Militant Journalist*. Chicago: University of Chicago Press, 1972.

Thurman, Wallace. *The Collected Writings of Wallace Thurman: A Harlem Renaissance Reader*. Edited by Amritjit Singh and Daniel M. Scott III. New Brunswick, N.J.: Rutgers University Press, 2003.

Tifft, Susan E., and Alex S. Jones. *The Trust: The Private and Powerful Family behind the New York Times*. New York: Little, Brown, 1999.

Tinney, James S., and Justine J. Rector, eds. *Issues and Trends in Afro-American Journalism*. Lanham, Md.: University Press of America, 1980.

Trachtenberg, Alan. *The Incorporation of America: Culture and Society in the Gilded Age*. New York: Hill and Wang, 1982; Hill and Wang, 1983.

Tuchman, Gaye. *Making News: A Study in the Construction of Reality*. New York: Free Press, 1978.

Turner, Richard Brent. *Islam in the African-American Experience*. Bloomington: Indiana University Press, 1997.

Tyson, Timothy B. *Radio Free Dixie: Robert F. Williams and the Roots of Black Power*. Chapel Hill: University of North Carolina Press, 1999.

Vogel, Todd, ed. *The Black Press: New Literary and Historical Essays*. New Brunswick, N.J.: Rutgers University Press, 2001.

Von Eschen, Penny M. *Race against Empire: Black Americans and Anticolonialism, 1937–1957*. Ithaca, N.Y.: Cornell University Press, 1997.

Voogd, Jan. *Race Riots and Resistance: The Red Summer of 1919*. New York: Peter Lang, 2008.

Wachsberger, Ken, ed. *Voices from the Underground*. Vol. 1, *Insider Histories of the Vietnam Era Underground Press*. Tempe, Ariz.: Mica Press, 1993.

Wallace, Mike. *Between You and Me, A Memoir*. New York: Hyperion, 2005.

Ward, Brian. *Media, Culture, and the Modern African American Freedom Struggle*. Gainesville: University Press of Florida, 2001.

Ward, Stephen J. A. *The Invention of Journalism Ethics: The Path to Objectivity and Beyond*. Montreal: McGill-Queen's University Press, 2004.

Washburn, Patrick S. *The African American Newspaper: Voice of Freedom*. Evanston, Ill.: Northwestern University Press, 2006.

——. *A Question of Sedition: The Federal Government's Investigation of the Black Press during World War II*. New York: Oxford University Press, 1986.

Washington, Robert E. *The Ideologies of African American Literature: From the Harlem Renaissance to the Black Nationalist Revolt*. Lanham, Md.: Rowman and Littlefield, 2001.

Wasserman, Ira. *How the Media Packaged Lynching, 1850–1940*. Lewiston, N.Y.: Edwin Mellen Press, 2006.

Waters, Enoch P. *American Diary: A Personal History of the Black Press*. Chicago: Path Press, 1987.

Wechsler, James A. *The Age of Suspicion*. New York: Random House, 1953.

Weingarten, Marc. *The Gang That Wouldn't Write Straight: Wolfe, Thompson, Didion, and the New Journalism*. New York: Crown Publishers, 2006.

Wells, Ida B. *Crusade for Justice: The Autobiography of Ida B. Wells*. Edited by Alfreda M. Duster. Chicago: University of Chicago Press, 1970.

White, Walter. *A Rising Wind*. Garden City, N.Y.: Doubleday, Doran, 1945.

Wilkins, Roger. *A Man's Life, An Autobiography*. Woodbridge, Conn.: Ox Bow Press, 1982.

Williams, Oscar R. *George S. Schuyler: Portrait of a Black Conservative*. Knoxville: University of Tennessee Press, 2007.

Williams, Robert F. *Negroes with Guns*. New York: Marzani and Munsell, 1962; Chicago: Third World Press, 1973.

Wilson, Clint C., II. *Black Journalists in Paradox: Historical Perspectives and Current Dilemmas*. Westport, Conn.: Greenwood Press, 1991.

Wilson, Clint C., II., Felix Gutierrez, and Lena M. Chao. *Racism, Sexism, and the Media*, 3rd ed. Thousand Oaks, Calif.: SAGE Publications, 2003.

Wilson, Sondra Kathryn, ed. *The Selected Writings of James Weldon Johnson*. Vol. 1, *The* New York Age *Editorials, 1914–1923*. New York: Oxford University Press, 1995.

Winfield, Betty Houchin. *FDR and the News Media*. Urbana: University of Illinois Press, 1990.

Wintz, Cary D., ed. *African American Political Thought, 1890–1930*. Armonk, N.Y.: M. E. Sharpe, 1996.

Wolseley, Roland Edgar. *The Black Press, U.S.A.*, 2d ed. Ames: Iowa State University Press, 1990; Ames: Iowa State University Press, 1971.

Wright, Richard. *Black Boy*. New York: Harper and Brothers, 1945; New York: HarperPerennial, 1993.

———. *The Color Curtain*. In *Black Power: Three Books from Exile*. New York: Harper Perennial, 2008.

Yette, Samuel F. *The Choice: The Issue of Black Survival in America*. New York: G. P. Putnam's Sons, 1971.

Articles

Baker, Ella, and Marvel Cooke. "The Bronx Slave Market." *Crisis* 42 (November 1935): 330–332.

Baker, Ray Stannard. "Gathering Clouds along the Color Line." *World's Work*, June 1916, 232–236.

Booker, Simeon. "1956: A Negro Reporter at the Till Trial." *Nieman Reports* (Winter 1999–Spring 2000), http://www.nieman.harvard.edu/reportsitem.aspx?id=100547.

Brown, Robert U. "The Negro Press." *Editor & Publisher*, July 18, 1964, 34.

Brown, Sterling A. "Negro Character as Seen by White Authors." *Journal of Negro Education* 2 (April 1933): 179–203.

Brown, Warren H. "A Negro Looks at the Negro Press." *Saturday Review of Literature*, December 19, 1942, 5–6.

Burma, John H. "An Analysis of the Present Negro Press." *Social Forces* 26 (December 1947): 172–180.

Caldwell, Earl. "'Ask Me. I Know. I Was the Test Case." *Saturday Review*, August 5, 1972, 4–6.

Calvin, Floyd J. "Who's Who: The Mirrors of Harlem." *Messenger*, February 1923, 610–611.

Chase, Allen. "The *Amsterdam News* Is Winning." *Nation*, November 13, 1935, 567–568.

Chase, Hal S. "'Shelling the Citadel of Race Prejudice': William Calvin Chase and the Washington *Bee*, 1882–1921." *Records of the Columbia Historical Society, Washington D.C.* 49 (1973/1974): 371–391.

Clark, Kenneth B. "The Crisis in the Civil Rights Crisis." *Negro Digest*, July 1964, 16–25.

Clarke, John Henrik. "The New Afro-American Nationalism." *Freedomways* 1 (Fall 1961): 285–295.

Cobb, Jelani. "The Matter of Black Lives." *New Yorker*, March 14, 2016, 34–40.

Dabney, Virginius. "Nearer and Nearer the Precipice." *Atlantic Monthly*, January 1943, 94–100.

Darnton, Robert. "What Is the History of Books?" *Daedalus* 111 (Summer 1982): 65–83.

Davis, Ossie. "Our Own Black Shining Prince." *Liberator*, April 1965, 7.

Diamond, Edwin. "'Reporter Power' Takes Root." *Columbia Journalism Review*, Summer 1970, 12–18.

Entman, Robert M. "Modern Racism and the Images of Blacks in Local Television News." *Critical Studies in Mass Communication* 7 (1990): 332–345.

Erskine, Hazel. "The Polls: Demonstrations and Race Riots." *Public Opinion Quarterly* 31 (Winter 1967–1968): 655–677.

Fleming, G. James. "Emancipation of the Negro Press." *Crisis* 45 (July 1938): 213–214, 216.

Friedman, Rick. "A Negro Leader Looks at the Press." *Editor & Publisher*, July 18, 1964, 13, 38.

Fuller, Hoyt W. "Editor's Notes." *Black World*, May 1970, 4.

———. "The Myth of the 'White Backlash.'" *Negro Digest*, August 1964, 10–15.

Gatewood, Willard B., Jr. "Edward E. Cooper, Black Journalist." *Journalism Quarterly* 55 (Summer 1978): 269–275, 324.

Gilliam, Dorothy. "What Do Black Journalists Want?" *Columbia Journalism Review*, May/June 1972, 47–52.

Gordon, Eugene. "The Negro Press." *Annals of the American Academy of Political and Social Science* 140 (November 1928): 248–256.

———. "Seven Years since Bandung." *Freedomways* 2 (Summer 1962): 298–306.

Hamilton, John Maxwell, and Jinx C. Broussard. "Covering a Two-Front War: African American Foreign Correspondents during World War II." *American Journalism* 22 (Summer 2005): 33–54.

Hanchard, Michael. "Afro-Modernity: Temporality, Politics, and the African Diaspora." *Public Culture* 11 (1999): 245–268.

Harlan, Louis R. "Booker T. Washington and the *Voice of the Negro*, 1904–1907." *Journal of Southern History* 45 (February 1979): 45–62.

———. "The Secret Life of Booker T. Washington." *Journal of Southern History* 37 (August 1971): 393–416.

Harris, LaShawn. "Marvel Cooke: Investigative Journalist, Communist, and Black Radical Subject." *Journal for the Study of Radicalism* 6 (Fall 2012): 91–126.

Haygood, Wil. "The Man from *Jet*," *Washington Post*, July 15, 2007.

Heard, LaRue. "*Inner City Voice*." *Columbia Journalism Review*, Summer 1968, 30–32.

Hedgeman, Anna Arnold. "The Role of the Negro Woman." *Journal of Educational Sociology* 17 (April 1944): 463–472.

Henderson, J. M. "The Need of a Monthly Magazine." *Alexander's Magazine*, May 15, 1905, 41.

Hernton, Calvin C. "Is There *Really* a Negro Revolution?" *Negro Digest*, December 1964, 10–22.

Hershaw, L. M. "The Negro Press in America." *Charities*, October 7, 1905, 66–68.

High, Stanley. "Black Omens." *Saturday Evening Post*, May 21, 1938, 5–7+.

Hunter-Gault, Charlayne. "I Remember." *Change* 11 (October 1979): 6–7+.

Johnson, Ernest E. "The Washington News Beat." *Phylon* 7 (Second Quarter, 1946): 126–131.

Johnston, Ernie, Jr. "Pioneering Black Newsman Writes 30 to Brave Career." *Editor & Publisher*, April 29, 1972, 34, 40.

Jones, Claudia. "An End to the Neglect of the Problems of the Negro Woman!" *Political Affairs* 28 (June 1949): 51–67.

Jones, LeRoi. "Communications Project." *Drama Review* 12 (Summer 1968): 53–57.

Jones, Theodore (Ted). "I Was Going to Be a Timesman." Maynard Institute (1999), http://www.mije.org/historyproject/Essay-IWasGoingtoBeaTimesman/.

Klein, Woody. "Survey Shows News Media Working on Racial Tension." *Editor & Publisher*, January 18, 1969, 40.

Klibanoff, Hank. "L. Alex Wilson: A Reporter Who Refused to Run." *Media Studies Journal* 14 (Spring/Summer 2000): 60–68.

Kotz, Nick. "The Minority Struggle for a Place in the Newsroom." *Columbia Journalism Review*, March/April 1979, 23–31.

Lee, Wallace. "*Negro Digest* Poll: 'Does the Negro Press Speak for Most Negroes in Its Opinions?'" *Negro Digest*, February 1943, 54.

Lomax, Louis E. "The Negro Revolt against 'The Negro Leaders.'" *Harper's*, June 1960, 41–48.

Martin, Louis. "Blood, Sweat, and Ink." *Common Ground* 4 (Winter 1944): 37–42.

Mayfield, Julian. "The Cuban Challenge." *Freedomways* 1 (Summer 1961): 185–189.

McCullough, Jim. "Not All Racial News Is Black and White, Says Negro Writer." *Editor & Publisher*, January 11, 1969, 17.

Meier, August. "Booker T. Washington and the Negro Press: With Special Reference to the *Colored American Magazine*." *Journal of Negro History* 38 (January 1953): 67–90.

Miles, Frank W. "Negro Magazines Come of Age." *Magazine World*, June 1, 1946, 12–13+.

Muhammad, Askia. "An Interview with Ethel Payne." *Best of Black Journalism Review*, November 1986, 6–7.

Murdock Larsson, Cloyte. "Land of the Till Murder Revisited." *Ebony*, March 1986, 53–54+.

Murphy, Carl, William N. Jones, and William I. Gibson. "The *Afro*: Seaboard's Largest Weekly." *Crisis* 45 (February 1938): 44–46+.

Neal, Larry. "The Black Arts Movement." *Drama Review* 12 (Summer 1968): 28–39.

Nishikawa, Katsuo A., Terri L. Towner, Rosalee A. Clawson, and Eric N. Waltenburg. "Interviewing the Interviewers: Journalistic Norms and Racial Diversity in the Newsroom." *Howard Journal of Communications* 20 (2009): 242–259.

Noall, William F. "Report on Rioting Doesn't Change Newspapers' Policy." *Editor & Publisher*, August 17, 1968, 18, 40.

Owen, Chandler. "The Failure of Negro Leaders." *Messenger*, January 1918, 23–24.

Padmore, George. "Ethiopia and World Politics." *Crisis* 42 (May 1935): 138–139+.

———. "The Second World War and the Darker Races." *Crisis* 46 (November 1939): 327–328.

Palmer, L. F., Jr. "The Black Press in Transition." *Columbia Journalism Review*, Spring 1970, 31–36.

Poston, Ted. "My Most Humiliating Jim Crow Experience." *Negro Digest*, April 1944, 55–56.

———. "The Negro Press." *Reporter*, December 6, 1949, 14–16.

Prattis, P. L. "The Role of the Negro Press in Race Relations." *Phylon* 7 (Third Quarter, 1946): 273–283.

Pride, Armistead Scott. "Negro Newspapers: Yesterday, Today, and Tomorrow." *Journalism Quarterly* 28 (Spring 1951): 179–188.

Randolph, A. Philip. "A New Crowd—A New Negro." *Messenger*, May/June 1919, 26–27.

Reid, Leahmon L. "Associated Negro Press Closes." *Grassroots Editor*, January 1965, 23–25.

Rhodes, Jane. "*The Black Panther* Newspaper: Standard-Bearer for Modern Black Nationalism." *Media History* 7, no. 2 (2001): 151–158.

Rouzeau, Edgar. "My Most Humiliating Jim Crow Experience." *Negro Digest*, January 1945, 63–65.

Sale, J. Kirk. "The *Amsterdam News*." *New York Times Magazine*, February 9, 1969, 30–31+.

Sancton, Thomas. "The Negro Press." *New Republic*, April 26, 1943, 557–560.

Schlesinger, Arthur M., Jr., "The U.S. Communist Party." *Life*, July 29, 1946, 84–85+.

Schudson, Michael. "The Politics of Narrative Form: The Emergence of News Conventions in Print and Television." *Daedalus* 111 (Fall 1982): 97–112.

Thornbrough, Emma Lou. "American Negro Newspapers, 1880–1914." *Business History Review* 40 (Winter 1966): 467–490.

Thornton, Brian, and William P. Cassidy. "Black Newspapers in 1968 Offer Panthers Little Support." *Newspaper Research Journal* 29 (Winter 2008): 6–20.

Tinson, Christopher M. "'The Voice of the Black Protest Movement': Notes on the *Liberator* Magazine and Black Radicalism in the Early 1960s." *Black Scholar* 37 (Winter 2008): 3–15.

Washburn, Patrick S. "'A Dozen Best': Top Books on Black Newspaper History." *American Journalism* 23 (Summer 2006): 124–131.

———. "The Pittsburgh *Courier*'s Double V Campaign in 1942." *American Journalism* 3 (1986): 73–86.

Watts, Daniel H. "Dream and Reality." *Liberator*, October 1963, 2.

White, Walter. "I Investigate Lynchings." *American Mercury*, January 1929, 77–84.

Wilkins, Roger. "Further MORE: From Silence to Silence." *[MORE]*, July 1975, 27+.

Wilkins, Roy. "The Negro Press." *Opportunity* 6 (December 1928): 362–363+.

Worthy, William. "The American Negro Is Dead." *Esquire*, November 1967, 126, 167–168.

———. "The Angriest Negroes." *Esquire*, February 1961, 102–105.

———. "A Negro Reporter's Dilemmas." *Esquire*, March 1968, 60+.

Young, Consuelo C. "A Study of Reader Attitudes toward the Negro Press." *Journalism Quarterly* 21 (June 1944): 148–152.

Young, P. B. "The Negro Press—Today and Tomorrow." *Opportunity* 17 (July 1939): 204–205.

———. "No Crusades, Please!" *Negro Digest*, January 1944, 69–71.

Dissertations and Theses

Hanson, John H. "An Evaluative Assertion Analysis of the Black Press during the Civil Rights Era: 1954–1968." PhD diss., Florida State University, 1997.

Lamphere, Lawrence. "Paul Robeson, *Freedom* Newspaper, and the Black Press." PhD diss., Boston College, 2003.

Murdock, Horace David. "Some Business Aspects of Leading Negro Newspapers." MBA, University of Kansas, 1935.

Thompson, John Henry Lee. "The Little Caesar of Civil Rights: Roscoe Dunjee in Oklahoma City, 1915–1955." PhD diss., Purdue University, 1990.

Index

FRED CARROLL is a lecturer at Kennesaw State University.

THE HISTORY OF COMMUNICATION

The University of Illinois Press
is a founding member of the
Association of American University Presses.

Composed in 10.25/13 Marat Pro
with Trade Gothic display
by Kirsten Dennison
at the University of Illinois Press

University of Illinois Press
1325 South Oak Street
Champaign, IL 61820-6903
www.press.uillinois.edu